RADICAL

BUREAUCRACY

by

MICHAEL D. HALLIDAY

SHARDS PUBLISHING

First Published 2011 by Shards Publishing.

Copyright©2011 Michael D. Halliday

The right of Michael D. Halliday to be identified as the author of this
work has been Asserted by him in accordance with the Copyright Design
and Patents Act 1988.

British Library Cataloguing in Publication Data.
A catalogue record of this book is available from the British Library.

ISBN. 978-0-9568124-0-7

Authors OnLine Ltd.
19 The Cinques,
Gamlingay,Sandy,
Bedfordshire, SG 19 3NU,
England.

The book is also available in e-book format, details
from www.authorsonline.co.uk

"RADICAL"

-    in favour of
     comprehensive reforms
     of political essentials

"BUREAUCRACY"

-    a complex system
     of administration
     within public bodies
     by paid officials
     at political command

ACKNOWLEDGEMENTS

As always my profound gratitude and admiration goes to my partner, Joyce Margaret Davies, who kindly typed the Manuscript and mopped my fevered brow.

ABOUT THE AUTHOR

Michael Douglas Halliday

- Born 25th August 1945,
Haslemere, Surrey.

Brought up in Elland, a small woollen town in the Yorkshire West Riding, and along the North Riding Coast on Teesside in the fishing village of Marske-by-the-Sea. Son of a secondary comprehensive school headmaster.

Educated at Sir William Turner's Grammar School, Coatham, Redcar, and Keble College, Oxford University. Graduated 1968 with a good honours degree in chemistry. Qualified as a teacher 1969, Nottingham University.

Taught science and English at a grammar school in Uxbridge, Middlesex, prior to a career in public administration.

A Chartered Secretary and Administrator, with an advanced Diploma in Education from London University, and a Masters management research degree, MBA, from Leicester University.

Worked in local government in the North West of England, in the College of Technology in Wigan, for the Metropolitan Borough Council of St. Helens and Cheshire County Council, in both district and headquarters, in middle and senior management.

Specialised in education, dealing variously with buildings and development, special education, nursery, primary and secondary schools, policy, adult-education, youth and community, and financial management.

Father to two graduate daughters, he retired in 2004 and lives in Heswall on the Wirral Peninsula with partner, Joyce.

CONTENTS

INTRODUCTION

A temptation has been resisted to call this book "Reflections of a Jobsworth". It aims to try to re-establish the importance and interest of public management in the public eye. Which may be a forlorn hope in our damaged and fragmenting society, yet there is so much at stake, if only the population would look up long enough from their own busy lives to realize it. For example, do they want to live in a democracy or a dictatorship, a free society or a police state?

It is notable that there seem to be very few books around in the country today on public management and bureaucracy as such. So the present work will provide a modest corrective. This is not the international experience, by the way. Spain, for one, teaches it prominently in the universities as a prelude to government employment. And there is a tradition of its importance in both France and Germany also.

Another purpose of the book is to try and dispel confusions. For instance, many make no distinction at all between civil servants, who work for central government, and local government officers, who are employed by councils. They believe that all are paid according to the same scales and subject to the same codes of practice, terms and conditions. Whereas in fact there is no connection whatsoever and no correlation in practice. It is also rare for public officials, which they both are, to move permanently from central to local government, or vice versa, although temporary secondments do occur, especially at times of local government re-organisation, when government wants to pick the brains of local officers to fill in gaps in the expertise of the civil service.

Prejudices abound wherever there is political subject-matter. Passions run deep because we have all suffered at the hands of politicians, all seen their promises broken and our hopes dashed. In very many cases ambitions and lives have been ruined, finances destroyed. This book attempts to engender some realism about politics and its administration; what we may reasonably expect and what is only pie in the sky.

Evidently most people do not understand public management, and because they don't, they are hardly likely to value it. So explanation is a necessary first step, which the book sets out to do, at least in part. Are

INTRODUCTION

you prejudiced about a term like 'bureaucracy', or are you willing to give it a closer look?

This is not a text book, however. Although it is set out reasonably logically, it does not attempt to go to the far end of everything, being content to sketch and illustrate important points, but not within a comprehensive framework for the whole public sector, which is very diverse. It is not intended for rigorous examination study. But it is hoped that it will speak to what is conventionally called "the intelligent layman", one with an interest in current affairs and a questioning turn of mind, as well as students, especially in the welfare services.

A personal spur to write the book is to some extent a kind of catharsis at the end of a career in public service in local government as a public manager. There was no especially dramatic experience, but the psychoanalytic notion of enabling suppressed thoughts and feelings to be expressed at last strikes a chord. A process of clearing out, sorting, and reflection, can be a healthy and satisfying part of moving on to a new life. Living with imposed change in organisations which already had too much on their plate in legal duties, and not the resources to see them through successfully, is undoubtedly stressful.

The author holds a desire to share experience in the hope and belief that, although the nation seems to be turning its back on the ways of the old, benign bureaucracies, with a sort of computer-obsessed sneer, the lessons available are still highly relevant and worthwhile.

Another of the personal reasons for writing is to discharge a common frustration of public office; local government officers of seniority tend to occupy what are known a "politically restricted" posts. This means that officers are disenfranchised from the extent of free speech enjoyed by the community at large. Whilst it is not as restricting as civil servants' signing of the Official Secrets Act, it nevertheless necessitates that the officer has to behave with complete neutrality. Not only must he be even-handed in his treatment of politicians from different parties, but he has to be inscrutable as to his own political leanings, and, significantly, he cannot stand for political office, unlike a teacher.

Less politically, there is a wish simply to share experiences from a world

INTRODUCTION

rather hidden behind the scenes and all too frequently away from the public gaze, as councillors take what limelight there is.

There is no synopsis here of the broad subject-matter for each chapter of the book.

Neither are summaries provided in the text, since inevitably with complex issues such as these there can be no substitute for full readings.

Notes are provided at the end of each chapter which acknowledge and detail the major sources of reference drawn on for the book. Where the books and articles have been more extensively used, such as having been sources for sources, they are marked in the notes with an asterisk. Other information is taken from the news and the journalistic comment around it in the media and mention is made in the text.

For each of the chosen chapter subjects there is a limited focus on given topics, which, as a result of his career experiences, are of some interest to the author. They are believed to be of considerable significance, at least in their totality, whilst falling intentionally short of a comprehensive account, if, indeed such is even possible in this rapidly changing world. In some instances they might be the standard topics, but their treatments will not be completely orthodox. The facts are led, when they are led, as a background to the author's radical personal agenda .It is naturally hoped that others will share and help to bring it about, in so far as this may be possible in a very imperfect world.

CHAPTER 1

MANAGEMENT, LEADERSHIP AND ADMINISTRATION

Preliminaries

Management -
               Roles
               Decision-making
               Strategic Management
               Theory -
                         The Classical School
                               Human Relations Approaches
                               Organisation Theory
                               Systems Theory
                               Contingency Theory

Leadership -
               Group-Think
               The Nature of Leadership

Problems with Management Theory

Administration

CHAPTER 1

MANAGEMENT, LEADERSHIP AND ADMINISTRATION

PRELIMINARIES

This chapter attempts to derive a working understanding of the meanings of the terms 'administration' and 'management' in practice and their interrelations. Along the way it finds it necessary to clear a path through the tangled forest of management theory, evaluating its use and also considering where the concept of leadership fits into the picture.

Some writers have been tempted to conflate the terms 'administration' and 'management', and even suggested it is a mistake to try to separate them. What they argue is that role diversity in organisations is just too great for precision. It is easy to sympathise, particularly when you consider the feats of imagination which go into the creation of job titles, and the development of new kinds of organisation as a result of changing technology or government fads.

Yet the task is fundamental to any understanding of public administration. Muddle occurs and much nonsense is talked as a result of the fact that the terms 'administration' and 'management' are bandied about without there being any common, underlying understanding of their meanings or interrelationship. It will therefore be necessary to stipulate meanings later, hopefully with a sound rationale. But not until some of the confusions have been discussed first.

MANAGEMENT

Cole[1] concurs with the view that there is no universally agreed definition of 'management'. Instead it tends to have a very broad range of meanings. That is rather a bad sign, so in this section management will therefore be looked at in more depth in an attempt to characterize it. It will be necessary to try a variety of procedures in our efforts to attain clarity.

CHAPTER 1

MANAGEMENT, LEADERSHIP AND ADMINISTRATION

Roles

The first approach is to consider the main roles and activities of management. This will hopefully throw some light on its intrinsic nature. Activities can typically include planning, controlling, organising, commanding, coordinating, leading and deciding staffing issues. These will mainly be associated with the exercise of authority, perhaps the popular view of management.

Mintzberg[2] identifies a variety of key managerial roles which have maybe less emphasis on authority. They involve resourcing, monitoring progress, negotiating agreements, trouble-shooting problems, liaising to aid communication, and disseminating information, as well as acting as spokesman. Mintzberg's roles are divided into three groups - interpersonal, decisional, and informational.

The traditional groupings of management activities are displayed by the mnemonic POMC:

Planning - Organising - Motivating – Controlling

This is manager-centred and focuses on their actions, as with Mintzberg. Since these are inputs, the approach fails to dwell on effectiveness, which can only be assessed by evaluating outputs as well.

Schein is able to show there are also other management roles not mentioned by POMC. These are:

leader, counsellor and mediator, catalyst and more generally facilitator, investigator, diagnostician.

Then there is Management by Objectives, MBO, a systematic method with its own sequential logic.

Starting from a strategic plan for the organisation, operating plans are devised. Each unit is given its own objectives, and within that frame individual managers' responsibilities are delineated. They devise key tasks to involve the staff.

CHAPTER 1

MANAGEMENT, LEADERSHIP AND ADMINISTRATION

The model is a feedback loop, with performance being reviewed regularly beyond the level of responsibility. Correctives can then be fed in to ensure progress is on track and timetable. Review may well identify shortfalls in resources - material, financial, or human. Staff training needs can then show up under the pressures and be addressed. Because the model is rational, it tends to have an integrative effect - staff can see where they fit in to the plan and how it pays to be collaborative.

So maybe 'management' does not have a discrete essence which exists separately in its own right, but instead is descriptive of a large range of possible actions undertaken by managers, whose responsibility they variously are in some organisational context, and to some degree? Definitions may miss the main point.

Of course, 'management' can also encompass the domains of specialist, discrete areas of activity, such as personnel (later called 'human resources'), marketing, and production. But these are outside the present scope, which is concerned with generalist conceptions.

Decision-Making

Decision-making[3] looks at that specific aspect of managerial roles which is to do with judgements and their effects. A distinction is usually made between 'strategic', or major, long-term decisions, and 'operational', or short-term, more routine decisions. Various tools have been devised, such as operational research, which use mathematical equations to model the decision variables. So-called 'administrative' decisions are also isolated, as being those which attempt to reconcile the strategic and operational modes, usually by framing organisational structures, with lines of command and formal communication pathways. The term 'administration' here is specialized, and far too restrictive in its meaning to be used in moving towards a working concept. That will be the subject of later discussion.

Although decision making has developed a whole set of techniques for making decisions, it also analyses types of decision and produces guidance rules. They can be 'strategic' - wide and long-term - or 'tactical' - shorter term.   They may be clear and structured, or the reverse. Their complexity will depend on the number and nature of factors affecting them and they will vary in their influence and how much they are affected by other decisions, now, or at other times. Conditions may be uncertain, whether in terms of incomplete information or unknown outcomes. Their purposes could be to deal with a crisis, solve a problem, or take an opportunity. Rules of decision-making invite optimistic or pessimistic stances, consideration of the likeliest eventuality happening, or looking at what opportunities are lost when a given direction is chosen.

What the field of decision theory serves to show is complexity, and the fact that whilst information requirements and thinking techniques can be scientifically developed, the context in which decisions have to be taken can be fraught with uncertainties and far from ideal.

Strategic Management

Nowadays, there is considerable emphasis on strategic management and a growing body of literature covers it.[4]

Strategic management theory concerns the so-called 'higher-level' functions of goal-setting and greatest generality in planning and policy-making. Johnson and Scholes, in a modern text on corporate strategy, see three strands of strategy- analysis, choice, and implementation. In the first strand the environment and resources are assessed in the context of power and desired outcomes. The second strand is about decision-making, following the promulgation of options and their evaluation. Thirdly, the implementation strand designs the structure and resources availability and deploys the requisite manpower.

Pettinger[5] regards strategic management as essential to the success of any organisation, within the private or public sector. He points to the importance of guiding and directing within a changing context, monitoring, priority-setting, and in general terms providing the clarity and understanding that all who interact with the organisation, internally and externally, need.

CHAPTER 1

MANAGEMENT, LEADERSHIP AND ADMINISTRATION

Theory

A second approach to explaining the nature of management uses theories from social sciences. Clearly, however, it is quite artificial to claim or imply that roles do not have their theory also.

Management theory has no universally agreed understanding about grounding effectiveness in practice. Rather, it has three broad strands within which various schools and individuals develop ideas. These are respectively the classical (functional), the human relations, and systems theories. None is the complete answer, neither can any be discounted either. All have something to offer in the right context.

The Classical School

The classical theories are associated with pioneers like Fayol, Taylor and Urwick. Fayol[6], and later Urwick[7], devised general 'principles' of management, not exhaustive, but important. Fayol's principles included a division of work, and unity of command and direction. There had to be authority in management to ensure discipline in the workforce. The importance of adequate remuneration was also noted for stability of the workforce and their good spirits. The organisation would be centralised, with a linear chain of command. Urwick's principles were different, however. He stressed objectives, specialisation, coordination, responsibility, and span of control, among others.

Both authors grasped the importance of having rules in organisations, and their lists have a sort of down-to-earth appeal. But they do not deal with external factors, and do not reflect the fluidity needed for coping with rapid change in the modern world. So they are incomplete at best.

There were other classical theories too. Taylor[8] was the founder of so-called 'scientific management', which attempted to design jobs and tasks so that they could be measured by methods called 'work study'. The idea was to ensure that optimum time was spent on tasks, neither too much nor too little, thus ensuring accurate time management of the labour force. A contract was negotiated, and frequently re-negotiated, between

CHAPTER 1

MANAGEMENT, LEADERSHIP AND ADMINISTRATION

management and workers with full cooperation. Performance was monitored and retraining provided where necessary. This was, of course, especially suited to elementary kinds of repetitive factory work, where a compliant, non-militant workforce was needed. The emphasis was on the organisation of labour, and was thus one-dimensional.

The profession of 'work study' in manufacturing industry and its office equivalent 'organisation and method' became very unpopular in the liberated 1960's, and beyond. The movement was famously satirised in the Peter Sellars' film "I'm all right Jack". People resisted being measured. They found it demeaning and dehumanizing.

No survey of classical management theory would be complete without reference to Max Weber[9], the sociologist, in his characterisation of 'bureaucracy'. Unfortunately, this has come in Britain to be a derogatory term supposedly demonstrating all that is wrong with the public sector in the jaundiced eyes of its users. When the word was coined, though, it was viewed positively as a great contribution to structuring (especially large) organisations so that they could function effectively. Bureaucracy was meant to deal with size and complexity by producing a hierarchical staffing structure with defined areas of responsibility and clear lines of reporting up and down the levels. Appointments to posts were on the basis of qualification and experience, and there was a prevailing culture of rules. Decisions and actions were formally written down, and were geared to the reaching of specified goals. The approach is still highly relevant in many organisational contexts today. Handy, for one, sees bureaucracies as generating role cultures which are rational and stable.[10]

Fair criticisms have included the tendency of bureaucracies in practice to become too rigid and impersonal, with rules acquiring exaggerated importance. Knowledge-based workers rather than generalists tend to thrive in such environments. The security traditionally afforded to civil servants and local government officers is characteristic, as are the restricted opportunities for personal advancement and radical change. Perhaps they are two sides of the same coin.

CHAPTER 1

MANAGEMENT, LEADERSHIP AND ADMINISTRATION

Human Relations Approaches

The second major movement in management theory was human relations, emphasizing psychological and social dimensions within the working experience. Typical approaches included studies of what motivates people, Elton Mayo's focus on the social group[11], Chester Barnard[12] bringing knowledge from the social sciences to bear on organisations and their structures, and Chris Argyris'[13] concentration on the way people have to modify their behavioural manifestations of personality in order to accommodate to the workplace. The industrial success of Japan during the 1970's and 1980's prompted a look at 'Theory Z', the all-embracing culture of care that firms provided for their core workers.

Many valuable insights have emerged from this field of research. For example, Herzberg[14] discovered features of motivation regarded now as commonplace. Achievement is generally the most important, followed by its recognition, and then the work itself, along with the people environment. So actual remuneration tends to be some way down the list, a fact much exploited. Mayo furthered the humanisation of work via the famous Hawthorne Studies in which control groups were used to test effects of improvements in working conditions, notably in factories. The importance of consideration of workers' feelings emerged from these early, scientifically limited experiments, as did the recognition of peer status, and the high influence of the unseen, informal networks.

Barnard saw clearly, among other things, how there could be a divergence of interests and aims between individuals and the organisation, with the onus on the latter to understand the hidden social dynamics and cultivate mutual cooperation. This implied, though did not only need, an adequate moral code.

Argyris took it further, showing and explaining workers' defence mechanisms when feeling threatened, their reactions to conflict, their behaviour when frustrated, and how to make people grow by removing negative elements and addressing repressed personalities.

Rensis Likert[15] pointed to the social changes expected of management. These would include producing employee-centred practices, general

CHAPTER 1

MANAGEMENT, LEADERSHIP AND ADMINISTRATION

rather than close supervision, employee consultation on major changes planned, employee-setting of work pace within targets for attainment and the encouragement of team working.

What was emerging was the realisation that managerial skills would need ratcheting up considerably to develop psycho-social knowledge and techniques. And that the authority of position was being challenged by a rising expectation that subordinates would be involved in negotiated agreements about the important matters affecting their working lives.

Organisation Theory

Organisation theory has risen in importance in the literature in contemporary times because of the influence of social science and the human relations school. Some regard it as the more fundamental framework, with management a subordinate discipline, a function only of organisations, and not the controlling dynamic within them. Others might argue that management serves as a valuable first-order simplification of ends and means, all that is usually necessary for focused performance. Most staff are pragmatic about their work, not believing that a complete psycho-social understanding is either necessary, or even desirable, for success. Whilst this may appear somewhat irrational, too much detail and complexity can undoubtedly be a dysfunctional distraction for practitioners.

There are obvious dangers with organisation theory. Does it, for instance, falsely suggest that the organisation is reified into being as an entity somehow capable of thinking and acting in its own right? Any organisation, however powerful, is only a social construct, a human invention. It may be simplistic to regard the organisation as having a small and clear number of goals, because the people in it are hugely influenced by the other environments they inhabit, and exercise varying degrees of free will within it. On the other hand, an organisation is rather more than the summation of the individual experiences and beliefs of its members. There are patterns of activities to monitor too, and a structure within which these are moderated and expressed. So the question is, really, how to harness organisation theory to make best use of it.

CHAPTER 1

MANAGEMENT, LEADERSHIP AND ADMINISTRATION

Systems Theory

The third approach to management theory looks at organisations as 'systems'. A system is a 'set of interconnected or interrelated parts forming a complex whole', so systems theory can apply to a great many more things, man-made and natural, beyond just organisations. Systems are characterised fundamentally as 'closed' or 'open'. Closed systems are self-supporting, and do not have any interactions with the world outside them. Whereas open systems do. They have 'inputs' from the 'environment' and 'outputs' to it, in systems parlance. Internal processes convert the inputs into outputs, and a good example would be a production line in manufacturing industry. Now the system is separated from the environment by a 'boundary', and the environment can be stable or unstable. Within the system there may be 'sub-systems' with their own 'interfaces' with each other and/or the system. Sophisticated systems will have feed back loops incorporated, so that information is fed back to improve inputs and their conversion to outputs where necessary.

The point about the abstractions of systems theory is that the model is very general as a result and so has many uses in the sciences.

Katz and Kahn[16] point to one very important feature of organisational systems and that is 'equifinality': the same results can be obtained by different paths from different starting points. This principle helps to explain why varied ways of structuring and working can yield acceptable outcomes, a point lost on many politicians, who often blame the structure of an organisation for its ills. Institutions can be usefully identified as 'dual systems' in which one stream operates the conversion of inputs or services, whilst the other manages the institution. This has been commonly reflected in staffing structures divided by function. Significantly, Katz and Kahn see social structures as contrived systems bound by psychology. They also identify organisational sub-systems variously as managerial, productive, supportive, maintaining and adapting.

Burns and Stalker[17] polarised two types of management system and suggested that 'mechanistic systems' were suitable for stable conditions, whereas changing environments were better dealt with by 'organic

MANAGEMENT, LEADERSHIP AND ADMINISTRATION

systems'. Mechanistic systems can be roughly equated with bureaucracies and have formal lines of communication. Organic systems, on the other hand, are comparatively fluid and flexible. Communication tends to be more lateral among colleagues than vertical within the hierarchy. In this model, control tends to be via loose networks of staff with mutual interests in a task. Individual initiative and self-organising is much in evidence, so managers advise more and instruct less. The model can also cope better with the informal lines of communication which always exist alongside hierarchy, an understanding of which can be crucial to the dynamics of the organisation.

Systems theory being a model, admittedly scientific, is nevertheless a framework constructed in an attempt to explain actual phenomena. In any model various elements will be used to represent the real thing, but inevitably only in what are deemed to be some of its key aspects. So something will be missing. The correspondence will not be exact. And in the gaps considerable error could lurk.

Contingency Theory

Beyond the three broad theoretical approaches there is yet another, born out of a desire to evaluate the impact of scientific and technological advances in the working organisation. This is the element common to many of the contingency theories. Joan Woodward was able to correlate the arrival of better technology with changed control systems and their staffing implications. Robert Merton studied technological effects on social interactions between workers, thereby anticipating change theory, with its psychological pathology.

Lawrence and Lorsch[18] stressed that organisations facing uncertainty had better success when they had less rigid structures and good interpersonal relations. Lawrence and Lorsch looked at what interactions there might be between types of environment and kinds of organisational structure, considering different market conditions for firms. They concluded that the more dynamic and complex the environment, the greater the extent of integration and differentiation needed by the organisation to succeed. It has to have shared purpose and good communication on the one hand,

MANAGEMENT, LEADERSHIP AND ADMINISTRATION

whilst being sufficiently separated in its functional sub-systems. This is a tall order, because the two requirements potentially pull the organisation in conflicting directions. Integration is always seen as desirable, but more differentiated structures might well be able to cope with stable environments.

The Aston Group research[19] highlighted the vital role played by size in prompting both organisational structural change and its nature. As the organisation gets larger it will eventually need to become more formal, more standardized, (more 'bureaucratic', if you like), but with greater differentiation into specialization of roles, and a dispersion of centralization.

Conventional contingency theories see the chosen mix of approach being influenced by three main variables - environment, human behaviour, and technology. But the author thinks this is unduly restricting. A wider theoretical framework might well be needed in order to do justice to all major, relevant factors. Organisation and structure are illustrations of the omissions and it rather looks as if some kind of eclectic mix will have to be the solution.

What is so very unsatisfactory about all this is that management theory appears to require the construction of theoretical frameworks which vary across institutions and purposes and levels. There is a deep irony here, since successful scientific theories are such because life corresponds to them. Whereas actual management 'theory' has to be fitted to actual states of affairs if it has anything worthwhile to say about them for the benefit of the hapless bureaucrat.

LEADERSHIP

As authority has become less acceptable in ordinary walks of life, with people less inclined than they were in previous generations to look up to others by virtue of the positions they occupy, and less willing to grant that others may be any better than they are, management of staff has become much more difficult. It is now a major and unsolved problem of the age, the source of much conflict and unhappiness.

CHAPTER 1

MANAGEMENT, LEADERSHIP AND ADMINISTRATION

The climate has changed. Instead of giving orders to exert control over subordinates, there is more equality of treatment, with requests and suggestions taking over from requirements to obey. To some extent this reflects the preoccupations of the human relations theorists, who might claim to have some answers. In local government the movement has been fuelled by human resources departments using human rights legislation and left-wing developments in employment law. These have had the effect of empowering staff to question more the instructions they receive, and to complain, sometimes by elaborate and long drawn out formal process, about the way they have been dealt with.

In this sort of climate organisations have tended to emphasize working in teams. The human relations school would suggest it is more effective in building good staff relations and harnessing staff in cooperative ventures.

What is not so commonly mentioned is the hidden dynamics of groups themselves and the fact that they doubtless do have influences on the nature and quality of the thought within them, whether the staff involved are aware of it or not. Group-think is another powerful reason why leadership is a very skilful and somewhat rare commodity. Some of the key sociological research conclusions will now be considered with that sobering thought in mind.

Group Think

Many people know, and suffer the fact, that there are considerable weaknesses in group thinking, enormous difficulties of communication between people meeting together as groups, especially large ones. Individuals with strong views often despair of being able to put them across in group discussions. Problems are frequently encountered in keeping to the subject-matter and agreeing on conclusions. Many are aware, also, that the manner in which they argue will probably be at least as decisive as the ideas they supply and the reasons which back them up.

In this regard there are two key facts. Firstly, humans are passionate, illogical animals, and therefore, much of our group thinking is confused,

MANAGEMENT, LEADERSHIP AND ADMINISTRATION

irrational, piece-meal, random and disparate. Secondly, weaknesses of group thinking are to an extent inherent within the systems of group activity themselves. It will be convenient, bearing this in mind, to divide our argument into two separate considerations, namely, those of human and systems weaknesses.

Homans[21] has developed hypotheses of human group interaction which throw light on our failings as human communicators. Obviously, groups meet because they have some purpose in view. The members of the group all have a motive or motives for joining the group and they interact with each other within it. Leaders emerge, sometimes formally appointed, often through popularity. This can conflict with official hierarchy, of course.

Firstly, by working together, members of a group identify with others and develop their own patterns of behaviour. Some may grow fond and this may lend to meetings quite outside the purpose of group activity! People tend to like those who agree with their opinions and dislike those who do not. Thus, friendships are usually made among those of similar views, background, and moral outlook. Bonds are quite likely to be strengthened if the group feels itself threatened by outsiders. Thus, there is almost immediate development of feelings with respect to members of other groups, so the group at once loses some of its objectivity.

Of course, people in the group may differ widely in character. Very different personalities are likely to oppose each other and this can generate disliking. Furthermore, a naturally bossy person who gives orders is liable to be resented.

It is important, too, not to see the group in isolation, but as inevitably interacting with others outside who must have at least indirect influence on it. Problems which the group is tackling are other potential sources of disruption and it cannot in general be legislated whether the accompanying tensions will unite or destroy it.

Secondly, the group naturally develops its own hierarchical structure. The higher in rank an individual within the group is, or hopes to be, the more likely he is to absorb completely its ethos, and the closer his

CHAPTER 1

MANAGEMENT, LEADERSHIP AND ADMINISTRATION

behaviour will correspond to its own accepted code. Conversely, lower ranking people frequently break the rules, as they have less to lose in position and prestige.

Thirdly, according to Homans, higher-ranking people in the group will initiate activities for others more often then the rest will for them. We are aware of the hierarchy and implicitly accept our own 'place' in it and corresponding level of power to influence events.

The fourth point concerns interaction between two individuals in a group. If one person starts the interaction more often, the other's dislike of, or liking for, him will be enhanced.

Finally, and probably self-evidently, feelings within the group tend to decline in strength when interaction becomes less and less frequent.

The messages are quite discouraging, because they indicate that most interaction is coloured by emotions, tribal rituals, 'pecking orders', rather than with scrupulous attempts to be objective in pursuit of problem solutions.

A major trouble is that working in a group often adversely affects the performance of individuals. Experimentally, it is realised that some individuals find an audience a stimulus to production. But social facilitation frequently shows itself as high output quantity, not necessarily quality. What spoils the latter is that the individual is only partly committed to the problem. He is also trying passionately to impress his audience.

Most people, however, lack security and self-confidence in a group environment and so suffer embarrassment. Unfortunately, the full and proper use of their intellect is inhibited by the situation itself.

In fact, very high attainment by individuals is prevented by a levelling process. People are reluctant, for reasons already stated, to risk disagreement with the majority. Especially if the group is confronted by an urgent or difficult task, there is frequently overt social pressure on the loner to conform. And if he refuses, ostracism may well follow. A

CHAPTER 1

MANAGEMENT, LEADERSHIP AND ADMINISTRATION

natural tendency exists to suppress, to censor, to impose majority dominance of minorities. They become generally more reluctant to speak as the group increases in size, and large groups also suffer from the great length of time necessary to canvass opinion.

It is obvious that for problem-solving the composition of group members is important. Sadly, ideal mixes are rare. Much more has to be taken into account than simply the intellect and relevance of expertise of participants. For instance, if we group together individuals whose opinions coincide, discussion will simply reinforce any errors of judgement on a collective basis. We need Belbin's awareness that team members should be picked to represent different qualities like those of coordinator, specialist, implementer, investigator, shaper, evaluator.[20]

Yet, too much conflict of opinions can also be destructive. Resolution of problems may become secondary, no matter how unconsciously, to a desire to win. It is the great weakness of debates that few ever vote for the side with the more powerful arguments. Most vote instead for those who support their own entrenched beliefs. This admission is disturbing enough in an alleged democracy and there will be plenty more about the follies of political thinking later in the book.

What is positively alarming, however, is the fact that weaknesses in group thinking are in any case inherent in the very techniques which we do, and must, use. Worse is to come.

Bales[21] has conducted important studies that indicate the ways in which group-think depends partly on the mode of seating arrangement of a group. He traces a variety of situations, from a 'circle' of people to the 'wheel'.

The circle is characterised by absence of a leader. Communication occurs in both directions and, although no consistent organisation emerges, at least there is an opportunity for fairly even participation by group members. At the other extreme, the 'wheel' structure imposes the organisation of a leader and members by having one person sitting centrally surrounded by the rest. There is a tendency for the members to

MANAGEMENT, LEADERSHIP AND ADMINISTRATION

send information to this central leader and await his instructions. Participation is unequal and, particularly if the leader is not liked, or displays incompetence, there will be dissatisfaction at the hub.

In intermediate shapes, such as a semicircle or the mode shaped like a letter Y, there is a tendency to take longer to decide on procedures than with the 'wheel', but efficiency is better than with the circle, where there is a higher rate of information flow, but more mistakes.

Seating arrangements and emotive forces between personalities have such a large bearing on discussion that they could easily override the best arguments mustered. With this in mind, a managing director would be well advised to regard his Board meetings simply as 'brainstorming' sessions for throwing up useful ideas. Before making an important policy decision he should always fall back on a close scrutiny of the arguments in the cold light of reason.

A final, disturbing observation is that from team-building sessions and other management games for staff. Most people there, especially among the lower echelons, will be going through the motions, paying lip-service to participation, waiting for the whole uncomfortable experience to pass so they can go back to their familiar patterns of work.

Team work is not a panacea and requires very careful handling for effective results, whatever the consultancy gurus choose to sell to the firm's hierarchy.

Nature of Leadership

Likewise, management training has an increased emphasis nowadays on leadership. Adair, for instance, firmly believes that every manager can learn how to lead, and needs to[22].

What light can theory throw, then, on the topic of 'leadership'? Traditionally discussions centre on the qualities which encapsulate the good leader and fails to find them. Trait theory looks at personality and speculates that such aspects as energy and intelligence are perhaps

CHAPTER 1

MANAGEMENT, LEADERSHIP AND ADMINISTRATION

significant. The trouble is, no qualities like this have emerged to separate leaders from the rest of us. Of course, charisma is a help in encouraging followers, but this is an elusive quality not tied to any given type of personality. And some of the most charismatic, like Hitler, have also been evil.

Style theory looks at the spectrum of behaviour between democratic and authoritarian extremes, and between being people-centred or task-centred. Much here seems to depend on other factors, like the culture within which the leader is operating, and the nature of the key tasks facing him.

Contingency theory seeks to judge leadership performance by how adaptive it is to changing circumstance. Adair models action-centred leadership as a balancing of needs, which change as between individuals, groups, and tasks.

Fiedler[23] reminds us that the leader cannot be properly effective without the requisite power and authority. His situation will be most favourable when he has, and when tasks can be well structured and he gets on well with those he has to reply on for action.

In spite of the above, opinions on the value of leadership courses, and even the need for them, can be very varied. For example, the Blair Government set up a National College for School Leadership in Nottingham in 2002, partly in response to head teachers' requests and to improve their professionalism. But it was not long before Chris Woodhead, the former Chief Inspector of Schools, accused the College of preaching "evangelical twaddle". He called it "a grotesque waste of public money" and expressed the hope that it would be closed down. His main objections were to its alleged use of jargon and its over-complication of matters. Woodhead, a controversial figure in his own right, regards leadership as a straightforward "question of common sense". You simply need to understand your own motivation and feelings, and to know the people you are working with.

But to many it might seem that great skills may be required to understand people and motivate them to follow the ways and direction of the organisation. Both insight into the psychology of interpersonal behaviour

MANAGEMENT, LEADERSHIP AND ADMINISTRATION

and the sociology of group dynamics would appear to be minimum requirements, either in a practical grasp of the theories, or, for the lucky few naturals, intuitively.

It is obviously a help if they have charismatic personalities, because people tend to be willing to follow such leaders in virtue of this. Warmth and enthusiasm are highly rated. It is an advantage, too, if the managers show the right strength of character, integrity, and moral courage especially.

Then they should learn their business and develop a flexible willingness to change. At the level of the group they need to be able to persuade the members to work as a team to achieve the common goal, respecting each other and trying to help them improve by positive encouragements, maybe to develop leadership qualities of their own.

So, 'facilitation' becomes a buzz-word for what 'new' managers do. They are enabling, prompting, advising, encouraging - the 'softer' arts. They address the three areas of need - individual, group, and task. As in school, sometimes the tasks will come a poor third if the other two are unwell.

A manoeuvre which has come to undermine managers and management in recent years is to play up leadership roles and play down management ones. Some even polarise the two concepts. Leadership is claimed to be synonymous with allegedly female virtues like empathy, whilst management is characterised by so-called male vices like being task rather than people-centred. The implications seem to include the idea that managers will fail, and that means most of them, if they cannot somehow inspire the workforce by their personal qualities as true leaders do.

So-called "hard skills" are contrasted with "soft skills", the former relating to technical abilities, the latter more about your interpersonal abilities and personality. Soft skills are increasingly emphasised, partly because of the rise of teamwork, often project-based, and partly with the formal emancipation of women in the workplace. A difficulty here is that all the skills required are rare to combine in one person. Managers who were taken on because of their strengths in hard skills might not have the

MANAGEMENT, LEADERSHIP AND ADMINISTRATION

kind of personality which makes for ease of transition to a soft-skills oriented culture.

Parts of the new approach can be quite unsettling for staff of a different mind-set. It is almost as though they are expected to improve as a person, with work as the means to this end. A self-improvement goal is supposed to motivate the worker in place of traditional hierarchical discipline, with 'human resources officers' acting as amateur psychological coaches, but it can be both threatening and a switch-off.

There must be doubts about Adair's optimism having read this formidable sketch of the required attributes. What it takes to be a good leader is in essence to be able to capture the hearts and minds of staff, so that they follow. And there will be many, the introverted and those lacking in self-confidence among them, who do not feel up to the challenge. You have to be likeable. You have to be trusted.

So whilst there can be rational characterisations of the qualities most likely to inspire, there is a basic emotional underlay. You can only lead if they consent to follow. They are thus in a position of empowerment - the paradox of leadership.

Therefore, if you are bewildered by the dynamics of relationships, think twice about becoming a leader. Staff will find you out. Try being human and approachable. Develop trust by not letting them down. Be honest and straight forward, open as opposed to secretive, direct not deviant, caring and considerate, respecting of confidences, very good at listening, clear and inspiring in what you say to them. Is this in your nature? Can you spread happiness? Are you that paragon of the virtues?

Leadership is also more difficult today for all sorts of other reasons: there is the rise of independent judgement and individualism with high general standards of education, the complexity of modern problems, often their interconnectedness, the diffuseness of power, rapid change, transient fashions, pluralism, and invasive influences of the media. A weight of expectation presses all the more when people seek to transfer over any personal responsibility they may otherwise have and lean on the leader instead.

CHAPTER 1

MANAGEMENT, LEADERSHIP AND ADMINISTRATION

PROBLEMS WITH MANAGEMENT THEORY

Well then, management is not now enough, it would appear. But is leadership too much?

The management guru, Peter Drucker, thinks so:

> "What seems to be wanted (in leadership) is universal genius......The experience of the human race indicates strongly that the only person in abundant supply is the universal incompetent"(24).

His practical conclusion is that:

> "We will have to learn to build organisations in such a manner that any man who has strength in one important area is capable of putting it to work".

So far we have looked at management via a selection from the many candidates for its true roles and theories. Obviously there will be omissions, perhaps very significant ones among them. We cannot be sure that they capture the essence, or even the flavour.

Also, are there any other 'lenses' through which we might envision further insights into the nature of management, but have somehow missed? The answer is probably yes- all too many for a coherent synthesis.

There will be problems of categorisation, too. Management theories can overlap the (artificial) boundaries between types, or 'schools', perhaps displaying facets of several.

Misguidance can stem from the mere fact that management texts are couched in abstract and technical terms, which necessarily lack the colour of practical experience within the jobs themselves, in the concrete reality rather than merely the cold concept.

As hinted somewhat earlier, the present author favours a (modified) contingency theory approach, following an acceptance, born out of

MANAGEMENT, LEADERSHIP AND ADMINISTRATION

experience, that there is just not one theory in existence whose appropriate use will ensure that an organisation is effective. Rather, the ideas to be used will have to be an eclectic mix which is both context-variable and situation-variable. This is disappointing to the purist, perhaps, but a recognition of the complexity of life. Management somehow has to choose a combination of theories which are effective in dealing with the internal organisation and external environment at that distinct time and place and set of resources. And that can be well-nigh impossible in a bureaucracy, where there are multiple and sophisticated goals.

So what are we to make, finally, of such a concatenation of ideas? The philosopher, Lars Svendsen [25] is very cynical about management theory altogether. He is disparaging about the large crop of popular books on management, viewing them as building case histories to illustrate a few catchy slogans, sometimes repetitive, often trite. He claims their advice has been followed with sometimes disastrous consequences, and cites the 1990's vogue for "downsizing" which cost a lost of capable people their jobs unnecessarily.

Understandably, he is annoyed that their authors often make philosophical claims for them, when in fact they embody elementary psychology at best. Needless to say, these works are much more influential than actual philosophy books, a fact which Svendson also notes with distaste.

That apart, the messages to take away for practitioners are mixed. Truth is hard to find given the relative lack of research evidence to back up the claims. A seeming paradox is that managers with good interpersonal skills and a sound general education might succeed well enough without any of them. But it is too risky to rely on.

The wider media literature is beginning to see through the management theory peddled by the gurus[26]. Targets are increasingly viewed with suspicion, for distorting effort and stifling professional initiative in favour of the easily measurable (often relatively trivial) objective.

It is well-rehearsed that the incentives, bonus culture of banking and other private sector concerns has been a disaster for the free world, with

CHAPTER 1

MANAGEMENT, LEADERSHIP AND ADMINISTRATION

reckless risk-taking propelled by personal greed a consequence and a major factor leading to the destabilization of whole national economies.

Pressure on employees by constant performance monitoring and review was driven by a belief in the uncaring wisdom of market forces to shake out the weaker brethren. It is now known, what child psychologists could long have told society, that such practices are liable to undermine collaboration between manager and staff, enhance suspicion and defensive feelings of insecurity, and reduce output quality.

In economically good times, when the organisation is expanding, sloppy thinking can create new posts which are costly to sustain during the downturn. The confusion mentioned above can produce less than optimal staffing structures. Hierarchies tend to generate too many layers. Lateral positions and reporting arrangements to superiors can be badly thought out, or simply not addressed, leading to anomalies and staff dissatisfaction.

Management gurus have attacked hierarchy (especially in the public sector) in the constant drive to reduce costs. This has led to the stripping out of some layers or tiers, especially in the 'middle' management posts, so that hierarchies have got flatter, with relatively few management positions. There has been a greater emphasis on effectiveness, with regular performance scrutiny in more organisations. Pay differentials have in consequence widened drastically, with fewer opportunities for promotion, and many basement salaries for the vast majority. Hope reduces and so can commitment. Accompanying delayering exercises is a stated justification questioning the value added by some management posts.

Which prompts some radicals to question whether we should even have managers at all, or, at least, to want to review what management should essentially be about. Some are turning again to old-fashioned ideas such as trusting experienced staff to use their professional judgement with more unfettered operational scope, subject, of course, to an environment of suitable regulatory controls.

CHAPTER 1

MANAGEMENT, LEADERSHIP AND ADMINISTRATION

ADMINISTRATION

Now that we have struggled, possibly surprisingly, to identify the essence of management, and to provide an underpinning theoretical framework for it with genuine explanatory, and maybe even predictive, power, what of its companion concept, 'administration'? We need to know in order to specify jobs accurately. Could it be just what is left over within an organisation apart from its professional functions?

Unfortunately not so simple. The matter of deciding what 'administration' is must also regrettably be far from obvious(27). The term has had a very long history, over the course of which it has acquired not merely nuances of meaning, but diametrically opposed ones as well! As early as Roman times administration had at least two senses: firstly, the giving of help or service; secondly, running or directing somebody's operations. One could consist of quite mundane chores; the other might occupy an important position at the heart of government. So the range could cover a very broad spectrum of possibilities.

The meaning of administration can also differ between countries. In the United States it is usual for the government of the day to be referred to as 'the Administration'. Hodgkinson, an American writer, admits that in practice the distinctions between administration and management are blurred, and sometimes deliberately so(28). Nevertheless, he sees a clear polarity between the two terms, regarding administration as the higher-level and management as the lower-level discipline. In his scheme administrators are concerned with the ends of the organisation; its values and purposes, and with the setting of policies and action plans. Their thinking is strategic and general, and tends to be more akin to an art form than a science. By contrast, management is seen as the business of implementing programmes, using scientific and technological techniques, thinking tactically, and deploying the means for success.

Another major semantic difficulty is institutional disagreement. Within the British Civil Service there has been a similar historical tradition and considerable continuity of various elitist notions to do with 'administration'. Recruitment to the 'administrative class' was by

MANAGEMENT, LEADERSHIP AND ADMINISTRATION

examination. The 'best' brains were taken on, with their merit being judged by the criterion of a first-class honours degree from Oxbridge. Administrators were relatively few in number, generalists rather than specialists, and not wedded to any particular professional backgrounds. In those days the Civil Service barely used the term 'management' for any reason at all. Everything was administration in some grade or other.

In practice confusions have developed because of the evolution of role requirements, the volume of work, and the development of 'executive' and 'clerical' classes. Executive officers came increasingly to be responsible for the internal organisation of a department, and its functional operation, including casework under existing regulations. Administrators, in contrast, dealt with interdepartmental affairs, and devising new regulations. The top ones even interfaced with Government Ministers and helped advise them on new policy development.

Drucker has an interesting definition of 'executive': "Every knowledge worker in a modern organisation is an executive if, by virtue of his position or knowledge, he is responsible for a contribution that materially affects the capacity of the organisation to perform and to obtain results." Such a definition is, of course, of little use in separating the respective natures of management and administration, so the Civil Service undoubtedly introduced needless confusions of terminology to service their grading structures.

A government report on the Civil Service in 1968 produced a further distinction. It said that administrative work could be placed in one of two categories. The first consisted of 'simple mechanical' tasks, namely 'the application of well-defined regulations, decisions and practice to particular cases'. The second category referred to much higher-order functions in 'the formation of policy, with the revision of existing practice or current regulations and decisions, with the organisation and direction of the business of Government'. To modern eyes this is going to look very simplistic.

In 1950 Bridges set forth qualities to be found in a top civil service administrator[29]. He (and it usually was 'he' then) should have 'the power of rapid analysis'. This meant ability to weigh up complicated facts and situations, place them in their correct interrelationship, and

CHAPTER 1

MANAGEMENT, LEADERSHIP AND ADMINISTRATION

explain them succinctly to the Minister, emphasising the essential points. He should also have a good sense of timing, for when it is appropriate to release information. He needs to be able to think ahead, and to balance principle with expediency. He requires 'imagination and perseverance'. He has to be able to understand people and to lead them. Ideally, he is able to spot the old problem in a new guise, which requires both experience and capabilities of abstraction.

It is rather strange that in different walks of British life there can be just about a complete reversal of the above roles as between administration and management. In business, for instance, the firm tradition in industry and commerce in the United Kingdom and in America is that administration refers to the internal running of the organisation itself, with financial and other recording and reporting, along with statistical and other management information, planning and programming. Management is concerned with policy determination, and it also runs key operations at the product or service interface.

Thus it is necessary to examine further meanings of the term 'administration' from the field of industry and commerce. As in the public sector, the historical development of the word is instructive. Much usage had come from the emergence in factories of record keeping needs, many being of a financial nature.

Brech(30) was later able to stipulate administration as corresponding to the techniques or procedures of management, thereby supplying them with information of various sorts. He it was who correctly illustrated the complete reversal of civil service meanings, where administration was the higher calling, to the private sector understanding, where it is the lower.

At one extreme, many businesses today, and other organisations too, regard administrators as clerical workers doing mundane tasks such as filing, answering routine calls, and manning reception, perhaps with a few higher-order skills like computer database or spreadsheet manipulation thrown in. On this reading, "management" is viewed as having elements of overseeing, frequently, but not always, with responsibility for staff and their supervision. In senior positions there is often a more strategic involvement, perhaps in policy-making.

CHAPTER 1

MANAGEMENT, LEADERSHIP AND ADMINISTRATION

Specialist professions contributing in organisations tend to have 'managers' qualified in those disciplines to run them, for instance human resources, marketing and accountancy, the day-to-day tasks can be 'managed' by an operations manager, and some 'managers' run projects with specified objectives. Very significantly, "management" has status; "administration" does not.

But in Local Government there was a different tradition. The various departments were led by professionally-qualified officers whose qualifications lay in the fields relevant to their department's functions. For example, the Town Clerk was usually a solicitor, the Director of Social Services a social worker, the Director of Education a teacher, and so on. In 1967 the Mallaby Report spawned a generation of elitist and patronising attitudes which riddle services to this day, although sheer need and a breakdown of respect for tradition is forcing pragmatic recruitment decisions which follow no clear pattern at all(31). The relevant section of Mallaby's Report is well worth reproducing here in full:

> "In the departments of a local authority there is an important element of administration work to be done at varying levels of responsibility which does not require professional judgement. While there is a shortage of professionally qualified men, this administrative work should be done by lay administrative officers who may be general graduates. This work can take many forms:
> > [a] specialist work in, for example, management services, and inpersonnel and establishment control;
> > [b] the drafting of reports and memoranda and the organisation of the flow of work in the department's headquarters offices;
> > [c] consultation and co-ordination with other sectors of the authority's activities;
> > [d] executive responsibility with powers for action in non-professional fields."

In reality, of course, the 'lay' and 'professional' lines of Mallaby become hopelessly blurred. There is an inevitable element of administration in the work of any professional.

CHAPTER 1

MANAGEMENT, LEADERSHIP AND ADMINISTRATION

And the complexity of institutional environments, sometimes with a political overlay, renders much higher-order administration subtle and difficult, requiring myriad skills and sound judgement. But the Mallaby agenda was set square against administration being seen as a profession in itself. And so it goes to this day.

It is not always easy to live in such a milieu as an administrator, working alongside the 'real' professionals, hearing their condescension, observing the performance of sometimes lesser minds, seeing promotion blocked by this unexamined and unproven canon. Most will be familiar with the impatient and superior cry of the teacher who considers paperwork as very much secondary to his calling, an unwarranted and resented distraction from his raison d'etre.

Similar tensions can, of course, exist between the civil servant and the minister, or the local government officer and the councillor. It is often the paid official who is the more able and knowledgeable; it is often the paid official who is fair and impartial; but it is the politician who has the authority, the public face, and any kudos going.

Returning to definitions, all this is confusing. It cannot be desirable in society to have such fundamental differences concerning the meaning of important practical concepts. Confusion in practice usually means confusion of thinking; and this can be dangerous ,not merely ignorant ,where public provision is at issue.

Yet try juxtaposing two traditional definitions. "Administration" is the "practical translation of policy into practice". "Management" is "the ensuring that the organisation gets things done". There is no insight here, either, as the descriptions could coalesce.

Collins for one takes the radical view that the terms administration and management are really synonymous(32). There is apparent support arising from a lack of consensus in society about their application. Some of it is driven by status considerations. Management would appear, in this country at least, to have much the greater prestige. This is to an extent tied to positions in the hierarchy. Yet in Collins' world the needs of organisations are very similar, so that the enormous diversity in structures

CHAPTER 1

MANAGEMENT, LEADERSHIP AND ADMINISTRATION

and job titles is not justified by the underlying reality. Part of the problem is: the word 'manager' is ubiquitous. No word sounding quite so good has yet appeared to replace it.

It does not help that there are other specialist uses of terms. For instance, 'administration' is used in accountancy. To 'call in the administrator' means that a firm is in very serious financial difficulties, so it can no longer trade and needs the immediate services of specialist accountants to resolve them. In the interests of pursuing a more coherent thread, this kind of usage will be set aside as unhelpful, even aberrational.

Obviously, for the term "administration" to have any useful meaning it needs to be rather narrower than one running the whole gamut from leadership and policy-making to working the franking machine.

Because management theory is very much more universally promulgated and understood, academically and in wider Anglo-American society, it will be stipulated for the present work that the meanings of 'administration' and 'management' which should be adopted are the private sector ones, notwithstanding hierarchical and functional overlaps in sundry posts. Public sector models have been shown here to be internally inconsistent and mutually conflicting. By pervading working practice they make roles and tasks, already onerous, more difficult than they need be.

Nevertheless, the above analysis points to a very heterogeneous, not to say disparate, set of theoretical approaches as the only underpinning we have for management. Nothing is resolved. In common with much of the social sciences the discipline is at an emergent, rather than developed, state. One which some day in the future may sadly come to be recognised as rather primitive. Unlike scientific theories they lack both explanatory and predictive power, especially the latter, and should give the practitioner a sense of unease and mistrust if he places reliance on them. Yet what else can the poor bureaucrat rationally do?

Finally, it should not be necessary, although it probably is, for administration to need a plug. So few people seem to have the imagination to appreciate it, which is why in general terms our society and its institutions are so badly organised.

CHAPTER 1

MANAGEMENT, LEADERSHIP AND ADMINISTRATION

Yet, as we could see by reflecting on the conduct of major events, such as, say, the Olympic Games, we can do it extremely well. The trouble is that all the glamour is up front, with the performers and presenters, whereas administrators for the most part work quietly behind the scenes.

As it isn't on the whole particularly well valued, it is hardly likely to attract many outstanding people. Its difficulty is greatly underestimated. We tend to assume that anybody with a basic school education can do it. Not so. In fact, on the contrary many professionals and gifted individuals have not the first clue. Their lives are a literal mess in consequence.

CHAPTER 1

MANAGEMENT, LEADERSHIP AND ADMINISTRATION

NOTES

*   1.   Cole, G.A., Management: Theory and Practice, D.P. Publications Ltd., London, third edition, 1990.

2.   Mintzberg, H., The Nature of Managerial Work, Harper & Row, New York, 1973.

*   3.   Proctor, Tony, Management: Theory and Principles, Macdonald & Evans Ltd., Plymouth, 1982.

4.   Johnson, Gerry & Scholes, Kevin, Exploring Corporate Strategy, Prentice Hall International (UK) Ltd., Hemel Hempstead, 2nd edition, 1988.

*   5.   Pettinger, Richard, Contemporary Strategic Management, Palgrave MacMillan, Basingstoke, 2004.

6.   Fayol, H., General and Industrial Management, Pitman, London, 1949.

7.   Urwick, L.F., The Elements of Administration, Pitman, London, 1949.

8.   Taylor, F.W., The Principles of Scientific Management, Harper & Row, New York, 1911.

9.   Weber, M., Theory of Social and Economic Organisation, The Free Press, New York, 1947.

10.   Handy, C.B., Understanding Organisations, Penguin Book, London, 1976.

11.   Mayo, E., The Social Problems of an Industrial Civilization, Harvard, 1945.

12.   Barnard, C., Organisation and Management, Harvard University Press, Cambridge, Massachusetts, 1948.

CHAPTER 1

MANAGEMENT, LEADERSHIP AND ADMINISTRATION

13.   Argyris, C., Understanding Organisational Behaviour, Dorsey Press, Homewood, Illinois, 1960.

14.   Herzberg, F., The Motivation to Work (with Mausner, B and Snyderman, B), Wiley, New York, 1959.

15.   Likert, R., The Human Organisation: its Management and Value, McGraw-Hill, 1967.

16.   Katz, D. and Kahn, R.L., Social Psychology of Organisations, Wiley, 1966.

17.   Burns,T., and Stalker,G.H, The Management of Innovation, Tavistock 1966.

18.   Lawrence, P.R. and Lorsch, J.W., Organisation and Environment, Harvard University Press, 1967.

19.   The Aston Group, University of Aston, Birmingham late 1960's.

20.   Belbin, M., Management Teams: Why they succeed or fail, Butterworth Heinemann, Oxford 1996.

*   21.   Sprott, W.J.H., Human Groups, Penguin, Harmondsworth, 1958.

*   22.   Adair, John, Effective Leadership, Pan Books, Macmillan Publishers Ltd., London, 1998.

23.   Fiedler, F.E., A Theory of Leadership Effectiveness, McGraw-Hill, 1967.

24.   Drucker, Peter, F., The Effective Executive, Pan Books Ltd., London, 1970.

25.   Svendsen, Lars, Work, Acumen Publishing Limited, Stocksfield, 2008.

CHAPTER 1

MANAGEMENT, LEADERSHIP AND ADMINISTRATION

26.   Billen, Andrew, 'From Man Management to Mad Management', The Times, March 9th, 2009.

*   27.   Dunsire, Andrew, Administration, The Word and the Science, Martin Robertson & Company Ltd., 1973.

*   28.   Hodgkinson, C., Toward a Philosophy of Administration, Blackwell, Oxford, 1978.

29.   Bridges, Sir Edward (Lord), 'Portrait of a Profession', The Rede Lecture, London: Cambridge University Press, 1950.

30.   Brech, E.F.L., ed., The Principles and Practice of Management, London: Longmans, Green and Co., 1953; 2nd edn., 1963.

31.   Report of the Committee on the Staffing of Local Government (The Mallaby Committee), Ministry of Housing and Local Government, London: HMSO, 1967.

32.   Collins, O.F. and Moore, D.G., The Organisation Makers, Appleton, New York, 1970.

CHAPTER 2

PUBLIC MANAGEMENT

A General Theory of Management

The Nature of 'Public Administration'

Historical Development of 'Public Administration'

Public Administration and Policy

Administrative Law

Problems of Practice

CHAPTER 2

PUBLIC MANAGEMENT

A General Theory of Management

The introductory chapter outlined a plethora of variously useful or credible approaches by management theorists, but was inconclusive about whether any grounded synthesis could emerge or be attained.

So does management have an internal coherence and integrity such that its nature is general to all contexts and all fields of human endeavour? Does it have an explanatory theory as well as a merely descriptive one?

Dahl in an article in 1947 called 'The Science of Public Administration'[1] attacked various then prevalent conceptions of the nature of management; the classical theory that management is just technical, a value-free endeavour unconnected with goals; the idea that managers always behave rationally; and its western cultural overlay.

In the 1950's there was a theoretical dispute about whether management could have a general theory, and, if so, the extent of it. Some went to the other extreme and said there could only be a 'hospital management', a 'school management', a 'business management', and so on, but no 'management' in the abstract, removed from an area of application.

Gulick was all for a general theory and famously identified the important elements, which he described as below:

> "Planning, that is, working out in broad outlines the things that need to be done and the methods for doing them to accomplish the purpose set for the enterprise;
> Organizing, that is, the establishment of the formal structure of authority through which work subdivisions are arranged, defined and co-ordinated for the defined objective;
> Staffing, that is the whole personnel function of bringing in and training the staff and maintaining favourable conditions of work;
> Directing, that is, the continuous task of making decisions and embodying them in specific and general orders and instructions

CHAPTER 2

PUBLIC MANAGEMENT

and serving as the leader of the enterprise;

Co-ordinating, that is the all-important duty of interrelating the various parts of the work;

Reporting, that is, keeping those to whom the executive is responsible informed as to what is going on, which thus includes keeping himself and his subordinates informed through records, research, and inspection;

Budgeting, with all that goes with budgeting in the form of fiscal planning, accounting, and control."

These we recognize, but do not regard all of them as necessarily managerial.

Gulick emphasized in a complex enterprise the crucial import of "coordinating". Coordination could be achieved in two main ways, he claimed, by structural organisation of responsibilities in a chain of command, or by the development of a group purpose which all strive to attain. Gulick seemed to think that coordination was most effective when both methods were in operation, suitably interacting.

Lichfield then pressed ahead with attempts to develop a general theory of management, but only got so far as a set of five working propositions, as follows:

A) The managerial process is a cycle of action which includes the activities: decision-making, programming, communicating, controlling, reappraising.
B) The managerial process functions in the areas of policy, resources, execution.
C) The managerial process is carried out in the context of different 'dimensions' from individual to institution to 'ecology', or environment.
D) Management and the managerial process occur in substantially the same generalised form in any organisation, public or private sector.

Lichfield's 'major propositions' were accompanied by so-called 'minor' ones. These made a range of ancillary points such as that decision-making can have many qualities from rational and

PUBLIC MANAGEMENT

deliberative to the opposite in any combination, the managerial process will differ in important respects depending on the personalities involved, the character of the institution and its environment, and the management itself, through its practitioners, will seek to preserve itself and perhaps aim to grow.

The approach is a non-rigorous one in which systems theory is mixed up with structural and normative elements. Whatever its merits, it did not have a lot of influence on subsequent events or theory. So we are left with an unfinished project in a world where such has gone out of fashion. Can it be done even in principle? We still do not know that much. However, the chapter will show some of the errors that do arise from its lack, thus allowing for intellectual and political expediency in the public sector.

The Nature of "Public Administration"

The opening chapter came to a decision to replace the word 'administration' by 'management' in relation to all activities above the purely clerical, in both private and public sectors, and across all organisations and institutions. This should be born carefully in mind in reading the present chapter, because it is time to turn to the public sector itself and to consider so-called "public administration", the traditional covering management discipline. After characterizing it, and giving a quick developmental history, a flavour is provided of its relation to the key topic of policy. The context chosen for this is specifically local government, rather than national government (which is discussed at length in later chapters), or other branches of public sector institutions.

The treatment then proceeds to a brief examination of administrative law, which provides the legal framework for the conduct of public administration. This is done from the perspective of the general public as clients or consumers of services.

Finally, the myriad problems faced by public administrators are introduced, though not exhaustively so. The term 'public administration' will often need to be used owing to its entrenchment in the literature of

CHAPTER 2

PUBLIC MANAGEMENT

public sector theorists, although they are really talking about management within a bureaucracy.

'Public Administration' was defined by Barber in the early 1970's as "the administrative side of government", as contrasted with the legislature and the judiciary, but the author then somewhat confusingly claimed "the impossibility of distinguishing conceptually between these functions of government in any conclusive manner"(2). He further contended that "the administration effectively exercises what can properly be classified as legislative functions".

Corson and Harris in 1963 were more explicit. Public administration was "the action part of government; the means by which the purposes and goals of government are realised". This fed readily into a list of specifics - "decision making, planning the work to be done, formulating objectives and goals, establishing and reviewing organisations, directing and supervising employees, exercising controls....".

Barber's textbook gives the typical nature of public administration via its chapter headings. The constitutional framework is outlined. Central government policy-making processes and machinery are discussed, as is the nature and organisation of the civil service. Public corporations and local government are treated, along with their inter-relationships with central government. There are chapters on finance, planning, administrative law, along with elements of sociology in the concept of bureaucracy, and management theory with particular reference to organisational approaches and managerial techniques. At that time there was also a flourishing comparative public administration, seeking to analyse different features in other nations, including those with more federal, or decentralized structures.

Today, the Royal Institute of Public Administration, RIPA, does not exist anymore, but its name lives on as RIPA International, an independent international training organisation. Specimen module titles give a broad idea of the current subject matter; Leadership, Human Resource Development, Organisational Effectiveness, Financial Management, Information Management and Systems, Justice Reform, Communication.

CHAPTER 2

PUBLIC MANAGEMENT

Definitions will vary, but the scope of the field is generally uncontentious. Public Administration is concerned with branches of government policy, its study, development, and implementation, whether at national or more local levels, and via a variety of organisations.

Notwithstanding it importance, in university bookshops in English towns you would now be hard pressed to find much reference. Public sector topics more widely are on the fringe, if they are there at all. Management tomes, by contrast, abound, strongly focused on a, usually generalized, private sector.

The nature of qualifications is also instructive. In the 1960's and 1970's 'public administration' was a recognised subject of study lectured on at polytechnics, and examined by the Local Government Examinations Board. For instance, the Diploma in Public Administration, DPA, was quite a prestigious in-service qualification, awarded to external candidates by London University. A new National Certificate examination in public administration was launched by the Government in colleges of further education, aimed at 16-19 year-olds in the main.

Postgraduate diplomas in Public Administration are still available, and an example is the PG. Dip. from the School of Sociology and Social Policy at the University of Nottingham. "Suitable for new graduates and those with managerial and/or public sector work experience" it takes "an interdisciplinary approach to issues facing public management". "Policy and management modules" are studied and it develops "skills to critically analyse complex managerial issues".

Notice once again the lack of purism. Management is discussed, as though it were part of administration. So, too, is policy.

But matters are still more confused. Consider the famous Master of Business Administration, MBA, which is a worldwide-recognised master's management degree, whose graduates are "well prepared to undertake advanced professional occupations in businesses". It originated in the United States as the country industrialized and companies looked for scientific approaches to management. Content comprises a variety of subjects including:

CHAPTER 2

PUBLIC MANAGEMENT

economics, organisational behaviour, marketing, accounting, finance, strategy, operations management, IT management, project management, decision sciences, marketing, human resources, as well as entrepreneurship and international business.

This is curious, because here we have a qualification termed 'administration', but also universally regarded as a management qualification, and a professional one at that. The difference is, of course, that it is from the orbit of private sector business.

If you secure an MBA it is said to open up many employment opportunities. Riches and high positions have been heaped on its graduates, with instant salary increases of five figures or more not unusual and significant promotions as well. Whereas within local government the award could meet with a reaction of indifference. The achievement may be thought of as good for personal development possibly, but not a key to the senior management door.

Perhaps a more notorious illustration of the status problems of the public sector is the qualification of Chartered Secretary and Administrator. This was billed as being at the level of difficulty of a first degree, and obtained by three phases of final examinations, each usually taken annually. Now it had parallel streams - private sector and public sector. If you were in the public sector the best the qualification might do for you would be a middle-ranking post; even in the central administration department, the Town Clerk's, where the top job would almost invariably go to a qualified solicitor. In other words, somebody from a different profession, the law, would rule the administration department. So what did that say about the status of public administration as a profession? And could it be called a profession at all, given the general lack of acceptance of the aspiration? By telling contrast, they very same qualification, within the private sector stream, was a well-recognised route to top jobs as company secretaries in industrial firms, sometimes with relatively vast levels of remuneration.

So, given the apparent ease of content interchangeability, are they all branches of the same basic subject - 'generic administration' -what is taught in Public Administration or Business Administration? Dunsire sums up:

PUBLIC MANAGEMENT

"There is so much that appears to be common to the two spheres (e.g. administrative techniques, decision theory, human relations, and organisation theory." He goes on:
"The consensus of opinion in Britain appears to be that the fundamental ethos of business administration and public administration are so different that each requires to be infused through all the teaching of the whole curriculum, not just 'optional' aspects. The atmosphere is of different composition, it seems; the public servant breathes social accountability, the businessman the keen airs of commercial competitiveness."

Some, on the other hand, might consider such a consensus to be a tradition based on thin argument and prejudice. Of course, there are many ingredients aside from paper qualifications which could go to the making of a career - interpersonal skills for one, patronage for another, sheer luck for the third. Yet the message by now must be all too clear. If you want to get on in life as an officer in local government other qualifications relevant to particular professions may be valued more than those in public administration.

Historical Development of 'Public Administration'

'Public Administration' is broadly to be contrasted with private sector administration, that is to say, business practice in industry and commerce. A brief history of public administration is instructive in throwing some light on its nature.

In the 1800's Von Stein is considered to have founded it as a 'science', one which integrated any relevant disciplines(3). It was not just a branch of administrative law; rather it encompassed informing material from subjects like politics and economics, but with a body of theory which led the practice. The field (or faculty) of public administration was to be scientific in the methods it adopted. It would come in time to include modelling, market research, and the use of statistics, for instance.

After 1945, Gulick and Urwick, building on organisational principles invented by Henri Fayol, produce a supposedly comprehensive theory of

CHAPTER 2

PUBLIC MANAGEMENT

administration. They thought this could also be applied to managing companies, but it later focused on the organs of government in the main.

The New Public Management Model, by Osborne and Gaebler, came into being in the late 1980's and early 1990's. As hinted above, and unsurprisingly in a right-wing political regime, the model advocates private sector models and methods, not to mention resources, all across the public sector. Whilst many twentieth century developments have originated in the United States, the United Kingdom has usually accepted them uncritically. This one was no exception, leading among other things, to a wholesale and doctrinaire attack on local government, its integrity, competence, and motivation. It says much for the resilience of local government, notwithstanding central government's reforming ineptitude and wavering resolve, that it survived at all, albeit in severely weakened and truncated form.

There have been critics of this approach, apart from those inside the public sector deemed to have vested interests. There is an unease that people are treated on an economic model as "customers" instead of "citizens". The populace are seen as end-users of services, not as participants in some progressive social engineering programme. The outlook is still commonplace among government departments and organs at all levels.

Somewhat in reaction to it, and the cold, uncaring treatment one can receive from those whose ideology it is, Janet and Robert Denhardt devised 'The New Public Service Model', placing the emphasis on 'citizens' rather than 'customers', and an ideology of engagement or participation, people as active democrats, not mere passive receivers.

It is obvious that such radical departures are far from easy for public administrators to adjust to. Some never make it, either in acceptance of belief or in practice. What government tends to want immediately has a time-lag in winning the hearts and minds of the staff who actually have to carry out the new roles and absorb the new attitudes. Unfortunately, few of the experienced ones believe that the practices will last long, before the next political fashion takes over. Further discussion will need to await the later chapters on 'Social Progress' and 'Public Policy'.

CHAPTER 2

PUBLIC MANAGEMENT

Public Administration and Policy

Appleby wrote a definitive American work in 1949 entitled 'Policy and Administration', which sought to introduce a practitioner's realism into debates about the meanings of 'policy' and 'administration' (management) and their interrelationship. This was regarded by Dunsire as the "scholarly death-blow to the simplistic formulation of the classic dichotomy."

He showed quite clearly that the words 'policy' and 'administration' cannot generally be distinguished by reference to level or status in a hierarchy, nor by type of issue. Practices vary enormously between different institutions in this regard.

And again "the level at which a decision is to be made....may be shifted downward or upward as evaluations point to less or more controversy, or to less or more 'importance'."

Finally, "importance within the administrative organisation turns in some part in the dimensions and scope of the action - the weight of impact it will have, or has had on citizens, and the number of citizens affected; in some part on ideal values."

The state of affairs in local government will serve to illustrate some of the principles.

The Maud Report (4) has been very influential to this day because it set out the respective roles of Council member and officer in local government, and the dividing line between them. There had hitherto been much confusion of roles and myriad problems of internal organisation which the report sought to redress. Repeatedly, the Committee tried to draw a distinction between 'policy' and 'administration', as the evidence to it pressed for, only to conclude that " 'policy' cannot be defined." Strangely (or possibly tellingly), the Maud Report had no such doubts about the meaning of 'administration'.

At any rate, whatever lack of objectivity there may had been, and for whatever reasons, the Committee did come up with a very workable

PUBLIC MANAGEMENT

formula to decide the roles; one which has been of considerable usage even to the present day.

The actual text is worth quoting in full here for the avoidance of ambiguity. It is all the more remarkable for not employing the word 'policy' at all.

> *We recommend that local authorities consider a division of functions and responsibilities between members and officers as follows:*
>
> *a) Ultimate direction and control of the affairs of the authority to lie with the members.*
>
> *b) The members to take the key decisions on the objectives of the authority and on the plans to attain them.*
>
> *c) The members to review, periodically, progress and the performance of the services.*
>
> *d) The officers to provide the necessary staff work and advice so that members may set the objectives and take decisions on the means of attaining them.*
>
> *e) The officers to be responsible for day-to-day administration of services, decisions on case-work, and routine inspection and control.*
>
> *f) The officers to be responsible for identifying and isolating the particular problem or case which in their view, and from their understanding of the minds of the members, has such implications that the members must consider and decide on it.*

Interestingly paragraph (*f*) has a way, in practice, of subverting all the others. The officers are revealed as having to provide the monitoring, guidance, and judgement that their employers are presumed to lack. It is but a short step from this to the realisation that in order for the members to do such grandiose things as 'ultimately control', or 'take key decisions', or 'review service performances', they have to be alerted, prompted, informed, and advised by their underlings, sometimes on the basis of considerable research, analysis, report writing and consultation. As so often in government, we have a convenient fiction.

Of course, the elected council do have the collective power to go their

PUBLIC MANAGEMENT

own way, with or without the advice of their officers. Sadly, the literature is littered with cases of the oft resulting excess. In 1974 some prominent North-East councillors were sent to prison for corruption, having obtained rewarding contracts for an (unqualified) private architect, John Poulson. The Clay Cross Urban District Council in Derbyshire in 1972 refused to implement Government housing legislation. They were disqualified from office and displaced by government-appointed commissioners.

Naturally, these are extremes, and still fairly rare. What could be a fruitful subject for study would be all those situations in which councils unilaterally acted, perfectly well within the law, and yet with appalling judgements, serving their local committees ill. To some extent these are a matter of taste and opinion on which rate payers will very likely have their own thoughts.

Administrative Law

Administration Law(5) is that which covers the public administration dealings of organs of state, such as the police, or local government, or quangos. It is to the purpose of the present work to consider what help it provides for citizens faced with dealing with these institutions when they have a grievance, because this is a very important strand to test how democratic the nation actually is in practice.

Historically it was a French idea to produce a separate group of legal rules governing how the administration is carried out. To its shame England went through a period before the Second World War in which claimants could not call on the aid of the principles of natural justice in cases that were deemed to be 'administrative'. Only where government had laid down a judicial procedure could they have recourse to a court.

Unfortunately for the citizen, government activity threatening individual rights then escalated. Even after the war the situation continued, so that by the 1960s there was little redress for individuals against the state. The venerated rules were out of date, and the widespread use of delegated powers by ministers was untouched by the courts, even in cases of alleged bias or error of legal interpretation.

CHAPTER 2

PUBLIC MANAGEMENT

As a kind of alternative, an ombudsman system was introduced to cover various areas of administrative activity. However, it is seriously to be doubted whether the idea achieves a great deal. For one thing, the system is far from covering every organ that needs scrutiny. Although there is an ombudsman responsible for local government, and he can review actions of councils and their individual officers, the schools, where there is much autocratic abuse, are exempt, probably because the government wishes for a different kind of relationship with its (frequently complaining) head teachers.

For another thing, access by the layman to the ombudsman is restricted. In local government, by way of example, you need to be able to persuade a councillor to take forward your case. Then, your grounds of complaint are narrow. You can find fault with the way officers have treated you. You can claim procedural faults, or delay, amounting to 'maladministration', but you cannot criticize policy, which is what most people are upset by, of course.

Perhaps conveniently, 'maladministration' is not defined in law. However, there are some pointers from practice and, most certainly, what does qualify is quite likely to be far removed from a complainant's perceptions. There can be maladministration by delay, bias, neglect, incompetence, failure to follow procedure, arbitrariness, bad rules, bad decisions, failure to tell people their rights, partial treatment as between like cases, misleading advice. What is not maladministration is a decision properly taken within a public body's area of discretion which the member of the public complaining does not happen to like. Experience shows that tends to be most of them.

If you win your case, what happens? Not a lot. The ombudsman will issue a statement giving advice to the council, but there is no legal obligation for it to take any notice. You may thus be left with a feeling that the procedural avenues are tokenism, that the government wants to claim publicly that you have democratic rights of redress, whilst in practice denying them in effect.

There is also an ombudsman with jurisdiction over Parliament. A notorious case is that of Equitable Life. The Parliamentary Ombudsman,

CHAPTER 2

PUBLIC MANAGEMENT

Ann Abrahams, produced a further special report into the Equitable Life Affair after earlier investigations when the mutual insurance company very nearly collapsed in 2001 ,taking substantial amounts of policyholders' money, which was being saved towards pensions. The report was critical of the government's role, found it guilty of maladministration, and noted that it had not produced a proper timetable for compensation.

However, the government steadfastly refused to accept some of the findings, rejecting the claim of maladministration, for instance, and it appointed another adviser to devise an alternative ex-gratia payment scheme. The chairman of Equitable Life called on the Parliamentary Ombudsman to resign if the government continued to reject her findings (she duly did so) and accused it of seeking to avoid payment to the policyholders, some of whom had died during the time of the lengthy dispute, and were now represented by their families.

So what else is available? Tribunals do exist, but they cover relatively small areas of activity within the many powers of public bodies. Some of the most developed concern local government, to which national governments from Thatcher onwards have shown varying degrees of vindictiveness.

A good example are the special needs tribunals in Education. The law requires local education authorities to provide each of those children with learning difficulties for whatever reason with a formal statement of their special educational needs, assessed by educational and medical experts. The statement has to recommend appropriate educational provision for the child and is legally binding. Since high cost implications are often involved, and the wording of statements could admit a range of interpretations, parents and local education authorities can often be in dispute, notably as to the nature of the proposed educational provision for the child. Originally, after the governing legislation, the Education Act 1981, the appeals were heard by an ad hoc committee of council members of the authority concerned. Later, independent (government-controlled) tribunals were set up regionally, with binding decisions. In effect the local government officers who attended to make their case could become directly accountable to the tribunal rather than to their own managers. However, the real villain in the piece is the perennial lack of resources.

Some progress in finding machinery for public redress has been made since the 1960s in that new influential judges like Lord Denning attacked the exclusion of administrative cases from the courts and so an Administrative Court was formally set up in 2000. It would seem that the great hope of the common man is now supposed to be a process called 'judicial review', to which he can only turn once any statutory procedures governing the area of complaint have been worked through and exhausted to no avail.

Judicial review(6) is a process whereby the actions of a public body are scrutinized by a judge to see if they are legal. It does not constitute an appeal against the decision of a court. No assessment of the merits of the decision is made, but the process by which the decision is reached is examined.

Joe Citizen faces barriers in the way of reaching a judicial review. First he has to apply to the Administrative Court for permission. Mostly this is strictly time-limited, usually to within three months of the grounds for the application arising.

Both features are designed to deter applicants. The Administrative Court examines their 'standing'. This means that they must be deemed to have 'sufficient interest' to pursue the case. The Court will exercise a judgement here, though there is case law to provide some guidance. Sometimes 'standing' will be granted if a person has no other remedy left open.

After that, the Court will look at the reasons presented for the action and decide whether there are sufficient grounds to allow a judicial review to proceed. These are roughly of three types. Did the public body act illegally? Was it irrational? Did its procedures breach statute or fail to honour the principles of natural justice? There is much development on the bald principles, but they at least give the flavour of it. They sound reasonable, yet anyone who has ever tangled with a public body, or a large private one for that matter, comes to realise just how many issues

CHAPTER 2

PUBLIC MANAGEMENT

will remain completely outside the purview. The government can also behave unscrupulously, writing statutes designed to exclude the possibility of judicial review, so that the matter is put beyond the consideration of a court altogether.

Anyway, let us assume that Joe Citizen has succeeded in overcoming all these not inconsiderable barriers and has been granted a judicial review. At the hearing his standing will be re-examined, now in greater detail. And at the end of the case the judge may dismiss it, make a 'declaration', which is not a remedy, but might find the actions unlawful, or he may even quash the public body's decision, or order them to take particular action.

So there is something in place, at least in theory. In practice it is only for the few, who have to be quite determined and not without courage. The process is costly, time-consuming, and very uncertain of outcome. And that is just the way the mighty state wants things to be, although you will never get a government minister to admit it.

Public authorities, of course, do many things, and the law has something to say about the circumstances under which members of the public affected may, or may not, have legal rights of potential redress. Such bodies are creations of statute and it is to the contents of these legal documents that we must go for enlightenment. If a nuisance is caused to a citizen as an inevitable consequence of an activity, which the public authority is authorised by statute to carry out, the citizen has no legal redress. Malicious decisions made for an improper reason, on the other hand, can be challenged via judicial review.

Even the fact that a public body has acted unlawfully is not in itself a sufficient ground for a legal action. If that body misunderstands its legal powers and acts beyond them there is no arising liability.

Some of the legal facts may strike citizens as surprising, even unreasonable. The police have no legal duty of care to protect victims and witnesses of crime, the stated reasoning being that public policy would not want the police to fear legal action against them which might make their behaviour defensive and so detrimental to the interests of society.

CHAPTER 2

PUBLIC MANAGEMENT

Where a citizen takes legal action against an organ of the state it is important to mention public interest immunity (PII), which it is for the discretion of the court to decide on application whether to grant. PII is used to prevent the content of documents being publicly disclosed during a legal case if this is deemed not to be in the public interest. Only the Crown used to be able to claim immunity, but now the contentious cases are usually ones in which the government seeks to keep something secret. A legitimate example would be the plans of a nuclear weapon, but government has sought to exclude whole classes of document, such as all those including advice to ministers. Normally, the court will want to look at the content of actual documents, but sometimes a judgement is made from a description of the contents of a document, rather than as a conclusion after actually examining it. Likewise, to be fair, the court has to consider whether a party to proceedings simply wants to trawl through a list of documents in the hope of uncovering something helpful to their case, the so-called 'fishing expeditions', which are not legally countenanced. Another restriction is on release of information as to the identity of police informants, who otherwise would probably not wish to risk coming forward.

The area is altogether clouded by controversy. Media frequently give the impression that government is hiding something purely for its own benefit, and is obtaining the compliance of the court to secure its position against legitimate public criticism.

So whatever the truth in distinct cases, it remains an unfulfilled aspiration that the citizen could acquire adequate legal rights and powers to assert his interests against the public bodies of the state. There is little chance, for the state palpably does not want it to happen. No wonder public servants are rarely popular ex officio and tend to carry the brunt.

Problems of Practice

So what are the major problems of working in the public sector? What is life like for the bureaucrat, in other words?

Barber classifies problems in public administration three-fold as "those

PUBLIC MANAGEMENT

of principle, those associated with the overall governmental context, and those of a more particularly administrative nature."

In the first category he has what is widely regarded as the cardinal value in administration, that of attaining 'efficiency'. Scientifically speaking, you are supposed to achieve your goal with the least expenditure of resources, be they man or material. Apart from the challenge of always having to do so, there is competition from other values, such as accountability, and social responsibility.

The public context throws up many a criticism which can lead to political review and change, whether justified or not. The political context and the governmental context both render decision-making in administration problematic at times, given the likelihood of political control and the certainty of the exercise of vested powers which may or may not carry democratic agreement within the society.

The governmental context is also permanently bedevilled by general dilemmas like how to balance freedoms with security, vested interests against the wider good, and current concerns against future needs.

When it comes to the fundamentally 'administrative' problems, they can look all too suspiciously similar to the ones nowadays listed under the management purview - matters like organisational issues, planning, decision-making and so forth.

The treatment following considers the governmental/political issues in more detail, but starts with its own category, that of the theoretical, which harks back to our earlier consideration of a possible general management theory.

Some of the theoretical tensions that emerged were unresolved and remain so. These were mainly the separation of politics from public administration, and the applicability of the theory from private sector organisations. Part of the problem here, in fairness, was the fact that political science, and indeed economics, were themselves emerging as disciplines, struggling against normative tendencies and dogma. But even where there is emergence, the gap between the interests of research academics and practitioners can be very wide.

CHAPTER 2

PUBLIC MANAGEMENT

The literature on public administration shows that the field is inevitably interdisciplinary in nature. While a few brave administrators might wish to delineate a boundary so that it becomes a separate subject in its own right, the plain fact is that in modern times, from around 1850, public administration has been seen as informed essentially by other subjects, some discrete, some not. Among the main influences are political science, sociology, constitutional and administrative law, management theory, public finance, and communication.

Therein lies part of the problem for both theorists and practitioners. Because public administration lacks coherence as a subject, and because government chicanery makes such studies unappetising for many, qualifications in it, even post-graduate ones, lack any tradition of high status, as we have seen. Allied to perceptions of low pay, and the enormous heterogeneity of the public sector, what have developed instead are practices with formal qualifications largely confined to the individual institutions, such as the Police, the NHS, or the Civil Service itself. Local government especially exhibits quite a different history, with separate, but parallel departments each representing a profession, like accountancy, law, teaching, social work, and civil engineering. Usually, the head of department has been a qualified, senior practitioner of the relevant profession.

This has many consequences, mostly bad. Prominent are how the situation encourages insularity, narrow thinking, and reduces the prospects for formally approved transfer of training and hence portability of qualifications across the public sector, or even across local government. The exceptions to this tend to be at both top and bottom. At lowest levels basic clerical staff roles can have a similarity of content or function. At the top politicians helicopter in acolytes of their choosing, whether qualified, relevantly experienced, or quite the opposite. These jobs are increasingly politicized, with tenure short (often fixed-term), targets to be met, and sometimes scapegoats to be found.

But the resulting mish-mash and confusions of thought have a deleterious effect to this day, a fact particularly true of the public/private sector divide. The relevance of theory and practice in one sector to the other has

PUBLIC MANAGEMENT

never yet been decided by evidence or argument. What we have instead are political fiats, again and again, based on a combination of opportunism and prejudice. Society is contested, and as things have gone, at least since the late 1980's, the insights and ideologies of the private sector have almost invariably been commended to, or even enforced upon, the conduct of the public sector. A notable feature of Thatcherism in the United Kingdom it has been continued, under Labour during the Blair and Brown years, with some further novelties of innovation, such as Public/Private Partnerships, used for the joint development funding, and transfer to private ownership, of large public sector institutions like hospitals and schools.

Because Government acts through many organs of State they all come within the broad scope of public administration. Some of the main institutions involved include the departments of central government itself, the councils in local government, the police and fire services, the National Health Service, and legions of "quangos"- public bodies which carry out government policies and laws in particular fields with accountability directly to government. Fragmenting has produced separate, isolated traditions leading to heterogeneity in both theory and practice. The field is consequently incoherent.

As illustration, the Education service is separate structurally and separatist by nature, even within itself. Private schools and the state sector do not mix. Universities, colleges of further education, local education authorities all have different administrative structures and recruitment patterns.

Finally, and fundamentally, there are even more profound problems with the underlying aims and assumptions of public administration than these, to be outlined below.

Public administration is the practical vehicle for improving society, but assumes, quite dubiously, that there is such a thing as the "public good". It is by no means obvious, and needs to be argued for and evidenced, in a pluralist society, except in extreme cases of emergency, such as a civil disaster, or a warring nation at the gates.

CHAPTER 2

PUBLIC MANAGEMENT

Even if there is a common "public good", can it be found and agreed upon, does it differ over time, and across the various fields of endeavour, and what would be the appropriate mechanisms for debate and decision?

It is further assumed that 'government' action via public administration can, and does, make a very significant difference in these matters. And that results can be, and are, accurately planned and delivered by policy implementation programmes. But is it so?

Some of these troublesome questions, and others, will be further explored in the following chapters. Pragmatically, of course, public administrators are no different from the rest of society; they proceed in hope, however considerable the odds against them.

CHAPTER 2

PUBLIC MANAGEMENT

NOTES

*   1.   Dunsire, Andrew, Administration: The Word and the Science, Martin Robertson & Company Ltd., London, 1973.

*   2.   Barber, M.P., Public Administration, Macdonald & Evans Ltd., London, 1974.

       3.   Public Administration, Wikipedia, 2009.

       4.   Maud, Sir John, the Committee on Management of Local Government, HMSO, London, 1967.

*   5.   Clements, Richard and Jones, Philip, Public Law, Oxford University Press, Oxford, 2009.

*   6.   Coles, Joanne and Reynolds, Jane, Constitutional and Administrative Law, Hodder Arnold, London, 2nd Edn., 2009.

CHAPTER 3

SOCIAL PROGRESS

Introduction

The Meaning of Progress

Science and Progress

Economics and Progress

Change

Human Nature

Theories of Social Progress

Fundamental Problems

Social Policy

CHAPTER 3

SOCIAL PROGRESS

Introduction

Social progress is a deceptively complex subject, and so a start will be made by looking first at the concept of progress itself, to try and pin down its meaning. Will it be fact or fiction? The strongest candidate among areas of human endeavour in which to find progress is feasibly science. Progress is therefore next explored in that arena. Coming to the social context, the subject among social sciences with the traditional claim to be pre-eminent in its scientific development - economics - is next discussed in relation to the prospects for progress. Many social ills, though naturally far from all, would crucially depend on adequate finance for their solutions. Thus, it is doubly apposite to look at the so-called 'dismal science' and what hope it may have to offer them.

Since progress by any definition involves change, it is fitting to examine the concept of change to see if it can throw any light on our subject matter.

The way humans behave, the way humans are, could in principle be a seriously limiting factor on the extent to which the human situation could be ameliorated. The concept of human nature is controversial and much will depend on what it is and whether/how it might be altered.

Previous discussion will then have highlighted major constraints and barriers to the way ahead. It is into that framework that exposition of the philosophical theories about social progress must be placed.

The chapter's penultimate section mulls over the fundamental problems that any realistic project for social progress has to surmount if it is to succeed.

A final section samples the sociological literature on social policy to see how it can try to make sense of it all.

CHAPTER 3

SOCIAL PROGRESS

The Meaning of Progress

It is desirable to focus the meaning of "progress" at the outset, since misunderstanding with an everyday, but complex concept like this is otherwise effortlessly easy. What are not meant are dictionary[1] characterisations like "movement whilst travelling in any direction", or simply a "course". "Progress" here is used, quite conventionally, to mean "movement towards a goal", "advancement", "development", "improvement", or "betterment".

'Progress' is founded on the belief that improvements can occur over time. Some take a wide view of progress, that it occurs in many fields of human endeavour, others that progress is restricted. Thorough-going sceptics deny progress altogether. So we have disagreement at the outset and are going to need evidence to resolve it.

Part of the trouble is that the word 'progress' tends to have connotations that are not neutral. When we call something 'progressive', we are often making favourable contrast with reactionary attitudes. It is good to move forward to, to change, to leave behind the out-moded past. On the other hand the word 'tradition' stimulates positive and nostalgic thoughts, beliefs that where we are is better than where we are going. So confusions can arise from the emotionally-laden baggage accompanying the words we use.

'Social progress' is itself a social construct, many would argue. What constitutes progress for me is anathema to you, so that there is normally no objective basis for it. Again the subjectivism can only be overcome in narrow contexts, where we can agree that, according to certain objective criteria, say of a factual or even measurable nature, there has been 'progress'.

Strangely, attaining agreement that all the issues are actually ills would be very hard, never mind obtaining resources for plans to tackle them. And in the same way there are profound disagreements about what are the social goods to be pursued also.

Social progress would have to resolve a whole series of tensions between

CHAPTER 3

SOCIAL PROGRESS

dualisms, each related to human propensities. The following list is not exhaustive but will illustrate:

self-interest	- versus -	community development
economic growth	- versus -	environment resource constraint
free enterprise	- versus -	the welfare state
nationalism	- versus -	international cooperation.

Great care is needed with the dualisms, since they are liable to be largely unexamined ghosts of upbringing in people's minds.

The climate of public opinion is no constant either, but changes quite irrationally over time. For instance, it ebbs and flows in sexual mores between extremes of permissive and controlling. When you are born can therefore in itself have a very significant bearing on your future sex life, its nature and quality.

There are other major differences of view about the meaning of 'social progress' relating to its geographical scope. Do locally, regionally, or nationally agreed developments constitute progress? Or can we envisage a global and universal, international destination which epitomizes world peace and has agreement over purposes, themselves planet-friendly and ethical? Is this the essence of the unattainable idealism, or something we can realistically strive for? The question, set against the tragic history of humanity, hardly seems worthwhile posing, sadly.

Looking at so-called fundamental goods, such as freedom, there is no common ground as to what it means - whether it is for individuals, or groups, for example. More widely, with goods like equality and justice - we have no consensus about which are the core values and how to prioritise them if they clash.

Without this, of course, presumably preceded by some kind of ambitious collective debate on a nationwide and international scale, we will not be able to agree where we want society to go and why. Never ending argument about methods is bad enough for public managers to cope with,

CHAPTER 3

SOCIAL PROGRESS

without the added nightmare of a plurality of aims, some of which will be mutually inconsistent.

But can we be this rational? Commentators vary on what they see as the main human forces involved in social change. Does reason play a leading part, or are irrational and emotional factors and selfishness paramount anyway? Some would claim that the moral capacities of human beings can be improved - really a question that underpins a later debate on whether human nature is a constancy. If the answer is found to be in the negative it obviously seriously curtails the potentiality for social progress, since right-doing has largely to follow on from right-thinking.

Science and Progress

Are there any fields, therefore, where the concept of progress is relatively easy to agree and apply, and where progress is clearly demonstrable?

The obvious candidate to consider is science and technology. Even here sceptics claim that truth is never attained. Rather, that science goes through a series of 'paradigm shifts', according to Kuhn, which lead to revolutionary changes in the tenets of scientific belief, but no final position of complete understanding[2].

They are inclined to cite Kuhn and distort his messages, casting the book as an attack on the rational or empirical nature of science[3]. What Kuhn actually said was that the history of science showed that science normally proceeded to be carried out within a 'paradigm', characterized as a previous major scientific achievement which the scientific community (tentatively) accepted as correct. If the work later threw up 'anomalies', that is to say, findings which did not fit the paradigm, then scientists would employ a variety of methods to deal with the problem. They may repeat their work, looking for consistency or otherwise with the original findings, or seek weaknesses in the experimental design, defects in their equipment. They might choose to proceed in the hope that further work would collapse the anomaly.

Eventually, if none of their measures worked, a 'crisis' would have to be

CHAPTER 3

SOCIAL PROGRESS

acknowledged. Key parts of the paradigm could then be jettisoned and a novel approach and understanding reached. If a new paradigm was the outcome, there was said by Kuhn to have been a 'scientific revolution'.

To suggest, as the critics have done, that the move to another paradigm is irrational, is false. The scientific community will have a great deal of both evidence and reasoned argument to use in their assessment of the position. Where Kuhn is weak is in not detailing just how the paradigm choice decision is arrived at. He did not deal sufficiently with another critique which (mistakenly) claimed the two paradigms as having no terms with shared meanings such as would allow a genuine evaluative comparison. To the challenge that the decision to change paradigms is ultimately a judgement standing outside any rules of method, scientists and philosophers are increasingly likely to retort, 'so what?' It will not have been taken without the best available intellectual support of the scientific community.

Besides, science and technology definitely do progress. This is indisputable fact. They progress in the sense that knowledge and understanding of the natural world advance, by empirical and rational means, even if tentatively and incompletely. This must be so because it brings with it a greater capacity to change that world and to exercise some partial control over it. We can test whether our scientific theories approximate to the truth by following their predictions. We can find out whether our scientific laws apply, and also their limits, by measurements of the interrelated parameters. We can see that a technology is soundly based when it delivers better practical results through its technical developments.

But scientific and technological progress must be distinguished from whether science and technology overall, or in particular key respects, bring about social progress or its opposite.

Whilst it is folly to argue that science and technology does not produce progress in the understanding and manipulation of nature, many voices do deny it as a progressive force generally due to society's obvious failures to harness it for good and against evil. It requires wisdom of a very high order, and superior moral strength, to ensure that most of its developments are in the human interest. The issues are many and

CHAPTER 3

SOCIAL PROGRESS

complex, from nuclear power and unrecycled waste, to stem cell research, and gene engineering in animals and crops, the social aspects of accommodating to computers, the uses and abuses of mass communication media, science in the service of weaponry.

Attitudes across societies on this question have varied over history. For example, at the end of the nineteenth century, electricity was new and there had been important medical advances such as antiseptics and anaesthetics, leading to very optimistic outlooks that science and technology could ameliorate the lot of mankind. By the time of the second-world war and the ensuing cold war, however, with the invention of the atomic and hydrogen bombs, it was all too apparent that they also had the propensity for terrible harm.

Nowadays attitudes are liable to be mixed, even contradictory. Science is difficult, so most people are scientifically illiterate. What you do not understand you tend to dislike, devalue, fear. The situation is potentially very dangerous, because the ignorant do not make enough good decisions.

Much scientific advance is now taken for granted because we lack the imagination to appreciate what is involved, our memories are short, and new inventions quickly become familiar. For instance, there have been steady breakthroughs in medical treatments, and we look to the scientists to find wonder cures for cancer. But in matters such as gene modification we are inclined to listen to religious zealots selectively complaining about our 'playing God', and meddling to prevent or hinder the legal reforms necessary to allow a framework for essential research.

Public concern about an unfettered scientific community is democratically legitimate. What especially does not help the scientific cause is the awareness of the ordinary citizen that he is squeezed out of policy influence between big business and big government. And people know that to proceed with caution in areas where there appear to be serious risks is both prudent and rare. Political and commercial pressures ensure that the onus is typically on detractors to somehow prove damage. Otherwise, projects tend to go ahead when there is an absence of existing evidence against them.

CHAPTER 3

SOCIAL PROGRESS

Economics and Progress

In addition to science and technology another field where there has been some optimism about progress is economics(4). This is a key issue for assessment of the feasibility of social progress, because unfortunately so many of its prerequisites rely on economics, the study of scarce resources and how to make them grow. Most areas of social policy, as we know, depend on finance, lots of it, to try and effect improvements.

A vexed question for economics relates to its concepts and measurements; how far they can be regarded as accurate indicators of economic progress. Economic growth is superficially equated with economic progress. The usual measure of economic growth is the gross domestic product, GDP, which is the total value of the goods and services the country produces in a year. To some extent, assuming it can be accurately estimated, it is an objective and useful index of changes in the real value of an economy's production of benefits.

Another common measure is gross national product, GNP. This measures the total income of the country, GDP plus net income added from abroad. If there are relatively large interest payments on foreign debt borrowings, as was the case in Britain following bank support action by the Brown government during the 2008 credit crunch, there will, of course, be a net deficit.

But the GDP omits some important factors. It excludes intermediate goods made for use in production, and also excludes consideration of the fact that goods sold to the final consumer are sometimes intermediate goods as far as they are concerned, since purchased as a means to a higher welfare end. There needs to be welfare adjustment depending on whether inequalities of income (and wealth) are reducing or, as in the United Kingdom, increasing. The welfare of future people is also discounted by GDP, wrongly according to those who stress the vital import of resource sustainability.

'Economic growth'(5) is glibly assumed to be a desirable objective, but it is in fact an open question dependent on a good deal of further information. Firstly, what is the growth to be of? The public in a

CHAPTER 3

SOCIAL PROGRESS

democracy would be entitled, and asked, to decide on the balance between public and private goods. In the second place, who is to benefit from the growth? The question points to deep- lying issues of whether one part of society or another is to be the receiver, and challenges policies on income and wealth distribution. Finally, what costs can acceptably be paid to attain economic growth? These will relate to the environment and to the quality of life, for example.

But many goods essential to our welfare and satisfaction are outside the economic markets entirely. They are non-traded goods like leisure, housework, child-rearing and community feeling.

So concentration on overall production as a social progress goal is extremely simplistic. The added contention that increased growth will lead to an automatic improvement in living standards is at best naïve. There is no substitute here for the kind of examination that is the *raison d'etre* of public management - what are the major underlying problems of our society and how may we solve them?

Capitalists, following the collapse of the Berlin Wall and the secession of some outer Russian states, tended to celebrate, very prematurely, the death of communism. China, for example, has continued its rise towards the status of a world power. Russia itself remains in its ideological grip. And Islamic states are rarely run on democratic lines.

However, Fukuyama(6) saw capitalism approvingly as prevailing endlessly, typified by mixed economies like those of the United States and Europe. He confused the fall of East European communist regimes with meaning that capitalism was instead the system, that it had somehow thereby succeeded, because it was the only other game. A sense of the moral superiority of the West was spawned, and an unfortunate element of complacency about the merits of capitalism set in.

Until the credit crunch of 2008/9, the conventional wisdom said that we in capitalist countries were living in managed economies with some kind of balance between the private (wealth-creating) sector and the public (welfare) sector, and with well-established economic theories which allowed us to control and prevent the main financial risks. We were told

CHAPTER 3

SOCIAL PROGRESS

that the tendency of the economy to swing between 'boom' and 'bust' could be managed, or even eliminated, so as to prevent serious problems. These economic cycles could be smoothed out by a combination of central measures involving changes to taxation and money supply, thus manipulating supply and demand.

The question has to be answered, however, as to whether economics in its present state of development is actually capable of managing a modern western economy. Do the theoreticians know enough, in other words, to allow for the requisite degree of control among all the main players?

What follows cannot be an exhaustive treatment of the question. A few key ideas will nevertheless be sketched in to leave little doubt that the answer must woefully be negative. We turn to Vincent Cable, the Liberal Democrats' chief economics spokesman, who had been called 'The man who gives politics a good name', and who provided 'the holy grail of economic comment'(7). (Unfortunately, these accolades did not survive long when Cable was appointed a   minister under the Con-Dem government and had to go along with polices he did not personally believe in).

The first piece of evidence to be led is the fact that there have been 'many boom and bust cycles in economic history'. If theory did exist to stop them, they were nevertheless not stopped.

Secondly, there has for very many years been an unresolved dichotomy between two fundamentally different economic approaches to the managed economy. On the one hand there has been the theory of John Maynard Keynes, which emphasized taxes; on the other hand the alternative use of monetary policy to control money supply. The practices adopted have sometimes been mixed. Sadly, they have typically been chosen by political rather than economic preference.

Thirdly, there are major dynamic factors which will have very large effects on national economies, and over which economists also disagree. One such is globalization, a complex admixture of factors whose good and bad points are endlessly debated without a consensus emerging. Another is protectionism over national trade.

CHAPTER 3

SOCIAL PROGRESS

Closer to home political commentators have elaborated copiously on what Cable called "the dangerous overdependence of the United Kingdom on the pretensions and 'short-termism' of the City". Robert Peston, for one, has discussed "the role of the City in influencing economic policy under New Labour".

Economists and politicians can no more agree over what needs to be done regarding banking regulation and how to do it than they can fly unaided. Which gives the City further respite and opportunity for selfish and irresponsible activity, needless to dwell on.

There has at least been a journalistic debate about the kind of capitalism we might like to see emerging. Although their seeming assumption that change will be major, and brought about by deliberate measures, remained dubious as the months slipped by after the credit crunch crisis reached its height within the financial institutions. And, of course, there was absolutely no agreement.

We have rehearsed the fact that waiting for capitalism to reduce the extremes of inequality within moderate limits, instead of adding to them, would be a triumph for naïve idealism. If wealth 'trickles down', that is all it does.

What people are also beginning to suspect is the key truth, as Cable pointed out, that "markets do not work when there is a collapse of trust". So the whole edifice is really a house of cards, depending on mass psychology as its backing.

For free-market enthusiasts the notion of some mysterious collective force somehow knowing better than actual people has been fashionable in liberal-conservative circles for hundreds of years since Adam Smith wrote 'The Wealth of Nations'. The further claim is that if people intervened in the market to try and control this force, the chances are extremely high that something will go wrong. How dangerous a view this should now seem, although socialists always knew it was ridiculous. To give them their due they at least tried to bring in a modicum of humanity by their corrective measures when in power.

CHAPTER 3

SOCIAL PROGRESS

Even without such a thing as a mild recession, with a temporary fall in demand and rising unemployment come the many individual tragedies that inevitably characterize capitalist systems. Unless personally affected, we tend to become inured to firms going into administration, thousands losing their livelihoods. The essential brutality of market mechanisms is glossed over in the good times.

To see the truly awful consequences of capitalism we need to look no further than the credit crunch of 2008 and the widespread international recession it precipitated.

The sheer scale of misery is worth reflecting on for those who say they prefer capitalism to more left-leaning options. Millions being thrown out of work, thousands having their homes repossessed, bear witness to a system that has worked only too well. Self-correcting, the unfettered market has no human feelings or face. It will be left for the next generations to pay off the massive national borrowing debt incurred in our names without our consent, whilst having their own life chances severely curtailed as a result of the long-term damage. That is altogether more serious in consequences than virtually all the crimes for which people have been sent to prison, and yet where are the laws to safeguard and punish? They are not there because the value systems of the ruling elites do not regard the actions as wrong doing.

When honest householders have their homes repossessed, when unemployment benefit is below the poverty line, and so on, who wants to live in a society that unjust? And who can afford to spend a life time being cheated, waiting around for an honest government that will actually help them rather than lie and deceive, tax and squander?

An irony is that although all are at risk, from rich to poor, from old to young, our personal stories are endlessly diverse and the economic impacts correspondingly varied. This both fragments our experiences and prevents an emerging commonality of views on remedial action. So long as those at the top continue to do well they will sing the system's praises and resist significant rather than merely cosmetic reforms.

Alas, we know now that the economy is fundamentally and essentially a

CHAPTER 3

SOCIAL PROGRESS

very complex and unstable system. Where financial value is decided, not on rational grounds, but by primitive emotions like fear and optimism in stock exchanges run like gambling casinos. Prices are created and destroyed at whim by imitative behaviour. Financial movements are generated by self-serving speculators who ought to be classified as criminals, yet are not, whilst underlying scientific valuations of the objective worth of firms are foolishly considered of little relevance.

Behavioural economics is an emergent, and long overdue, subject, which explores the way that strong psychological factors affect the subject and the financial world. John Maynard Keynes was convinced that 'non-economic motives and irrational behaviours' actually controlled the economy, for good and ill[8].

The possible psychological factors involved are many and various. Notable, though, are confidence, fear, fairness, corruption, greed and anti-social attitudes, ignorance about money causing delusions, the effect on our views of other people's stories. Akerlof and Shiller have revived Keynes' expression 'animal spirits' to refer to 'a restless and inconsistent element in the economy', which is the collective way we think about it, in effect[8].

People do not always act independently ,as economic theory supposes. They can sometimes be influenced by others. They can act unselfishly, exercise mutual cooperation.

If we are uncertain of the worth of things we tend to value what we have the more. So this can reflect in prices. There is a rationality to it, but it is not the simple surface phenomenon of orthodox economies.

In this spivs' culture we have come to realise, all too belatedly, and then only some of us, in spite of everything that has happened, that you do not even need villains to corrupt the system. There are plenty such around, probably outweighed in number by the simply ignorant and incompetent, and speculators who make judgements with our money, mostly without our knowledge or consent, but emphatically at our expense. The computers they use are capable of moving billions of pounds sterling around the entire world in a matter of microseconds, so tragedy can strike very fast and big-time.

CHAPTER 3

SOCIAL PROGRESS

Is not the rule of law being used perversely to protect the vested interests of the guilty? When loan sharks exploit the weak-willed, with exorbitant interest rates, when banking chiefs starve companies of cash-flow into receivership, when they bring their banks to the brink of collapse and walk away with golden handshakes and opulent pensions?

The origins of the credit crunch of 2008 are well rehearsed. There was irresponsible bank lending to feckless mortgage borrowers, who had no potential to repay their debts. It occurred in both the United States and in Western Europe, including the United Kingdom, and it was on massive scale. Greed and incompetence among investment bankers was such that packages were traded without any regard to their underlying value.

There were warnings given, notably by those who saw some negative elements in globalization. They included large multinational firms deceiving national governments through tax evasion, and the avoidance of pollution penalties, and moving their manufacturing plants wholesale to areas of cheap labour in third-world countries. It led to rounds of competitive cost-cutting in the West, driving down real wages, reducing hierarchical structures and opportunity. To stimulate demand, credit was encouraged to fill the gap. Both government and financial services were complicit. With advertising continuing to create wants, many people soon overreached themselves with debt. Rulers had not in a generation or more bothered to set up frameworks that would classify publicly acceptable limits to financial actions or develop a system of proper legal penalties for transgression, together with effective regulatory rules and monitoring agencies, to ensure compliance and punish miscreants.

So what about the role of political leaders in managing the economy? Even allowing that there can be states of affairs within it from time to time which are in principle manageable, within existing economic theory. Politicians would at some stage botch things up, through doctrinaire notions, response to pressures, or sheer incompetence.

When, however, it comes to a situation as complicated and wide in scope as the credit crunch, the lessons have just not been understood or adopted. Among them are the fact that western governments lack the expertise or will to cope with the much greater degree and nature of regulation

CHAPTER 3

SOCIAL PROGRESS

required in the financial industries, the laws are too woefully inadequate even to characterize the excesses as evidence of fraud, and the regulatory failings are wrongly deemed not culpable in the legal culture. Politicians in government do not have the authority needed (since too ignorant) to stop the rogues in the private sector, and the hapless taxpayer remains backstop, the ultimate, impotent, source of funding.

All sorts of desperate remedies have been tried, from reducing bank rate virtually to zero, to underwriting toxic assets, printing money, direct funding in selected industries, pseudo-nationalisation of banks. Nobody know whether they work, or to what extent over how long.

The culture of our ruling elite is so sick that they frequently struggle to see the excesses of bankers as morally corrupt. Neither, of course, do the bankers, who instead demand further bonuses, light taxation and regulation, and threaten to move their operations overseas.

So all in all, the many casualties of the economic fall-out are adding, in complex and numerous ways, to the existing aggregate of financial problems, ensuring, at least for the present and foreseeable future victims, considerable social regress, not progress, nor any hope of it.

Change

Social progress, or any sort of progress for that matter, would naturally require that something changed. Could an analysis of the nature of change therefore illuminate our subject?

'Change' is making or becoming different, according to the dictionary. It is everywhere. It may or may not equate with progress. Much change is completely or partly outside out control. Some worry about this; others take the view that there is nothing they can do.

If the change is big enough, human reason might fly out of the window. Adverse shocks in a life, as well as major civil crises, such as environmental, or man-made disasters, can disorientate and unsettle an otherwise balanced and moderate disposition. On a society level, change

CHAPTER 3

SOCIAL PROGRESS

appears to be accelerating, and the pace of modern life speeding up generally. Some may be comfortable with this, but it is out of our control and for the most part, we cannot be sure where it is all going. This can be a psychologically disturbing experience. Outlook and mental make-up is likely to influence our perspective too. For the eternal optimists there will, of course, be the prospect of progress. But pessimists would deny it.

So what is emerging, then, is the notion that social change is capable of exerting profound influences on the psychology of individuals. There could be a whole spectrum of reactions to just one such change, let alone the myriad of changes we inevitably experience.

The fact is bad news for anyone seeking an objective and dispassionate account of social change whereby the progressive, regressive, or neutral quality of the change would be apparent. We shall all make judgements, probably the vast majority of them coloured in some way. The task is by orders of magnitude more difficult than first acquaintance might suggest.

Now psychological effects of change are quite often considered by management theorists, because many institutions today undergo a great deal of it. Those in authority need to know how to drive it on, whilst minimising the upset to the workforce. And there is plenty of evidence around of what it does to people. Thus we will go there next, for it serves as a social microcosm.

Scott and Jaffe characterise what typically happens to staff undergoing organisational change of a major kind(9). They are inclined to go through various stages from denial, then resistance, to exploration, and finally commitment. If they are lucky, that is. Many can get stuck at any of the earlier stages and never move on in their minds.

The change does not need to be a negative one, like staff reductions, for it to be badly received. Even with desired movement, there can be a feeling of loss associated with the old ways. Sense of loss is not necessarily a simple thing; it can have elements of insecurity, a reduction in confidence or the ability to cope, anxiety about familiar colleagues going and unfamiliar ones moving in, perhaps a reaction to changing territory, and disorientation - an unease that they no longer know where they are going.

CHAPTER 3

SOCIAL PROGRESS

The ones more likely to embrace change, on the other hand, are the young and the uncommitted, as well as relative newcomers to the set-up, the multi-skilled, the ambitious and the self-assured.

The ability to adapt is important on more levels than the psychological, of course. Human resources and/or management may terminate your contract if you are not seen as being made of 'the right stuff'.

There are invariably those who do not sign up. They have their own agendas and usually have to remain with a low profile for these obvious reasons of possible persecution. Their role play will not be genuine, so the prospect of being found out can set up personality strains. They may become ill with the stress.

It is thus easy to see change happening in wider society as a result of a very complex interplay of forces, only some of which are under human control. Consequently, outcomes are uncertain. Even with the human factors, they and people behind them, do not all pull in the same direction.

When politicians talk of having a political consensus, there will usually be a substantial minority opposed to the change, some of whom will be minded to try and subvert it.

In conclusion, then, what can we say about our social progress, given our very different attitudes to our experience of the change allegedly bringing it about? It will obviously not be satisfactory to let our leaders have the last word. Nor will we be content to listen to the sociologists decree when social progress has been made. So how do we, as a social collectivity, actually know if it has happened?

Before we can answer that it is fitting to look first at human nature. We know that society can be changed. But can we do so as people?

Human Nature

You can usually tell when science is struggling to explain something which would appear to be at least in principle within its compass. That is

CHAPTER 3

SOCIAL PROGRESS

because the ancient philosophies are still being trotted out, have not yet been debunked. 'Human nature' is a classic case, but it has not been for the want of trying.

'Human Nature' is itself a controversial field, one closely related to assessments of social progress and its possibility. The fundamental problem is that, strange as it may seem, we do not know whether there is any such thing as human nature. Many philosophers and humanists are inclined to postulate that it exists, is a positive force, and provides a basis for social progress. Postmodernists think human nature is endlessly alterable and so has no essence. The conjecture tends to be reinforced by recent psychological findings, which indicate that, although we have a sense of self, there is no core identity. The molecular brain is forever changing, as are its functions and capabilities. As Ford puts it; "the human self...can be seen as a bundle of conditionings, drives, and attractions which under modern conditions is fragmented or even shattered. There is no centre of a person's identity; many pressures overwhelm us from outside us and from parts of ourselves (especially the subconscious); and in the midst of all this we are continually trying to invent and reinvent who we are in fairly arbitrary ways"(10).

So where does this lead ? If the postmodernists are right, human nature slips out of the picture as a relevant factor in influencing social progress. We can conveniently forget it. But if they are wrong human nature does exist and has to be taken into account.

Essentially, there are three crucial aspects of a putative human nature which we have yet to resolve in relation to social influence according to the literature (11):

(1)   how much is 'in our genes' and physiology and how much is environmentally influenced;

(2)   to what extent is human nature, however based, fixed;

and (3)   are we mainly motivated just by our own human condition, or do we give much weight to the plight of other people, specifically or generally.

Questions (1) and (2) are in principle amenable to biological research,

CHAPTER 3

SOCIAL PROGRESS

though have so far defied it. Question (3) is the province of psychology, except as framed, it would seem incapable of any sort of universal answer.

The same dilemmas are naturally to be found in the field of ethics. In both politics and ethics, for instance, there is no point in making someone liable for conduct if it is not in his nature to control it. So the whole prospect of legal responsibility and punishment could be cast into doubt.

Now, should there be such a thing as human nature, and if it is fixed enough to be accurately characterized, then we can properly try to assess what effects it might have on social progress. The fact that we do not know either way, but what is worse probably think we do, and may even have strong views on the subject, is a serious drawback for our project at the outset.

Historically, those who would find a constancy in 'human nature' included Enlightenment figures. Societies and cultures do differ, certainly, but this is a mere gloss over the common elements, they argued.

Their outlook then was an essentially optimistic one, that 'human nature' contains mostly positive elements such as lead to social cooperation. There would, for example, be altruistic tendencies based on a natural understanding of people's life problems occasioning sympathy, perhaps even help. One conclusion sometimes drawn was that our 'human nature' would limit the kind of political and social institutions and procedures under which we could thrive (though not unfortunately those which we might produce).

The idea was that if human nature were essentially good in a moral sense, and human mental capacities were capable of considerable improvement in attainment, then social progress could be driven forward over time. There is ample evidence about intellectual capacity being adequate. The brightest among us continue to achieve wonderful things. Yet the issues surrounding human nature never get resolved, even where it is agreed we have a common core. Some say that human nature is good, certainly. Others agree, but take the view that society itself undermines this. Still

CHAPTER 3

SOCIAL PROGRESS

further beliefs are that society provides the civilisation without which human nature's essential badness would prevail.

One famous philosopher of this latter persuasion was Hobbes. His view of human nature is notoriously pessimistic. Essentially, we act on our desires. We do show a limited benevolence to our close family and friends, but our altruistic feelings are too weak to bind us voluntarily in civil society. The logic leads to the law of the jungle; hence the necessity for strong authority over us in the form of a powerful ruler. Hobbes' own preference, set against the age he lived in during the 1600's, was monarchy, but other kinds of political system could have delivered the same requirements. We can improve society by strong government, though not, seemingly, the people within it.

The sentiments were much later flatly contradicted by Hegel's(12) principle in the 1700's and 1800's that 'human nature' is changeable, not by individuals, but by social circumstances over the sweep of history. There is little scope in the thesis to help the student of social progress, because an almost mystical view is taken of the 'progressive force'. It does not come about by human agency, intentional or otherwise, rather by certain abstract historical principles working outside our control or even influence.

It is notable when surveying the options of political philosophers that they are usually very well aware of human nature as a concept, whether they specifically address the point or not. All visions of human nature remain controversial, of course, so it may pay politically not to dwell on them over much.

A key point to note about human nature theory in any political work is to mention the fact that some political ideologies are broadly compatible with whatever view of human nature is taken, whilst others might not be. The problem for the latter is that if ever their assumed position on human nature turns out to be false, then the political ideology itself may collapse alongside it, at least in part.

So, not for the first time, we are left with a conundrum. What, if anything, can we take forward from human nature theory to inform our

SOCIAL PROGRESS

hopes for social progress? If human nature were quite malleable, we could be optimistic over time about harnessing people's better feelings to some altruistic cause. If human nature, on the other hand, was largely constant, we could still do the same, but would have to be much more wary of the negative side and set more modest goals. On pessimistic models of human nature this would be an uphill struggle in itself, with much prospect of recidivism. On other models, those that deny there is any such thing, we would be off to the happy realms of fantasy.

Blackburn is unsure whether it is even a respectable concept, because Darwinism and genetics both point to an evolving, changeable human species(13). Moreover, there are profound cultural overlays for the individual, and other effects from the non-human environment too. The ultimate problem, however, is the consciousness leap, the incommensurability of insights about electrochemical activities in the brain translating into specific thoughts and behaviour at the level of being.

Ford refers to 'overwhelmings' that have always affected the human condition and always will. They include 'disease, war, wickedness, sexual passions, love of money, fame and power, over-drinking and over-eating'. And old age and death, he might have added. It is important to acknowledge the formidable nature of the list and to accept, realistically not with resignation, that there is a limit to what can be done by way of remedy. Even where the overwhelmings are of individuals, they are usually destructive in their effects on friends and family also. There are others, beyond the capacity of individuals to influence which might be ambitious long-term targets for a plan of social progress. The message is clear, nevertheless, that human failings of a persistent kind, physical and mental, are always going to impose rather severe constraints on social progress in practice. In the last analysis the best it could ever be is an abstract state in which an ever-changing set of actors must participate.

Theories of Social Progress

We have seen that even such an obvious candidate for the accolade of

CHAPTER 3

SOCIAL PROGRESS

'progress' as the natural sciences is not without its doubters and detractors. So much the more so have we found it to be true within the social sciences, with economics, arguably its best prospect, failing spectacularly on all the tests.

Turning next to the phenomenon of change, we found a multitude of reactions to it, so as to cast grave queries over our capacities to view it without detachment and without bias.

That our feelings were bubbling along the surface of some still fundamentally hidden nature of our humanity, with no general agreement as to what we are in essence, then perhaps came as little surprise.

Given the problematic context, therefore, what do the social theorists make of it all? Can they find a path through the maze?

A few models of social progress will be briefly set out below in order to give a flavour of the unhappily great disparity in viewpoints.

Religious ideas will not be considered here. Their primary concern, by definition, has to be with God, and the afterlife they believe in. The prospect for the righteous of a utopian post-death existence in the next world has led to a variety of stances about this one. They can include a passive acceptance that the world is a very imperfect place and likely to remain so. Some would therefore advocate a stoical outlook. Toughen up and experience your fate with resignation would be their motto, with their interest in the prospects for social progress very much a secondary consideration, if one at all. Other religious people might be quite intensely political in arguing for the kind of society they would like to bring about on earth. The Church of England, as the legally established religion of the land, uses its privileged position to interfere. And it is not alone there.

There are some social theorists who believe profoundly that social progress is possible. Some would say inevitable. Others are pessimistic. Some deny the possibility at all, except for individuals and groups.

Philosophers like Hegel, and Marx who was influenced by him, thought that history itself would make progress. They saw it as moving in a given

CHAPTER 3

SOCIAL PROGRESS

direction, which they favoured, and as imbued with rationalism. The view was highly politicized, picturing an inevitable movement towards a classless society with common ownership. A trend like that ,of course, many would not wish at all to see and would challenge the progressive character of.

In any case most philosophers do not nowadays believe that the developments of history are either predictable or inevitable. To think so is merely another act of faith, for which there is scant evidence. History is no abstract entity with a life of its own. It is common for those who see a march of human progress sustainable into the future as being determined by 'laws of progress'. Unfortunately, despite the best efforts of many sociologists, no laws of progress beyond the merely trite have yet been discovered, as Popper has decisively demonstrated in his classic work "The Poverty of Historicism"[14].

After Victorian times the theory of evolution was very influential. Although a purely biological theory, it was applied by analogy to society as a whole by some, leading through economic and cultural stages to more developed states of society of increasing fitness to realise potential ideals. There were formulated on some subjectively desired levels of freedom and self-fulfilment. 'Social Darwinism', as it was called, was a false trail. Based on Darwin's biological principle of evolution a crude parallel was drawn with the social world. 'Survival of the fittest', a mechanism whereby individuals either thrive or die out, and the same applying to species, is concerned with relative success in adapting to the changing environment. But application to the social world is quite simplistic and without evidence. In the wrong hands it has led to suggestions that we should increase competition within and between societies to encourage the process. The irresponsibility of that in a world already full of conflict needs no further demonstration.

The contemporary social theorist, Jurgen Habermas, also believed in social progress[15]. He pointed to that fact that human individuals from childhood can learn about moral issues and develop a more rational conscience. And he thought the same could be true of societies. He saw stages in the moral development of children, such as the early-life phase where moral concepts are not understood, through the uncritical acceptance of family and societal norms, to more advanced positions

CHAPTER 3

SOCIAL PROGRESS

where people can think for themselves and use rational principles to argue for their view, even in the face of opposition.

Critics point out that apart from the complete lack of evidence, in what relevant ways does society parallel an individual? After all, there is no such thing as a collective social consciousness. Society is a concept, not a learning entity. Mrs Thatcher famously said it did not exist, and, certainly, it would be a grave mistake to imbue it with any sort of anthropomorphic qualities.

However, the philosopher, Blackburn is scathing about Mrs. Thatcher's negation of the existence of society. He saw her as slave to the economic capitalist idea of a nation of self-reliant (and self-serving) individuals, making it on their own with little or no help from the state. This would be a minimalist entity because the markets would have little use for government and would provide the things we needed.

A moment's reflection will reveal that even economic man requires the cooperation of his fellows. Some kind of community will be its mainspring, quite inevitably so, to provide a framework for practical conduct among the people, behaviour which is almost never completely, and oft times not at all, of a commercial nature.

'Modernism' is a new outlook which replaces the old ideas of conserving traditional values and ways of life. It has a confidence that social progress, or improving the human condition, can come about through better knowledge and rational methods. We have seen that change is an inevitable feature of the modern world, so we can use it to develop facilities and improve people's lives. Giddens[16] is a contemporary sociologist who was closely involved in the creation of the Blair government's so-call 'third way', which seemed basically to be an attempt to reconcile socialism and capitalism. His view is that sociology has a dual function, not only to describe society through its scientific study, but to change it. In other words, sociology should have a normative role in evaluating how we should live. The 'project of modernity' is to analyse society's problems and suggest ways of solving them. The short steps from such a view to a practical political programme need little imagination to conjure.

CHAPTER 3

SOCIAL PROGRESS

To some extent social progress comes down to a belief. Societies have differed greatly as to their strength in this belief. During the Enlightenment, for instance, there was widespread confidence, at least among intellectuals, that knowledge and reason would lead us there. For some supreme optimists social progress was not merely movement towards a set of ideals actually to be manifest in practice to an increasing degree, but to perfectibility itself. Nowadays we live in a much more pluralist society and confidence in Man's capabilities is waning.

Fundamental Problems

Whatever our social plight, we humans are the sole guardians of the health of our planet. We now know it through science to be in a delicate state of balance. That we are causing serious damage to it is beyond dispute. That we are plundering its non-renewable resources is a measurable fact. So irrespective of the state of our current lives, the risks for future generations of a terrible future are probable. As it is, the vast majority of the world lives in poverty and squalor. It is only in the developed industrial nations that a minority of the people enjoy a good standard of living. This can distort our judgement of the prospect for social progress into a hopelessly unrealistic optimism.

The eradication of social ills, the ultimate object of social progress presumably, seems inconceivable on any rational view. We have had already thousands of years of recorded history, but human misery is almost everywhere still firmly entrenched.

So let us examine our husbandry of the planet in a little more detail(17). Much of the world is over-populated and so cannot ward off famine. Education in contraception makes inadequate headway against entrenched religious forces of darkness and dogma. Although notable improvement has been made with the control of some diseases, such as small pox, the burden worldwide is overwhelming, with epidemics rife, and new illnesses emerging. Many cannot be supplied with basic sanitation or clean water. The world's supplies, other than rainfall, are running out.

When you look at poverty, which affects up to three billion already, it

CHAPTER 3

SOCIAL PROGRESS

does not seem possible to eradicate it, since the distribution of wealth is so uneven, and no society ever properly addresses it to bring the differences within moderately egalitarian limits. In every society there is an irreducible element of crime, whatever the penalties.

Over-fishing, enhanced by advanced recovery techniques and vast factory ships, has depleted the oceans of all but a small residuum of edible species.

The rainforests are being cut down; soil erosion is producing large new deserts out of once good arable land.

The dangers of global warming through over-use of fossil fuels for heating our homes and driving industry are very well-documented. Many experts warn that the demands to maintain advanced western economies, and those of the economically emerging nations, will triumph fatally over the restraint and sustainability urged by conservationists, unless concerted and radical international remedial action is taken urgently.

Apart from the legion man-made ills, with wars, and even genocide, showing no sign of disappearing, there are the natural disasters, major and minor, which continue to devastate the communities they hit - from earthquakes and volcanoes, to droughts and floods, to forest fires (when not caused by arson), avalanches, rock falls, tsunami, meteor collisions, and hurricanes. Many others must have been missed out. As it is, the list is very sobering.

That we can regress, in probably incalculable ways, all in a matter of a few moments, with great suddenness, is testimony to our civilization's physical fragility on the planet. Challenges to the social fabric and our technological infrastructure are daily occurrences somewhere on Earth.

There will doubtless be progress here and there with some of these difficulties in limited and specific ways. For example, understanding of causes will improve, we will develop better warning systems, technological tools to aid disaster recovery will advance, and maybe even organisational procedures and the skills of the authorities too. By the same token, matters as we all know, can also deteriorate. We make

CHAPTER 3

SOCIAL PROGRESS

financial cuts, we disband useful institutions, we fail to plan ahead to the appropriate event horizons.

But, away from the global scale, when we see the decline of a nice housing estate, or the renovation of a run-down one, we are using particular criteria of progress which are much more limited than the rather vague and general nature of the term's usual use. A comparison may be made over time on certain specific factors like the state of the building fabric, or the statistics on reported crime. These are objective rational criteria, the sort of things that can be measured. They are not a tenuous matter of opinion, but have a factual basis in reality. They are akin to the scientific progress previously acknowledged.

Unhappily over-riding this, what seems to be the case is that advanced societies, so-called, have become too complex to run and small gains too costly to maintain. There is neither the concentration of expertise, nor the power, nor the right foci for coordination of our efforts.(Just consider ,for instance, how it takes years to deal with the flooding of a small town.)

Quite apart from the mind-boggling irresponsibility and folly displayed by bankers and others in the financial sector, the credit crunch and subsequent depression discussed earlier highlight a crucially important factor in politics; namely, that our political leaders and systems may not be fit for purpose. It is very hard to envisage how society can put things right. At the very least it would have to involve a complete overhaul and redesign of many key institutions and the eradication of others. There is not the recognition, not the knowledge, nor the will. Perspectives are too narrow; visions short-term and piecemeal.

It will be expected, perhaps almost encouraged, that in a capitalist society there will be those who make their money by exploiting others - the weak, the poor, and the gullible being relatively easy targets. So attempts to improve matters for the benefit of the community may be undermined by the fast-buck brigade. There are inevitably people, some ruthless capitalists will be among them, who do not give a damn about anyone or anything else. So ameliorating society always has to contend with this drag-back factor.

CHAPTER 3

SOCIAL PROGRESS

Social Policy

As we have a multitude of problems and major confusions on our hands, let us turn finally at this point to the research literature of the social sciences in a search for clarification and enlightenment.

'Social Policy' is both an academic study and an intensely practical subject where political measures are used to change society[18]. Its scope can be shown by any reputable text book and is both vast and multifarious. Certain individuals will always have social problems. The human condition ultimately defeats us all, as has been outlined earlier. Additionally, specific groups are identified for addressing by specialist agencies. These will include children, youth, the elderly, the disabled and lone parents. Some of the services are grouped by categories such as social security, employment, health care, education, and housing. Various endeavours will be slanted towards families, communities, racial minorities. Political ideologies applied will include conservative, socialist, liberal-democrat, and feminist. Welfare is provided by both private and state organs, as well as through voluntary bodies, and people's informal efforts. Social policy has also to be understood in relation to available resources, economic policy, the legal context. In addition there are political fads which come and go. Current organising principles among the institutions include welfare rights (awareness promotion) and the social inclusion movement (designed to reach the disconnected).

In short, 'Social Policy' is multidisciplinary and is concerned with: the welfare of individuals and social groups; the nature and theory of welfare, its policy analysis and impact; and the institutional organisation and implementation of policies.

Social policy as a formal, but rather loose, collection of concepts and aims, is very instructive from the standpoint of those who would assess the chances for social progress. For one thing, there is the brute fact of long-term under-resourcing. Secondly, the heterogeneous nature of organisation and effort means that virtually nobody has an overview. Thirdly, it is entirely likely, never mind possible, that some of the applied principles will be in conflict, or at least based on different beliefs and moving in different directions. And nowhere can we say that what we are

CHAPTER 3

SOCIAL PROGRESS

trying to achieve was a democratically agreed intention of society as a whole.

As the theoreticians put it:

"Social needs and social problems are subject to contested definitions. In both cases a major debate concerns the relative weight to be given to objective or subjective factors".
"These points lead us back to the nature of policy as a subject. The word 'policy' implies that it is a part of the political processes and institutions of modern society, and that social needs, social problems and social welfare are similarly political."

A few illustrations, all from academic papers, should suffice to show that actual understandings of the concept of social progress are very diverse, as is contended. Numerous studies and articles abound comparing the impact of one factor or another on 'social progress', which may or may not itself be defined as a term, and may or may not be in line with conventional understandings.

An example is Luo Guojie, whose paper addresses social progress in relation to morals in the context of modern China[19]. A notion of social progress is tied to improved industrial productivity raising living standards. The assertion is that the process has been accompanied by the arrival of 'moral degeneracy', a common enough result, but not inevitable, the author argues. Yet here we have a narrow view of social progress as equating with economic betterment, where it is seen as a concept somehow outside moral considerations. But not all view social progress as being about money, and substantial numbers would regard moral degeneracy as one important element within social regress, rather than progress!

Secondly, the Centre of Analysis of Social Exclusion at the London School of Economics has examined Labour's record in power from the standpoint of social progress, measured as movement towards a more egalitarian society[20]. Evidently, for those not politically persuaded that we need a more equal society, such movement would not be said to constitute social progress. Even for egalitarians, evaluation of whether

CHAPTER 3

SOCIAL PROGRESS

the findings demonstrate social progress is difficult. Essentially, the picture has been mixed, with reductions in numbers in child and pension poverty, improved measured education outcomes of the poorest children, though with increased poverty for the childless unemployed, wider health and income inequalities generally.

A third treatment is Charlton and Andras's paper claiming that social progress is consistent with modernizing societies[21]. Their purpose is political. They do not like socialism, but they do like education, which they controversially assert has replaced it as 'an instrument of political reform'. Their treatment of 'modernization' is worthy of note in the present context. It is characterized by processes of separation and specialisation of functions as society grows in complexity. Thus, there is the division of labour, and the division of institutions within systems like politics, the economy, the legal system, the health service, and so on. The systems "are themselves becoming increasingly more complex, subdivided and sub-specialized". They claim "modern societies are no longer hierarchical" (which is highly dubious), but resemble "a 'mosaic' of functions each with different internal rules". "These systems interact and shape one another's growth".

This is relevant, if true, because it bears witness to a rising modularity of structure. We all live in separate working boxes, so that a unifying overview and coordination of effort becomes very difficult to attain. It may increase the likelihood of more limited and polarised outlooks.

Penultimately, to clutch at straws, social progress is sometimes conceptualized in terms of 'social mobility'. The idea is that in some societies, the progressive ones, individuals and groups can better themselves socially and economically by taking advantage of opportunities to improve their position. Naturally, fluid societies allow the possibility of downward movement as well as up, but this is strangely less dwelt on. And again, the movement only affects certain people-relatively small numbers out of the total population. If it applied to very many at any one time, society would be a very unstable entity indeed.

So a long perspective is needed when being optimistic about cases of social mobility. We are mostly familiar with the saying: rags to riches

SOCIAL PROGRESS

and back   again in three generations. Experience shows this to be a common fate of upwardly mobile families that cannot sustain over time the economic edge that got them up the slippery ladder.

The main findings from sociological studies of social mobility in the United Kingdom are bad news for those who nurse hopes of some kind of utopian equality, or even equality of opportunity(22). What we find instead is that, compared with their previous generation, over one fifth of men are falling on the socio-economic scale. Even within an individual's working life downward mobility is commonplace. Redundancy is a major reason, as are problems of psychological adjustment to the pressures of modern life.   Women frequently sacrifice careers for motherhood, returning to the workforce, if at all, later in life, in more junior capacities and often part-time.

Overall numbers in upward social mobility are low.   Most of the population remain close to the level of their family of origin. Where there is movement, it tends to be modest, usually the result of changes in the occupational structure of their work place, rather than through meritocractic advancement. The societal trend of the expansion of white-collar jobs has provided opportunities, but major progress is illusory, the mobility remaining 'short-range' and sometimes temporary.

Finally, using the long perspective, the Joseph Rowntree Foundation has for over a hundred years studied the problems of United Kingdom society and regularly produced reports. The social weaknesses the Foundation identified in its first report of 1904 were:

> "poverty, war, slavery, intemperance, the opium trade, impurity and gambling".

Now, it is notable that all these ills are very much still with us (for 'opium' read 'drugs' in the modern situation). And formal slavery today will have fewer victims, though many contemporary lives have other rigid constraints. Some of the items are inevitably damaging others, or morally disapproved of even when they are not so.

A comparable report in 2009 from the Rowntree Foundation still singled

CHAPTER 3

SOCIAL PROGRESS

out 'drugs and alcohol', and 'poverty'. But the rest of the list was significantly different, namely personal greed, family breakdown, failed institutions, declining moral values and social behaviour, such as growing intolerance, bad manners, lack of mutual respect, dishonesty.

Between the two reports society has changed a great deal, including attitudes to social ills and which are the most serious. Nevertheless, both have very formidable problems.

Many people are latching onto a realisation that social problems are usually deep-seated, very resistant to treatment and maybe even incurable. The Foundation noted widespread public scepticism and some despair.

Professor Glatter of the Open University(23) has pointed out that nobody knows how to solve the major educational and social problems. All too often some politician has his hour and comes forward with an idea, which he presents with passion and conviction. But the initiatives usually run out of money and drive soon enough. Although presented quite otherwise, they are just like amateur experiments. They may set targets, or involve the private sector, but we never systematically explore whether the changes improve or even hinder their chances of success. Constant political obsession with structure rather misses the point. Effective change cannot be forced. We are not able to rule by mandate and edict. Initiatives need time and resources, as well as hearts and minds. Guidance is probably more effective than coercion, and changes need absorbing in small chunks slowly.

So should we have a council of despair, faced with such an impressive catalogue of woe? Is there any point in the humble public manager trying to give effect to the social policies which politicians dream up? Would they, or even could they really work? With that sobering thought in mind we turn next to an examination of key disciplines as potential informants for a radical public management. 'Radical' because, whatever we do as a community, we just cannot afford in terms of the quality of lives to continue as we are. It isn't working. Of course, if the analysis of the chapter is correct there may be no universal salvation and this is the real radical message.

CHAPTER 3

SOCIAL PROGRESS

NOTES

1.   Giant Dictionary and Thesaurus; Chambers, Harrap Publishers Ltd., 2007.

*   2.   Kuhn, T., The Structure of Scientific Revolutions, University of Chicago Press, Chicago, 1970.

3.   Gutting, Gary, What Philosophers Know, Cambridge University Press, 2009.

*   4.   Bronk, Richard, Progress and the Invisible Hand, Warner Books, 1998.

5.   Donaldson, Peter, Economics of the Real World, Penguin Books Ltd., Harmondsworth, 2nd Edn., 1978.

6.   Fukuyama, F, The End of History, The Free Press, New York, 1992.

*   7.   Cable, Vince, The Storm, Atlantic Books, London, 2009.

*   8.   Akerlof, George A., and Shiller, Robert J., Animal Spirits, Princeton University Press, New Jersey, 2009.

*   9.   Scott, Cynthia D., and Jaffe, Dennis T., Managing Organisational Change, Kogan Page Ltd., London 1990.

10.   Ford, David F., Theology, Oxford University Press, 1999.

11.   Concise Routledge Encyclopaedia of Philosophy, Routledge, London, 2000.

*   12.   Blackburn, Simon, Philosophy: The Big Questions, Quereus Books, 2009.

13.   Blackburn, Simon, Oxford Dictionary of Philosophy, Oxford University Press, Oxford, 2008.

CHAPTER 3

SOCIAL PROGRESS

14. Popper, Karl, The Poverty of Historicism, Routledge and Kegan Paul, 1957, 2nd ed. 1961.

* 15. Finlayson, James Gordon, Habermas; A Very Short Introduction, Oxford University Press, Oxford, 2005.

* 16. Jones, Pip, Introducing Social Theory, Polity Press, Blackwell Publishing Ltd., Oxford, 2003.

* 17. Martin James, The Meaning of the 21st Century, Eden Project Books, Transworld Publishers, London, 2006.

* 18. Alcock Pete, Erskine, Angus and May, Margaret (Eds), The Students Companion to Social Policy, Social Policy Association, Blackwell Publishers Ltd., Oxford, 1998.

19. Goujie, Luo, 'On Social Progress and Morals', International Journal of Social Economics, 1991, Volume 18, Issue 8/9/10.

20. Hills, John, Sefton ,Tom and Stewart ,Kitty, Towards a more equal Society? Poverty, inequality and policy since 1997, Centre for Analysis of Social Exclusion, LSE, The Policy Press, 2009.

21. Charlton, Bruce G. and Andras, Peter, 'Universities and social progress in modernising Societies', University of Newcastle upon Tyne, Critical Quarterly, 2005; 47: 30-39.

22. Giddens, Anthony, Sociology, Blackwell Publishers, Oxford, 1989, reprinted 1992.

23. Glatter, R, 'Governance and Educational Innovation', in The Handbook of Educational Leadership and Management, eds. Davies, B., and West-Burnham, J., Pearson, 2003.

CHAPTER 4

SCIENCE, PHILOSOPHY, AND MANAGEMENT

Introduction

Science and Management

Political Science and Management

Philosophy and Management

Philosophical Analysis

Management Defects and Computers

CHAPTER 4

SCIENCE, PHILOSOPHY, AND MANAGEMENT

Introduction

Management may be informed by many disciplines, but two of the most likely candidates (to provide its main methodology) are science and philosophy.

Attention is drawn to the role that science, as the empirical approach to knowledge and understanding, can play in forming the theory and practice of management. Particular consideration is given to the nature and application of the social sciences. One of them, political science, is then introduced, as obviously relevant to management within bureaucracies.

Philosophy is similarly considered here as exemplar of the rational approach to thought and its relevance in practice to the pursuit of management is assessed, branch by branch.

There follows an appraisal of the applicability of analysis, as a philosophical tool, for use in the managerial field.

A brief characterisation of the many weaknesses of modern management concludes the chapter, and throughout there is a tacit assumption that the public sector is the main subject of consideration.

Science and Management

The author takes no scientism stance, that only science can deliver knowledge because only science uses 'scientific method'. Philosophy has played a very important role in demonstrating that there is no such entity as 'scientific method'[1]. Rather, such is the range and diversity of problems and subject areas that there have to be different approaches across the sciences for solving them. Even within one particular science that will be true.

CHAPTER 4

SCIENCE, PHILOSOPHY, AND MANAGEMENT

Some sciences have a considerably developed mathematical basis; others do not. The branches of mathematics useful for a given science also differ greatly. For example, growth in bacterial systems uses exponential equations, whereas chaotic systems like turbulent flow in rivers and gases, or weather variation, require non-linear equations.

In extreme cases we cannot directly observe the phenomenon under investigation, such as subatomic particles, so we have to infer their characteristics by experiment indirectly from their effects on other things.

Where you have observations of some phenomenon leading to a discovery, the evidence may be very strong indeed. Other explanations might need more support from a theory, which could later turn out to be false. And it is now thought to be impossible to develop universal criteria for determining the complex relationships between phenomenon, theory, and truth in any general way applicable to all cases. One aspect of what we are saying is the unsystematic variability of theory-dependence of observations. There could also be competing theories to contend with.

There are scientific explanations that depend on a known law of nature which covers certain kinds of events in specific situations. So if we know the circumstances and the law we can explain the event, perhaps even predict it in advance. And we can test the limits of applicability of the law in addition.

However, with a 'law' such as the principle of conservation of energy there are no recorded instances of it being breached, so it is 'fundamental' in the sense that it just is and explanation probably has to stop.

Note that the present treatment does not make any distinction in meaning between the terms 'explanation' and 'interpretation', although some philosophers of science would.

In various areas of science there are no clear laws to support our explanations. Where there is more than one interpretation, deciding on the best requires the exercise of judgement. So complete objectivity cannot be attained and the matter is open to become one of legitimate dispute.

CHAPTER 4

SCIENCE, PHILOSOPHY, AND MANAGEMENT

But the fact that there may be a subjective element to a scientific explanation does <u>not</u> let in post-modernism, a blanket denial that anything can be known. It lets in rational arguments instead, with objective criteria for deciding on their relative strengths and weaknesses.

It is hard to discount the impact of psychological influences, when there is much at stake especially. And the less our results provide concrete evidence for the explanation, the more scope there is for individual manoeuvre on the outstanding questions.

Dewey, a philosopher, had a pragmatic approach to the improvement of society. He believed in democracy, which he saw among political systems as the most suitable for developing, criticizing, and testing ideas for reform.

Society was to be subject to experiment. Learning would be by trial and error. Natural sciences could help by their rational and systematic methods, and by technological developments invented to aid the process. There was an implied optimism here, given that many social problems had remained unsolved for hundreds of years.

Dewey's approach is altogether too elementary. Methods in natural science cannot glibly be assumed to apply in social science just like that. In fact, there has been endless debate in the modern world about whether social science, owing to the nature and intrinsic difficulty of its subject-matter, may not require different methods entirely, or to some extent at least. There has been further scepticism set against the idea that there can be social sciences at all. Apart from the (defeatist) arguments of cultural relativism, suggesting the non-existence of universal social truths, there have been (more reasonable) suggestions that social subject-matter is over-complicated for scientific method to investigate, that there are legal and moral barriers too onerous to transcend in some cases, and that a novel and sophisticated methodology appropriate to the challenges has yet to be invented.

The social philosopher, Roger Trigg, has some crucial observations on the nature of social science and the profound research dilemmas it faces[2]. He quite rightly dismisses postmodernism, a corrosive and entirely negative movement, because:

CHAPTER 4

SCIENCE, PHILOSOPHY, AND MANAGEMENT

"A full assault on the possibility of rationality undermines the possibility of all science, including social science."

Postmodernism(3) is very difficult to characterize, and has forms of application to many a subject, but its theory is frequently said to be relativist, the belief that knowledge is not universally true, but only applicable in its context in relation to something else. Postmodernism is more concerned with temporary situations and surface appearances. It sees representation as crucial for reality, pointing out that much of our world we construct ourselves by the use of signs.

At least the post modernists do us a favour in highlighting "a deep problem with social reality". The trouble is, they provide no basis whatsoever for solving the problem, except as numerous individual ideas the relative values of which, they contend, cannot be apportioned.

So at this first stage those who espouse postmodernist tendencies will have accepted that there can be no such thing as scientifically attested social knowledge.

For the ones who still hope, another type of attack on the social sciences is that which says "that sociology is particular, and social science in general, are not proper intellectual disciplines". The argument is that they have no content to study because it is disputed "whether society means anything more than the conglomeration of individual action".

We can concede part of the postmodernist agenda which says that society is humanly constructed without concluding that this means it has no subject-matter. There are broadly two possibilities: either 'society' does not exist, or individuals construct social structures which themselves have effects on us and which we in turn also affect.

Thinkers who are wedded to human reality being 'atomistic' will again, like the postmodernists, not see the point, or indeed the possibility of collective success in political ventures that try to ameliorate national conditions, or in a public management discipline, an admixture of social sciences among other influences, being any useful help in what they regard as an inevitably foredoomed enterprise. Some faults in the

CHAPTER 4

SCIENCE, PHILOSOPHY, AND MANAGEMENT

outlook have already been highlighted in the earlier chapter on social progress.

For the remainder there is at least a starting conviction that 'society' does exist. Opinions will differ, however, on whether the physical and life sciences have appropriate methodology to investigate it. The normal situation there is for some material or living objects to be studied, and the matter can be taken up without any prior consideration or assumptions about the nature of the researcher. But with society, as Trigg points out, it greatly matters what view we take of the nature of our object of study. Because not to do so means we cannot even decide the purposes of our research, since we do not know what is feasible. As we do not already know what sort of something society is, we have to be guided by our philosophical assumptions about it, as well as what we already know scientifically about human beings' needs, interests, wants, and behaviour in general. There will be an unresolved tension about the respective weightings to be given, in variable contexts, to concepts of self and social structures. There will be a particular difficulty about objectivity. We must study society, if we are to be scientific, as it is, not as we would want it to be.

Given all the above, a realistic social science programme will look for explanation on a theoretical basis, beyond a neutral description. Meanings and interpretations are very likely to be contested, still more so any claim to be able to use emerging 'facts' and measurements as tools for future prediction, or even perhaps political control.

Political Science and Management

Be that as it may, Lasswell(4) tried to take the social science and management project forward. He stated *"Sciences are policy sciences when they clarify the process of policy-making in society, or supply data needed for the making of rational judgements on policy questions"*. He went on to clarify that the 'policy sciences' are the subjects which explain how policy is created and implemented, how the data are found and the results are interpreted.

CHAPTER 4

SCIENCE, PHILOSOPHY, AND MANAGEMENT

Now a scientific approach requires objective methods with the best technical aid to all projects. These are designed to solve particular problems in given social situations. A policy science will thus aim to bring together what is rational in the approaches of all the relevant actors, professional and otherwise, and from whatsoever specialisms. The policy process is studied, as are the policies themselves, in order to acquire knowledge. And the ultimate goal is the improvement of society in some regard.

Policy science can be seen as a branch of 'Political Science' which will operate mostly in the arena of public management, rather than administration, or management in industry or commerce. Heywood[5] defines it as:

> *"The study of government, the state, and politics; more narrowly, the application of empirical theory and scientific theory and scientific methods to the analysis of political matters."*

Social sciences will be relevant to management since they variously address the study of society via independent, but related disciplines like economics, sociology and social psychology.

However, the increasing criticism of the sciences generally, seen as dangerous when exploited for antisocial purposes, became a crisis of faith in the power of such methods, especially since the management problems still seemed to be with us for the most part. Better information and techniques had not noticeably improved the performance of the policy makers and implementers.

Newby[6] pointed to an increased realism about what the social sciences can achieve. Over the years from the 1960's to the 1990's, social science changed from maintaining it alone could solve socio-economic problems by a sort of 'social engineering', to a recognition that policy problems depend greatly on their context. They are also defined in relation to their historical background. Perceptions of the nature and importance of the problems differ. Those concerned in the policy process make their own changes too. This implies, of course, that social scientists cannot afford to stand remote and aloof from the citizenry (and neither can the bureaucrat.)

CHAPTER 4

SCIENCE, PHILOSOPHY, AND MANAGEMENT

Time was that the German sociologist, Max Weber regarded the ideal as a value-free social science, including political science. But this seems a pipe dream now. The very concepts of political discourse are not value-free, just the reverse, although political science can and does seek to give neutral descriptions, and explanations free from any particular political standpoint.

Delanty[7] asserts that social science is like the other sciences in being both a system of knowledge (and its acquisition) and an institution itself within society. *"As a socially constructed discourse, the crisis and transformation of knowledge in contemporary society has major implications for the identity and conduct of social science".*

He locates much more in this "crisis" than just the faltering of confidence in 'scientific method' and its practitioners, although that alone would be gravely serious. He points, in addition, to *"new issues relating to power and identity", "the decline in the sovereignty of the state",* and *"new conception of democracy"* (presumably such as direct action and participative movements.) He might nowadays also have thrown in pluralism, some of it arising from accelerated immigration from very alien cultures.

Reacting to Lasswell, the limitation of his model of scientific management in practice led Dror[8] to advocate the inclusion of irrational elements alongside the scientific ones, and, although values need not be in that category, they have to be included too to be a realistic model for actual life. His ideal is 'comprehensive rationality', yet it is obvious that the irrational elements can, and often do, get the upper hand. He wants it all ways, though. The policy model should reflect reality, whilst guiding us to do better in our methods and results. This is all very well, but danger lurks here, when the unscrupulous can claim that life is too complicated to be effectively informed by better evidence and reasons.

Dror was a 'managerialist', someone who believed that the management theory which was applied to running businesses and organisations was also highly relevant to public policy. He predicted a merger between management sciences and policy sciences.

CHAPTER 4

SCIENCE, PHILOSOPHY, AND MANAGEMENT

But what happened in the public sector, politically driven, was that management theory came to dominate. Whereas Lasswell tellingly thought that the policy sciences were vital to help the leaders first come properly to know "their values, intentions, motives, and perceptions" before they made the important decisions. He saw this as an essential defence against irrationalism, sadly undermined today by gurus and fashionable views.

There should be enough here to convince, or at least sow seeds of doubt, about the feasibility of management as a pure science, or even as a social science, somehow eliminating all that is not factual and certain.

This is emphatically not an argument against using the virtues of scientific practice and ways of thinking within management. Nevertheless, when you do, certainly at the higher levels of responsibility, there will always be trans-scientific elements of importance to consider as well. The old adage that management is both science and art is not unpacked, but true as far as it goes.

The 'artistic' elements will not be considered in detail here. They have dominated for far too long. Even so, it may be worth posing the question as to what kind of training/education would increase the odds on producing the right kinds of managerial mind? In former days it was usual to assert the claims of the classics. Nowadays, with so few studying it, other candidates may be offered, like history. Certainly, some of the subject-matter of history could be useful, notably those elements referring to 'contemporary' politics, perhaps. Though much would be lost without a grasp of historical research methodology, which needs, of course, to be as scientific as one can make it if even partial truth is to be uncovered.

So we must end on a pessimistic note. Science, to conclude, is very relevant to good managerial theory and practice, yet it encounters conceptual and methodological problems of application in the field. To add to the difficulties, certain non-scientific elements may also be advantageous, but there is no consensus at all on what these aspects may be, or how they might be learned. Any accommodation between the two is a matter for judgement, and how do you teach or acquire that?

CHAPTER 4

SCIENCE, PHILOSOPHY, AND MANAGEMENT

So we have seen that management cannot completely become a science, because it inevitably possesses too many non-scientific elements. But we have also seen that the study of management can to some extent be made scientific, and the author contends that this is a benefit, helping to rationalise and systematize its practices, and to make improvements based on an unbiased appraisal. It is to 'management science' itself that we now turn for further enlightenment.

'Management techniques'(9) are used by managers in almost all areas of their work, and constitute those of their methods that are systematic and analytical. All techniques attempt to be as objective as possible and a lot of them are quantitative, relying of mathematical theory and numerical calculation. They are to be contrasted with ordinary administrative procedures and functions, as well as managerial skills demonstrated in management activities such as coordination, communication, and negotiation, for example. The methods are analytic in their examination of complex situations, fragmenting them into their key aspects, and organising relevant data accordingly to inform decisions.

Out of the plethora of management techniques 'management science' has developed, giving insights in such diverse areas as production planning, quality control, cost-benefit analysis, job design, salary structure design, training techniques, simulation, decision theory, resource allocation, project control, efficiency and effectiveness measurement.

A difficulty with management science arises out of our cultural traditions, sadly. To be fully understood and applied it requires scientific and numerical literacy which many managers do not have. There has thus been a deleterious tendency for the arts-based educated to assume positions in senior management, where they can handle the more obviously people-related skills of general and strategic management at a high level of abstraction. Whilst management science is relegated to 'management services', whose specialists turn data into information for senior managers to make judgements about. The dangers of an advanced society run by the scientifically illiterate will keep on growing.

CHAPTER 4

SCIENCE, PHILOSOPHY, AND MANAGEMENT

Philosophy and Management

It is next appropriate to examine the relevance of philosophy to management, precisely because scientific approaches need something more. The argument here is that the extra dimension has to be provided by the other path to truth, namely the use of reason. Among the subjects which could be used to provide reasoning power, philosophy in the author's opinion, is pre-eminent. This is because of its depth of logical methods and enormous breadth of scope. It can be applied in any field.

The word 'philosophy' has a popular usage which can be quite misleading in a managerial context. It means not a subject of study but an attitude of mind, particularly in adversity. If you are 'philosophical' you are not necessarily cerebral and reflective, but you do display a spirit of calm resignation. You do not get emotionally steamed up. Rather, you accept the pain and suffering with fortitude. The view was probably associated originally with the ancient philosophical school of stoicism.

Another way in which there is a confusingly incorrect juxtaposition of 'philosophy' and 'management' is in the so-called 'mission statements' and their attendant documents beloved of industry and public sector institutions. An American example from Wyoming[10] is:

> ### "Statement of Philosophy and Vision Vision
> *The Administration Division, by the way it delivers services, should enable all internal agencies to perform audits and examinations in an effective, efficient, and accountable manner.*
>
> ### Philosophy
> - *Using current and future technology, IT staff can provide the tools and technical assistance necessary to allow the agency's divisions to produce quality work in an efficient manner.*
> - *Through management support, training and development provide employees an opportunity to advance their skills so that a quality product is delivered.*
> - *By processing transactions in a timely manner and fiscal*

SCIENCE, PHILOSOPHY, AND MANAGEMENT

> *monitoring allows the Department of Audit to operate in an accountable manner.*
> - *Administration provides human resource support by informing employees of benefits, maintaining employee records and assisting the divisions in hiring competent and motivated employees.*
> - *People are our most important resource within the Department; therefore Administration must respond to their needs in a positive and attentive manner so full attention can be placed on the audits."*

Administration is here cast in a support role, to enable Audit to operate better. The above list of homilies serves to remind staff of their purpose, but the values of the audit function, this particular organisation's primary rationale for existence, remain unexplored. There is no philosophy here as such, since the staff purposes are instrumental, not ultimate goals of the organisation as a whole.

A different kind of confusion about the use of the term 'philosophy' is demonstrated by a further example from America[11]. A computer manual sets out its 'philosophy of system administration':

> *"Although the specifics of being a system administrator may change from platform to platform, there are underlying themes that do not. It is these themes that make up the philosophy of system administration.*
>
> *Here are those themes:*
> - *Automate everything*
> - *Document everything*
> - *Communicate as much as possible*
> - *Know your resources*
> - *Know your users*
> - *Know your business*
> - *Security cannot be an afterthought*
> - *Plan ahead*
> - *Expect the unexpected".*

CHAPTER 4

SCIENCE, PHILOSOPHY, AND MANAGEMENT

Once again, although the word 'philosophy' is used here, there is no philosophy in the content. The word is probably intended to aggrandize what is in reality a rag-bag list of working tips of things to do or keep in mind, as is the use of the term 'themes'.

So, having demonstrated that it is easy to misconstrue, what then are the connections between philosophy and management?

Examining first the nature of philosophy, inevitably briefly, it has a core of logic, metaphysics, epistemology, and value theory, the latter being traditionally split between ethics and aesthetics.

Logic is perhaps seen these days as more affiliated to mathematics and science than to philosophy, out of which it grew historically. Logic is concerned with 'inference'. It has two forms, deductive and inductive logic.

In deductive logic we 'infer', or 'deduce' a conclusion from a set of 'premises' (a starting point of hopefully true statements, or at least presumed to be true for the purposes of argument). The steps of this deduction proceed like a mathematical proof. If we are right to start with, and then we follow the steps accurately, the conclusion cannot be in error, or, at least, cannot be inconsistent with the premises.

In inductive logic, the premises still support the conclusion, but the truth of it depends on the real world out there rather than being contained in the meaning of terms and the nature of the method, as in deductive logic. The key difference is that the truth can never be conclusively established by such a method. Instances may all be consistent with it being so, but we cannot rule out the possibility of encountering a future instance which is contrary.

Philosophers and logicians study the rules of inference, but these do not necessarily reflect people's actual processes of thought. The relevance of logic to management is therefore complex. It has to rely on an underlying assumption in management that practice should proceed scientifically and logically, except that large ranks of managers are not trained to behave that way. Mind-sets forged in the humanities still dominate the

CHAPTER 4

SCIENCE, PHILOSOPHY, AND MANAGEMENT

managerial world, especially in politics and government. Nevertheless, the subject has spawned many a useful primer on how to reason and argue, and how not.

Moving on with the assessment of parts of philosophy potentially useful in management, we turn next to value theory, which comprises aesthetics and ethics.

Aesthetics is the branch of philosophy that considers the nature of art and its values. We may, perhaps, seek beauty in management, and some public administrators come to love it, no doubt!

Even so, it is ethics, not aesthetics, which is the dimension of value-theory suitable for informing management. Ethics, the study of morality and the good, is fundamental to management by reason of values being implicit in all policy, even if there is time and again political capital to be made out of concealing them. It cannot ultimately be avoided and will be considered in depth in a later chapter.

Metaphysics is the branch of philosophy which attempts to decipher the nature of ultimate reality. Clearly, this project is a matter for science, if for anyone, and few modern philosophers might claim to go beyond it, except perhaps in the clarification of concepts and the examination of method. To put management in the metaphysical category stretches credulity, since it is, albeit a vital human endeavour, nevertheless just that: a (hopefully sophisticated and effective) set of social constructs.

Some could argue plausibly for the inclusion of at least two other branches of philosophy as relevant to philosophy, namely philosophy of language and the philosophy of mind. Nonetheless, they are arguably subsumed under logic and science respectively and are more remote than their parent disciplines, language and psychology, which obviously have a bearing, so they will not be treated here.

Finally, there is epistemology, also called the theory of knowledge. This subject spends its time agonising about such matters as what knowledge is, what truth is, and whether either is actually attainable. Application to

SCIENCE, PHILOSOPHY, AND MANAGEMENT

management in its purist form is thus hard to see specifically, since management necessarily has to proceed as though these sorts of question are uncontentious. And were they not, the implications would cover every field of endeavour, not solely management, making life even more difficult than it palpably is.

Nevertheless, social epistemology is a relatively new sub-discipline which could be very insightful for management in time. Helpfully to the cause, social science has been very thoroughly worked over by philosophy, albeit with fractured results on major questions. Goldman(12) is a philosopher in the forefront of the development of social epistemology. It is predicated on a realisation that ways of knowing face new problems (and opportunities) from change in society, both cultural and technological. He is optimistic, seeing hopes for the promulgation of values and the changing of misguided beliefs. Social institutions like the legal system, schools, the scientific community, and political arrangements too, are scrutinized, as Goldman identifies their capacities for improving or distorting knowledge. The approach can be extended to all socio-political institutions, and concepts like democracy also, the while evaluating them in ethical terms. It is a recognition that we do not just have individual knowers, but institutions collectively possess knowledge , or at least beliefs and policies. Additionally, institutions themselves are social constructs, or human inventions, and develop by processes independent of the individual knower. So we can have very complicated interactions hidden beneath their development.

To summarize, then, apart from ethics, which is intrinsic to management (and subsumes political philosophy), not many other branches of philosophy would appear especially applicable to it, other than the emerging social epistemology, with which ethics is complementary, together with practical logic - the study of reasoning and argument.

It may be different when we come to apply philosophical methods, even so, and it is to a likely candidate (analysis) that we now turn.

CHAPTER 4

SCIENCE, PHILOSOPHY, AND MANAGEMENT

Philosophical Analysis

As philosophical analysis has developed, it has provided useful clarifications of concepts in all the major fields of intellectual enquiry, so it is reasonable to speculate that it might do the same for management. The prospect is quite plausible in principle.

Analysis has been a major approach to philosophy during the twentieth century, where there has been ample opportunity to assess its strengths and weaknesses as a methodology. Essentially, philosophical analysis is the taking of a (complex) concept and splitting it up into simple parts. It could be a key aid to understanding, seeing that concepts can be notoriously subject to differences of view about their meaning. It has nothing to do with analysis in the psychoanalytical sense of lying on Freudian couches and baring your 'soul'.

Unfortunately, 'analysis' is itself a contested term in philosophy, even nowadays, and any practical application of it to management is bound to be a bit on the loose side(13). We are seeking the essence of things by reducing them to their component parts and studying their characteristics in detail. We are decomposing compound thoughts to more simple ones, maybe looking under their surface appearance to discover their essential nature. In the process we must be careful to use words carefully and accurately, not to be led astray by syntax and forms of expression. In the endeavour we shall look at 'contested' concepts, among other things, seeking to clarify ideas whose meaning is not universally agreed. We shall aim at truths which are not narrowly linguistic, but are actually grounded in reality, despite there being no one general way in which this might be achieved.

Though it has many detractors, without a shadow of a doubt the method has been of enormous value in the development of contemporary philosophy, and still is. Of exceptional worth is the fact that it is painstaking and detailed, giving rigorous attention to meaning throughout. It can thereby aid clear thinking. And these virtues carry over into managerial analysis too.

Purely conceptual analysis, however, can be limited by the discovery that

CHAPTER 4

SCIENCE, PHILOSOPHY, AND MANAGEMENT

the meaning of a concept is not really clarified by virtue of becoming unambiguous. What tends to happen is that you get a layering effect; the concept is shown to have depth, nuances, and context-dependent applications. It can also gain much of its power by connection with other concepts in a wider network. Nor is it always clear which direction to proceed in, or where to stop. Quine [14] is a critic of philosophical analysis in that he says it seeks a structure in language which does not exist. Therefore, it must fail. But another way of looking at matters is to say that analysis offers the hope of avoiding language's 'bewitchment' (Wittgenstein), so keeping our meaning precise ,whilst recognising the limitations of our language (indeed, any language) and not being carried away by its capacity to generate misplaced emotions.

There are close connections between philosophical and managerial analysis through their essentially logical approach. Management analysis does not, of course, use mathematical logic, like philosophy can, with its deductive lines of formal reasoning from axioms, such as in a proof. Rather, it operates with looser notions like systematic approaches, categorisation, linearity, sequence, delineation of scope. Managers are often engaged in looking at aggregated issues or situations, rather than concepts as such, and reducing them to their component factors. Sometimes they are faced with a great deal of 'data', in no particular arrangement, so it has to be ordered, perhaps into logical or other patterns, identifying what is important, and so translating it into useful 'information'. Communication and decision-making are thus aided, and if the analysis occurs in a neutral way, then the account is purely factual, not opinion-laden.

As the dictionary has it [15], analysis is *"the detailed examination of the structure and content of something"*. In other words, analysis is a process which looks at documents and their ideas from a standpoint that separates the constituent parts. The enquiry may have myriad different purposes, such as reviews, testing against criteria, comparison, evaluation of merit. And so it involves judgement. The approach is essentially rational, critical, in-depth, methodical, detailed, questioning, interpretive and explanatory. It is often solitary, leading to written reports for senior management, and in the public sector for politicians too.

CHAPTER 4

SCIENCE, PHILOSOPHY, AND MANAGEMENT

However, analysis is frequently disparaged by those whose habits of thought are jumbled and unsystematic. They talk of 'paralysis by analysis', pointing to the risk of over-complicating matters, and the excuse of delay afforded, at least in principle, by such techniques. In a political context the criticism may frequently to be true. Politicians can find advantage in delay, setting up commissions and enquiries essentially to buy time and postpone decisions, especially in controversial or uncertain arenas. Politics is very relevant to management, of course, and political philosophy is as old as the hills, dealing with such concepts as 'justice', 'equality' and 'freedom', all important as guiding principles.

Pertinently, the policy-making side of management is concerned with matters like devising objectives within general aims or goals. These are highly abstract and value-laden, yet they have an intensely practical purpose. So it can be argued that policy and philosophy coalesce within the socio-political arena: that policy is about philosophy in action. This would have appealed to Marx, who claimed that the function of philosophy was not so much to understand society as to change it.

Hodgkinson[16] for one views the manager(or as he would term it 'administrator ') as a practising philosopher. Given that he may be involved in policy development and/or policy implementation, he works in an intensely value-laden environment, where ethical considerations are paramount. In clarifying, analysing, and assessing practical options he would benefit from certain philosophical tools and disciplines. Notable among these, referred to in earlier discussion, are logical reasoning, ethical knowledge and theoretical understanding, critical thinking skills, honed abilities with language and meaning, and awareness of socio-political factors and the institutional context.

Hodgkinson has a mission and zeal of his own, regarding management as a humanistic activity whose overall goal is to ensure that power is exercised in a civilized way. This is no bad credo for any manager, at whatever level, because the potentiality for social ill is boundless and there is a heavy burden of responsibility to advise and warn, given the temptations afforded to their political masters.

CHAPTER 4

SCIENCE, PHILOSOPHY, AND MANAGEMENT

Management Defects and Computers

We have seen how the domain of management can be informed and possibly improved by the insights and usages of scientific and philosophical methods, and especially analysis.

Haplessly, there is usually too big a gap between theory and practice. Research insights can seem very remote. One valuable role for philosophy would be to develop, if it is possible, a body of theory which finds broad agreement as characterizing the subject of management in its fundamentals, including the scientific aspects. There is at the present no such theory.

Even if there were, Hodgkinson rightly points to various weaknesses in practical management as a result of human frailties. He believes philosophy can cure these, firstly by setting them out so that we are all aware, secondly by arguing against them to expose their deficiencies. The optimism is questionable and all remains to be seen. In what follows there is no attempt to be exhaustive.

It may be said, of course, that many of the other sicknesses of management relate to the faults in particular human beings. Management is common to most fields of endeavour and so it has a great many practitioners of variable quality. Some of these are politicians, some are 'amateur' managers in the sense that they have not been trained in managerial principles and techniques, but merely work in management as their paid employment. A relative few have 'qualified' as managers by passing relevant examinations and accumulating appropriate experience. Quite a lot will not have arrived there through choice of preference and their hearts may not be entirely in it.

Along with a lack of grounded theory, it is common in any case to find anti-intellectual attitudes to the subject. Management often attracts doers rather than thinkers when it really needs both.

Where it is politically controlled, management will be derailed at times by politicians who place self-service above that of the public. Even when they do not, their quality of decision-making can leave much to be

CHAPTER 4

SCIENCE, PHILOSOPHY, AND MANAGEMENT

desired, stemming from a poor education and unreasonable attitudes. A disturbing illustration occurred late in 2009.

When David Nutt, the chairman of the government's Scientific Advisory Council on the Misuse of Drugs, was summarily dismissed by Home Secretary Alan Johnson, a whole can of worms was opened regarding the relationship of politicians and scientists. Johnson claimed that Nutt had crossed a divide and was openly campaigning against government policy. But several other members of the committee then also resigned and Lord Rees, President of the Royal Society, stressed the importance of respecting scientific input. A draft code of practice was drawn up and agreed by the parties, but not before some had seen the incident as indicative of a fundamental lack of willingness by government to make its decisions on the basis of proper evidence.

With politicians there are always Machiavellian tendencies to be aware of, so that straight-dealing is uncommon instead of the norm. The evaluation of people is accordingly suspect. We have the fallacy of paragons, and the distorting influences of charisma and egotism to contend with.

Plato sought even in ancient Greece to curb these tendencies by eliminating the claims to service by volunteers in favour of very experienced and wise (as well as philosophically educated) members of the community, who might rule for a while, even though reluctant to do so. Of course, there aren't enough of such exemplars of excellence to go round, to provide a complete antidote to careerism, certainly in a modern state, which has very differentiated and dispersed activities. And it is far from having been demonstrated that the cadre of philosophers would be the best place to look!

In any walk of life there are naturally ambitions and ,in reasonably large organisations, hierarchies to climb too. Much positive behaviour can stem from this; dysfunctionality also. One hierarchic problem is that cream does not always rise to the top. Good people may be wasted in subordinate roles , owing to poor judgement, and even favouritism, in preferment by those higher up. They say that appointments tend to be in the appointer's image, so mediocrity in an organisation can be self-perpetuating.

CHAPTER 4

SCIENCE, PHILOSOPHY, AND MANAGEMENT

Since management malfunctions in myriad ways, they cannot all be catalogued here. Suffice it then to characterize just a few more. It is commonplace in organisations for structures to be unsuitable for function. There can be other difficulties too around ineffective or inefficient lines of reporting and communication. Organisations may come to seem as though they are themselves a force beyond the people in them. It can result in members of the organisation suspending their own moral conscience and committing unethical acts in its name.

As staff become elevated they come to have more discretion as to how to organise their time. A price is that job descriptions can become quite vague as to purpose and criteria of success. This is notoriously true in local government. What tends to happen is that a climate of industriousness prevails which emphasises meetings and visits. Officers are reluctant to spend time at their desks. (Some behave as though the very prospect is anathema). Key reports and reading round the subject to keep up to date fall to a low level of priority. Time for reflection is minimal, as is opportunity for writing, research, and reflection. Difficulties are deferred or avoided. There is typically much computerised information flow, nevertheless, dealing with the here and now in a shallow and transient manner.

For one technological advance threatens the world of management like no other ever has. It is the rise and rise of the computer. The ramifications of the device are endless, and being played out with ever-increasing speed, of course. Such is their complexity, and radical difference of operation from what went before, that staff educated before the revolution on the whole fail to adapt completely to them. It will take a new generation, brought up in the digital age since early childhood, to get the best out of the new machines.

Yet at what cost? Offices are being dehumanised, as face-to-face contact is replaced by monitor screens. A strange breed of staff is in some cases happy to spend all day interacting with them to the exclusion of almost everything and everybody else.

Data is transformed across cyberspace, in larger and larger volumes, and still there is a question mark about how much of it informs, just what extent and quality of real communication is actually going on.

CHAPTER 4

SCIENCE, PHILOSOPHY, AND MANAGEMENT

Some of the changes are potentially an improvement, on the other hand. Statistical data can be processed faster and more accurately by computer, allowing greater facility of financial reporting, for instance. Files are made available more widely and easily, although contemporary leakages of sensitive data in public and private sectors have highlighted the urgent need for much tighter security measures, including evolutionary encryption.

The key to a mature accommodation to what is after all only a sophisticated tool, will be to use computers only where they are a decided improvement, not all the time for (virtually) everything, and to escape from their thrall to a critical awareness of their strengths and weaknesses.

The design of computer operations has been very clever. Instead of producing software whose usage is just about self-explanatory, the internationally adopted standards ensure a perpetual need to training. Given that the functional procedures lack logic, they have to be learned. In the nature of things, the learning is unlikely to be retained without dint of very regular usage, because it will mostly comprise variously long sequences of function keys best internalised if they are ever to be used efficiently.

Consequently, we are far from attaining the point where the computer becomes only another, albeit important, aid. It tends to dominate the working environment, profoundly altering the way people interact with each other. This is not a sensible or healthy state of affairs. Many traditional, and valuable, managerial and administrative skills are in danger of being devalued , or even lost, as a result. Bureaucracy was never noted in the public estimation as especially human. Now it has a new potential to become completely remote and unresponsive to feelings.

CHAPTER 4

SCIENCE, PHILOSOPHY, AND MANAGEMENT

NOTES

*   1.   Philips, Michael, The Undercover Philosopher, One-world Publications, Oxford 2008.

*   2.   Trigg, Roger, Understanding Social Science, Blackwell Publishers Ltd., Oxford 2nd Edn. 2001.

*   3.   Ward, Glenn, Postmodernism, Hodder Education, London 1997.

*   4.   Parsons, Wayne, Public Policy: An introduction and practice of policy analysis, Edward Elgar Publishing Limited, Cheltenham, 1995.

*   5.   Heywood, Andrew, Politics, Palgrave, Basingstoke, Second Edition, 2002.

6.   Newby, H, Social Science and Public Policy: #'The Frank Foster Lecture', RSA Journal, May, 1993.

7.   Delanty, Gerard, Social Science, Open University Press, McGraw-Hill, Maidenhead, 2005.

8.   Dror, Y, Public Policymaking Re-examined, Transaction Publishers, New Brunswick, 1989.

*   9.   Armstrong, Michael, A Handbook of Management Techniques, Second Edition, Kogan Page Ltd., London, 1993.

10.   Administration Division, Department of Audit, Wyoming.

11.   Red Hot Enterprise Linux 3, Introduction to System Administration, Mirror Service, 2009.

*   12.   Goldman, Alvin I, Knowledge in a Social World, Oxford University Press, Oxford, 1999.

CHAPTER 4

SCIENCE, PHILOSOPHY, AND MANAGEMENT

13. Glock, Hans-Johann, What is Analytic Philosophy?, Cambridge University Press, 2008.

14. Quinne, W.V.O., Word and Object, The MIT-Press, Cambridge, Massachusetts, 1960.

15. Chambers Dictionary and Thesaurus, Chambers Harrap Publishers Ltd., Edinburgh, 2007.

* 16. Hodgkinson, Christopher, Towards a Philosophy of Administration, Basil Blackwell, Oxford, 1978.

CHAPTER 5

VALUES AND IDEOLOGY

Preliminaries

Values
      Introduction
      Meta-Ethics
      Grounds for Values
      Modern Ethicists
      Politicians and Values

Ideology
      Introduction
      General Features of Ideology
      Ideology and Politics
      Coping with Ideology

CHAPTER 5

VALUES AND IDEOLOGY

PRELIMINARIES

The book is trying to explore the struggles faced by bureaucracy as a discipline whose practitioners have to live and work in the real world of politicians and problems.

The present chapter seeks an understanding of, and accommodation with, two of the great and probably inevitable filtering devices thorough which all our social perceptions come to be distorted. These are respectively 'ideology' and 'values'.

In a way this chapter is about attitudes; attitudes that we all have and which may, and frequently do, hopelessly cloud our vision of certain kinds of reality. If we can come to understand 'ideology' and 'values' as concepts, see how they tend to be applied, we might just about escape their clutches for long enough to be able to look at the objective truth with our own eyes, instead of peering all the while through their distorting lenses.

If we cannot the world is always going to be very imperfect and to seem that way too to all who do not happen to share the prevailing orthodoxies of value and ideology in their society.

We shall start with values, because this is the more basic of the two concepts and quite fundamental. Ideology is always based on some type of value, or collection of values, and so is a derivative concept.

VALUES

Introduction

At a theoretical level, if public management can be viewed as a kind of applied social science, it is subject to a major doubt within these disciplines that questions whether they can be free of values to any extent at all, and if so, to what degree. Weber's optimistic dream was that social

CHAPTER 5

VALUES AND IDEOLOGY

sciences could be value-free. Then they would be capable of an objectivity to match the physical and life sciences. Once values intrude there is a parting from the natural sciences. It becomes dubious whether the social sciences are sciences at all, or if they can attain truth, frame testable theories, derive experimental laws which have both predictive and explanatory power, and the like.

Value-laden social science would also bring in many people without any scientific background and some whose motives are anything but scientific. But the question can also be posed as to whether it is desirable for the social sciences to be value-free, even if they could be. This in itself is, of course, a value judgement.

Nevertheless, on a practical level, if an administrator is to operate, he needs goal-direction. This implies that at least someone in authority has decided a particular course of action is worthwhile. Whether directly, indirectly, or even in the remote subconscious, there has been a value judgement. Administration in practice is connected (often obscurely) with values in theory, albeit they may not be explicit and can remain hidden. So the key question here is: what is the basis which 'grounds', or justifies, a value? Because without such a basis we are flying blind, with only faith and hope to sustain us. It seems ironical that the administrative processes themselves may well be intensely rational when the values that drive them can be contentious.

So we had better start by considering what a 'value' is. Most of us probably regard it as some principle which has intrinsic worth. If we looked at aesthetics, this would take us into the philosophy of art, to study value in the context of the various artistic media. But here, in the world of ethics, the principle is usually perceived as guiding conduct and our decisions about life. We talk about concepts like 'good', 'merit', 'standards'.

As soon as we do this, we find a fundamental split. There are those who believe values are objectively true - based on some kind of legitimating authority - usually a God, or the requirements of rationality. The rest think values are subjective, because they cannot see any source of legitimating authority. Values to them are personal choices based on preferences and emotional stances.

CHAPTER 5

VALUES AND IDEOLOGY

So it is necessary to examine further the problem of values. Not at this stage the individual qualities of worth that we may espouse, like equality before the law, or free speech, and so forth - but the nature of the possible bases for believing in this value or that. And whilst ethics is the subject which studies values, it is meta-ethics that considers the possible ways of explaining what kind of things values are, looking for the logical possibilities regarding their place in reality. It is therefore to meta-ethics that we now turn in the hope of demystification.

Meta-Ethics

Miller[2] produces a classification which, if not completely comprehensive, certainly attempts to characterize the majority of meta-ethical theories. He poses a series of questions the different possible answers to which delimit separate meta-ethical positions. The fundamental question is: do moral judgements express beliefs? And the two definite answers to this logically are 'yes' (cognitivism), or 'no' (non-cognitivism).

So the main meta-ethical theories conform to two deep categories; namely, whether moral judgements are deemed to express beliefs (cognitivism) or not (non-cognitivism). The former category opens up a prospect laymen tend to take for granted, that some of the moral beliefs expressed could in principle actually be true. Non-cognitivism denies this altogether.

We shall look at non-cognitivism first, because most people will want it to be false. There is a lot at stake. The non-cognitivists say that moral judgements do not express beliefs. In that case what do they do? One well-known version is Ayer's 'emotivism', the claim that moral judgements express emotions instead. A similar line is that they set out our approval or disapproval. There are other variants, such as quasi-realism, the claim that values are the projections of our own sentiments, which can include attitudes. Gibbard's theory suggests that values are a reflection of mental states, and that they assert someone's acceptance or rejection of social norms.

It is important to note that subjectivism is <u>not</u> the same as non-

CHAPTER 5

VALUES AND IDEOLOGY

cognitivism in that the former claims that moral judgements are statements about emotions. Non-cognitivists say that moral utterances do not make statements, but just express people's sentiments.

So how may the claims of non-cognitivism be challenged? Firstly, there may be no such thing as a moral emotion or feeling. Secondly, why would we all take right and wrong seriously if they were just merely such? Thirdly, if it were true, would not morals disappear if our sentiments did? And, finally, wouldn't we therefore be in error to speak of values as though they did exist in the world? There are other arguments, but these in combination are weighty, although not decisive.

Even if non-cognitivism had been disproved it would not be a justified conclusion to say that cognitivism must thereby be true. Nevertheless, for anybody who wishes to cling to the notion that ethics has some meaning based in truth with which to underpin society, it is to cognitivism they must turn. They would still need to filter out those theories which deny that 'moral facts' exist independently of human opinion and so cannot be true. Prominently, we have Mackie's error theory, which discounts the possibility that there are such things in the real world as moral facts. His conclusion is then that any moral judgements we make must be in error because nothing exists to make them true. He goes further, using his 'argument from queerness': *"If there were objective values, then they would be entities or relations of a very strange sort, utterly different from anything else in the universe."* But states of affairs we find in the world are 'normatively inert'. That is, they do not come with any kind of built-in demand that we take a particular (moral) action in regard to them. Again, Mackie's position may not be unassailable, but it is very difficult indeed to find convincing arguments contrary to it.

It is against this uneasy background - where philosophers have thus far failed to unseat both non-cognitivism and Mackie's error-theory - that we resume consideration of those forms of cognitivism which claim there are moral judgements that can be true in some cases and independent of human opinion.

Another two-way split then claims either that these independent moral

CHAPTER 5

VALUES AND IDEOLOGY

facts are natural features of the world (naturalism), or that they are not (non-naturalism).

Dealing with non-naturalism first, such theorists regard moral properties and moral facts as really existing, and quite independently of human opinion, but they are claimed to be simple, not analysable any further, and 'non-natural'. Non-natural means they are not 'natural', which is to say that they do not form part of the subject-matter of the natural sciences, including psychology. The most famous version is due to G.E. Moore who coined 'the naturalistic fallacy'. Essentially, although the argument is complex, and inevitably open to criticism, Moore takes the word 'good' in its moral sense and says it cannot be defined at all, never mind even in terms of non-natural properties. Anyway, assuming Moore is wrong, and stretching many a point along a tangled way, what we are left with is 'naturalism'.

Looking at naturalism further, devotees do all agree that there actually are such things as moral facts, and that they exist in the world whether humans have an opinion about them or not. They are called 'moral realists' accordingly. However, they disagree with each other over whether moral facts can be reduced to other natural facts or not. Those who say they can are called 'reductionists'. Railton's theory is a prominent example. Moral facts, he contends, can be defined, and a definition of one is appropriate if it contributes to the successful explanation of a feature of our experience. In this way moral properties can be reduced to complex non-moral properties. Yet doesn't an unwarranted role for subjective judgement become introduced in the process? Anyway to illustrate, Railton defines 'moral rightness' as 'what is instrumentally rational from a social point of view' . Another immediate objection here would be that the juxtaposition of the words 'social' and 'rational' is not a happy one, but Railton would make the more optimistic claim that moral norms evolve for the better, albeit with 'numerous reversals', surely an unsound reading of history.

A final type of theory we will consider is that of Cornell realism. Cornell disagrees with Railton and denies that moral facts would be reduced to any other kind of fact. So are they out on their own, then, some unique kind of metaphysical furniture within the unexplained part of the

CHAPTER 5

VALUES AND IDEOLOGY

universe? Well yes, except that Cornell says moral facts are also 'natural', which is to claim that they can play their part in explanatory theories of the world. To Harman, a critic, the operative word is 'can', because they are superfluous to requirements. You don't need to postulate any of them to explain the world. Scientific facts are what you need. Moral properties just don't exist, he concludes.

Grounds for Values

So meta-ethics has served to demonstrate that, although values are important to us, there are very deep-seated problems with current endeavours to explain their nature. Far from clearing confusions they will have compounded them among the open-minded.

Turning instead to ethics itself, if we cannot discover what 'ethical' values are ('moral' is used here synonymously), perhaps we can at least fathom out what grounds them in truth, if indeed anything does.

Blackburn looks further at the possible objective grounding of values(3). He indicates no less then seven major threats to the claimed objectivity of ethical values. Traditionally, it was widely believed that religion provided their foundation through God. But which then is logically prior? We cannot obey God just because we are afraid of his power, but because it is somehow right to do so. But then ethics is logically prior to God, so what grounds ethics?

Secondly, relativists maintain that there is no such entity as a universal good. This is something which varies from society to society. Worse, subjectivists argue that good is not out there at all, but in the mind. It is therefore a creation of many individuals, and their opinions on the subject will differ widely.

A third threat is egoism. Ethics comes down to what a person wants. And so there is no basis for deciding which is true, if any. We may want very different things.

Another attack on the objectivity of values is that, since we have

CHAPTER 5

VALUES AND IDEOLOGY

biologically evolved, there is a basic sense in which we do what our nature makes us. So what seem like 'good' and 'bad' are really related to species survival imperatives in some way, it is claimed.

A similar idea, that we are not really responsible for our actions, and thus cannot fairly be held accountable, is implied by a philosophical theory, which has not been reasoned away over hundreds of years, that there is no such thing as free will. In other words, our actions are determined in accordance with laws of nature, and choice is only apparent, not real.

Blackburn points to an objection to the existence of objective values arising from realism about how our conduct can cope in the face of the many demands placed upon us and the varied roles society expects us to play. It is all too much, and the more we meet them the more we unfairly disadvantage ourselves.

Finally, how do we know we are not being conned by society at large, as Marx would claim? Although often upheld as noble sentiments and behaviours, aren't morals just devices for denying our own interests and keeping us in line. They are really not about "the good" at all, but designed to cement the power and control of the ruling group.

So in conclusion, then, although the force in each of these positions has not been worked through fully here, there is surely sufficient cumulative doubt, based on the fact of these fundamentally very varied approaches, as to the veracity of each of the claimed grounds for the existence of objective ethical values. We are therefore in a serious mess.

Modern Ethicists

Having signally failed to discover what values actually are, and how they may have any relation to truth, will we fare any better when we look at what the sages have to say about them? What follows is a brief account of the views of three very modern and influential moral philosophers - Parfit, Nagel, and Williams. These have been chosen for originality, to get away from the polarised and moribund debate of the traditional thinkers, and to see if they provide fresh prospects for progress with the problem.

CHAPTER 5

VALUES AND IDEOLOGY

Derek Parfit(4) has made a major contribution to ethical philosophy in the later part of the twentieth century. He classified what he termed 'normative practical reasons', as concerned with self-interest, or beneficence. These reasons refer to what we ought to do, or ought to care about; in other words to value judgements. However, it is only matters of beneficence that can be regarded properly as moral. Our own self-interest lacks the necessary social dimension of consideration for the well being of others.

Parfit's discussions are of labyrinthine complexity, liberally interspersed by theoretical scenarios and constructed to test, through the use of thought experiments, the tenability of one position or another. He is concerned to try and show that some moral theory can encompass the reasons for benefiting others and indicate their content sufficient at least to be able to discriminate morally between courses of action. This might not seem to the layman a particularly ambitious project. After all, we tend to take it for granted that we should and could be doing something for others, especially those near and dear to us, perhaps. And a great deal of beneficent behaviour is quite natural. For the sticking points we tend to have a conscience whispering in our ear. So what is the problem?

Well, the arguments are very technical, but seem to conclude, somewhat counter-intuitively, that we cannot successfully ground beneficence in any moral theory at all!! That is to say, ethical theory lets us down in failing to find a framework within which beneficent acts can be systematically and coherently justified. All relevant reasons for rational principles to demonstrate moral obligations have to be shown. But their sheer number and variety, and the infinite nature and complexity of possible scenarios in the world, render the task beyond our whit. Don't forget that situations of moral choice are not confined to those of intimate or close relations among family and friends in everyday life, intractable though these may sometimes seem. A moral theory also has to cover the bigger picture, including our moral stances towards strangers, people in other places, different countries, and even across the centuries. It also has to be able to cope with conflicts of interest, and variable scale from small numbers of people to whole populations. Such vastness of scope tests to destruction the potential choice of candidate moral principles, noting additionally that

CHAPTER 5

VALUES AND IDEOLOGY

such a set would have to be compatible, cohesive, non-contradictory, and comprehensive, whatever else.

The philosopher, Thomas Nagel(5), is also pessimistic, but for different reasons. He regards ethics and politics as inevitably entwined and asserts:

> *"It is clear that we are at a primitive stage of moral development. Even the most civilized human beings have only a haphazard understanding of how to live, how to treat others, how to organise societies."*

On the oft-claimed objectivity of morality, he has this emphatic denial:

> *"The idea that the basic principles of morality are known, and that the problems all come in their interpretation and application, is one of the most fantastic conceits to which our conceited species has been drawn."*

He talks about the "sickening" moral differences we display, so concluding sceptically that we are quite unable to invent appropriate political institutions that would allow for harmonious living, underpinned by a rational and agreed morality. Ironically, this does show the vital importance of public institutions, even though Nagel is defeatist on the chances of success of any project that would seek political legitimacy, which he (exactingly) defines as the arrival of community unanimity.

Bernard Williams(6), an extremely influential contemporary philosopher, also attacks what he sees as bogus ethical objectivity in society. Duties morally binding on us he claims it is beyond philosophy, or any other method, to demonstrate the existence of. Some of the reasons he considers at length. Essentially, they are very powerful, ranging from individuality, pluralist culture, and the fact that some people are amoral. There is not the remotest chance that we shall as a society reach a consensus on ethical questions, although we can be forced by state power to behave as though we have.

Williams looks at the major schools of moral philosophy, undermines

CHAPTER 5

VALUES AND IDEOLOGY

their basic arguments, and comes to a broadly critical and sceptical position.

Even if we did arrive at a consensus view on the application of ethics in society, this would not entail that it had any status, other than a democratic one, as a collection of universally true, objective moral norms. All we can reasonably hope for, and even this ebbs and flows, and is consistently observed nowhere, is a set of simple rules for the practical conduct of everyday life, to try and ensure that we see to our basic needs and can get by in social situations with minimal conflict. If we have disagreement and contradiction in science it indicates theoretical flaws. This is also true of ethics, but sadly, unlike with science, the flaws cannot be removed. Maybe not even in principle, certainly never in fact thus far in history.

For example, he considers "Socrates' Question", namely, how we should live. Socrates himself concludes that we have moral obligations to act and desist from acting in certain ways towards people and that these transcend all other considerations. Whereas, Williams does not regard the question as having any one definite and unique answer. He attacks the idea of the supremacy of obligation among moral kinds, pointing to important matters such as welfare as also being relevant. And he would bring to bear non-ethical factors on the question too, not forgetting self-interest in the balance.

Turning to Aristotle, he seeks a foundation for ethics in the personal. By acting in our self-interest we are being both rational and ethical. Again, Williams is unimpressed. We don't always know our self-interest, it is not necessarily the same as for other people, and contemplation of it is ultimately confounded by the mysterious complexities of human nature, as we have already seen when considering prospects for social progress.

He looks to Kant, who attempted to found ethics on practical reason. There is a 'categorical imperative' to behave in certain ways which you would want to apply to everybody, treating people as ends not means, as you would have them treat you. The view has been profoundly influential, and gels with many people's intuitions about right and wrong. But its major flaw, according to Williams' argument, is that the theory equates acting and thinking when they are fundamentally different.

CHAPTER 5

VALUES AND IDEOLOGY

Rational thinking is conducive to believing the truth. But rational acting could merely be about satisfying desires.

So Williams' is a profoundly pessimistic conclusion to arrive at. And it is all of a piece with the scepticism that claims that social progress is ultimately a chimera. For what social progress worthy of the concept could claim to exist if the moral progress on which its values were based did not?

Politicians and Values

So this leaves us without any known path forward. Clearly the way we do go on at present is palpable nonsense, so we need to change both direction and process. And since we have had hundreds of years of short shrift, a paradigm change is long overdue if we want to have any pretence to being a civilized society.

Unfortunately, we cannot look for leadership from the top in United Kingdom politics, for a lot of very poor quality thinking goes on there. An illustration is of the Brown government's some time Communities Secretary, Hazel Blears[7], (before her political disgrace) making statements urging people to defend 'core British values'. This was in part a welcome challenge to the straitjacket imposed on free speech by the political correctness movement, and a usefully defiant thrust against the dangers of Islamic practices being imported into the country along with religious extremists. Nevertheless, its fundamental assumption that there are any British values, and its further assertion that these are commonly held, and that those who do not can be branded 'extremists', are pathetically unargued.

It is revealing that Ms Blears did not go on to list these values in any detail, or to say in what way they could be seen to be essentially 'British'. You could also reasonably conclude that she was being intolerant. Is that perhaps one of her British values?

By referring to 'British values', Ms Blears was, of course, playing the well-known nationalism card. Appealing to people's sense of patriotism (or possibly xenophobia), she was seeking the kind of unthinking

CHAPTER 5

VALUES AND IDEOLOGY

agreement of the herd, or possibly the football crowd. Once you do that, your problem is intellectually much more difficult. Before-hand, you might have cited some generalised value you hoped would curry favour. Now you have to justify nationalism as well, (a very difficult project in its own right) and additionally say just how and why this value is uniquely and only British.

Nationalism[8] is an 'ideology' which is to say that it is subject to the analysis in the second part of the chapter of ideologies as concepts. However, it might also be said of this particular ideology that is has spawned intolerance and many a war. Sometimes a people's feelings of commonality derive from an identity of race and descent, but clearly not in Britain, which is very heterogeneous these days.

Nationality can spring from a variety of factors, usually in combination, like a common geographical location, similar language and religion. Legally, the nation-state has an existence in which it is allowed to coerce its citizens through rights of political sovereignty. Probably one of the strongest factors, though, is a sense of emotional bonding arising from a shared history and set of collective experiences. Needless to say, the concept, being complex, is contested, and its value is subject to much disagreement.

Unfortunately, a great deal of political speech material relating to values, is cant. Darling's budget[9] in April 2009, the first following the credit crunch, could hardly have been a more significant occasion, yet is was marked with superficial comments like being "guided by our core values of fairness and opportunity". Fairness for whom? Opportunity for what? It might sound all right, but it is quite empty. And if these are "core values", can we also have non-core values? What judgements would lead to values being placed in either category? Are core values the most important, or just the most firmly held? And so forth.

Finally, returning to the vexed question of choosing and using values as a nation across the whole of society, the likelihood seems to be that it isn't going to happen. We cannot rely on the politicians; for the most part they would lack the calibre even if they could earn our respect. We cannot rely on the churches, who only convince small minorities and put faith before reason. So who?

CHAPTER 5

VALUES AND IDEOLOGY

An illustration of how we do not agree on values is that of 'tolerance'. Opinion is very much divided over its practical exercise, whether to allow the militant, anti-British dissent of Muslim extremists in the community to be openly expressed.

Yet if we can justly claim to live in a properly democratic society, we should enjoin a very serious root and branch national debate, led by our best brains in the various relevant fields of human endeavour. To do it we would have to invent machinery that does not exist. Ends and means would then have to be monitored continuously, regularly reviewed, and improvements factored back into process.

From what has been said, our journey needs to use ideas which we are prepared to discard in the light of better ones. They have to serve us as tools, not come to rule us and ossify our thoughts and actions. Ultimately, the courts of reason and experience are the only ones we have that are worth the candle. Values, whatever they may philosophically prove to be, are always appellants in those courts. And because values can obviously conflict one with another, their worth and relative importance will change not just over time, but in the myriad different contexts too.

IDEOLOGY

Introduction

Following the analysis of values, and the rather pessimistic conclusions about uncertain meaning, lack of connection to truth, social disagreements, and want of clear applicability, we turn next to values in a socio-political milieu. Here they are usually to be found wrapped up, and sometimes hidden in, something called an "ideology". The aim will be to see to what extent, if at all, we can prevent ourselves being seduced away from right thinking and acting by false ideologies once we have explored their complicated and deceptive nature, and their stranglehold on political life. We can easily be caught unawares.

CHAPTER 5

VALUES AND IDEOLOGY

General Features of Ideology

Ideology is yet another complex term on whose meaning there is no universal agreement. It has numerous strands, some of the main ones being discussed below, and they are adequate for a working understanding.

As has already been indicated, the concept is normative; that is to say, it is value-laden, not neutral.

A second key strand is the view of ideology as a comprehensive way of looking at things.

Opinions differ on what things, but it has been espoused by some forms of literary theory and regularly applied to religions. Marx in a famous quotation said that "religion was the opium of the people". He brought religions within his own idea of ideology, asserting that they fulfilled the ideological function of deceiving people into acceptance of the established order as appropriate and natural. This was in the interests of the ruling group rather than theirs.

Some neo-Marxists and other modern writers have cast the term even wider, so that it comes to denote any belief system in whatever subject, and all world views(10).

Sometimes the underlying claim is that elements of the truth are captured by these systems. But this outlook is considerably misguided.

Ideology as a term is rarely neutral and rarely pure. Readers should be on the look-out for its derogatory uses. This has happened ever since Napoleon, to discredit rivals views.

So there can be undertones of propaganda and brainwashing in ideology to persuade people of the truth of something for which there may be no scientific evidence. Seductively, it can be called 'common sense', and when it is, minds close against those who would argue against it. Since we frequently criticize folk for not having common sense, evidently it is not that common. One of the misleading features of ideology is that it seems (to some) to be true, but only seems. If you are not careful, its hold on you goes unnoticed. Ideology can be very deep-seated, habitually colouring your views.

Ideology tends to be one-dimensional. The world is regarded from one point of view in preference to all others, which are then disparaged. The view is both partial and selective.

Because there will be different collections of values within an ideology, it will tend to contain contradictions if they conflict. Various smokescreen activities may well be generated to conceal this fact, so as not to undermine the ideology. Deflection is a common tactic, getting large numbers of people interested in relative trivialities, like football, say, or celebrities, to keep their attention away from the big issues in society.

Another confusion, and one that emerges from the literature, is that some academics may seek to impose their own ideology on the meaning of 'ideology'. An instance is the sociologist, Peter Berger, who uses the world 'ideology' about an idea that supports a vested interest in society. The function ideology performs is thus to interpret social reality in such a way that it appears to justify that interest. The underlying assumption is that the vested interest is not really defensible, although that does not strictly follow in the argument.

So we have already seen that ideology is complex and problematic. It can be powerfully influential, have appealing values, and yet be quite dangerously wrong. Needless to say, its main use as a concept has been, and is, in the world of politics, to which we now turn for its further consideration.

Ideology and Politics

It may be relatively uncontentious to claim in its political contexts that "ideology" means a political, social, or economic belief system, or set of ideas(11). One definition has ideology as a 'political orientation', which is characteristic of the beliefs of a group, or even a nation.

CHAPTER 5

VALUES AND IDEOLOGY

Ideologists are commonly not satisfied with their (narrow) explanation of the world, but seek to impose it through political action. Ideology, as Marx said, is about changing the world. It purports to give a justification to programmes of action in the political and social spheres.

There can be a thought gap, arising owing to ideology being a system of abstract ideas, such as the above, but having to be applied to down-to-earth public affairs.

Since Marx and his disciples were mainly responsible for developing the concept of ideology, it is to them that we now return for further insight. According to Marx, by persuading people of the rightness of its values, an ideology enables the ruling class to hold onto power by minimizing opposition. The people become socialized in a process whereby the ideology shapes their understanding of, and feeling towards, society. The socialization process is carried out by ideological organs of the State, which include schools, churches, family, as well as cultural forms, such as the arts and media more generally.

A possible problem with Marxism is that it provides just one motive for ideology, namely, that of concealing the true sources and structures of power and exploitation in society.

This may encourage a revolutionary view: that society is not so much being interpreted, as constructed. In a battle of wills to impose a particular vision on the community, political power is essential and the only justification. And it is where the bad name of ideology came from: association with domination and oppression of the people in pursuit of an unattainable, minority dream.

In reality, despite their grip, ideologies do develop over time. Disciples come along and change aspects of the theory, as with the history of Marxism. They comprise not only the grand principles that attract followers, but often detailed practices as well. Nor are they always mutually exclusive, tending to overlap, certainly at the level of method, in addressing issues.

Louis Althusser(12), a neo-Marxist, had an instructive conception of

CHAPTER 5

VALUES AND IDEOLOGY

ideology as a special kind of discussion: some statements are given which suggest other statements. An example is the statement 'all are equal before the law'. This is trotted out as a basis for our legal system, but is essentially a lie. Private property legal rights, and the high cost of legal dealings, ensure that the affluent get better treatment.

The concept of 'hegemony', written about by Gramsci, may be very important too. It refers to a state of society in which most of the populace think alike about the main matters of how it is run, or even forget that alternative modes of organisation are possible. Then, you may think, we have either arrived at Utopia, or ideology has truly worked its evil magic.

But one powerful agent for change is the dynamic tension that can ensue between the ideology and the real problems a society faces. This may be illustrated by one or two examples relating to Conservative and Socialist ideologies of the parties.

We can to an extent comprehend some of the underlying mindset tendencies which have an effect on whether someone becomes a socialist, liberal, or conservative in their politics. Pivotal are attitudes to the place of individuals within society. If the community is accorded more importance than the individual, socialist, or even communist outlooks are liable to result. If, on the other hand, the individual is given pride of place, liberalism will be preferred, with its emphasis on personal choice and freedom. Society is likely to be seen as a threat with all its constraining influences. Conservatism is a kind of middle ground, recognising the tensions between individuals and society, but seeing worth in according rights to both. More often than not, it will be accompanied by a belief in the continuing value of existing traditions and institutions (unless these were established by the political opposition).

The connection between ideology and political parties can vary. Some parties follow an ideology quite closely; others choose from a range of ideologies. And a good deal of opportunist pragmatism may fly in the face of all the sacred ideological cows when a party is in desperate need of bolstering support.

Traditional Conservative ideology is fundamentally in favour of a status

VALUES AND IDEOLOGY

quo that approves elitism, a pronounced division of wealth and power throughout society, capitalist values, and a minimalist government to encourage personal freedoms and self-reliance. But confronted by the plight of the poor, let's say, graphically demonstrated to the public through a persistent media, the Tory party feels forced to develop putative welfare schemes. Conversely, Socialist ideology seeks an egalitarian society, but balks at the undoubtedly major redistribution of wealth which would be needed to bring it about. These approaches to a complex pluralist and rapidly changing society are, of course, hopelessly inadequate. At worst they spawn exercises in applied prejudice.

Coping with Ideology

In so far as people in the United Kingdom generally tend to understand the term, which is generally not a lot, they may well associate "ideology"[13] with the beliefs of Karl Marx. Which is sensible because, as we have seen, Marx did much to develop ideology as an operational societal concept. However, since they are not communists, and regard extreme left-wing thinking as deeply damaged and dangerous, they can fall into the trap of dismissing the invaluable lessons of ideology owing to a dislike for its messenger.

Whatever you might think about Marxism, then, the nature of ideology, and in particular its psychological and sociological dimensions, is more than a worthwhile study; rather an essential one. And as already stated, some suspicions about ideology focus on it as a mask to conceal meanings. Its study therefore aims to serve other useful purposes like decoding the messages and exposing any concealed motives.

A great problem of fusion exists in political thought, because every political tendency entails an ideology interlinked. Some are not even explicitly acknowledged to be such. So whilst the need to unravel is crucial to understanding its meaning, we mostly do not make the efforts we should. The task is difficult, though, and might at times require professional analysis by neutral political scientists.

Now if you look at all the main political ideologies the world has so far

CHAPTER 5

VALUES AND IDEOLOGY

invented, the main thing they have in common is that they are wrong; wrong in theory and wrong in practice. In other words, they are rationally unsound, neither do they actually work. We know this because we all live in hopelessly inadequate societies.

So how do we come to believe in ideologies? This might be a hard question, except that most people do not learn about such things in school, where teachers, through fear of the consequences, are reluctant to get involved, and politicians rather see the advantage in discouraging political science as an unfit subject for the masses, especially in their tender years. It is therefore likely that their family situation and its beliefs will be the biggest influence on many.

Partly for such reasons a potential problem with ideology is that it can arouse powerful emotions. The views of its followers will then be much harder to shake. They may become inflexible and unwilling to compromise. So there are understandable psychological reasons why we may be reluctant to critically examine our position. It is probably a mass of contradictions, but it is also rather close to our innermost beliefs, so we can feel very threatened by even a smidgin of criticism. We may fail to realise that, while we might be disparaging this ideology or that, we too have an ideology. It is quite the sort of thing others could know about us rather better than we do ourselves and inevitably it will colour their judgement.

So people will tend to hold the notions of their ideology very dear, and often too deeply for close examination. They will be inclined to believe them implicitly and argue for them passionately. They will reflect people's values and will be strongly believed to be true.

It goes without saying that for the most part the vast majority of people live removed and aloof from politics; that is to say, they will pay it very little attention in their daily lives unless it directly and obviously impinges on them, or perhaps at general elections, when the media clamour becomes almost too loud to ignore, or maybe some dim sense of public duty obtrudes at last.

This is a bad thing. Apart from the rather obvious fact that developed

CHAPTER 5

VALUES AND IDEOLOGY

democracies cannot thrive without a committed, interested, and astutely-informed electorate, there is the danger that ideology gets in the way of reasoned debate and constructive dialogue. Because we usually talk through our hats on most things.

There is an attitude to ideology which sees it as rather too abstract to succeed in characterizing social reality without distorting simplifications. Ideology is dismissed as unduly dogmatic: the world needs to be approached pragmatically, using history and experiences as the best guides to judgement. It is therefore very tempting instead to want to expunge ideology from politics altogether. Sadly, it seems very doubtful whether this can actually be done. No matter how neutral political plans may appear to be, they must all rest on assumptions, probably confused or underdeveloped, about the nature of human beings and society.

So some would say it is impossible, but perhaps to proceed we need to try and rise above ideology as much as we can. Or at the very least to have a thorough grasp of where we stand and why, its strengths and weaknesses, its likely social consequences, and how it might be brought about in what timescale and with what resources and costs, financial and otherwise.

Could we even find a proper way to build an ideology worthy of serving our developing society? The view here is pessimistic. A fundamental dilemma is that whilst insights into the (very diverse) nature of ideologies are attainable using the empirical and rational scientific approach of political science, the same methodology cannot be wholly successful in constructing a suitable ideology for a nation to follow, because an ideology has to be value-laden. We need to know where we are going, and why we want to go there, as well as to decide on how to do it. And this implies that we uncover and critically consider values. Ultimately, when we follow values back to source, in a secular society where we have mostly seen through religious 'justifications', we have found that there just aren't any. It seems inconceivable, even if there were, that a heterogeneous, pluralistic society would agree about them. People are usually too preoccupied by their own lives, and narrow focuses of family, friends, jobs, health, and hobbies, to be genuinely altruistic, although many are in principle and a few in actual practice.

CHAPTER 5

VALUES AND IDEOLOGY

Finally, there can be an insidious complacency among democrats. They incline to believe that democracy is the 'best' political possible system, the one which suits human fulfilment. Once a nation has attained some kind of democratic system, they would see it as regressive if it became non-democratic. Conversely, movement would be regarded as desirable if it led towards a democracy being established where there was none. When we have become a democracy, we have in a sense arrived. There is nowhere more suitable to go. So many become blind to the manifold needs for its improvement.

The dilemma is that complacency, and these assumptions, are still ideological. Democrats do not escape ideology. They are embedded in it up to the hilt, just like everyone else.

CHAPTER 5

VALUES AND IDEOLOGY

NOTES

1.   Blackburn, Simon. Ed., Oxford Dictionary of Philosophy, Oxford University Press, Oxford, Second edition revised 2008.

*   2.   Miller, Alexander, Contemporary Meta-Ethics, Polity Press, Blackwell Publishing Ltd., Oxford, 2003.

*   3.   Blackburn, Simon, Being Good: A short introduction to ethics, Oxford University Press, Oxford, 2002.

*   4.   Parfit, Derek, Reasons and Persons, Oxford University Press, Oxford, 1984.

*   5.   Nagel, Thomas, The view from Nowhere, Oxford University Press, Oxford, 1986.

*   6.   Williams, Bernard, Ethics and the Limits of Philosophy, Fontana, London, 1985.

7.   Blears, Hazel, 'British values must be defended', BBC News, 25/02/2009.

*   8.   Thomas, Geoffrey, Introduction to Political Philosophy, Duckworth & Co Ltd., London, 2000.

9.   Darling, Alistair, Budget Speech, BBC News, April 2009.

10.   Lye, John, 'Ideology: A Brief Guide', Brock University, California, 1997.

11.   Chambers Dictionary and Thesaurus, Harrap Publishers Ltd., Edinburgh, 2007.

*   12.   Freeden, Michael, Ideology, Oxford University Press, 2003.

13.   Ideology, Wikipedia.

CHAPTER 6

DEMOCRACY, LAW AND CONSTITUTION

Introduction

Democracy
  Definitions and Types
  Strengths and Weaknesses

Law
  Some Defects of Law
  The Rule of Law
  Erosion of Freedoms
  Separation of Powers
  The Police

Constitution
  The British Constitution
  A Bill of Rights
  Devolution

Public Participation
  Elections
  Referenda
  Participative Deficits
  Civil Disobedience

CHAPTER 6

DEMOCRACY, LAW AND CONSTITUTION

INTRODUCTION

During the writing of the publication there coincided a period of singular and dramatic happenings in the political firmament of the United Kingdom. It is fair to say these were impossible to keep up with fully in terms of their complexity and speed. The backdrop was the international financial crisis, which had especial impact here at home, and which fully engaged and extended the political classes way beyond their previous experience. Then there were the media revelations in the Houses of Parliament, both the Lords and the Commons, of dishonest and even criminally fraudulent behaviour, regarding respectively cash for legal influence and unacceptable expenses claims. The issues raised revealed scandal on a very wide scale, a corrupt system of deliberate abuse of public funds, probably going back many years, and not subject to proper scrutiny. They went to the heart of the political system. In exposing serious weaknesses, including constitutional ones (in the opinion of some) and engendering almost universal public outrage, they threatened, the media claimed, to undermine our very system of government itself. It would be many years before the dust would fully settle. Meanwhile, Parliament, many now believed, would have to be aided by a kind of external force, because no longer to be trusted to put its own Houses in order. The public clearly saw that many who they had thought were upright and honourable were in fact greedily feathering their own nests and had with the connivance of the Speaker and the government, sought to conceal the truth and prevent corrective reforms.

The subject-matter of the chapter is what is usually called 'British Constitution', or 'Constitutional and Administrative Law'. It starts with a discussion of democracy, which the United Kingdom system of government supposedly (but mythically) is, as a background and framework, governing the nature and development of the country's constitution. Certain technical terms are used as guidance principles, such as the 'rule of law' and the 'separation of powers', which are then explained and commented on in an intermediate section which sets discussion within the context of law. The constitution is critically

CHAPTER 6

DEMOCRACY, LAW AND CONSTITUTION

considered, its recent changes examined, and exposed as the dog's breakfast it is. The hopes for reform, and the limits of what these might do for us, are looked at.

Since the purposes of all this are ostensibly to provide a basis for governing with the consent of the people, methods of public participation are evaluated. Both legal and illegal options are considered, together with a variety of novel ideas yet to be tried out here.

DEMOCRACY

Definitions and Types

"Democracy" is one of those apparently simple, but actually very complex, words. You can always tell when philosophers argue interminably over a concept and its meaning that you have such a word.

There is the added difficulty with "democracy" that it is a word people tend to use very readily, and as a matter of course. The unspoken assumption is that we all know what we are talking about. But do we?

If we are going to be able to communicate with each other using "democracy" as a term, it is first incumbent on the thoughtful to try to define it, or at least, if this is too difficult, to assemble a collection of broadly agreed key ideas setting out its approximate meaning.

Looking at so-called democratic states around the world, it will prove an exacting challenge to extract the essential elements of "democracy" from all the disparate practices and institutions. The dictionary says it is "rule by the people", but what rules and what people? The idea is too vague to be very useful, because in some places not many will be involved in any capacity. Even in Athens, the ancient cradle of democracy, slaves and women were disenfranchised.

Another approach would be to search out the ideas or principles which are essential to it, but people tend to disagree about these. Commonly proposed are notions of 'liberty' and 'equality' ; only opinions differ on what even these mean, let alone whether or not they are essential elements of democracy.

Warburton contrasts two main forms of democracy(1). One apparently relates to the population having some kind of participation in the government of the country, commonly by a vote. Another argues that a democracy must act in the 'true interests' of the people. But this latter mode could be associated with totalitarian regimes where dictators claim to be acting 'in the public interest', whether or not the public agree. Even if they do not, it is sometimes said that they are not aware of their own best interests. It is not known, though frequently assumed, whether there is such a thing as 'the public interest', except in broad terms at times of national crisis perhaps, and if there were it is rather less likely that it would be a politician who would find it. Since such an approach has very obvious dangers of manipulation and oppression, and can at best produce a kind of paternal benevolence, it will not be regarded as 'democratic' here.

Returning to the first meaning of democracy, much dispute can centre around precisely what we can in theory and practice mean by 'participation'. There are four key questions of feasibility, namely, does a majority wish to participate in government, can decision-making be made participatory, is it possible with very large numbers of citizens, and could a system be invented that will deal adequately with the inevitable conflicts? This is an ambitious and slow-moving model, requiring much knowledge and skill from very many people. Therein lie some of the ingredients of weakness in what is sometimes called 'direct democracy'.

Hence, the more usual form of democracy is characterised by the people taking a step back from actual participation, except at elections, by appointing 'representatives' to act politically on their behalf. This in itself is an almost complete fiction, of course, because the group being represented will largely disagree on many things and so cannot really be represented most of the time. However, in order to be able to proceed, it will be held here as a working hypothesis that "democracy" contains legal rights to much individual freedom, formal opportunities to influence the make-up and behaviour of government, and a notion of persons being political equals with only the criminal and insane among adults being

DEMOCRACY, LAW AND CONSTITUTION

disqualified from voting. The formulation is perhaps on the right lines, but lacks the detail required to look at the concept of democracy in operation across society. A systematic and thorough approach which is in similar vein to the above definition is that of Saward(2). It also throws light on the feasibility of democracy. Saward's definition is: "a political system in which the citizens themselves have an equal effective input into the making of binding collective decisions".

Saward sets out no less then twelve requirements for the "necessary conditions" of democracy. These relate to his "four stages of collective decision-making" as follows:

" A) Agenda-Setting
- (1) A set of equal procedural rights common to all citizens;
- (2) equal and regular opportunities for all adult citizens to set the public political agenda;
- (3) formal provision for notification of citizens concerning options, arguments and relevant previous outcomes with respect to public political issues: and
- (4) formal provision for freedom of information from all government bodies;

B) Debate and Discussion
- (5) equal rights to basic freedoms of expression and association;
- (6) equal social rights to adequate education and adequate health care;
- (7) a basic income, or guaranteed minimum income;

C) Decision-Making
- (8) citizens, votes to be decisive;
- (9) majority rule procedures to be employed for the resolution of public political issues;
- (10) direct democratic mechanisms be given formal and systematic priority over indirect mechanisms;

CHAPTER 6

DEMOCRACY, LAW AND CONSTITUTION

D) Implementation

    (11)   appropriate time limits for the realization of the substance of public decisions;

    (12)   adequate appeals and redress mechanisms with respect to public bodies and their functions."

Looking through the list several thoughts may strike immediately. One is that we have here in effect a blueprint for at least part of a full constitution. Another is that the wording would have to be tightened to give effect to the intention as well as the letter of the proposals. Politicians are adept at lip service and the convenient image hiding the uncomfortable reality beneath.

It will be instructive to keep the list in mind as a template by which to consider how far the various examples of political behaviour and machinery in the book measure up to, or more likely fall short of, these great ideals. For that is what they are. Nowhere at all exists, or ever has, where they are all in operation.

Saward goes on to produce a catalogue of "institutions and mechanisms" which are directly or indirectly implied by his terms of democracy. It is unexceptional and could easily be superficially argued to exist here in the United Kingdom, at least for the most part and in some quasi-equivalent form. The courts required would be for procedural rights, basic rights and freedoms, appeals and redress, constitutional, civil and criminal. Agencies would be responsible for initiative and referendum, education, health, income, implementation, taxation, police and rehabilitation.

Saward looks at the construction of political units, usually regarded as problematic, but concludes positively that, while they may take many forms consistent with function, what essentially matters is that they are run in accordance with democratic principles. Now that is a challenge indeed, for it would be hard to think of a single one in the United Kingdom that currently meets such a test.

Saward's terms of democracy, as he freely admits, are very demanding and "no doubt difficult to realize". This is an understatement. They may well prove to be impossible.

CHAPTER 6

DEMOCRACY, LAW AND CONSTITUTION

Be that as it may, Saward concedes that his ideas of direct democracy (for people's participation) are "core" elements "rarely employed to any great extent in modern democratic polities". He rightly regards them as crucial, since democracy in its essence has to be "responsive rule". By this is presumably meant government listening to, and changing its policies in response to, the criticisms by the public at large (not a few self-opinionated media pundits in the tabloid newspapers).

Saward's analysis points out practical limitations to democracy through the consideration of 'constraints'. He sees these as 'natural' or 'systemic'. The natural we can easily dismiss because they are features beyond human control, like the inevitable delay between a policy decision being implemented and having results, like some past choices reducing present options (where they actually do).

What needs studying carefully, though, are the systemic constraints, because these are cultural and institutional features which we have mostly come to accept largely unquestioned. Some will be very old and may be taken for granted as inherent or natural. Whereas they emphatically are not. The category is obviously one subject to a great deal of political chicanery. All manner of excuses can be given for preserving a status quo and not every opponent comes from government either. The United Kingdom is brim-full of the sacred cows of history, such as religions.

Saward cites three other major examples of constraint on the attainment of democracy in contemporary society. The first is complexity, distinguished into structural, functional, and technical, which can all be systemic. The second is individual liberty, and the third ecological sustainability.

He quotes Zolo as an illustration of an extreme pessimist regarding complexity as putting paid to prospects for democracy, partly because it ensures, in effect, that the public inevitably remain largely ignorant of what is going on and have insufficient understanding to formulate appropriate needs. Link that to a sort of political over-class that looks after itself and the situation may seem hopeless.

Individual liberty is also a constraint on democracy, but it is really a case

DEMOCRACY, LAW AND CONSTITUTION

where values come in. Liberty and democracy have some principles in common, like free speech and association with others. The question is where you want to draw the line between freedom of the individual and the powers of the state. There are circumstances when the values clash. Unchecked individualism will lead to vast inequalities of wealth, which a democracy would have to work much harder than our governments do to moderate in the interests of social cohesion and justice.

Finally, ecological considerations could also easily be in conflict with a democracy that practised unsustainable use of resources. There is nothing in the theory to say that it would or it would not, but in the event of a conflict ecology would have to win. Failure to comply with it might damage the planet, whereas only individuals suffer (where they do) in a less than democratic country.

A further problem exists for commentators about democracy, and that is its status as a set of values. In short, people, often encouraged by politicians, be they in Britain or banana republics, tend to assume uncritically that it is universally a good thing. Which is highly contested, though many critics would accede to the view that it is nevertheless the least bad system of government available. The matter will be set aside here for others to mull over, after a brief discussion of its pros and cons. System is one thing, of course, and behaviour is another.

Strengths and Weaknesses

A possible paradox is that it seems easier to find flaws in democracy than trumpet its virtues. For example, the freedom that supposedly arises from not being in a dictatorship can be negated if you are in a minority with a feeling of persecution by the prevailing majority. Majority rule sounds noble, but it can be the yob voice of the crowd, the populist line of lowest common denominator, the aired prejudice of an infective tabloid newspaper. But in any case, how can we argue that a majority in favour of a policy (or government) actually legitimizes it? What is the connection? There was a time when a majority believed the Earth was flat. But they were wrong.

CHAPTER 6

DEMOCRACY, LAW AND CONSTITUTION

Again, if you go with equality as a democratic virtue, how do you feel as an intelligent, politically informed citizen whose vote counts for no more than that of the ignorant moron next door? A fundamental weakness of democracy is surely that it gives equal say to the experts and the educated on the one hand, and to the ignorant and/or prejudiced on the other. There is just too much at stake now.

So the 'paradox of democracy' is that the will of the majority should prevail even when their decision can be shown to be wrong and irrational. It does not seem to have a solution, unless the democratic or the rational requirement is dropped. Either alternative might seem invidious, but logically this points up a limitation beyond which democracy cannot correctly go.

Democracies are sometimes lauded for being a rule by consent. The authority of the state derives from a sort of contract with its subjects, but then if you are born into our kind of society, in what sense can you be said to have agreed to its methods and institutions? If in your relatively powerless condition you do not risk or cannot afford leaving your friends and family for the uncertainty of an unknown country, you may perhaps be deemed to have at least acquiesced. Yet, realistically, what can you do about it?

As a Marxist you may argue that the so-called choice of electors in a democracy is an illusion anyway. What we see are entrenched power relations which we just have to live with and cannot unseat.

It has been remarked that in a dictatorship you are just a number, whereas democracies do at least respect the individual and give his voice a chance of being heard. The problem is, of course, that on a mass scale such a chance is almost vanishingly small.

And a critic of democracy might argue for the moral superiority of communism, which ostensibly sets people as equals. It has not had a good press principally because notorious dictators have used violent means to bring it about and run communist states. Yet there is nothing in the theory which necessitates such methods; rather, the ends of community sharing and egalitarianism are noble. Whereas, democracies

CHAPTER 6

DEMOCRACY, LAW AND CONSTITUTION

in the west exhibit a fundamental tension - between the inhumanity of capitalism, with its brutal economic system, and some of our other, civilizing, values. There is, certainly within the United Kingdom, a seemingly steadfast resolve not to address systemic problems and contradictions. But then, perhaps, neither is the link between democracy and capitalism an essential one.

In perhaps a similar vein Slavoj Zizek, a Slovenian philosopher and cultural critic, points out that a democracy can be heterogeneous because most people do not want to be told[3]. Any ruling political elite has to learn to accept that it does not know all the answers. Faced with a palpable need for a new system, between the Scilla and Charybdis of capitalism or state bureaucracy, is there in fact any acceptable solution, given that revolution is presumably not an attractive starter? Or are we really at the end?

Zizek would see suggestions of greater involvement for the citizens as being ineffectual so long as no major reforming measures are planned for the long term. He has in mind such items as "limitation of the freedom of capital" and the "subordination of the manufacturing processes to a mechanism of social control". He has given up on the typical two-party system that is dominant in the United Kingdom as polarising false choices that do not really exist. There is pessimism, too, about the proletariat. Fighting for the interests of workers seems lukewarm today, because they only want to bring about their own interests, not those of the community as a whole. How to reconstruct the social framework when its parts are so selfish, so atomized?

As Estlund has pointed out, democracy, if it is ethically evaluated, will be seen to depend on some values outside itself[4]. By emphasizing democratic deficits in the United Kingdom, the present work does not seek to imply that democracy is somehow the supreme value. A 'radical' democratic theory might contend that, but the author sides with Estlund. We might see democracy, rather, as a means, whereas a higher ethical value could be placed, say, on some ends-driven hypothetical arrangement whereby the people were ruled by others, but in accordance with noble purposes, using principles to try and ensure just outcomes.

CHAPTER 6

DEMOCRACY, LAW AND CONSTITUTION

Some departures, though, can seem either misguided or incomplete. Social choice theory, for instance, is a model of politics that concentrates on fair and scientific methods of aggregating the preferences of individuals. It is a proceduralist conception which attempts to develop reasonable methods of voting, but what if the preferences themselves are confused, erroneous, manipulated, motivated by evil intent, and so forth?

So-called deep deliberative democracy, on the other hand, stresses the claim that political legitimacy will depend on the views and wishes of the populace, as gleaned by egalitarian debate and the application of intelligence and evidence. These again go beyond the somewhat limited requirement for democracy of some kind of expression of majority will to embrace normative aspects of its qualities.

Gordon summons powerful arguments against democracy, whilst counselling that our democratic assumptions as a society are so ingrained that criticism tends to be summarily dismissed(5).

Firstly, to recap, it fails the test of inclusion to vote, since its own ideal rules out the sensible principle of competence as a valid qualification. Secondly, it acquiesces in majority rule even when tyrannical. Thirdly, it does not empower the people. They can neither elect their leaders nor make policy. A further argument is that its methods for determining laws are fundamentally irrational. Finally, the State itself is a problem, one which democracy does not address.

A key strength of democracy would appear to be its capacity to limit power in single hands and to diffuse it among individuals and institutions so that no one person or organ can do too much damage. Dictatorships may sometimes be benign, but power has an established tendency to turn corrupt and despotic.

Possibly the best argument in favour of democracy is that from theory of knowledge, namely the scientific justification that all ideas need to be scrutinized without fear or favour by the razors of reason, and all plausible policies subject to the practical test of unbiased trial before adoption, rigorous monitoring afterwards, and regular review, with

DEMOCRACY, LAW AND CONSTITUTION

revisions and new policies then emerging in the light of experience against objective criteria of success. However, this is so far removed from the way in which real politicians behave at present, as to be regarded as a hypothetical model for an imaginary utopian world.

LAW

Some Defects of Law

From what we already realise about the law, it is no doubt unlikely that we shall find here much of comfort for the ordinary citizen, but it may be a start at least to 'know thine enemy'.

Law is too vast a subject to be treated fully in a chapter, however attractive the proposition may be, given the appallingly inadequate state of development of law at the present time. There is so very much wrong with the law, both in theory and practice, that it is time long overdue for its many expert critics to be listened to. Be that as it may, the legion problems must remain for the most part outside the scope of the present work, a disgrace as they are to any democracy worthy of the name.

Whilst some laws are quite elaborately developed, such as contract law, which you might expect in a capitalist society, obsessed and driven by deals, usually with hidden values, others are very weak, like international law, and consumer protection. No right to privacy exists, actual law is often morally offensive, administration is cumbersome and over-elaborate, the wheels 'grind exceeding slow', the system of courts is an over-complex and confusing set of structures, the penalties are inconsistent and incoherent, the sanctions mostly inadequate, or irrelevant, the judges little accountable, and the barrier between public interest areas and private matters ever unclear and contested, with civil liberties being eroded rather than enhanced the while.

For a start, there are far too many laws, leading to ignorance and bewilderment on the part of the general populace. And laws are in desperate need of simple codification, so we could all see, if we had a

DEMOCRACY, LAW AND CONSTITUTION

mind to, what are the different areas and how they have gaps and shortcomings. In general a constitutional assumption against the proliferation of new laws would help public knowledge to catch up with what is an appallingly over-complex situation.

Jamie Whyte specialises in advice on clear thinking. Government legislators would do well to heed him(6). In a changing society there will be a need from time to time to pass new laws - to deal with possibilities that have arisen from the invention of new technologies, for example. But an advanced society will otherwise have quite quickly gone through the main areas of need and passed relevant laws to cover them, Whyte argues.

So why is it that our politicians never stop legislating? Whyte concludes the reasons are mostly to do with their interests, but very little concerned with ours. He points to an initiative in New Zealand designed to stop the rot. They plan to have a law of 'regulatory responsibility', which would act as a template against which every potential new law would have to be measured before it could be actively considered for enactment. Law proposals would first have to accord with laid down principles of reasonableness, such as disqualification if it reduced freedom of contract, or disqualification if it diminished the rule of law. So long as society does change more rapidly in the modern world, it behoves government to be methodical, circumspect and deliberative, which it usually is not, before it legislates. Fast law is commonly bad law and may even be unworkable. However, Whyte realises that MPs would not comply with such procedures willingly. So his solution would be the transfer of politicians' legislating powers to an independent panel of experts, who would review and decide on political proposals for any new laws.

After law is enacted not enough attention is paid to what its effects are. It may not be working, or as intended, so there need to be put in place post-legislative standing committees (but with changing membership) to provide scrutiny and feed back. They would also take evidence, in public, from interest groups and others especially affected. That would be a scientific-like process reinforcing democracy in action, as the book so often advocates.

So some law will inevitably be tainted and ignoble where decided on by

DEMOCRACY, LAW AND CONSTITUTION

political leaders. Another sorry state of affairs in our nation is that sometimes politicians who are legally responsible fall short of abiding by those very laws. The Attorney General, Baroness Scotland occupied the position of chief law officer in the country. In September 2009 it came to light that she failed to exercise due care, in making the legally required checks, before employing what subsequently turned out to be an illegal immigrant, who deceived her about her residential status. She was duly fined (only half of the maximum penalty) and refused to resign, having not complied with a law she herself had helped to enact. She was backed in this stance by the Prime Minister on the irrelevant grounds that her intentions were stated to be honourable and that she had acted in ignorance of the applicant's position .This defence will not, of course, help you, the citizen, should you ever come to trial.

Another kind of problem about the law is that of any unstated government intentions behind a piece of legislation. For instance, the anti-fox hunting laws were passed in a climate of considerable controversy among the interested parties, but the government in reality was paying lip-service to the pro-animal lobbies, without any desire to implement the law in practice through the vigorous prosecution of the hunt. So a citizen may be quite in the dark about the consequences of breaking the law, and kept so deliberately.

A notorious illustration is the problem of assisted suicide, which is illegal and carries penalties. The media have drawn attention to a trend for United Kingdom citizens who wish to end their lives of going to special medical clinics in Switzerland, where such practices are legal. But many doubts have persisted as to whether their close relatives may then be prosecuted back home. That they are liable is clear enough if they have collaborated over the plan. What has queered the pitch, however, is the uncertain behaviour of the Crown Prosecution Service, CPS. That led to "clarification" of the law by a public statement from the CPS in September 2009. It was stressed that the CPS was in no way making the law, nor was it empowered to. Quite right, but what was not said so loudly was that the CPS was carrying out, contrary to the letter of the law at least, a covert (political) policy of going easy on miscreants. It acted to publish, seemingly, because of the public anguish expressed by a string of high-profile cases, but has yet to come clean. How could it?

CHAPTER 6

DEMOCRACY, LAW AND CONSTITUTION

Another piece of legal nonsense is the popularly believed adage, that people are innocent until proven guilty. It can be true, but confusingly not always. One group of exceptions is that the police can give spot fines for certain minor offences, like litter dropping. Other examples include driving behaviour such as failing to stop for red lights, where a letter is sent imposing a fine and uttering legal threats of dark consequences if payment is not made within a specified short period of time. When a defendant does go to court the onus is on him/her to disprove guilt.

Then there is something funny going on across the whole of business life. You can get the feeling that so many unacceptable behaviours are either not illegal, as they should be, or the law is not being enforced by the authorities. In America we are told that there have been many prosecutions as a result of the banking debacle, whereas in the United Kingdom - almost nothing. In Parliament we see hundreds of bent MPs fiddling their expenses, and literally less than a handful being threatened with court action. Even there, disreputable lawyers seek to claim immunity for their clients through 'parliamentary privilege'. Is it a matter of too much being conveniently classified as a civil wrong rather than a criminal one?

Another dispiriting matter is the ludicrously high standard required of evidence in criminal cases - something like 95% certainty as opposed to just on the balance of probabilities. Many a theory of science is accepted as true on much less weighty grounds, so criminals go free, and the police can have an easy ride, batting away large swathes of difficult-to-prove practices as beyond their purview, putting the onus on John Citizen instead to come up with the goods if he can. (And the authorities say they do not want vigilantes!)

A serious issue is that the law does nothing to prevent innocent citizens being abused by the principle of presumed guilt in their working lives. If allegations are made against staff, it is common for them to be suspended pending investigation. If staff are found innocent of a crime in a court of law, it is common for them to lose their jobs anyway. It seems that institutions are free to set their own internal rules that play with quasi-legal concepts and enable them to moralise and to judge with impunity. (Whoever gets their job back if they win in an industrial tribunal case against their former employer?)

CHAPTER 6

DEMOCRACY, LAW AND CONSTITUTION

The principle may be worth elaborating from the bizarre field of sports' governing bodies. Almost every week professional footballers will kick and maim each other for a great deal of money and receive little more in the way of sanction than fleeting media notoriety and possibly a brief suspension from the game. The yobo-land incidents, recorded on a screen for all to see, could easily lead to custodial sentences if committed in the street by ordinary members of the public. So why is the law of the land apparently inoperable on the pitch?

Worryingly too, why are Muslim communities seemingly being allowed to run their own courts based on Sharia law, which contains unspeakably barbaric punishments?

One of the biggest drawbacks with the law as conducted is its massive irrelevance to much of what matters most to us all in life. Decent societies are largely self-regulating; people who live in them on the whole behave towards others with civility, tolerance, and respect. They do have a sense of fair play and can imagine themselves in others' shoes. But when things go wrong and there are disputes and dishonesties, how many are going to be confident enough, trusting enough, and patient enough to resort to law? Only the very few. And they will need to be intelligent, resourceful, and persistent. To most of us, a very slow, uncertain and probably inappropriate legal remedy will seem like no remedy at all.

A few thoughts will be provided next on the topic of legal reform. Everyone has their own ideas of laws they would like to see repealed or reformed, the author being no exception. But this could take us into a wholesale critique of modern society which, although sorely needed, is too large a subject. So the matters to be raised here are, somewhat arbitrarily, confined to a few issues of principle of wide scope and application.

We are told we have recourse to law to safeguard our interests, but this is a pipedream for most people, because they cannot afford its vast cost. Powerful vested interests have for centuries built up an elaborate edifice within which lawyers can get rich at our expense. Legal aid is available to the very few. There are perceptions that it sometimes goes to the

DEMOCRACY, LAW AND CONSTITUTION

undeserving, like applicants for immigration, or people of means and influence who can exploit loopholes in the system.

Law is always going to be a matter of dread and hatred. However "just" it is, it nevertheless symbolises compulsion, the framework by which the state restricts people's freedoms, decrees punishments, and carries them out. Whilst there are those who are reassured by this, and so presumably sleep more soundly in their beds as a consequence, there is perhaps a majority that do not really believe in justice except for themselves, or maybe as an abstract philosophical concept, an ideal that actual life rarely brings about. They have come to doubt whether the State is really interested in protecting them, and have no feeling of confidence that the organs of the law could achieve it anyway.

But they do know that law is done unto them. And that the legal system is unfriendly, powerful, and unpredictable.

One of the hindrances, which goes along with the archaic and silly wigs, is 'contempt of court', which is what you can be found guilty of if you cross a judge. Now all that is supposed to create a climate of respect for the law and obedience to the procedural farces of the case being tried, no doubt. By why? Are we still expected to be the cap-doffing serfs of old? How insecure is the state that it must seek to impose such genuflecting coercion on an increasingly educated and self-reliant populace? Let respect be where respect is earned. When, in other words, the legal system does a worthy job, which is far from always.

A large flaw at the heart of the United Kingdom legal system is the adversarial nature of proceedings. Specialist lawyers - the barristers - act out roles in representing either the prosecution or the defence, whilst the accused is largely reduced to passive observer of verbal combat between the two. Out of this circus the truth is supposed to emerge concerning his guilt or innocence, though it is hard to see how. Who wins could be largely a matter of the relative performance abilities of the two lawyers. A barrister may know his client is guilty, but nevertheless succeed in getting him acquitted. Far from seeing a moral dilemma here, he is likely to regard it as a noble duty.

CHAPTER 6

DEMOCRACY, LAW AND CONSTITUTION

Instead, what is needed is to strip away the stultifying and anxiety-inducing procedural straightjacket, negotiable only by legal practitioners for the most part, and get round a table with all the interested parties and every scrap of available information, watched by a jury, to thrash matters out. In general, the so-called trial would proceed like a scientific investigation. Defendants who maybe lacked confidence, or the requisite degree of intelligence, would be able to call on a friend to accompany them and act as interlocutor when necessary or desirable. Barristers and solicitors would be a duality of the past. As in America, we would have generalised lawyers, bridging the gap between the public and the courts. Barristers should not be a remote distance from their clients, but rather in a professional relationship where trust can be fostered.

One final illustration of distance will have to suffice. The issue of social justice and people's wellbeing and their relation to family courts is shrouded in mystery because family courts still effectively operate in secrecy. Would-be reformers nevertheless paint a very disturbing picture of parents in effect being on trial to justify maintaining care and contact with their own children, of social workers and child psychologists largely getting their own way. The system is one in which judges are largely lacking knowledge of the areas of concern, with hopelessly ill-defined regulations to guide them, and can be unduly credulous of professional claims.

Somewhat surprisingly, other problems of the law include the widespread ignorance of it by lawyers. If Joe Citizen wishes to employ an ordinary solicitor, woe betide him if the issue is not a bread and butter one. This is even more the case when it involves the European Union, because neither government nor lawyers have in general come to practical terms with it yet, over 35 years or more.

But for the hapless citizens, on the other hand, it is a long-standing principle of United Kingdom law that ignorance of it is no defence. The onus to be aware of the nature of the laws and their requirements is placed by the State squarely on the shoulders of Joe and Josephine Citizen. That is, of course, very convenient for the State, but in this modern world the position is worth challenging in the opinion of the present author in the light of a variety of relevant factors, some of which will now be briefly considered.

CHAPTER 6

DEMOCRACY, LAW AND CONSTITUTION

Firstly, the State makes every effort to impose a national curriculum on those who are not affluent enough to be sent by their parents to private schools. Yet it does not formally prescribe that children are taught the law of the land, or the realistically likely penalties for transgressing it. It could be postulated that the State has a duty here and fails it, which might be construed as an argument in mitigation of the citizens' ignorance.

Secondly, the Government today legislates extremely quickly in comparison with former times. New laws roll onto the statute books more and more frequently, so that the ability of even professional lawyers to keep up with them, aided as they are with summary notes and conferences, is gravely taxed. We need a standing panel of experts to review all law periodically in order to consolidate, simplify, and recommend removal of anomalies, anachronisms, and failings of effectiveness.

We do not see systematic media campaigns to inform the population as to the nature and details of these new laws, in spite of government running advertising on selected narrow topics, such as an aspect of health like the dangers of obesity. It is, of course, true, that some information (and disinformation) percolates through the national press, but only on legal topics that are seen by the editors as particularly newsworthy, like the scandalous and the controversial.

Finally, what also confuses is that different aspects of a law may come into force at different times, whereas no notice is usually posted of the fact.

In addition, ordinary folk tend to be bewildered and dissatisfied with sentencing and their seeming inconsistencies. They are frequently scandalised when custodial terms like 'life' end up meaning just a few years, where lenient sentences are meted out for very serious crimes, such as sadistic tortures and murder. They do not accept it when prisoners are released for political convenience such as shortage of cells. They cannot understand why some types of sentence are even regarded as punishment. Notorious in this category are police cautions and the infamous anti-social order, ASBO, which young hoodlums seem to wear like a badge of honour.

CHAPTER 6

DEMOCRACY, LAW AND CONSTITUTION

Another problem is confused logic. For example, one 'punishment' is a community service order, by which the offender has to undertake a number of hours of unpaid work on behalf of the community. But do we really want to convey the impression that helping our fellow man, as many charities and volunteers willingly do, is somehow an unpleasant set of chores? What does that say about social (or is it political) values?

The Rule of Law

So it is to a quaint constitutional idea that we now turn, the so-called 'rule of law'(7). This is given enormous significance at least in the utterances of government politicians.

What it means is that, in effect, law supposedly transcends government, at least to the extent that there are legal limits on the powers of governments over their citizens. The implication is that the people have what the Americans are fond of calling 'certain inalienable rights', which governments must respect and protect.

It is probably fair to say that most people in the United Kingdom do believe they have rights. They might not consider the country to be a democracy if there were not some reasonable balance between the rights of the State and those of the population at large. So once they know what it is, most ordinary folk will be in favour of the rule of law.

But they might be horrified to learn that in the United Kingdom it may not actually exist. Because the Government's ability to arrogate powers and practice them is legally unfettered, except for those laws of the European Union which may conflict. Even then, the United Kingdom remains a sovereign state, in that it could secede from Europe should it so wish.

When the 'rule of law' is trotted out as something true democrats live by it is seldom questioned. Yet the rule of law is only another social construct. There is no such thing as the mystical 'natural law' that Catholics would have you believe is part of the metaphysical furniture of the universe, like rocks undoubtedly are. And because it is a social

DEMOCRACY, LAW AND CONSTITUTION

construct there is no reason to respect it unless it is any good. Since the state of law is pretty mediocre, and officialdom shows little serious inclination to acknowledge, let alone ameliorate, the shortcomings, loyalty to the abstract and somewhat ideal principle could be argued as counterproductive to the pro-democracy cause.

Now there are legal theorists who point to certain disadvantages of having a rule of law. They say it is financially costly because some independent bodies are needed to adjudicate in case of possible breach or dispute. These tend to be courts of law, so we know the criticism will be valid! They also say that the litigation is time-consuming, so that Government business is slowed down undesirably. This may also be true, but the seriousness of the consequences will be situational and variable.

If you do have a rule of law there should be a fundamental, and normative, question for prior national debate as to where the line is to be drawn. What should governments be able to do to their populace and what should they not? And are there circumstances, say of national emergency, when this line could reasonably be moved on a temporary basis? Many of us no doubt have our own prescriptions, but to inform the reasoning processes it would be highly appropriate to lean crucially on the secular arguments of contemporary applied ethics in a modern society.

Moving away to the legal theorists, they are inclined to fall into one of two camps. Minimalists argue for unconstrained government powers, trusting in a benign State. Sceptics, on the other hand, wish to curb the State, seeking serious limitations to its powers and machinery to enforce whatsoever controls may come to be necessary to reduce its abuses. Surely there is no contest here for the humanitarian, or even just the prudent? From time to time history throws up truly evil people in positions of political authority. And the endless inventiveness of circumstances may tax even good leaders to subordinate means to ends.

Apart from being a lofty matter of principle, the rule of law is regularly fought over in practice on the ground. Tensions have arisen ever since the Human Rights Act 1998 came into force in an attempt to provide court remedies for United Kingdom citizens in British courts, who felt that their rights under the European convention on Human Rights had

DEMOCRACY, LAW AND CONSTITUTION

been breached. Previously, they had had to go to Europe to seek justice, because the United Kingdom had scandalously refused them access to our own courts. The public did not acquire new rights, however.

Soon the problems mounted. The government refused leave of appeal of failed asylum seekers through the courts, thus bypassing the protection of the Human Rights Act. Detention without trial for terrorist suspects was another bete noire, with the judiciary again being critical as the length was increased from 28 to 42 days under the Terrorism Act 2006.

So Parliament is still demonstrated as very willing when it suits to subvert, or even disapply, the Human Rights Act, whereas the judges demand that such matters are for resolution in the courts under the rule of law. What the public need to remember is that government treatment of terrorists and immigrants may enlist these groups little sympathy, yet turning away from the rule of law offers scant protection to the ordinary citizen either.

Erosion of Freedoms

Basic freedoms are under threat. Baroness Helena Kennedy QC has made an impressive list of freedoms which the United Kingdom public have lost as a result of government legal reforms in recent years(8). They include attempts to reduce trial by jury for a range of topics, including those of technological complexity, serious restrictions on access to justice by cuts in legal aid, huge expansion in the powers of the state to invade privacy, proposed introduction of identity cards, tightening extradition so that British subjects can be removed abroad for trial with inadequate protections. What specifically needs monitoring includes government usage of new technologies, like DNA, where records are kept of innocent people contrary to European (and hence United Kingdom) law, phone-tapping, CCT, and other surveillance techniques involving computers.

Another attack on personal freedoms is the Brown plan to change the law regarding organ donation to one of presumed consent in the absence of a positive decision to opt out, rather than the choice being for individuals to consider whether to register as donors.

CHAPTER 6

DEMOCRACY, LAW AND CONSTITUTION

The same Brown government that emphasised restrictions on private freedoms, ostensibly to further our protection through enhanced national security, had a terrible track-record of losing citizen's private and personal data. For example, when in 2008 a laptop computer was stolen from a naval officer's car, the records of 600,000 recruits were lost. Sir Edmund Burton's independent report, as chairman of the Information Advisory Council, said the loss was inevitable at some point because of poor management and systems. Independent reports, covering data losses in other government organisations, such as the Police, HM Revenue and Customs, drew similar conclusions, citing lack of staff awareness and training, with fault covering many, not just a few. At least 25 million children and parents had their personal details released in one scandal after another, because senior civil servants did not communicate to their staff how to protect sensitive material.

The Home Secretary, Jacqui Smith, proposed to change the law so that men who paid for sex from a prostitute commit an offence if the prostitute has been 'trafficked', even if they are not aware of it. This is revealing and dangerous. On numerous occasions government ministers claim ignorance of a situation as defence against any culpability. In logic the relative feasibility of knowing would have relevance and weight.

Political correctness is undermining free speech, a matter of democratic concern. When, in February 2009, Goert Wilders, a Dutch MP, was banned from the United Kingdom, where he wished to show a film associating the Koran with terrorism, opinion was divided. The Home Secretary did not have the power to exclude him merely because of his views, but where there was believed to be a threat to national security, public order, or public safety. These outcomes seemed unlikely, apart from the risk of minority protest from volatile Islamic factions already living in this country. And their reaction was within the scope of their free decision and had to comply with the law. As a result of cases such as this, the feeling persisted that government was not being even-handed as between the indigenous and immigrant communities.

Freedom of information is snuffed out by the Official Secrets Act, which uses the expression 'the interests of national security', to conceal whatever information the government want suppressing for whatsoever

DEMOCRACY, LAW AND CONSTITUTION

reason. The government does not have to declare its reasons, or justify its conduct.

A typical illustration of government secrecy and lack of public accountability in this regard is the episode in February 2009 when the Justice Secretary, Jack Straw, vetoed publication of Cabinet minutes which might have shed light on the nature of the government's deliberations leading to their controversial decision to invade Iraq. The so-called Freedom of Information Act had a convenient clause in it allowing 'national interest' to override public interest (in disclosure). Of course, government is usually the sole arbiter of national interest. Such decisions are not uncommon and invariably invoke the suspicion that government has something to hide and is really just acting in its own interest, not that of the country.

In that particular case, the Information Tribunal had ruled that the information should be disclosed, but the law simply allowed the Justice Secretary to veto its decision, leaving grave doubts as to the integrity of decision-making processes in Cabinet. That suspicion was amplified by the later open deliberations of the Chilcott enquiry.

For most people law is a backdrop to their own lives, only noticed in media coverage of celebrated court cases, or at rare personal times, concerning wills and house purchases. Despite such appearance, law is potentially far from peripheral. By bounding allowed behaviour it mostly protects us from others without our noticing and renders community life more feasible.

It is, as Helena Kennedy said, too important to be left to lawyers or to politicians, both of whom have vested interests that can make some stray from the principled. Like plans to reduce the areas of operation of trial by jury on spurious grounds of complex subject-matter. "Our only hope is an order governed by law and consent". But to consent you have to know, and to know you have to watch and be vigilant.

The Separation of Powers

The idea is a very old one and is based on the assertion that there are three

CHAPTER 6

DEMOCRACY, LAW AND CONSTITUTION

main functions of government, which are to legislate, to take executive action in carrying out policies, and to judge transgressions of the law(9). The principle of separation of powers claims that too much power would be vested in one body otherwise, so the best defence against maltreatment is to separate the powers under different bodies. These bodies would be quite distinct, in both membership and roles, but there is nothing in the idea as such to prevent them going their own ways and developing corrupt practices not in the wider interests of society.

So it is commonplace for commentators, and even those opposed to the separation of powers, to speak of the need for a system of checks and balances. Governments may also do other things, not confined to the three functions, since they are not constitutionally fettered, and this also is a grave potential threat, but within the functions themselves the idea would be to ensure that each body could keep a check on the others. A further set of procedures is obviously also needed in order to produce requisite reforms.

Now the United Kingdom constitution does not enshrine the principle of separation of powers, nor the system of checks and balances either. What exists in practice is that the three bodies exist, and there is some separation of powers and personnel, but there are also considerable admixtures. Some come from tradition; some by design.

For example, the government has established many administrative tribunals outside the court system to decide disputes between the individual and the State. The government, in addition to running the country through its executive functions, also acts as the legislative body. The judges, as well as deciding legal cases that come to trial, also create common law, by setting precedents which are to be followed in subsequent, similar cases. And they are appointed by the prime minister, not by Parliament in open hearing, which would be importantly transparent.

One of the most fundamental planks of constitution with formal checks and balances is for the judiciary to be able to challenge government legislation where it would be unconstitutional, perhaps via a standing independent committee enshrined as a constitutional requirement, which there is not.

CHAPTER 6

DEMOCRACY, LAW AND CONSTITUTION

Technically, the legislative comprises both Houses of Parliament, the Commons and the Lords, since all decisions are taken on the basis of majority vote across the whole membership of each house, whether government or opposition. As a first-order approximation, however, except when the government holds a slender majority, it out-votes overall opposition at will, and the Lords can merely delay its intentions.

Now there is already supposed to be considerable separation of powers in the structures. As a first-order approximation the Prime Minister and Cabinet makes policy, Parliament scrutinizes it and passes the laws, the civil service advises and implements policy - as the practical arm of the executive - and the judiciary decides cases which breach the law and in the process in effect interpret it.

Of course, there is serious blurring of the boundaries. Ministers direct the executive and are also part of the Cabinet. Fundamentally, why are MPs, collectively as Parliament, allowed to pass the laws? Surely they are only competent (if even there) to take charge of the operational functions of government? The strong argument is for a properly professional, and, of course, independent institution, to draft and decide the laws. The idea is so out of keeping with our experience in England that it takes some grasping.

One potential improvement in the direction of further separation of powers was for the House of Lords to cease being the highest court in the land and to be replaced by an 'independent' Supreme Court. That happened nominally in October 2009, when the Supreme Court opened in a building (conveniently) across the road from the Lords, but what needs watching is how long Law Lords will continue to sit in it. To be anything better than a sham change and a public relations stunt, there needs to be an appointment body genuinely independent of Parliament altogether and senior judges selected by it from outside of the House of Lords, which is supposed to happen when vacancies arise. It would also be wise to make the appointments time-limited, perhaps for five years, with a view to bringing in fresh expertise on a regular basis. However, as matters stand the Lord Chancellor, a Cabinet minister, (whose conflict of interests is obvious) and whose post was due to be abolished, still has some kind of role, as do the other senior Law Lords in the Supreme Court. But at least they are no longer allowed to sit in the Lords now.

CHAPTER 6

DEMOCRACY, LAW AND CONSTITUTION

A real unresolved problem is that, whilst it is a good thing for the judiciary to be independent, it would not do for it to be unaccountable. But they mostly are. At present Parliament cannot censure individual judges, either for their behaviour or for their legal decisions, it has no say in the appointment of judges, nor can it remove them from office. On the other side, judges, in addition to having a powerful influence over the direction of the law, sometimes promulgate their views to the general public. So what is the solution? Is it sufficient to wheel their representatives out now and again in front of Parliamentary Select Committees, so they can be fearlessly questioned? Or is that in itself a threat to the separation of powers principle?

A mature constitution would have thought these things through and have enacted balancing measures long ago. Fine in principle, judicial reforms nonetheless generate the possibility of too little dialogue between the judges and the government. When there are constitutional battles to be fought over the implementation and scope of the Human Rights Act, relations could degenerate harmfully. Which perhaps demonstrates that it is not always wise to allow rule by an abstract principle. Or maybe that the doctrine of the separation of powers is flawed, or at any rate more limited in its applications. Somehow, mechanisms of dialogue need to be designed and set up to mediate between different arms of the constitution. But what kind of dialogue would be appropriate? When does it turn into influence and what kind of influence would be legitimate? Can there even be such constructs as valid general prescriptions here?

The Police

Finally, discussion of the law would not be complete without some reference to those responsible for enforcing it - the police.

One of the comforting myths used by the ruling classes is that policing is by consent of the people in this country. It sounds reassuring. It isn't true. If we don't like what they are up to, there is precious little we can effectively do about it. And public approval for policing in this country is breaking down for a variety of reasons. The public are losing trust in police motivation and confidence over their performance.

CHAPTER 6

DEMOCRACY, LAW AND CONSTITUTION

Why? The story is complex, and very possibly distorted by media coverage of a series of high-profile cases; nevertheless, they cumulatively add up to grave issues to address.

Crime statistics are bandied about like political footballs and it is hard to make any sense of them, whereas the public perception is that serious crime is getting worse and that the police are largely ineffectual in bringing criminals to justice, or providing public protection.

The government's own watchdog on bureaucratic red tape in a December 2009 report wanted a return to "common sense" policing which would allow officers to exercise more discretion. The public perception is that more 'bobbies' are needed on the local beat, whatever the evidence over how effective that may actually be in reducing crime. The Tsar's report made it clear that two years of effort had not reduced the problem. Activity is skewed to meeting targets so that the separate forces compete to look good in the league tables. For all that the new cadre of community officers may chat and smile, the actual police force is apparently no more public-centred now than it was when it became part of the social malaise, rather than a partial cure for it.

We know that there are too many controversial cases. A sad illustration is that of Commander Ali Dizaei, the matter coming to a head in 2009. Dizaei, an Asian, had been in the Metropolitan Police Force for almost twenty-five years, during which time he had risen to a very high rank. A jury convicted him of corrupt and bullying practices, abusing both power and position, and he was imprisoned for four years. The Metropolitan Police then formally dismissed him in 2010.

But In May 2011 there was another twist to the long-running saga when Dizaei won his appeal. Judges quashed his conviction on the grounds that " it cannot be regarded as safe " and released him on bail. He faced the prospect of a retrial to try and clear his name, having already served thirteen months of his sentence.

Another way that the police have undermined public trust in them is how they behave as distrusting of the public themselves. They are developing into a very sinister and shadowy organisation. In October 2009 the

CHAPTER 6

DEMOCRACY, LAW AND CONSTITUTION

Guardian ran a major feature in which they explained that the police had coined the term "domestic extremism", which has no legal force, to cover their operation in monitoring and exchanging computer data on members of the public involved in protest groups or their activities.

Most of these people had not committed crimes; they were often ordinary families with young children, but frustrated by the fact that their more conventional protests seemed to fall on deaf ears.

And it should not have been necessary for the Home Secretary to issue ,as he did in December 2009 ,a statement clarifying that the police "must start" from the point of supporting citizens' rights to peaceful protest. That came in the wake of public and media criticisms of the way they handled security at the G20 international financial summit and the climate conference in London. A man in the crowd died of a heart attack in mysterious circumstances and an officer faced criminal charges for an alleged assault on a protester. Although caught on camera, he was predictably acquitted by a magistrate. A code of practice was to be introduced, since society is neither "open" nor "democratic", as Johnson claimed, but further atrocities unfortunately seemed inevitable under the prevailing terror-struck climate.

Regarding the blurring of the separation of powers principle in practice the suspicion exists that the police is increasingly a politicized service. This has particularly been alleged of the Metropolitan Police because of its geographical proximity to the seats of government and various notorious events.

A series of controversies occurred in 2008 and 2009 involving Bob Quick, Assistant Commissioner and Head of Counter-Terrorism. For instance, he was widely blamed or authorising the arrest of Damian Green, MP, in the House of Commons and ultimately had to resign when he unwittingly allowed the media to photograph secret papers he was carrying to a meeting with the Home Secretary.

Massive security raids by police forces in the north of England were compromised and they had to be brought forward. (Subsequently arrests failed to result in any charges, although the government then sought to

CHAPTER 6

DEMOCRACY, LAW AND CONSTITUTION

deport the Pakistan university students involved). Quick became overtly politicized by publicly criticizing the Tory Party accusing them of moving against the Green investigation "in a wholly corrupt way", an allegation he later had to withdraw after the howls of protest.

The Metropolitan Police have been involved in a succession of heavy-handed and failed operations which carried high suspicion of political motivation. In the de Menezes case notoriously an innocent Brazilian national was hunted down mercilessly across London and shot dead at a tube station because of a climate of terrorist threats. The police were trigger-happy and panicked with tragic consequences. The ensuing inquests and enquiries were hardly less unsavoury, with the de Menezes family quite unable to obtain justice and none of the police involved disciplined. However, for their part in the affair, the Metropolitan Police eventually paid out an undisclosed sum in damages to the family behind closed doors, presumably in lieu of acknowledging their guilt and to shut them up.

Police attitudes are increasingly sick, with protection of criminals the priority and help for victims a seemingly lesser consideration. A symptomatic case involved the arrest and prosecution of a man who chased down the street and beat up an intruder who had attacked him and his family at home, tied them up, and threatened to kill them. The law is also at fault, because it preserves intact a criminal's rights even when he has wilfully undertaken illegal activity. Because Police policy concentrates on certain activity driven by targets and political steerage to the exclusion of dealing with some crimes altogether, it enhances the likelihood of vigilante groups filling the gap. They have developed a range of responses to public requests for support, largely designed to fob them off, or divert their enquiries elsewhere.

Scandalously, when we are looking for improvements, the police are not immune from cutbacks in the wake of the credit crunch in order to help pay for the bail-out of banks. Home Secretary, as early as December 2009, announced a need for the forces to make annual savings of £550million, mostly from overtime, with more expected after the 2010 General Election.
One mooted remedy for ills would be to put the police under democratic

DEMOCRACY, LAW AND CONSTITUTION

accountability to the local people. Something of this sort has been supported by the Liberal Democrats. And it makes sense in principle, since the public expectations of the police have not been met. Catching local villains in a spirit of political independence is what they want, not chasing government targets and buck-passing.

CONSTITUTION

The British Constitution

It is common for a club to have a 'constitution'. This is a set of rules under which the club functions. The same idea generally applies to a very wide range of institutions and organisations. A State is no exception.

Its constitution will be a document or set of documents that specifies as a minimum which body can pass the laws of the land, which body is to carry out the business of government, and which is to be entrusted with overseeing the operation of the laws and passing judgement on the conduct of the people when they transgress them. In addition a country's constitution will have to make provision for resolving disagreements about its interpretation, and machinery for making changes to it.

To quote from Bogdanor, a leading expert, "Constitutions are concerned with the grandest and most important of issues - the relationship between the individual and the state, the conditions of political order, and the methods by which men and women are ruled"(10).

In spite of its nature, the study of constitution rarely excites. Perhaps in part because it is bandied about with indignant vagueness whenever it suits a politician so to do. Indeed, the word 'unconstitutional' sometimes seems to be a mere term of dislike for whatever political activity is being criticized and an implication that it should be stopped or altered.

There are quite a few different ways of classifying national constitutions, and these serve to shed further light on their nature. Constitutions can be 'codified' or 'uncodified'. A codified constitution is written in one document, or one set of documents, whereas in an uncodified constitution

DEMOCRACY, LAW AND CONSTITUTION

there is no one identified source, despite the existence of rules.

Constitutions may likewise be 'rigid' or 'flexible', referring to the ease of change. Rigid constitutions can only be changed by special arrangements, but flexible constitutions can be altered by ordinary laws.

Another relevant classification is the dualism between 'unitary' and 'federal' constitutions. A unitary constitution has all government power vested at the centre. Federal constitutions divide up legislating power between the centre and individual areas, as in the United States of America.

The nature of the United Kingdom's constitution can be generally characterized as a unitary system with unlimited power to make laws over its devolved regions, and with a Parliament that is supreme. It is a formal monarchy, with the monarch as titular Head of State and succession to the throne being through the royal family heredity. The powers of the present Queen are, however, mainly nominal and historically residual. Most are exercised by the government directly, so why bother?

The body which undertakes legislation is Parliament, which is composed of two chambers in a system known as bicameralist. The lower chamber, with the main power, is the House of Commons; the upper chamber, is the House of Lords.

The constitution is 'uncodified', and tends to be buried within law and 'convention'. It is said as a result to be 'flexible'.

It is something of an indictment that a book published in 1885 remained until 1997 the definitive work on the United Kingdom constitution. This was Dicey's "An Introduction to the Study of Law of the Constitution". Along with Walter Bagheot's book "The English Constitution", written in 1867, it has been a key source of reference. Whilst there needs to be a certain amount of continuity and resilience to a constitution, so that it does not break under every gale, it is also supposed to be a great reforming instrument in a dynamic democracy. Ours has become moribund as a deliberate and positive device for improvement, for all the chorus of criticisms, except in so far as minor changes are expedient for

DEMOCRACY, LAW AND CONSTITUTION

the rulers.

Then there are its innumerable "conventions". Bogdanor usefully defines convention as "a non-legal rule which supplements legal rules, imposing non-legal rather than legal obligations". As he rightly observes: "They are likely to play a more important role in a country without a codified constitution, such as Britain, than they do in countries with".

In other words, we presently have a vague constitution, which is added to by a plethora of other conventional practices, rendering the actual position even more complicated and difficult to follow, tangled up in law as it also is.

It might be argued, perhaps, that it does not matter unduly, because conventions do not have to be followed. But if not, why not? What would be the legitimating criteria for their breach?

Let us be clear: this is no trivial matter. The role of the monarch is largely based on conventions, and there are very many others that play a significant part in the conduct of Parliament.

Conventions have insidious effects. Their relative lack of explicit quality, or embeddedness in the constitution, allow all too easily those in power to make unaccountable changes.

Should some conventions be formally included in the constitution? And if so, how would we be able to decide among their different kinds? It would help if they could first all be written down and their constitutional contexts and purposes explained. The people would be entitled to a justification in each and every case.

Now it is a common misunderstanding that the United Kingdom does not have a written constitution. The constitution is written down, but in so many different documents and types of document that it would take real experts to fathom it completely. Some is enshrined in laws, while other elements come from rules which are conventionally followed, but not binding, or from the European Community. It contains writings by scholars, not to mention the Queen. Whilst this sorry state of affairs is

DEMOCRACY, LAW AND CONSTITUTION

endlessly convenient for those with power or influence able to exploit it, it is hard to see how it could be in the interests of ordinary people. Changes can all too easily be made without our support, or even our knowledge. And the ability of the courts to declare practices unlawful is obviously very weak in such a system. Shamefully, the United Kingdom is about the only developed nation left in the world without a so-called "codified" constitution, one written down all together in one place and available to its subjects.

Bogdanor has interesting and depressing things to say about developing a codified written constitution. He agrees there should be one, yet argues against now being the time, for the specious reason that we are allegedly in constitutional ferment. Since he concedes a written constitution would inevitably be normative as well as factual, surely the currents of change could usefully try to foster consensus on key issues, and to galvanise a reluctant people and polity into actions already hundreds of years overdue? Well, they could in a 'proper' democracy, where even written constitutions are seen as development tools, tentatively adopted and all in principle subject to future betterment. The fact that it would be prodigiously difficult bears witness to the appalling hotchpotch we have indolently and abjectly allowed the system to become.

Professor Anthony King's position with regard to the question of a conveniently available written constitution also appears unduly tolerant 11). He concludes his analysis of the new British Constitution by admitting it 'remains a mess'. But thinks it is "probably.....benign". His argument that people could accept it has to be judged in the context of hundreds of years of unwritten constitution, which the people, some of whom have been vociferous critics, have at least apparently not sacked governments over. That does not mean they like it, or deserve it necessarily, even if their behaviour appears largely indifferent.

King compounds the seeming complacency by claiming there is still no need for a written constitution. His reasons are various. One is that there has been a period of major constitutional change going on since the 1960s, so a rest period is needed for them to settle. This is bunkum. Few politicians accept that teachers need a break from the constant changes foisted on schools and children. The important thing is to get matters

CHAPTER 6

DEMOCRACY, LAW AND CONSTITUTION

right. While they are not injustice follows.

King also lobs in two hypothetical arguments: that consensus would probably not emerge and that, if it did, it would produce a "bad" constitution. Finally, he claims there are more "pressing problems", something that can probably be said at any time regarding matters of urgency. But good government always has to have the capacity to plan longer-run as well as immediate change. It could, and should, have standing panels of experts and lay people working on constitutional reform as a bedrock necessity of democratic process. Why would we want to wait for a 'crisis' before taking action? And do we even know, given our eccentric, not to say idiosyncratic, traditions, just what a constitutional crisis might look like, anyway?

Reading President Obama's comments on constitution is to note a striking difference from British politicians(12). He speaks of the American constitution in tones and terms of reverence. It is clear that he sees the, as he freely admits, flawed efforts of the founding fathers to be ennobling of purpose, a continuity for bringing out greatness in the people and to ensure the smooth and honest running of the government. These, of course, are somewhat lofty ideals in the modern world, and have perhaps always been so. Yet he is one of those rare politicians who carries the constitution around with him for reference, to touch base when considering policy. For in America (unlike here) it is actually written down, briefly and clearly, in one portable booklet.

Obama has wrestled, as all in high office must, with the practical meaning of a fixed constitution in a rapidly changing environment. How, then, is it to be interpreted? There is the usual polarity of positions to consider. On one side are the strict interpreters, for whom the constitution has an unchanging and transparent meaning which must be taken literally. The other side regards the constitution as simply time-contingent and ripe for rewriting, a very useful but not gospel, guiding framework. Obama's conclusion is that the constitution is a set of rules within which we must conduct our democratic processes. It checks and balances the power and moderates our deliberations.

Ironically, in spite of the clamour from some sections of the media, and

CHAPTER 6

DEMOCRACY, LAW AND CONSTITUTION

even opportunistic politicians, for constitutional reform here, it has in fact been going on under our noses, although without our consent and dubiously in our interests. Bogdanor claims that: "We have been living through an unprecedented period of constitutional change, …which began in 1997 and shows no sign of coming to an end".

In his view there have been major new elements in recent years which have turned the constitution on its head - the Human Rights Act, devolution to Scotland and Wales, House of Lord reforms, Mayoral government in London. Strangely, he adds the referendum, which was only used in relation to canvassing public opinion over the European Economic Community once we had joined it! This last organisation forms the other major "new" constitutional factor, with its powers of precedence over United Kingdom law. These aspects will be discussed later in the chapter.

So how may we characterize the so-called 'new constitution'? It is unprincipled, its developments haphazard, lacking continuity of direction or theme, difficult to understand either in its institutions or in their interactions. It lacks, and this would be laughable if not so dire, any coherent intellectual justification. And yet, like an irrational monster, it rules us.

Perhaps a mitigating consolation about the new constitution is that it is inherently unstable in some important regards. But this simply means that the instabilities might be removed over time by their controlling forces without any regard at all to constitutional improvement. Some at least of the unstable features are the devolution arrangements to the home countries of the United Kingdom, showing desirable laws being passed only outside England, and having major unresolved issues concerning respective powers and revenue-raising for the devolved countries. Another is the raft of major tensions between the European Union and the United Kingdom over legal sovereignty and funding. A third is the no longer compliant judiciary when armed with a weapon like the Human Rights Act. A fourth is what to do with the House of Lords as second chamber of government. A fifth is the kind of central-local government relationship there should be. One glaring inconsistency is that the devolved Parliaments of Scotland, Wales, and Northern Ireland are given

CHAPTER 6

DEMOCRACY, LAW AND CONSTITUTION

large amounts of money from UK taxation over which they have spending autonomy within their areas of responsibility. By disgraceful contrast, local authorities in England are told in great detail by Whitehall how to spend their revenues and are never given enough by which to achieve all their imposed targets.

There are so many glaring faults in the British Constitution that it is a constant source of complaint by some politicians, whilst no doubt a comfort and protection for others.

Ben Bradshaw,as a junior minister, said in the wake of the MP's expenses scandal: "It's not just Parliament that's outdated, but the whole constitution".

Vincent Cable, the Liberal Democrat, saw another fundamental weakness: "there is no mechanism in the constitution to replace the (parliamentary) system".

For would-be reformers, then, the whole area of practice needs to be very carefully and comprehensively looked into. Public controversy erupts from time to time on a constitutional issue, where it becomes evident that historical arrangements are inappropriate, be they lacking in certainty about rights, procedures, or penalties, but too rarely to be properly effective.

The Damian Green affair in 2008/9 is instructive. Mr. Green was the shadow immigration minister, arrested in the House of Commons by the Metropolitan Police, without a warrant, and with the acquiescence of the Commons Speaker. The action was considered unconstitutional by some, but not by all. The allegation was that Mr. Green had obtained confidential information from a civil servant, who was also arrested. Subsequently, the Crown Prosecution Service announced that it had insufficient evidence to mount a legal case against either man, but the civil servant, who admitted aiding and abetting Damian Green, was then dismissed for breach of the Official Secrets Act.

Green had a reputation as something of a thorn in the government's side, a serial leaker of uncomfortable material. What concerned many MPs was that their own confidential dealings with constituents could be compromised by such police actions. The Conservative opposition argued that Mr. Green had used the material in the House of Commons, where it should have been covered by parliamentary privilege.

The constitutional disarray and lack of certitude for proceeding was shown up during the affair. The Speaker, smarting under attack from all sides of the Commons for his decision to allow Green's arrest in the House by police without a warrant, announced he was referring the matter of the police seizure of Mr. Green's belongings, to an ad hoc committee(13), (14). He would nominate seven experienced MPs to report to him as soon as possible. But the government did not back him, saying that the policy inquiry should occur first without prejudice. The opposition parties then boycotted the proposed committee, anyway.

Further ramifications of the case are that democratic rights to information could well be compromised in future, that it reduced the accountability of ministers, in this instance the Home Secretary, who would probably have much preferred to keep the information from the public gaze. Where, too, do journalists stand in law, given their role in reporting on the leaked documentation and its contents, (which did not, incidentally, constitute any threat whatsoever to national security)?

Despite government denials, the uneasy feeling persisted that they were using the police as instruments to cover up their actions, where disclosure could be compromising. Of course, the government, once it felt it could do no other, responded with the usual promises of legal reform. Some hoped that the public attention, reliably short-term, would move on, so that the changes might be modest.

We are regularly asked to believe that the United Kingdom is not only civilized ,but also a highly developed democracy that has led the world in political reforms. Yet, the general public at large do not know what the constitution consists of, nor do they understand its principles either. This is a very serious matter in a supposedly democratic state, because it undermines the capability of the electorate through its ignorance of basic legal rights and powers.

Obviously, a constitution may not be effective in preventing abuses of

CHAPTER 6

DEMOCRACY, LAW AND CONSTITUTION

State power even if it is known. The Government could flout it and the courts could let them. In the United Kingdom such scenarios are rendered less likely by active and potentially hostile media. On the other hand, atrocities are being committed on a daily basis whilst people play the ostrich.

Bogdanor accepts that constitutional reform is not a panacea. We will need to go beyond it to involve people more in 'direct democracy'. The electorate is still too passive for the requisite tasks. Somehow, the public has to become involved. They have got to feel a strong sense of belonging in order to become motivated. So what can channel and focus such a collective feeling?

Bogdanor names three "institutional instruments" as methods for increasing participation - party primaries to choose political candidates, proportional representation, and referenda. These measures will be discussed elsewhere, and each could have a partial role, whose totality would require to go much further for ultimate success.

There is an important proviso about the limitations of constitutions, as Graham reminds us. Unfortunately, it is not, and could not, be a preventative for all departures from democratic practice. Whilst constitution should be set out, principle by principle, even if defined with philosophical rigour and then cast into law, outrages will still occur. We also need a society-wide desire to see that the constitution is upheld and we have to put in place measures to ensure it. Much scope exists for coming up with possible candidates for the measures. One key one is to limit periods of office. Another is to prevent patronage. The latter requires both independent monitoring and severe sanctions, neither currently more than rudimentary.

Bogdanor claims that changes in the constitution have had the effect of dispersing power. That may be, yet it is screamingly obvious more needs to be dispersed still. The prime minister, for one, has far too much power, especially when you consider that there have been many cases of the incumbents being incompetent and others where they were mentally ill. (It is said that on some medical opinion, Sir Anthony Eden might have been certified temporarily insane at the time of the Egyptian War and

CHAPTER 6

DEMOCRACY, LAW AND CONSTITUTION

Suez crisis). And, needless to say, the constitution is weighted heavily against shifting power from the politicians to the people, which has to be a key objective towards setting up a truly democratic State.

It seems inevitable that we shall continue to experience constitutional controversies. To some extent they could be seen as a healthy sign of a developing nation. But this is the charitable view. The vested interests are powerful guardians of status quo and it is often in their interests to leave matters in obfuscation. Also, governments see little public interest, and hence votes, in such matters, which tend to be arcane. Reform is bound to be complex if systematic and widespread. But governments are usually in a hurry, with little time to address or impress. Even if they have the ability, which is seldom, few will stick to a plan of systematic constitutional reform with zeal. Much more likely are put-downs, fob-offs, cosmetic statements, long-term promises, and quick-fix patch-ups.

Considering the overarching importance of constitutional reform, it is highly significant that over ten years in office as prime minister Tony Blair was silent on the subject.

Gordon Brown, his successor, at least seemed to start with other ideas. He said in May 2007:

> "I want to build a shared national consensus for a programme of constitutional reform that strengthens the accountability of all who hold power".

Brown's asserted interest was therefore welcome in principle, except that it soon became likely that it would be largely superficial and cosmetic if it happened at all.

One of the troubles with consultative group meetings around the country, apart from their obvious lack of balanced representation, is that politicians will set them ridiculous agendas. Thus, the first proposal was for the Ministry of Justice to lead a debate about "British values", hopefully leading to an agreed statement which Parliament could endorse. The idea has understandably led to much criticism. Fundamentally, how could we separate out uniquely British values from the universal ones we will also wish to embrace? And how would the resulting statement then be useable?

The Queen's Speech of proposed government legislation, announced in December 2008, did not contain the promised plans for a Bill of Rights. Along with plans to change the constitution to require Parliamentary approval to any proposal to go to war, the proposal was ditched.

This was predictable. Even if we take the charitable view that the government was overwhelmed by events, it remains unproven whether there was a serious reforming intent.

Some commentators strike a note of warning that the constitutional reform agenda of political leaders is a way to create machinery of patronage and influence for interest groups and powerful individuals. The following statements of the position from King are apt.

"We have got to understand that safeguarding a liberal democracy is not a job that can be hived off to politicians who, once elected, are left to get on with it. We're all in this together. This must be a properly national project, to reinstitute principles both in the private and public spheres…".

And again, "there are…signs…that the mass party, plagued by falling membership and a weakening sense of party identification, is dying on its feet… . Yet the grip of the parties on the institutions of government remains as strong as ever". That goes for their influence over the constitution too.

What can we expect of a central government? The simple answer, sadly, is less then we used to, realistically, although we probably claim more, egged on by the media. For government power has weakened, for various reasons and in different areas of operation. To illustrate: much sovereignty now rests with the European Union regarding the making of laws. As has been amply demonstrated by the recession of 2008/9, the government cannot stand up to banks and other multinational firms in practice, whatever its constitutional position. The market economy is now too globalized for Britain to be able to insulate itself from the trends either. Devolution has delegated quite a lot of power to Scotland, Wales,

CHAPTER 6

DEMOCRACY, LAW AND CONSTITUTION

and Northern Ireland, and the Human Rights Act has given many an individual the ability to defy the government, notably on matters of immigration and the inciting of politico-religious intolerance.

Frustration and resignation are common reactions among the populace, given that the constitutional changes that are made are not of our choosing. One suspects from the lesson of history that future constitutional changes will continue for the most part to be event-driven rather than principled, and will be as piecemeal as before.

The power of the party machines at the present time seems unstoppable, and with it their self-serving tendencies to conservatism and modest pragmatism on constitutional questions.

Harking back to our study of ideology, it is a gloomy thought, if true, the Bogdanor claim that "in the last resort, ideological forces determine constitutional forms"

Finally, and to recap, in the United Kingdom, constitutionally, the government can do what it likes. The constitution does not safeguard the people's " rights". There is no simple summary of it in written form, to enable the constitution to be taught to our citizens as of democratic right. Powers of the executive, legislature and judiciary are not properly separated for the avoidance of corruption. We have inappropriate historical institutions like the Crown and the House of Lords, which are anti-democratic, idiosyncratic, and quite anachronistic. We are in a deep and complex legal relationship with Europe, which we can neither control nor make our minds up what we want it to become, or what we want to contribute to and take from. Constitution could help more than a little if we could only address it properly.

A Bill of Rights

Attention turns to considering the concept of a Bill of Rights.

Believe it or not, there was a Bill of Rights enacted in 1689. The main historical importance arises from the fact that at that time Parliament was

DEMOCRACY, LAW AND CONSTITUTION

wrestling authority from the Crown, so the Bill of Rights allowed Parliament to operate without undue interference from the monarch. If the King acted with the support of Parliament his powers remained unlimited, but it did force him to cooperate with Parliament and no longer act unilaterally, as a dictator who thought he had the backing of God. The ancient Bill of Rights has mostly done its job in reducing monarchy to a largely symbolic and titular role, where the great damage the Crown has historically wreaked is now minimized.

To a modern democrat, however, a bill of rights is something quite different from a set of privileges for a narrow group of people. It is a law which would set out rights which ordinary citizens would be accorded and which could not then be taken away from them, so long as the Bill of Rights remained in legal operation. The focus is at once shifted from royalty, from government, down to the people. The United Kingdom has no such bill of rights.

The model to watch for the British is the United States Bill of Rights, which gives the people rights against the government. It also builds in rights to prevent majorities behaving tyrannically to the rest. And it has resistance to alteration at government whim, requiring substantial majority support in each state and the Congress for every proposed change.

A complication arises in practice owing to the fact that there are other legally significant entities that might vie for similar ground. These are the European Convention on Human Rights and the Human Rights Act, 1998. Although the United Kingdom is signed up to the European Convention, as a member state of the European Community, it illegally refused citizens access to its own national courts for redress in cases of breach.

Such a state of affairs could in principle be rectified under a Bill of Rights as part of a constitution that was legally supreme, transcending any contrary will of Parliament. At the present time, however, a citizen has only such rights as allow him to do what the law has not made illegal, this scope literally changing on a daily basis, for the most part without his knowledge, never mind consent.

A potential pressure for a Bill of Rights may come from operation of the

CHAPTER 6

DEMOCRACY, LAW AND CONSTITUTION

fact that the European Convention on Human Rights is now built into the law governing the devolved actions of both the Scottish and the Welsh Parliaments.

Turning to the Human Rights Act, 1998, this potential helpmate came into force in the United Kingdom in late 2000, and it will take some time before a full assessment of its effectiveness becomes possible. It actually brought the European Convention on Human Rights within United Kingdom law, thus making it operative in practice here, rather than merely in principle. Unfortunately, once again the same serious loophole remains: the Human Rights Act is subordinate to Parliament, which can with impunity pass laws incompatible with it. So it hardly seems likely that we have here the answer to the problems we are seeking to solve by a constitutionally paramount Bill of Rights, in spite of Government reverses in the courts.

Care must be taken not to fall for fob-off deals, such as the Conservatives offered in 2009. A Bill of Rights would be introduced, they said, instead of the existing Human Rights Act, which would be repealed. In fact, the country needs both, particularly if politicians can do without either. The Conservative proposal has been widely criticized as unworkable, given its incompatibility with the constitution of the European Community. It is recognised that the Tory Party has been hopelessly divided over United Kingdom membership of the European Community, so the ploy had more to do with their prospects of advancement than any desire to increase public rights. Indeed, without the protection that Europe can afford these rights are liable to dissipate further.

Whether or not reluctantly, the Brown Government, unlike Blair's over ten years, talked about (modest) constitutional reform. However, as a prelude the constitutional minister started a debate about producing a United Kingdom 'statement of values'. This process, involving some (restricted) public consultation, was a false step for more reasons than one. Firstly, are there any such things as specifically United Kingdom values, especially in our immigrant-driven pluralism? Secondly, what will that mean for the utility of universal values, or those applying in some other countries too, in a revised constitution? Thirdly, how will the statement of values be used in producing a Bill of Rights? Similar

CHAPTER 6

DEMOCRACY, LAW AND CONSTITUTION

initiatives have been seen in industry when there was a fad for so-called 'mission statements'. Local authorities aped the practice, but so often staff did not know what to do with them. The statements tended to stand alone, difficult to connect with either policy or procedure, for all their high-sounding rhetoric.

An interesting comment by Jack Straw, the Justice Minister in Gordon Brown's Labour Government, is that a Bill of Rights could be used to introduce a balance between citizens' rights and our mutual duties and obligations. It is often said that every right also imposes a duty as its converse. That then produces further complexity and there is the added dimension that rights are increasingly seen as not just political, but at least also economic, social, and environmental. The path ahead will therefore not be easy, and the prospects for ready national consensus would appear to be slim. That such changes can even be contemplated without the parliamentary rulers allowing a plebiscite shows just how inappropriately paternalistic our sovereignty has become, and how depressingly compliant the public.

So what, specifically, is at stake? The main elements of the Human Rights Act can be seen from the following list:

> right to life, except provision for death penalty in time of war,
> prohibition of torture,
> prohibition of slavery and forced labour,
> right to liberty and security,
> right to a fair trial,
> no punishment without law,
> right to respect for private and family life,
> freedom of thought, conscience and religion,
> freedom of expression,
> freedom of assembly and association,
> right to marry,
> prohibition of discrimination,
> restrictions on political activity of aliens,
> prohibition of abuse of rights,
> limitation on use of restrictions on rights,
> protection of property,

DEMOCRACY, LAW AND CONSTITUTION

> right to education,
> right to free elections.

At first glance it might seem an impressive collection of rights already. But it has to be remembered that it is how they are upheld in life that counts. Currently, the Human Rights Act is able constitutionally to be disapplied by Parliament. Statutes are passed actively fettering its application, or denying citizens appeal to the courts. It is a crucial challenge to the so-claimed independence of the judiciary, and their strength, to ensure that the intentions of the Act, and of the European Community behind it, are upheld.

So far the auguries have not been impressive. The Human Rights Act has not, for example, safeguarded:

> respect for private life and privacy
> (now invaded with impunity by tabloid newspapers);

> freedom of expression
> (look how whistleblowers are persecuted by their employers);

> a severely limited period of detention without trial
> (debated by Parliament during 2008 and 2009 with widely varying, lengthy, time periods being mooted using terrorism as the pretext);

> peaceful assembly in public places
> (the police have powers to impose conditions relating to the size, location, and length of demonstrations);

> protection of personal data
> (the government, and public and private organisations, lose it for you without redress);

> fair hearings before imposition of penalty
> (unlike speeding fines).

Any Bill of Rights to be enacted in the United Kingdom must legally be

CHAPTER 6

DEMOCRACY, LAW AND CONSTITUTION

compatible with the Human Rights Act and not seek to undermine it, but rather to extend people's rights still further. Only in an ideal world there would be no need for the Human Rights Act. It, and other additional rights, would be part of a Bill of Rights enshrined in a written constitution and buffered from state interference.

For what it is worth, and as a taster for what is still missing, such a Bill of Rights could well supply us with such emanations as:

no retrospectively operating legislation
(such as occurred with government plans in 2008 to severely tax vehicles bought after 2001 which were not fuel-efficient);

no entitlement to legal assistance and representation
(currently in effect denied to those not rich or poor);

the right to a healthy and sustainable environment
(instead of endless dithering on energy policy whilst hectoring the world at international conferences);

right to fair and just administrative action;

democratic rights of voting and direct action short of legal breach;

special protection for weak or disadvantaged groups, such as children, the disabled, minorities, and crime victims.

Whilst a Bill of Rights should be a good thing for the people, like a sensible Constitution would be, both projects can easily be ruined, by intention or ignorance, or both. It ought to be very clear what they are there for, what they can and cannot do.

In the case of a Bill of Rights, its purposes should be for the benefit of all citizens, not just those belonging to some minority group or other. The main broad requirements are to protection from those in power and to fair and equitable treatment. It is worth remembering that governments have a track record of being untrustworthy in relation to reforms that would surrender some of their powers to the general public. Also that a

DEMOCRACY, LAW AND CONSTITUTION

tendency to favour interest groups would play out differently under Conservative and Labour, with each favouring a different patronage.

Devolution

Great strides were made by the Labour Government in devolving at least some power from Whitehall to national assemblies for Scotland and Wales in the ten years or so after 1997. What was followed was the restoration of the Stormont Parliament in Northern Ireland, with an accommodation brokered between the Protestant and minority Catholic factions which time and history will have to give the verdict on.

However, devolution has itself de facto created a great many serious problems which will provide the London legislature with headaches. Because the situation is quite new, everyone, including electorates, is inexperienced, and thus mistakes are made. Even so, an unstable situation has been produced.

One such, arguably, is that Scotland has been given more powers than Wales. Is that either just or sustainable?

Cynics, and others of more even outlook, claim that devolution was only ever a sop to the militant voices of nationalism in these countries, yet it remains theoretically quite possible that they will eventually curry sufficient support to be able to press for complete independence.

Then again, much resentment has been generated in England by what is called "the West Lothian Question", wherein Scottish MPs vote in the House of Commons on matters affecting England, without English MPs being able to do likewise in the Scottish Parliament. The challenge is there somehow to limit the rights of Scottish MPs to voting on legislation which concerns just Scotland.

The enthusiasm of the Welsh and Scottish peoples for devolution has been uneven and mixed before and after it. Nevertheless, there is a perception that somehow to go back to what went before would be regressive and not to be countenanced. It may be a case of letting the

DEMOCRACY, LAW AND CONSTITUTION

genie out of the lamp.

Also remaining to be played out is the reaction of the English. There is certainly anger at funding arrangements, seen south of the border as unduly generous to the Scots. Pressure may mount for the Scottish Parliament to raise its own revenues through local taxation.

The Calman Commission, which reported on the first ten years of Scottish devolution, recommended a new tax for national funding. The arrangement proposed was a complicated one, involving creaming from the upper rates of income tax in Scotland, and allied to the block grant from London. However, the machinery would operate through the Whitehall Treasury, not locally. Reform proposals, hailed as radical, were actually very cautious, and did little to shift the burden of taxation closer to the Scottish people.

But will the English follow suit and press for their own Parliament? The precursors are difficult to read. Certainly, in the early years of the Blair government there was much flirtation with notions of regional government. Referenda were held in various parts of the country to test public interest, but only in the very integrated North-East was there much display of enthusiasm. Any movement to regional assemblies with significant powers would also cause something of a crisis with over layering, in that the various tiers of central and local government would get in each other's way and need to be thinned out. That might see off the remaining counties, but even in the case of local unitary authorities there could be a conflict with regional powers. Much would depend, as always on the degree of genuine delegation from the centre.

It is vitally important to be clear what devolution has meant so far. It is emphatically not a system of federal government. In devolving powers to Scotland and Wales, the United Kingdom has reserved the legal rights not to recognise any of the laws these countries pass, and to pass other laws of its own to overrule them. Fundamentally a reason why Scottish Nationalists continue to press for independence, it will be interesting to gauge wider public reaction once instances of dispute over sovereignty begin to appear. In the last analysis the Scots and the Welsh are completely at the mercy of a foreign government. This is their legal

DEMOCRACY, LAW AND CONSTITUTION

position today.

So far what has lacked has been any sort of public debate about the kind of powers it would be appropriate to have situated at each stage of the continuum from locality to region to national centre. The debate is fundamental, non-negotiable, and would be unavoidable in a genuine democracy facing the prospect of major and radical change.

Once again, unless the peoples assert their collective wills and come to realise where their interests lie, they will receive whatever political whim decides to foist on them. Albeit the justifications will sound oh so noble.

PUBLIC PARTICIPATION

Elections

We turn next to elections, that heralded bastion of democracy. Yet how could you call it 'democratic' if the government of the day, or even its Prime Minister, can decide within very wide limits of duration, when to hold a general election? Unless the government loses its majority in the House of Commons, and is defeated on major policy issues or confidence votes, it matters not one jot that millions of good citizens out there think they are well past their sell-by date. Not only do they go to the country when they want to, they do so at a time they best calculate to serve their own personal interests for re-election. This cannot be right. When the Blair New Labour administration fell from grace, and its popularity declined sharply further under his dynastic successor, Gordon Brown, various landslide by-election defeats, and accurate opinion polls showing the nature and depth of public discontent, all failed to unseat the regime with two years to go before the absolute deadline was reached. Even fixed- term Parliaments would be unjust ,as they would conveniently allow a Government immunity for the duration, unless proper constitutional safeguards allowed for earlier dissolution in relevant circumstances.

But when Joe Citizen actually gets to exercise his vote, this is so much of the time a pointless gesture of very limited and rather blunt effect. If the

DEMOCRACY, LAW AND CONSTITUTION

government stays in office, the general election is only once about every five years. Typically, with the first-past-the-post system this means that most votes are wasted. If you are in an area that is always Labour or always Conservative, your vote for the other side will not count as he is well beaten, but neither will your vote for the winner, since very many others have already voted him in. Should you wish to vote for some minority party, this is meaningless, too, for it cannot lead to office.

The British voting system is technically called the single-member plurality system (SMP) (15). It suits the two main parties because it keeps one or the other of them permanently in power, usually with a clear majority allowing for strong government. It should not suit the electorate for the same reasons. Most of their votes are wasted, on non-elected candidates, and about three seats in every ten never ever change the colour of their party control. Small parties, which could provide radical alternatives to the present duopoly, are under-represented.

The British system is an example of a 'majoritarian' system. These distort the result in favour of the larger parties, giving them many more seats than warranted by their proportion of the votes. So blatant is it that no government has been elected on a majority of the votes cast since 1935!

Distortions in the voting system for our first-past-the-post elections are little understood by the public at large. If they were, they would probably be scandalised by the palpable unfairness of it all. Quite simply, a party can win more seats than another although it receives fewer votes. The reasons are that no value is placed on votes in seats you do not win, so they are in effect discarded, and no additional value accrues for your extra votes if you do win a seat and your majority increases. These votes are wasted too.

On the national scene, when you have a party like the Liberal Democrats who have support across many constituencies, yet with few areas where it is really concentrated, their vote is less effective. The distortions are very considerable and grossly undemocratic. Approximately, a thirty percent vote for Labour would give them around 230 seats, a thirty percent vote for the Conservatives about 170 seats, and a thirty percent vote for the

CHAPTER 6

DEMOCRACY, LAW AND CONSTITUTION

Liberal Democrats some 85 seats only.

In appraising voting systems there are broadly two sets of consideration: how 'effective' they make the government (in the sense of providing a clear party majority, which could be a very different thing); secondly, what is the quality and extent of proper representation. Governments stress the importance of the first, claiming wildly that coalition governments are weak and would result from other voting systems, so the people need to concentrate on the latter.

Recognising some measure of public disquiet, Brown made tentative moves towards a system called the alternative vote (AV) if the electorate bought it. Not a good idea and for the simple reason that votes can be redistributed against the voters' best wishes among other candidates, so that all drop out apart from the two with most votes.

In any electoral system the rules will ask voters to choose between candidates or parties. If candidates, which seems more democratic, voters will either be asked to choose one, or put a list of them in an order of preference. In proportional representation the idea is to ensure that the number of seats a party receives is in direct relation to their proportion of the total vote, which would seem eminently just save only that it can be more or less achieved in practice by the operation of a suitable method. There are various possibilities available, all with their strengths and weaknesses and operating across Europe. But the point is that in the United Kingdom they never get a fair crack of the whip because of the powerfully entrenched self-interests of Labour and Conservative alike.

A kind of proportional representation is therefore needed to be consistent with democratic ideals. Voters are likely to get at least one MP from a party they support under the single transferable vote system but with larger constituencies. What the main two parties are afraid of here, for they both oppose it, is ending up with less power and influence, or more sharing. They are at pains to describe coalition government as some kind of an ogre, suggesting these arrangements are intrinsically unstable and indecisive. But if it is not in the interests of the main parties, the citizen might be wise to conclude that there would be something in it for him.
In local council elections, too, the council tax payer is frequently

CHAPTER 6

DEMOCRACY, LAW AND CONSTITUTION

disenfranchised despite his vote. For instance, in many councils there is no overall control by any party and, unfortunately, no proper rules exist to guide the conduct of the parties in such a situation. It is simply left to the party leaders to negotiate pacts, or working arrangements, if they can or will. It is not unknown for there to be a Council with a majority of Tory Councillors, but outvoted by a Lib-Lab pact, a clear frustration of 'the will of the people' as expressed through the ballot box.

It is an illusion, and an argument used for 'gentling the masses', to claim that the people have power if they have the vote. One serious mistake is to assume that the voting result, which is the aggregation of large numbers of individual (and secret) decisions, provides evidence for a collective intention. Yet that is what the ruling party will always claim.

It is logical nonsense to conclude from the premise that individual voters putting or not putting an 'X' in a box for just one candidate adds up to the nation consciously and collectively deciding on whatever the outcome. So that if the result is, say, a hung parliament, that is what the country wants. And it is worse than a disgrace that, in such an eventuality, the constitution leaves what happens next to the political parties, to make out they are serving public intention by trying to carve up the governmental arrangements between them.

A coalition is a reasonable democratic outcome in principle if no party commands an overall majority in a general election, but the coalition was then constitutionally required to be made up of all the different parties according to the proportion of votes cast for them (not seats won, which can be very unrepresentative, as we have seen).The monarch should play no part, neither should party leaders be allowed to horse -trade over selective pacts with only some of them to 'form a government in the national interest'. In their interest more likely.

Likewise ,in such a situation no decent constitution would allow the party with most votes to impose its manifesto on the country ,although unelected in its own right, and on the rest of the coalition. All votes would have to be free votes without whips and every policy would have to be so decided.
Finally, the public do not get a look-in when it comes to choosing candidates

DEMOCRACY, LAW AND CONSTITUTION

to stand in either local or national elections. The parties have it stitched up, so all people can do is vote for someone else's idea of who the candidate should be - another lack of fundamental democratic influence. Then, there is the local grass-roots party machine, where the faithful work tirelessly for the greater good. Their (undemocratic and unrepresentative) choice of candidate, or short-list, is increasingly overseen and overtaken by the central dictat of the national party hierarchy.

The Totnes by-election in 2009 broke interesting new ground when the Conservatives, possibly as a gimmick to distance themselves from the MPs' expenses scandal, selected their candidate by a postal ballot of the whole local electorate (and won). Some hailed it as a democratic move, but one person's enfranchisement can be another's denial. True, Tory Central Office apparently surrendered their usual unhealthy control of decisions, but the local party faithful were also removed from main influence. Another, perhaps laudable, feature was that you did not have to be a Tory to have a say. On the other hand, might not some supporters of other parties have voted mischievously for a poor quality candidate. The stated cost of proceedings was as much as £40,000, so the 'experiment' was not a serious starter for future use in national elections. And is it all that democratic? Who, for example, chose the short-list of Tory candidates, and on what basis?

A key question is: would the process extend the range of candidate choice into strata of society usually under represented?

A good and related democratic idea which can be adopted from the United States is the use of 'open primaries' to hold elections. All the voters in a constituency would be invited to choose the candidates who stand for each party. Party selection committees would, presumably, still choose the short-list of candidates, but there could be enforced public criteria rather than the usual party political chicanery.

There are various unsatisfactory conventions which operate around elections to frustrate the will of the people. One illustration is that an elected MP may change his mind about the political party he wishes to support and stay in office.

Another silly, undemocratic, convention is that because the Speaker is

CHAPTER 6

DEMOCRACY, LAW AND CONSTITUTION

supposed to be above party politics, he is not opposed by the other parties at the general election. The practice appears to give no consideration at all to the rights and wishes of the local electorate. A new departure ,however, because the Speaker, John Bercow, was himself regarded as tainted by some in regard to events in the Commons, was that the Leader of the UK Independence Party, Nigel Farage, an MEP, announced his intention to stand down so he could oppose Bercow in the voting.

And beyond the actual election, of course, it is clear that the ordinary citizen has little say either in the choice of political leaders or the making and changing of policies.

Regarding elections, though, if we are seeking an indication of the 'general will of the people', in other words a majority view, we do not need them at all. These days we could find the information out much better, and a lot more finessed, by scientific approaches to statistical sampling via opinion polls.

Government business is very fast-moving today, which is part of the general acceleration of the pace of life. Yet this is not reflected in the electoral system. In these times of instant computer voting on television game shows, a progressive democracy would introduce regular referenda on a whole range of important developments, thus moving people towards participation, rather than their usual role of disgruntled, and ultimately switched-off, passive subjects.

What is inappropriate is that, in desperate attempts to curry support, all the major political parties encouraged unregulated registration on the electoral roll and postal voting. In both cases no identity checks were made and no particular credentials, such as medically attested illness or disabled status, were required for qualification. To the country's lasting shame, reports and complaints of alleged ballot-rigging were rife and international monitors arrived to monitor the 2010 elections, as though Britain was a banana republic like Zimbabwe. The situation was potentially even more serious in local government elections, where wards are small and a handful of votes can sometimes determine the outcome.

The police were said to be undertaking around fifty investigations

DEMOCRACY, LAW AND CONSTITUTION

nationwide, though the practices have not been effectively combated in the past and are unlikely to be in the future without a very different climate of determined political control. The police are reluctant to do anything which requires large-scale resources and is not among their own priorities. In this situation they were even more reluctant owing to the fact that the fraud allegations mostly involved Asian immigrant communities, who would brand them racist. There were local residents claiming to have been intimidated into voting in the way the local tribal elders dictated. And the system was pathetically lax, and open to easy abuse, with anyone from Commonwealth countries eligible to vote in a general election if living in the United Kingdom, whether actually present or otherwise!

Referenda

One seemingly no-go area for democratic reform is that government will have no truck with plebiscites (referenda). Essentially it wants the relatively undemocratic option of a vote every five years to continue. This disastrously gives carte blanche to ruin the nation in between with little in the way of effective challenge possible, short of media campaigns and civil disobedience. The latter has only very rarely been tried, and then on a comparatively small scale, so it is still a tantalising and open question what could thereby be achieved in terms of reform. The forbearance and docility of the population is wondrous to behold. Certainly, it is not a phenomenon our politicians have been effective enough to have engendered. Set against the records of certain other advanced societies, it is perhaps not something to be relied on indefinitely, either.

A referendum is a vote of the people on a single issue. One difficulty with referenda is that, however intense the desire of at least some United Kingdom citizens to have them at times, there is no constitutional basis for them, because the system here is one of representative government on the 'evidence' of elections. A difficulty, however, for those in power is that some of the populace have acquired a taste for it after one was held, allegedly without establishing a precedent, and with its outcome not legally binding, just after our joining the European Community in 1973,

DEMOCRACY, LAW AND CONSTITUTION

to see if we should stay in! Further referenda have been held subsequently in those countries over devolution for Scotland and Wales. And the public should know it is a common practice in Europe. Embarrassingly, most civilized democracies already use them, albeit some quite seldom. They tend to be utilized on major constitutional issues and to settle some moral questions perhaps, such as can crop up with medical breakthroughs.

It is clear from the enormous reluctance of both the Conservative and Labour parties to hold referenda - one notorious example being over the ratification of the Lisbon Treaty (effectively a new and more federal constitution for Europe) - that doubtless they are gravely concerned at the possible erosion of their power by the machinery.

Yet the measure is not intended to supplant representative government. And its results could be made advisory only, at least to start with. It might slow legislation down, especially if used regularly on a range or issues, but it is far from clear that the United Kingdom public en masse would actively participate anyway.

There are as usual patronising arguments against referenda, of course. Some issues are said to be too complicated for the people to understand. The same argument is unsurprisingly adduced to undermine the jury system, especially in complex technological cases.

In our political culture, there is little doubt that governments would abuse the principles of referenda in practice. One obvious ploy is to load the questions and to restrict their nature and range. Another is to have a re-run if the outcome is deemed uncertain or unfavourable. There is always a chance that the verdict will be different the next time, or they might say conditions have changed and question how long a referendum's outcome continues to reflect the will of the people.

The referendum undoubtedly does have dangers, especially in a country like the United Kingdom where direct democracy has scarcely been tried. The people's judgement could be poor. The turn out could be low and cast doubt on its representative nature. It might actually ignore the issues altogether and act more like a vote of no-confidence in the government.

It is little use, from the perspective of a disenchanted electorate, in conceding the theoretical possibility of using the referendum in uncertain future circumstances, like Brown did for a voting system review after the 2010 general election. What they need is the written constitutional guarantee that the referendum will be held for specifically listed eventualities and that it will have a definite, pre-set force in regard to subsequent decision-making relevant to its outcome. Such matters are not easy to frame; neither are they beyond the wit of man.

We must also seek to limit, within new constitutional safeguards, the scope of governments to use the referendum as a tactic, and only when it suits them. Scandalous to say, at present, the referendum is only a politician's tool, not the people's.

Politicians, if they had the genuine interests of the public at heart, would be pleased, not disconcerted, at the knowledge of public opinion which a referendum, scientifically used, has the potential to reveal.

Participative Deficits

When in July 2009, in the immediate aftermath of the MPs expenses scandal becoming public knowledge, a disgraced Labour MP resigned in Norwich North, the results of the ensuing by-election were arguably very depressing for democrats. There was a large swing to the Tories in spite of their being just as much implicated in the scandal, turn-out was only about 45% of those entitled to vote, and the anti-sleaze voters did not support any particular party or individual in large numbers. Perhaps it showed a mixture of resignation, a simple knee-jerk reaction for change, even unconvincing change, and the woefully inadequate crudity of the vote itself.

Two generations of representative government have amply demonstrated the inadequacy and folly of leaving politics to the politicians. The public, thoroughly disgusted and largely disenfranchised, would have surprised Marx by turning apathetic instead of militant. The sad consequence is the

DEMOCRACY, LAW AND CONSTITUTION

perennial see-saw of governing parties between Labour and the Conservatives.

Yet how do you energise and involve the electorate at large? Assuming it is at least worth a try before even our semblance of democracy disappears, what kind of measures can be realistically used?

"We will begin a massive redistribution of power in our country, from the powerful to the powerless, from the political elite to the man and the woman in the street".   So said David Cameron, Leader of the Conservative Party, in May 2009. Many a political leader in the wake of the MPs expenses scandal, and with the prospect of a general election looming, has made similarly dramatic and sweeping promises. And as the saying goes, there's one born every minute. Another observation is that tyrants do not willingly surrender power. Just look at President Gaddafi of Libya..

Michael Mansfield Q.C., a radical defence barrister, has suggested a variety of ways in which members of the general public can participate in democratic protest to seek change(16). Joining organisations like 'Liberty' or 'Amnesty International' will heighten awareness and aid their campaigns, at home as well as abroad.

In addition to local radio and television, the press can also be informed of issues and arguments.   Organisations need to be challenged, with questions asked of their conduct and for the disclosure of withheld information that should be in the public domain.

People can even participate in local politics, by joining a public forum, or trying for election to the local council.

The Calman Commission gave evidence during 2009 to the Scottish Parliament after a two-year study recommending aspects of reform (notably on tax and funding powers) for this relatively new body(17). It is already in some ways much more far-sighted than the United Kingdom Parliament - for example, in making regular use of the referendum on major constitutional matters.
The need for this is accepted by most who are not already holding power,

CHAPTER 6

DEMOCRACY, LAW AND CONSTITUTION

or likely to do so, but how about an independent standing committee to monitor and recommend reforms of the United Kingdom Parliament, with special reference to public education and participation? And what about an English Parliament, as campaigners press for?

Another useful democratic measure which the English should not be reluctant to introduce is the people's petition. Any Scottish voter can take up a matter personally and directly with the Scottish Parliament by using the device. In England the nearest equivalent would be the much more remote private member's bill, which an MP may introduce, usually on behalf of a group of constituents he feels are getting a raw deal, under the ten-minute rule, which is obviously a time-limiter. He faces stiff competition, needless to say, from other MPs, so very few of these bills ever become law. They need the provision of adequate Parliamentary time, not as a favour from government, but by constitutional right.

Civil Disobedience

Civil disobedience is widely disparaged by ordinary people, and obviously frowned upon by the authorities. Though it claims to be a kind of law-breaking which is morally justified, and it is typically peaceful. Occurring in public, it aims to generate considerable publicity for what is usually a single issue over which it seeks to change the law, or at least government policy.   So the challenge is to a particular law. Paradoxically, while breaking the law it still upholds the rule of law in general terms.

The conventional reaction is to say that there is no excuse for civil disobedience. If you want to change the law you have to campaign legitimately within it. Counter arguments say that this usually has no effect, consumes a great deal of time and effort, and that civil disobedience has sometimes been known to succeed, as, famously, with the suffragette movement.

The main arguments against civil disobedience are that it could escalate to a point where it is undermining of government, and, again, that it is undemocratic. The first is unconvincing, in the sense of being speculative

CHAPTER 6

DEMOCRACY, LAW AND CONSTITUTION

about both its development, and their effects. The second is true in the case where a small minority believe in the cause and the vast majority do not. But if the status quo is objectionable perhaps civil disobedience can be justified in encouraging the government to give the matter further thought. Democracy is not the only value, and law-breaking is not a threat to the fabric of society when honest citizens of integrity press a point on behalf of their community. Of much greater concern, it could be argued, are the ways in which the forces of law and order respond, proportionately or otherwise, in suppressing the expression of dissent.. …

When the Coalition Government decided on a very tough and unprecedented policy of allowing the cap on university fees to almost treble, there were bitter student demonstrations around the country in response.(Tellingly, most of the anger was directed towards the Liberal Democrats, for having reneged on the pre-election pledge not to put them up, rather than at the Coalition playmakers, the Conservatives ,whose policy in effect it was.)

All that was perhaps predictable. But from the standpoint of 'people power', the reaction of the Establishment to the unrest was interesting. The usual mystery men were invoked. If not the Afghanistan 'insurrectionists', well then 'professional agitators'. It was also quickly asserted that the student argument somehow fell (un-debated) ,because a few of their number had resorted to vigorous measures outside the law (of peaceful protest). The authorities seemed genuinely shocked and even apprehensive. Which rather shows we need more of the same.

CHAPTER 6

DEMOCRACY, LAW AND CONSTITUTION

NOTES

*   1.   Warburton, Nigel, Philosophy: The Basics, Chapter 3. Routledge, London, Second edition first published 1995.

*   2.   Saward, Michael, The Terms of Democracy, Blackwell, Oxford, 1998.

     3.   Dean, Jodi, 'Zizek's Politics', Routledge, London, 2006.

     4.   Estlund, D, 'Making Truth Safe for Democracy', in Copp, D, Hampton, J. and Roemer, J.E. (eds), The Idea of Democracy, Cambridge University Press, 1993.

*   5.   Graham, Gordon, The Case against the Democratic State, Societas, Imprint Academic, Thorverton, UK, 2002.

     6.   Whyte, Jamie, Bad Thoughts: A Guide to Clear Thinking, Corvo Books, 2003.

*   7.   Honore, Tony, About Law: An Introduction, Oxford University Press, 1995.

     8.   Kennedy, Helena, Just Law, Vintage, Random House, London, 2005.

*   9.   Coles, Joanne, and Reynolds, Jane, Constitutional and Administrative Law, Hodder Arnold, London, 2nd Edn., 2006.

*   10.   Bogdanor, Vernon, The New British Constitution, Hart Publishing Ltd., Oxford, 2009.

     11.   King, Anthony, The British Constitution, Oxford University Press, 2009.

     12   Obama, Barack, The Audacity of Hope, Canongate Books Ltd, Edinburgh, 2007.

CHAPTER 6

DEMOCRACY, LAW AND CONSTITUTION

13.   Riddell, Mary, 'Our society is indeed broken - but at the top, not the bottom', Daily Telegraph, 9/4/09.

14.   Johnston, Philip, 'What happened to Westminster', The Daily Telegraph, 11/5/09.

15.   Heywood, Andrew, Politics, Palgrave, Basingstoke second edition 2002.

16.   Mansfield, Michael, Memoirs of a Radical Lawyer, Bloomsbury, London, 2009.

17.   Commission on Scottish Devolution (Calman), Serving Scotland Better: Scotland and the United Kingdom In the 21st Century, June 2009.

CHAPTER 7

CENTRAL GOVERNMENT AND DEMOCRATIC DEFICITS

Introduction

The European Union

The Crown

The House of Lords

Political Parties

The Prime Minister

The Cabinet and its Office

Ministers and Departments

The Speaker

Members of Parliament

The Media

Reform

CHAPTER 7

CENTRAL GOVERNMENT AND DEMOCRATIC DEFICITS

Introduction

We have seen in the previous chapter how glaring constitutional deficiencies seriously undermine any realistic claims for the United Kingdom to be regarded as a functioning democracy, given that its citizens in general count for so little. The next task is to sketch out and evaluate the various organs of central government. Is it the well-designed and smoothly-oiled machine that most of us would like it to be?

The treatment starts by a first look at the European Union, since the United Kingdom is but a member of this body, whose laws are sovereign over us, although this fact will come as a shock to many.

The European Union

Europe, and membership of it, poses numerous further responsibilities and problems for the UK citizen, if he did but know it. There are some 492 million people in 27 member countries in the European Union, with others, such as Turkey, a vast nation with a potentially Islamic government, having also applied [1].

European Union political parties do not really equate with those in the United Kingdom, but in 2007 the broadly Conservative, or right -wing elements, formed the largest group, followed by Socialists, Liberals, and a significant number of Greens.

As at 2007 the United Kingdom had 78 seats in the European Parliament, the same number as France and Italy. Germany had most, with 99, and the overall total was 785.

In the European Council, France, Germany, Italy, and the United Kingdom each had the maximum votes, 29 out of a total of 345. The larger a country's population the more its votes, but there was a weighting towards favouring nations with lower populations also.

CHAPTER 7

CENTRAL GOVERNMENT AND DEMOCRATIC DEFICITS

The political structure of the European Union has the European Parliament, an elected body composed of MEPs from each member state, and the European Commission, a civil service bureaucracy. The most important other bodies are the Council of the European Union and the European Court of Justice. The Council (which used to be called the Council of Ministers) has representatives of each state. These are sent by government and change according to subject-matter. The Council is the law maker, with Parliament playing a second-chamber amending role, whereas the Commission drafts the legislation and acts as the executive, implementing policy.

Parliament in theory controls the commission, but not in reality, although it does approve the EU's annual budget. The European Union's finances are reportedly in a dubious shape, with repeated refusals by the auditors to sign approval to the published accounts. Their probity is often in doubt.

Note a fundamental difference between the EU and UK governments: in Europe it is the serving officers in the European Commission who initiate and draft legislation, not the politicians. It is also the same bureaucracy that implements policies, and programmes, exercising management and control, and deploys the budget, which are not the roles of departments of state under ministerial direction, as they are in the United Kingdom.

The founding document for the European Union was the Treaty of Rome back in 1958 when the originating nations were France and Germany. In the years since then there has been a complex history of attempted constitutional reform, including notably the Maastricht Treaty agreed in 1992, then the Lisbon Treaty, finally ratified by the last country in 2009, unanimity being a requirement for its adoption.

The Lisbon Treaty had the effect of centralising more powers, member states will have weaker powers to veto EU laws, and a European Foreign Office has been created for the first time, with embassies around the world. The prospect of the EU signing its own international treaties moved closer.

The current scope of the European Union's activities is vast and covered by around twenty policy committees. These are concerned with many issues relevant to our daily lives, including the environment, public

CHAPTER 7

CENTRAL GOVERNMENT AND DEMOCRATIC DEFICITS

health, food safety, consumer protection, fisheries, gender equality, agriculture and rural development, culture and education, employment and social affairs, as well as civil liberties.

Their work also encompasses international trade, economic affairs, transport, regional development, energy, industry, and foreign affairs.

The purposes of the European Union are described in the advertising literature as: *"Security, stability, and prosperity"*, beyond, presumably, anything that an individual nation could hope to achieve on its own. Now arguments still rage about the desirable purposes of the European Community, be it a trading and economic group of nations, or a federal government of Europe, perhaps even an assembly for collective defence. Europhiles have a variety of positions, ranging from retention of national sovereignty in all important areas of law, to Europe as a complete political entity subsuming constituent nations apart from their cultural differences.

Be under no illusions: the European Union is far from being a loose affiliation of independent nations in intention. Crucially, all the major parties represented there believe in the same goal - federalism. They want full integration, a European constitution, a common foreign policy, all undermining the sovereignty of their constituent countries. What may have started as a small number of nations clubbing together over a few mutual interests has moved a long way away. Is this what United Kingdom citizens want? It would seem rather unlikely.

A fundamental problem exists in relation to the law, now that United Kingdom is subject to European Law. This is owing to there being a major rift in the way continental legal systems and the English have evolved (2).

In this country we pass laws in statutes. After a while they can overlap, be mutually inconsistent, and lack overall coherence. Attempts at "consolidation", or tidying up the mess, are themselves unsystematic, and only occur from time to time. Just as the law lags behind technology, and, indeed, behind society in general, so do consolidation exercises. Often our laws are badly framed, drafted in a hurry by inexperienced junior lawyers at political whim, and unclear.

CHAPTER 7

CENTRAL GOVERNMENT AND DEMOCRATIC DEFICITS

The interpretation of the courts plods along, case by case, as the law just happens to be tested, so we may wait years for enlightenment as to their practical meaning, and the outcomes can be quite unpredictable. 'Common law' is formulated by the judges' elite. It is to a considerable extent unwritten, a very unsatisfactory state of affairs for those outside the profession.

Typically, in an English court, the lawyers will search for a 'precedent'. If there has been a similar case, what was decided there is likely to be very influential in the present one (whatever the quality of the judgement and however long ago).

By contrast, Continental law, often called 'civil law', sets out in written "codes", devised by academic lawyers, not politicians, the main principles of each branch of law within which further legislation must fit. These codes at least attempt to be comprehensive and to be easily understood. And the general principles have great influence over interpretation when cases come to court. Then continentals will tend to look at the facts, find out who suffered damage, who was at fault, and whether the fault caused the damage. The approach is much more scientific and more likely to uncover the truth.

So it may seem somewhat bizarre to the layman that with the United Kingdom being in the European Union, and laws being passed there which have force within the United Kingdom, we have two fundamentally alien systems of law, and approaches to laws. But then democratic ideals require democratic methods. And there is nothing remotely democratic about the Dickensian autocracy of the English judiciary.

Regarding the law of the European Union, the reluctance to come to terms with it in the United Kingdom is seen at all levels, despite the fact that it binds us in many areas transcending national sovereignty. It is estimated that over three-quarters of our laws are now passed in Brussels. For years the government of the day has played on perceived public sympathy by asserting our 'national sovereignty' and being vague on the very great extent to which this has been supplanted by rule from the European Union.

CHAPTER 7

CENTRAL GOVERNMENT AND DEMOCRATIC DEFICITS

A serious loophole for non-compliance by a member state with European Law appears at the level of 'secondary' legislation: that is, those subordinate to the 'primary' law of the main Treaties. Whilst there are 'regulations', which have general and direct, binding application in full in all member states, there are also 'directives', where the choice of form and methods of implementation are left to individual countries to decide for themselves. The latter are a source of much abuse, both wilful and through ignorance, where the equally binding directives are flouted in practice. The United Kingdom government redrafts them into its own language, which can conveniently wander from the original intent. A prominent example was that of DNA databases. In 2008 the European Court of Human Rights ruled out as illegal the indefinite retention on databases of the DNA of innocent people, a practice undertaken presumably on the off-chance that some of them might offend in the future, and despite the fact that arrested suspects routinely have DNA samples taken. The government's predictable response was to disagree with the ruling and propose a compromise of retaining the DNA of the innocent for up to twelve years instead. The Commons Leader even accused those opposed to the measure as being "against justice".

So does Joe Citizen fare any better when he fails to find justice at home and seeks it instead via the European Court?

Protocol 14 was introduced into European Law early in 2010, partly as a matter of expediency (3). There were so many cases backlogged in the European court of human rights that something had to be done. The answer was to have weak cases filtered out by a reviewing judge and no system of appeal.

But there was another intention. Protocol 14 gave the Committee of Ministers greater powers over member states reluctant to comply with court rulings. The previous position was that a United Kingdom citizen who won his case in Strasbourg would have to take it all the way up through the domestic courts to the United Kingdom Supreme Court, and the domestic law, even though contrary to European Law, would still be applied to other litigants. Protocol 14 would allow the Committee of Ministers to refer the case back to the European Court, who could in theory enforce sanctions against the United Kingdom government.

CHAPTER 7

CENTRAL GOVERNMENT AND DEMOCRATIC DEFICITS

Regarding finances, Coleman indicated in 2002 that each English citizen was paying around £450 per year for membership (4).   Although some money is gained by England from the European Union, every £1 cost the English taxpayer £4.15, and the money received is allocated for expenditure on specific objects decided by the European Union.

What needs to be borne in mind is the fact that the United Kingdom government only has a very limited say in regard to the funding it is required to put in and is allowed to take out. EEC project funding is bid for by local areas in the different countries and regions according to preset criteria, and is competitive, so there are no guarantees of success.

The European Union is frequently talked up as the international organisation that can have the clout individual European countries lack. When it comes to the economy, though, what happens when the richer nations in the community are suffering recession, or even modest growth? If there are weak economies within the European family of nations, and there probably always will be, there will be a pressure, possibly an onus, on the stronger to bale them out. Even if these countries fail to take the recommended austerity measures. That happened in reality during 2010 with Greece and there was an enormous reluctance on the part of Germany in particular, to provide the needed aid. In April 2010 the Greek national debt was branded by Standard and Poor, the respected credit rating agency, as no better a risk than junk bonds! Is this the kind of financial stability and international obligation that the United Kingdom wants, or needs?

So what of the public's rights and involvement? The constitution process of treaty agreement has always been riven by controversy, not least because some nations have given their citizens voting rights via referenda, whereas others, like the United Kingdom, have not.

The United Kingdom joined what was then known as 'The Common Market' in 1973. The people were not consulted prior to this momentous step by the then Conservative Government of Edward Heath, but a referendum was held in 1975! Although they voted two to one in favour of staying in, the people did not really have much democratic scope. For all three main political parties were in favour of retaining membership.

CHAPTER 7

CENTRAL GOVERNMENT AND DEMOCRATIC DEFICITS

There was no radical alternative movement to rally around. Since then, major constitutional reforms have occurred, notably the Maastricht and Lisbon treaties, without any public consultation, even though many politicians are now opposed to membership, including much of the Conservative party. It is usual for the government of the day to play down the significance of the new treaties so as not to alarm, or perhaps even interest, the public.

What citizens need to be able to evaluate is the nature and quality of the governments they elect and pay for, be they national or European. At the present time the latter cannot be done for the European Union owing to the lack of available information and the remoteness of the representation. In effect the MEPs, each covering a vast constituency, are not accountable to the electorate. Yes, they will write back and give out information, but they have to be asked first. There are no required reporting processes, few forums for discussion in comparison with the national scene. That at least will have to change, even if most citizens in the United Kingdom, if not actual Europhobes, are (dangerously) apathetic about EU politics.

When it comes to elections for political representatives the democratic deficits of the European Union are all too obvious. In June 2009 Britain was asked to vote. Very few parties bothered to send out election leaflets in the author's area. Unnamed people decided who would be the candidates in each party. We knew nothing about them. They had never been seen on the doorsteps, hardly surprising since the constituencies are huge regions, not closely-knit towns and their hinterlands. Local television showed little interest. When the votes were cast publicly unaccountable people behind the scenes had already decided a batting order of candidates to receive them. If the party managed to secure a large enough proportion of the total votes, their second choice would then be given an allocation. So in no real sense were the voters choosing actual people. It was all about parties.

So what is the role of MEPs, those shadowy figures who nominally represent our 'regions', but are usually very little known there by the ordinary citizens of the United Kingdom? Well, they spend a lot of time sitting on one or more of the many policy committees. MEPs also work

CHAPTER 7

CENTRAL GOVERNMENT AND DEMOCRATIC DEFICITS

in the United Kingdom in their regional constituencies, and periodically vote on proposed legislation in Brussels.

Financial abuses by MEPs may even be worse than in the United Kingdom because, not only is public scrutiny of the claims banned, but also they do not render internal accounts for most of their expenses. They are generously paid by average standards.

Are MEPs worthwhile? Do we get value for money? The last word will be left to Jeffrey Titford, one of their number:

> *"Individual MEPs are not an essential, nor even an important, part (of the European Union)...Oratory plays no part. Reason plays no part. Our votes cannot change a directive. We are there merely to furnish an illusion of democracy, providing a veneer to conceal what is a fundamentally undemocratic process".*

In conclusion, then, what is the United Kingdom citizen to make of the European Union? If he believes in national sovereignty he is likely to want out. Even if he does go along with the concept of individual nations disappearing into a massive European one, he will not know, and may not be able to estimate for many years, whether the trade-off will be worth it in terms of enhanced benefits.

If he puts participative, or even representative democracy high among his list of values, he will see the shortcomings of Europe to be on an even bigger scale than at home, with prospects for continuing corruption accordingly at least as great.

If he worries about the financial subsidy burdens of membership to our small nation he will be wary of plans for continued expansion to include very large and some economically less well-developed countries.

And the many legal and political incompatibilities and anomalies will be of concern, as he struggles to know his rights and obligations, and to lead a free existence without threat from the governments that purport to safeguard his interests and well-being.

CHAPTER 7

CENTRAL GOVERNMENT AND DEMOCRATIC DEFICITS

The Crown

Within the United Kingdom there are still important constitutional organs to do with royalty - namely, the Crown and the Royal Prerogative (5). It is unfortunately necessary to distinguish the two owing to historical developments.

The 'prerogative' is just what is left of the power of the Queen and it comes from the common law, not from statutes. The term is very far from appropriate because the Queen does not exercise the prerogative. By that unsatisfactory concept 'convention', these powers are used by the government, often by the prime minister in person. They cover crucial areas like defence, foreign affairs, and justice. The Crown, on the other hand, has powers derived from statute law.

Now, for the protection of the people it is clear that prerogative decisions should be challengeable in the courts, typically by the process of judicial review. Yet the law lords, who decide such matters, do not agree on which prerogative powers can or cannot be judicially reviewed. Decided cases have suggested that only minor uses may be, but not the big issues, such as national security, or going to war. Obviously the position needs rectifying. Whatever should be the law it is palpably a nonsense that even the experts do not know. It inevitably results in a serious lack of public accountability.

Until 1947 the situation regarding the Crown in law was wholly unsatisfactory to the people, since historically 'the King could do no wrong'. He wore an evil cloak. This meant that the Crown was mostly immune from legal liability, as the King's exemption also applied to any powers he exercised through is servants, whatever their individual liability might be. The Crown could not be sued for tort (civil wrongs). It could not be sued in contract either, unless the Attorney-General allowed a petition of right. Although wrongdoing by Crown servants was actionable, unless the Crown stood behind them to pay any damages, a plaintiff was unlikely to receive proper compensation.

However, the Crown Proceedings Act, 1947 brought in reforms designed to meet public criticism of the injustices that arose. In tort the Crown is

CENTRAL GOVERNMENT AND DEMOCRATIC DEFICITS

now vicariously liable for civil wrongs committed by its servants, it has employers' liability, and that stemming from property ownership or occupation. But there are still serious exemptions. For instance, the Crown is only liable under statutes that specifically say it is. Until modern times this did not happen. Now most new statutes do, but there is no constitutional safeguard, another example of bad lawmaking since the framework does not guarantee consistency. Anomalies will persist for years to come.

A further major loophole is that the Crown is not liable for torts committed outside the United Kingdom. Cases will commonly involve the Armed Forces. The Crown is in a strong position generally here because it has the legal power to revive its immunity in time of war or national emergency. There is also 'combat immunity', under which no duty of care is owed by the Crown to its military personnel in active combat. Exceptions are policing and peacekeeping military operations, also likely to be subject to liability under the Human Rights Act, 1998, so it could become a legal battleground.

It is sometimes claimed that the dignity of the monarch has to be preserved, so he is conveniently immune against actions in tort in his personal capacity.

The Crown does these days have liability in contract law, except again that actions against the monarch in person require permission via the quaint old 'petition' procedure. The Crown tries to settle matters out of court, by negotiation, or arbitration, but a sticky area is that of contractual obligations as employer. Scandalously, military personnel are employed at the pleasure of the Crown and the relationship is not contractual. They could be dismissed at any time without warning, which may be news to the grieving relatives of soldiers wasted in the Afghan campaign. At least normal employment law, such as it is, protects civil servants.

It is said that the Courts are willing to restrict the privileges and immunities of the Crown. Conway v. Rimmer in 1968 actually removed the Crown's absolute right to withhold evidence. Yet why do they have to operate in an area where historical curiosities remain within the law, which the Crown may or may not decide to take advantage of? Where is

CHAPTER 7

CENTRAL GOVERNMENT AND DEMOCRATIC DEFICITS

the political resolve to sweep away the inconsistencies and drag the whole institution into the modern world? Assuming we still need it, which is highly dubious. There is a lot of inertia, even complacency. Concerning the monarchy itself, even minor reforms are considered as if revolutionary steps.

To illustrate, in 2009 the distinguished journalist, William Rees-Mogg wrote an article in the Times in all seriousness about the Act of Settlement, 1701, which he described as "*a central constitutional statue; it determines the succession to the Crown of England*" (6). He claimed it as a success, although noting its venerable age. He credited it with helping to develop what he amazingly described as a "*democratic monarchy*", not evidently a contradiction in terms.

The Act of Settlement discriminates by religion against Catholics, as it does not allow for a Catholic, or a person married to one, to become monarch. It also discriminates by gender against women. Although a royal princess can attain the throne, only in the event of no male heir. And a younger brother has precedence over an older sister. The Act is thus in conflict with human rights legislation.

Rees-Mogg nevertheless argued against reform, at least for many years to come. He pointed out that the whole Commonwealth would have to agree on any change for it to come about, and would be likely to see some wavering countries like Australia off into republicanism. He claimed that women and Catholics are not too bothered about the position, and so he seemed to elevate political expediency above moral principle.

Simon Heffer, of the right-leaning Daily Telegraph, wrote a piece in May 2009, when he argued that the monarchy still had a "vital role to play" in rebuilding British politics. He first suggested that the Queen had been active in private by providing advice to the prime minister following the public reaction after the MPs' expenses disclosures. He believed (without putting forward evidence) that what the Queen said would have reflected the mood of her subjects. Why, given her rather different background and position in life? And if she had said something quite otherwise that would also have been consistent with her present constitutional entitlements.

CHAPTER 7

CENTRAL GOVERNMENT AND DEMOCRATIC DEFICITS

The fact that she is able to say what she likes in private, with a view to influencing events, and without any public scrutiny, ought to be unacceptable if we have any pretence to being a democracy. According to Walter Bagehot, in his 1867 book 'The English Constitution', and henceforth by the unsubstantiated power of the tradition he created, the monarch has *"three rights - the right to be consulted, the right to encourage, the right to warn"*.

But why should the monarchy have any rights, even if allowed to exist at all, in a democratic state? How are the two in any way compatible? And what if the Queen's judgement was faulty, or her motives other than those of public duty? What could the citizen do about it, even if he was allowed to know?

Heffer makes another extraordinary claim, which is clearly a contradiction: he said that the *"monarch is guarantor"* of *"our democratic institutions"*. The point of the piece seemed to be really that he wanted a new government, a Conservative one, and was rather hoping that the Queen had advised Brown to dissolve Parliament. He went so far as to concede that if she did not warn in such extreme circumstances, there would be no point in having a "constitutional monarchy".

It is tempting to say that the Crown is an irrelevance, a mere privileged quirk of British life which will disappear if society ever matures, and is meanwhile mostly harmless.

Some of the flummery, it is true, is laughable genuflection. There is the demeaning custom, for which there is no warrant save to acknowledge that the monarch is somehow superior, in the weekly practice for the Prime Minister to call on the Queen and report when she is in London. Bagehot in his day called it "dignified", yet it is surely sycophantic.

Anthony Howard, the former editor of the Spectator, and distinguished political commentator, described on Radio 4 the convention of the year's planned government legislation being read out by the Queen in her annual speech in the House of Commons as a "feudal farce".

There are dangerous nonsenses about the monarchy. The Queen could in

CENTRAL GOVERNMENT AND DEMOCRATIC DEFICITS

principle refuse to assent to a law passed by Parliament. The last time that happened was in 1707, so it is statistically rather improbable, but it is offensive in principle and could do real damage if ever invoked.

A more feasible worry is that in a hung parliament, the monarch could become quite a player behind the scenes, unless legally written out. To whom would he/she be accountable through these secret acts?

What is also not known, and clearly needs to be sorted out sooner rather than later, is under what circumstances, if any, the monarch can herself take back her legal powers of prerogative, and what would be the extent of them? Could she, for example, actually dismiss the government herself and call for a general election if the government was behaving 'unconstitutionally'. But then, how on earth could she tell?

In all it is a sad reflection on what a rum old backwater the United Kingdom has become in many important respects that the Crown continues to exist at all. Supported at great cost by the taxpayer, it is still not constitutionally irrelevant, despite the appalling behaviour that generations of royals and their families have displayed and continue to demonstrate (with the ironically honourable current exception of the present Queen). The obviously marginal value of having this bunch of privileged oiks nominally preside over us is talked up by armies of sentimental traditionalists, who weep ostentatiously at their funerals.

The House of Lords

Some national constitutions are 'unicameral', with one legislating chamber, and others, such as the United Kingdom, are 'bicameral', with two.(7) Although the House of Commons is the main legislating chamber here, where all the elected MPs deliberate, the House of Lords has a secondary and related role. An unresolved issue is whether to continue being bicameral. Almost every country that has such a system is unhappy with it, and there is endless debate about what reforms would be the most desirable. In looking at the problem here, there is, of course, the theoretical opportunity of using some kind of democratic template. Abolition would be the simplest structural solution, although it requires

CENTRAL GOVERNMENT AND DEMOCRATIC DEFICITS

some adjustments to the way the House of Commons functions. It is also the least likely because of the deeply entrenched forces of tradition and vested interest.

The House of Lords in its current rôles is supposed to function mainly to scrutinise draft legislation from the Commons and to suggest modifications to it as appropriate. Supposedly non-controversial legislation may also have its 'first reading' there to take working pressure off the lower house. Ministers could be appointed from its ranks (and often are). And it is to act as a 'constitutional watchdog', to keep an eye on government and squeal if it misbehaves.

Traditional membership has developed in an odd sort of way. Originally, the monarch would have advisers whom he rewarded with land and titles. That is the origin of the House of Lords, where their hereditary descendants sat as of right, the peerage having passed down the generations. There were over 750 of them.

The Life Peerages Act, 1958, gave governments the ability to create life peers to sit in the Lords, but without a hereditary passage of the privilege to their offspring. Frequently, this is used to provide further political involvement to former Commons MPs, but it is also a way of promoting non-elected people into the machinery of government, an undemocratic power if ever there was one.

As well as hereditary and life peers, the Lords also contains 'law lords', who are senior judges, and the bishops and archbishops of the established Anglican Church.

The conditions of 'employment' of members of the House of Lords have generated a good deal of heat in the years of the Brown government because of the behaviour of some of their number.

They are not paid a salary, unlike MPs, but receive a generous daily allowance just for turning up and signing in. The Lords were effectively non-accountable and that had to change without delay. As with the Commons, the House of Lords suffered grievous blows to its reputation because of an utter failure properly to regulate the conduct of its members. Several peers early in 2009 were exposed as receiving large consultancy fees, in addition to their normal remuneration as members, from firms seeking to buy influence. Some were alleged to have sought to amend Bills, or try and initiate legislation favourable to their 'sponsors'. This threw into turmoil both their role and that of lobbyists. It was not helped by the brazen behaviour of some of the accused, who claimed to have done nothing wrong. But their argument was largely on the basis that they were acting within what turned out to be very thin rules indeed. It also emerged into the public domain awareness that even if they had transgressed what rules there were, no constitutional sanctions existed. They could not be suspended or expelled, nor could their titles or ill-gotten gains be taken away. Apologize was all that an honourable member could be required to do.

Hurriedly, the Justice Minister announced that he would bring forward proposals for reform and punishment..... .

When the massive extent of unseemly financial conduct was exposed in Parliament it was an amazing indictment of our so-called justice system that only one peer, Lord Hanningfield, was charged with criminal behaviour, the accusations relating to six alleged instances of dishonestly submitting expense claims to which he knew he was not entitled.

To grasp the extent of the gravy train, it emerged that for the period of the 2008/9 financial year, no fewer than 103 peers had claimed over £50,000 in expenses. Some hardly ever even contribute in the debates and there have been many suspicions about attendance fiddles because the recording arrangements are so lax. Some scams are actually built in, like the rule which allows attendance claims for forty of the days a year when the Lords is not sitting.

The Senior Salaries Review Body reviewed Lords expenses in late 2009 and made a raft of sensible recommendations for reform. Unfortunately, the constitutional machinery to introduce and enforce them is as usual non-existent.... .

Dishonest attempts to avoid removal of what ordinary people will regard as unfair privileges is still going on in the House of Lords. Wherever you

CENTRAL GOVERNMENT AND DEMOCRATIC DEFICITS

see self-regulation there is temptation. A blatant illustration occurred in February 2009 when they changed their rules, thus allowing peers the right to designate which of their residences would be classed as the main one.

The Director of Public Prosecutions publicly expressed disapproval, as he was unable to charge Baroness Uddin with criminal conduct when she designated as her main residence a house in Kent she rarely visited, despite having lived at her family home in London for ten years. By such device she was able to 'legitimately' claim and receive more than £100,000 in allowances. So, in spite of the fact that the Commons is now externally regulated by an independent Parliamentary Standards Authority, the Lords has resisted attempts to make it subject.

Paradoxically, in the face of those who may still clamour for appropriate and effective reform of the Lords, politicians can argue that much has been done already.

Some inroads have been made into House of Lords reform, albeit like pulling teeth. Significantly, the House of Lords Act of 1999 removed all 'hereditary peers', apart from the obvious number of 92! It is claimed that the triumph of vested interest is only temporary and that they will all go eventually. Quite simply, for the sake of public credibility they have to.

Most of the Lords are now 'life peers', so their membership dies with them and cannot be passed on to progeny. However, they are political appointees, voting and sitting in parties, with relatively few being independent. It is hard to see how that arrangement is in the public interest. In practical terms, it serves mostly as a vehicle to smooth the passage of government bills, not improve them.

In 2000 a Royal Commission ('Wakeham') reported with proposals for 'reform' of the Lords. Various white papers followed, with government proposals. Characteristically, the Conservative Wakeham was not radical. He favoured a second chamber appointed wholly or mostly, and a majority of the Commons agreed with him. So there seemed to be little imminent prospect of elections. Patronage would probably continue

CENTRAL GOVERNMENT AND DEMOCRATIC DEFICITS

unabated under a system of appointment. Government would no doubt seek to control the choices as ever.

After most hereditary peers were removed, the second stage of proposed reform was to come in March 2007, when the Commons then voted for an elected upper house, four-fifths or in total. However, progress towards the stated goal is likely to be slow, if the size of the obstacles is anything to go by. Brown said in March 2009, two years later, that plans would be laid "soon".

Even as it stood, the achievement to change the composition of the Lords was very significant, because all through the twentieth century two thirds of the members had been hereditary peers. The great bulk of them being Conservatives, there was a perennial Tory majority in the upper house, quite irrespective of the voting preferences of the people for a party to form the elected government.

When, in July 2009 a Constitutional Reform Bill was put before Parliament, it proposed to give life peers the right to resign from the House of Lords, something not previously possible, although hereditary peers have been able to do so since 1963. The measure was cynically seen in some quarters as smoothing the way for the unelected Lord Mandelson to become prime minister. In fact, a rather important clause proposed the end of the hereditary principle. After Blair's first reforms of the Lords, some 92 hereditary peers were left. Amazingly, if one died a by-election was held to provide a replacement and keep the numbers constant. That custom would cease under the Bill, so that the hereditaries would gradually die out. As matters stood members could then all be appointed by some kind of political patronage.

Further reforms have occurred in relation to the Law Lords. Traditionally, certain lawyers who are members of the House of Lords sit to form the country's highest court. They presided in judgement on cases referred by the Court of Appeal. Note this conflict of interest. The same lawyers who form an important part of the judiciary deciding cases were also members of the forum which seeks to amend prospective legislation passed to it by the House of Commons.

CHAPTER 7

CENTRAL GOVERNMENT AND DEMOCRATIC DEFICITS

The Constitutional Reform Act 2005 made provision for the House of Lords to be replaced as highest court in the land by a new, independent Supreme Court. That was needed to enhance the separation of powers.

The Supreme Court was duly set up in 2009, tellingly just across the road from the House of Lords, and heard its first case in October. But it still consisted of three Law Lords, judges from the House of Lords, and appointed by the Lord Chancellor, himself a Cabinet Minister.

It will therefore be important to watch how the so-called independence of the Supreme Court can develop from an origin of old-fashioned political patronage and whether future appointments to vacancies will see the judiciary at large responsible for the choice, according to publicly available criteria that would satisfy employment law and personnel practice in ordinary walks of life. Superficially, of course, the Court will have a more friendly and approachable public face than before. The population will be allowed into the building, for instance, and will be able to play law games on their computers!

Regarding future reforms, there is surely the prior question to be addressed as to whether we need a second chamber at all. The case for it only convinces on the assumption that it can act as an effective corrective to the totalitarian, and sometimes tyrannical, decisions of government. To do this it may even need a new power of veto, perhaps when government seeks to transgress a cardinal constitutional principle. Clearly, a workable balance is required, and that is a very difficult piece of machinery to devise.

If the obstacle could be overcome in practice would its possible purposes suffice as a justification? One function could be to bring professional expertise and advice to bear, perhaps through select committees, which the 'career politicians' of the Commons lack. We have mentioned its role to act as a check on the power of the first chamber, a delaying conscience which asks the Commons to think again at times of controversy. Subjecting proposed legislation to detailed scrutiny is difficult and time-consuming - something which the Lords could aid the government with. More controversially, a second chamber might help the media scrutinize the executive, which is, of course, the government in management mode.

CHAPTER 7

CENTRAL GOVERNMENT AND DEMOCRATIC DEFICITS

To consider whether we should have a second chamber it is also necessary to look at its possible composition. For a democracy the legislature should somehow be representative of the people. If there already is a 'representative' first chamber, the second one needs to be representative in a different way, if that is realistically possible. Geographical divisions are one commonly used method, although, of course, not in the United Kingdom. A danger is that local politicians would predominate. There is another prospect - specialist expertise in the key fields of human endeavour.

Reform of the House of Lords requires a systematic alteration not only of its membership, however, which is where public emphasis has tended to be placed, but also of its powers.

Concerning reforms of membership, if the body is to be retained (at the public's choice, not that of the establishment), much has to be put right.

For example, there is a continuing legal right for the 26 Church of England bishops, as a privileged narrow interest group, to retain membership, in a country where most people do not attend places of worship, and where there are many other religious bodies, Roman Catholics notably, in numerical terms. The country is statistically secular, yet the Lords has no formal representation for agnostics and atheists as it must. An appropriately democratic response would be disestablish the Anglican Church, removing its unhealthily close relationship with the State, and provide instead a handful of seats for the different main denominations. Of course, a powerful case could be made out that religious interference in law-making tends to have unfortunate results for those on the receiving end, so their contribution needs to be kept small and proportionate, if it is even relevant and legitimate.

Other unwholesome patronage has also developed. Life peers are created by government, enjoying the privileges of membership on the basis of cronyism with the prime minister. Such people only hold office for life, and mercifully, do not pass on the office to their offspring, but they can exert an influence which is difficult to justify by their selection process. A notable illustration is Lord Mandelson. As plain Peter Mandelson, he was forced to resign as MP and minister under Blair, after a series of

CHAPTER 7

CENTRAL GOVERNMENT AND DEMOCRATIC DEFICITS

scandals, but was later brought back by Brown to be a cabinet minister sitting in the House of Lords. The government also uses its appointments to the Lords to manipulate the conduct of business and to ensure powerful advocacy sympathetic to its causes, as well as stacking the second chamber with numerically strong support. It goes without saying that all these practices and their ilk would have to cease, and indeed be constitutionally barred, under a corruption-free second chamber regime.

Vincent Cable, the Liberal Democrat MP, was clear about life peerages that "they should not be a perk for public office". William Hague, a former Tory leader, made the assertion that some MPs retired to become life peers, then made no contribution in the Lords. So there ought to be mechanisms for evaluating performance, rendering peers accountable, then unseating the unfit. And these would have to include those non-domiciled life peers who refused to pay United Kingdom taxes on all their earnings. Titles should be stripped, too, not kept as badges of status and privilege by the disgraced.

Imagine that we had instead an entirely elected second chamber, suitably renamed, with representatives of all the main fields of human endeavour, as nominated and voted for by their respective professional and other parent bodies.

There would still be a need to produce a suitable balance between the House of Commons and the House of Lords, so that prospective legislation is thoroughly and expertly examined and appropriately amended, but without holding up the process of legislating disproportionately.

Until 1911, when the Parliament Act removed it, the Lords had the power of veto over 'primary' legislation - the statutes. It still has an absolute veto over 'secondary' legislation, such as statutory instruments and regulations, frequently tabled by Ministers concerning the operations of their departments. These oil the wheels of government and in many cases, such as in local government, provide officers with detailed instructions on how to carry out national policies.

Under the so-called Salisbury Convention the role of the House of Lords

CENTRAL GOVERNMENT AND DEMOCRATIC DEFICITS

was seen as ensuring that the government's legislative plans were mandated, not opposed, but again the folly is shown of relying on a convention, which can easily be breached, instead of a definite constitutional law. Not surprisingly, after 1999 when the majority of hereditary peers had been removed from the Lords, the House became much more openly critical. It also seems likely that a professionalized membership would come in time to demand significantly important roles.

Undeniably, there is a fundamental problem in making the House of Lords both democratic, representative, and effective, and it is one that many nations have struggled with.

Concerning composition, some elusive principle is required to provide a set of members who can be successful in their roles. Unfortunately, what categories we may need or could agree on remains a mystery once each of the rational suggestions have been made.

The fundamentally hereditary basis of peerages passing down the generations within an aristocratic family would never have had any place whatsoever in a real democracy. Merit does not enter into it. It is unjust, and in no way representative of society at large.

What is so undemocratic here, in the last analysis, is that the vast majority of the population find the House of Lords anathema, and yet the elected politicians neither abolish nor fundamentally reform it. In defying the will of the people, in effect, they display a complex mixture of incompetence and self-interest.

Regarding the method of choice, the people want the members to be elected, but are less trusting of political parties and politicians to do it. So how would an effective and agreeable mechanism be decided upon?

The public dilemma, again and again, is that whenever it feels government cannot be trusted, and major reforms are mooted, the task of implementation seems to fall, one way or another, to that very body. Nothing transcends it, either in constitutional theory or practice, and the more it talks about independent bodies being given the task and responsibility, the more it turns out that their members are political

CENTRAL GOVERNMENT AND DEMOCRATIC DEFICITS

poodles, or the terms of reference do not meet the case, or the body is purely advisory, anyway, and most of the deliberations go on behind closed doors and are little divulged.

To develop a totally elected chamber would require very careful monitoring by democrats to ensure fair play.   There are many fundamental and formidable issues that would have to be debated regarding the election process, such as how would candidates be chosen for consideration, and by whom, who would vote to elect them, for what term of office, what institutions and interest should we seek to have represented in the reformed House of Lords, what size ought it to be, and what proportions should the various groups enjoy and why? In particular, the political affiliations of all members would have to be carefully scrutinized.

Will it happen? A resigned constitutional adviser to the government said on Radio 4 in July 2009 that Lords reform "should be about combining democratic accountability with expertise and it won't be".

The incoming Coalition government immediately engaged in double-speak over constitutional reform proposals designed to reduce the number of Commons seats, and hence constituencies , to 600,by rather less than one tenth of their number. This was said to be in the democratic interest, by recasting constituencies of roughly equal population size. Yet at the same time , Prime Minister Cameron appointed no fewer than 53 new peers in the Lords, in order to bolster support for the Coalition in the upper chamber. It brought the size of the House of Lords to nearly 750,or 150 more than that of the senior body, the Commons itself. This was risible, the more so because of election promises to reduce the cost of politics.

When the Lords are observed in action as a collective, some apologists say they are independent in spirit ,dispassionate in judgement, and watchful to safeguard the ancient liberties of the people in the face of sometimes dictatorial government. They would claim credit during the Brown-Blair years for supporting principles such as trial by jury ,religious freedom of expression , and incarceration without trial. This may be so ,but it is not even a plausible theory to suggest that it results, as no other

CHAPTER 7

CENTRAL GOVERNMENT AND DEMOCRATIC DEFICITS

method could , from the appointment processes of inheritance and patronage.

Discussion next turns to the workings of the heart of the government, within the House of Commons itself. The view taken looks at various prominent organs or government, not comprehensively, but in order to appraise their effectiveness in broad terms. And, of course, to see their contributions to democracy, if any.

Political Parties

Perhaps the biggest anti-democratic practice of all is the party political system itself. So powerful is it that it effectively polarises the national, and usually local, debates along left wing and right wing lines. Nobody else gets a look-in for long. The parties themselves are held together by coercive practices from the whips which deny free speech and personal conscience in the interests of solidarity. If these are virtues at all, they are not democratic ones.

Commentators have remarked that the main party of opposition is not so much elected to office as the government of the day is defeated. Whatever the merits of the opposition seem to be, there is bound to be a credibility gap because they have not done the job. Therein lies a reluctance of the electorate. It has gelded liberalism in modern times at the national level because of it. The country has never trusted the Liberal Democrats to form an administration on their own. Nevertheless, there comes a point where the government has wreaked too many disappointments on too many people, so out they go, and people pray that the next lot are better (or at least, not as bad).

There is an idea that is sometimes appealed to by our politicians when they seek to defend some element of government policy currently under attack. They are then inclined to say that what they are doing is in keeping with their party manifesto at the general election. It is scarcely necessary to point out that for a member of the public to actually find one such manifesto, let alone all of them for the main parties, may in itself be quite an achievement. They are very unlikely to be down at the local newsagents, and rarely in practice figure at all prominently in an election campaign. What we get instead is increasingly broad-brush in approach,

CENTRAL GOVERNMENT AND DEMOCRATIC DEFICITS

dealing with vaguely-applicable principles within a cult of personality, centred on the party leaders.

Ruling parties after successful elections are apt to cite the manifesto as being what the voters have chosen, and accordingly credit it with being their mandate for action. When events render parts of the manifesto unfeasible, or the leadership simply decides to do something else, there is no shortage of creative excuses shy of admitting that the manifesto just might be flawed, or even lack relevance to the emerging problems of the day. What they rarely admit is that the manifesto is not a mandate.

And that, at heart, is what is unacceptable about political parties: they think they know best. As paternalistic guardians of the wisdom, they prejudge issues from some abstract and generalised standpoint. They also have the amazing gall to believe they should be given the right to impose their ideas on society, and the startling self-confidence to assume that they actually have the (extremely high order of) ability necessary to do so. When just before the 2010 General Election there was the prospect of a hung Parliament, the Tory and Labour parties inveighed against it, having the effrontery to admit they would find cooperation with the others difficult.

Political parties are also internally centrist in behaviour. The national leadership effectively calls the shots to the constituency parties even on local issues.

A further illustration that it will take more than a furore over expenses to really change such bedrock political behaviour is Labour's choice of Tristram Hunt as their candidate to fight the seat of the Stoke-on-Trent Central. The local Labour party constituency secretary announced his intention to stand in opposition as a protest: the government had produced the short-list for them and it did not contain a single local candidate. The Tories act in a similar way when it is expedient to do so.

What we have come to is a situation so accurately characterized by Professor King, namely, that on the whole people dislike both the major parties and their policies (8). In other words, the so-called 'two-party system', not admittedly by any means for the first time, has again become dysfunctional.

CHAPTER 7

CENTRAL GOVERNMENT AND DEMOCRATIC DEFICITS

One of the things people do not like is internal squabbling between factions within a party. They like them to be united ,or at least cooperative, and they have a suspicion of extremists. Political parties are haunted by the spectre of damage from division within their ranks. They seek to attain, or at least maintain the illusion of, what in an official dictatorship would be called 'solidarity'. The claim is, and the media support it, that a divided party is weak, unstable, and not fit to govern; or, at any rate, that the people will draw all these damning conclusions about them. Some would say that the state of affairs is evidence of a lack of political maturity within society. After all, in our everyday, largely politically uninvolved lives, do we not readily see that some of the most infuriating and misguided people are the ones who always know all the answers?

Another thing people do not like is the fact that there is no continuity when one party gains office and sets out reversing the actions of its predecessor. How can you plan ahead in such needless climates of uncertainty?

When both parties perceive that the public favour the middle ground, principled opposition to the government tends to reduce, so the public observe the spectacle of opposition for its own sake and are not impressed.

Commentators such as Peter Hitchens have drawn attention to decline in the 'adversarial politics' that used to characterize dealings between the main left and right parties on major issues. Now we are left with a Prime Minister's Question Time, which is ritualistic and showman-like in its staged disagreements. The parties struggle to distinguish themselves from each other's position, offering the public little alternative except of personality. As they both struggle to occupy the centre ground, conceived essential to their winning chances at a general election, they jettison interest in many an important question and become fixated on a dangerously narrow range of issues.

Naturally, the opposition has to characterize itself in a certain way to get in by default. Extremes, particularly of the left, are out. And so, both Blair in the 1990's and Cameron in the 2000's seemed to go to elaborate lengths to conceal specific policies and implementation plans from a hapless public. Strategists gave them a better chance if only the superficial and favourable aspects of their personalities were known.

Rather as with the American Presidential elections, speeches are made full of vague intent, sweeping generalizations, abstract principles, when not actively side-swiping at the opponents. There is, admittedly, undeniable risk in making generous promises ahead of knowing precisely what financial state of affairs you will inherit on assuming office, or what background events await. Yet the public are woefully short-changed, and seem resigned to being powerless to do anything about it.

So voters are constrained by a paucity of choice among invidious alternatives, each with their incompatible views of society and sterile philosophies. We have lurched and swung each way so often to little positive effect and much disappointment, underachievement, and disillusionment.

Virtually the only effective action the populace has so far taken has been to leave party membership in droves, or be resistant to joining in the first place.

A powerful argument for abolition of the parties does arise from their very low membership among the population at large. We are just not interested or committed enough to bother joining. Or it seems such an unsavoury preoccupation to have.

Yet another argument for their abolition is that nobody appears to have devised a fair and adequate way of funding the parties. The Conservatives always have more rich benefactors. The Labour Party has to rely mostly on undemocratic block donations from unions. The smaller parties always struggle financially. And it seems outrageous to pay the parties out of public funds when the public is at best apathetic about their value.

So this has precipitated funding crises. The manner of political responses is a further argument for abolishing the parties because various high-profile cases of corruption have been the result. Would-be donors have

CHAPTER 7

CENTRAL GOVERNMENT AND DEMOCRATIC DEFICITS

sought, quite illegally, to obtain favours for finance, usually of political preferment, abusing an already discredited system of 'honours'.

Michael Ashcroft, with the connivance of the Conservative political establishment, entered into an unsavoury and semantically deceptive arrangement in 2000 whilst living in Belize and representing them in the United Nations. He undertook to resign representation in exchange for a peerage in the House of Lords and "taking up permanent residence in the United Kingdom again". He then proceeded to become a very influential party adviser as Deputy Chairman, whilst also turning into their largest single financial donor. Unknown to citizens he retained 'non-domiciled' status for tax purposes. This is a convenient loophole whereby he was able to avoid paying tax in the United Kingdom on his considerable earnings abroad. So some at least of what he might have owed the exchequer found its way into party coffers instead. The matter blew wide open in early 2010 in the run-up to the general election as commentators and political opponents vied to expose how much of this marriage of convenience had been known to the Tory hierarchy and for how long. Lord Ashcroft and others were quick to point out that two of Labour's own, somewhat lesser donors, Lord Paul and Sir Ronald Cohen, were in the same position. Once it had been exposed, the Conservative Leader, David Cameron, called for a change in the law so that any member of either house must be treated as resident and 'domiciled' in the United Kingdom and pay tax accordingly. And so it goes.

Lord Hailsham, a former Conservative cabinet minister, wrote: *"if democracy, which demands a change of government from time to time, is condemned for ever to oscillate between two factions with opposing philosophies... , I cannot see much prospect for its future".* That was way back in 1978 and we are still enmeshed in the same rotten dilemma.

The Prime Minister

If we lived in a democracy wouldn't the Prime Minister be elected by the people and not by the MPs of the ruling party? When Tony Blair resigned as Prime Minister during the term of a Labour government with a strong majority in 2007, his successor, Gordon Brown, was 'chosen' by

CENTRAL GOVERNMENT AND DEMOCRATIC DEFICITS

the sitting Labour MPs in some dark process. They did not even have an internal election. He had been heir-apparent for so long that it surprised nobody. And he did not then call a general election to secure the people's mandate, because he did not have to and might have lost. There is no constitutional safeguard, as there should be, against this kind of totalitarianism.

Even worse, from the point of view of those of a republican disposition, is the fact that a conservative MP, Sir Alec Douglas-Home, became Prime Minister in 1963 when the Queen chose him. That happened because his party, then in government, could not agree on who should fill the vacancy! There was no suggestion of asking the people, of course. That would have seemed a strange course indeed to a non-elected monarch.

As we may recall, there have been many monarchs in English history who have been quite tyrannical and wielded awesome power. Much of that power is now vested in the Prime Minister today.

He is completely dominant at times of strong majority over the policy decisions of the government. And, as long as the government has a working majority in the Commons, the prime minister could decide the election time within the five year term. Members owe their appointments and tenure to him - the Cabinet, other ministers, and the party whips.

Other key appointments he either makes or sanctions include bishops, senior judges (where is the separation of powers here?), ambassadors to foreign countries, peers to sit in the House of Lords, and members of quangos.

Increasing use is made by the prime minister of another specific device for getting round democratic process. An unpopular figure and prime example is Lord Mandelson. A former MP, subject to several government sackings for being central to high-profile scandals, he was next made a life peer by Brown, after a brief interval, then helicoptered straight back into government, effectively in charge of the industry brief. He was far from alone. Another was Baroness Scotland, the Attorney General, famously fined for breaking her own law on immigration.

CHAPTER 7

CENTRAL GOVERNMENT AND DEMOCRATIC DEFICITS

Far too much is within the personal gift of the Prime Minister. He can, for instance, devise departments and their internal structures, creating posts of junior ministers and appointing by preferment, building up a coterie of non-elected personal advisers, unlikely to be, on recent performance, career civil servants, but outsiders chosen at his whim on made-up salaries paid from the public purse.

Special advisers are an influential group rather hidden from the public view, except perhaps for the Downing Street press office, which under Alistair Campbell became very high in profile during the early Blair years. They represent something of a wedge between the Whitehall politicians and their civil servants. Unlike the latter ,they do not have to remain politically impartial and ,in fact, are usually brought in for just that reason , so that they can help with political judgements regarding policy or media presentation.

Some regard their lack of public accountability and burgeoning numbers (not to mention the cost) as serious problems. Prime Minister Cameron, for example, (once one himself) employed an army of them, whilst disparaging bureaucrats. The main worry about them, however, is that they are becoming a fast and inside track to recruitment as national politicians themselves. They inevitably acquire useful knowledge and make influential contacts along the way. Frequently, they are recruited straight from the prestigious universities, where they have studied for degrees in politics and related subjects, but what they do not know about the outside world of work ,lacking personal experience of it, damages their credibility.

At times of strong majority the power of the Prime Minister has become much greater than that of Parliament itself. A democracy would seriously fetter his powers, whereas we have become quite used to seeing him function without recourse to Parliament at all. At the height of the credit crunch crisis in September 2008, for instance, whilst major banks were threatened, and even crashing, on either side of the Atlantic, it was not even a requirement for Parliament to be recalled from holiday! The party conference season was in full swing and Gordon Brown operated 'alone'. The media speculated about whether this display of 'leadership' would enhance or reduce his public standing in the opinion polls, whilst glossing

CHAPTER 7

CENTRAL GOVERNMENT AND DEMOCRATIC DEFICITS

over the incongruity, not to mention the risks, of one-man oligarchy in a supposedly democratic state.

This matter of the Prime Minister's increasingly dictatorial role is so important it will be dwelt on. Some call it 'presidential style', but the parallels with the United States' system of government are not all close. Arguably, the Prime Minister has more power, albeit as de facto head of a decidedly less mighty country, because he does not have to carry the consensus of his cabinet, never mind the Commons, except at times when his credibility has been seriously weakened by previous behaviour or events.

Especially dangerous is the fact that the prime minister decides on when the United Kingdom goes to war and deploys the armed forces. Should nuclear weapons be called upon it would be he that would authorise them. He also signs treaties with other countries committing the country to international obligations which most of us never know about.

In April 2009 the Damian McBride affair presented still further evidence for justifying parliamentary reform. McBride was forced to resign as close political adviser to prime minister Brown when he was accused of writing e-mails attempting to smear various politicians and their relatives by inappropriate personal disclosures. Brown reacted by ordering the rules of conduct of special advisers to be tightened up, although many said they were already adequate, and this was just a gesture too late. Brown was tarnished because McBride worked closely with him and the style was said by critics to be characteristic of the way both of them operated. It drew additional comment about the (unhealthily) large increase in the numbers of special advisers, brought in above career civil servants, under modern governments, starting with Harold Wilson. This is not just at number 10, but has invaded the ministries also.

A vital area to reform is to alter the fact that Parliament has no role in approving expenditure. The Prime Minister exercises the so-called Royal Prerogative and does what he likes, so any scrutiny will be after decision, frequently after the fact. If there were any concept of a nation becoming bankrupt then that would have been the effect of Gordon Brown's actions. So the stakes could hardly be higher.

CHAPTER 7

CENTRAL GOVERNMENT AND DEMOCRATIC DEFICITS

The upper house is concerned that the prime minister's accountability is inadequate. In January 2010 the House of Lords constitution committee called for him to be "subject to appropriate parliamentary accountability mechanisms".

They also wanted to curb his powers to make constitutional changes. Legally, these should not occur, in their view, without prior consultation of Parliament, presumably through both its Houses.

Yet, in a curious way, there are some limitations, or at least restraining influences on the Prime Minister. A key one, increased in significance by media interest and television coverage nowadays, is Prime Minister's Question Time in the House of Commons on Tuesdays. This provides a public forum for a kind of Punch-and-Judy knockabout style of questions and rejoinder, which largely takes place between the Leader of the Opposition and the Prime Minister. It can be entertaining, but insights arising about actual issues are sadly few and far between. Questions and answers will mainly be from pre-prepared written scripts in anticipation regarding the burning issues of the day. There is no debate, but a kind of public school-boy point-scoring , accompanied by cheering and jeering from backbenchers on all sides of the house, which some commentators regard as a debasement of democracy and our national dignity. A few other MPs may get a small look-in with a question of their own, but much depends on who can catch the Speaker's eye. In any case, some of the questions are government plants, designed to provide the Prime Minister with the opportunity to make a statement, perhaps about policy or performance, helpful to their cause.

How does this jamboree, which has to be couched in quaint old-fashioned phraseology ,emphasizing just how out of date the machinery of government can be, serve to rein in a Prime Minister's undoubted excesses? Essentially, by the onlookers' collective perceptions of how he is performing at the despatch box. It is a matter of style over substance. He has to appear to be on top of the issues, not to be weak or hesitant, or lacking in fluency and so forth in comparison with his opposite number. In times of national difficulty when a Prime Minister is on the defensive you can visibly see the confidence of his supporters withering away behind him. Too much of the same and mutterings to unseat him can start. But it takes

CENTRAL GOVERNMENT AND DEMOCRATIC DEFICITS

one hell of a lot, because in politics the consequences of being on the losing side can ruin careers. Just remember how damaged Brown became, presiding over one debacle after another, yet how he clung on.

And in life, or at least in politics, we seem to find few heroes. And that is not all. A constitutional atrocity came to public light when opinion polls suggested quite a likelihood of a 'hung parliament', with no party in overall majority, at the general election in 2010. Many unsatisfactory elements emerged, including the fact that the Queen apparently has the power to prevent a second election, and the suggestion that Gordon Brown would be able to stay on as prime minister perhaps for weeks, if he was narrowly defeated, in order to try and do a deal with other parties to form a government. (In the event he felt the pressure and resigned after a few days). Another ridiculous problem is the cumbersome machinery for getting Parliament up and running again. MPs are required to be 'sworn in', which takes days, and a new Speaker has to be elected, again a potentially lengthy process.

The Cabinet and its Office

From a professional management point of view, we have the Prime Minister, the Cabinet, with its Ministers of State, and the Departments they are responsible for. A crucial question is: how to design and administer a system which can operationally handle the communication of the business, as opposed to political, side of all their interactions?

The traditional answer is to have a Cabinet Office, run by a Permanent Secretary, a very senior civil servant. So it would appear that a discussion of its role is pivotal.

The former mandarin, Michael Barber, saw the Cabinet collectively identifying the key priorities of government, with Prime Ministerial backing to the Cabinet Office to lean on departments of state to deliver. Professor Peter Hennessey, a contemporary British historian, thought the Cabinet should produce systematic, formal agendas and minutes. He would argue that Departmental Ministers are mostly weak and looking to Downing Street for approval at every turn.

CHAPTER 7

CENTRAL GOVERNMENT AND DEMOCRATIC DEFICITS

Simon Jenkins, the Guardian political journalist, was pessimistic. The Civil Service's noble tradition of (fearlessly) 'speaking truth to power' had been eroded. There was an obsession with structures and procedures, whereas good people of intelligence and integrity were the answer. British government became worse than most in Europe (in the Blair/Brown era) and the Civil Service demoralised, no longer feeling they could exercise their professional discretion.

Whilst there is a select committee to look at the role of the Cabinet Office, there is no guarantee that any proposed reforms will be adopted, still less enshrined in the constitution.

Jenkins wanted to abolish the Cabinet Office altogether. It has an irreconcilable conflict of interests, trying to give support to the Prime Minister, the Cabinet, and the Civil Service.

A key problem is how to get strategic direction to a government run on a departmental basis. There can also be an unhelpful overlapping of functions, or lack of role clarity.

Many pundits seem to respect the right of the Prime Minister of the day to have his own system. That is questionable because of the cult of personality, and it is moot whether the structures should be laid out constitutionally instead. Mrs Thatcher, for instance, was reputedly an intuitive leader, unsystematic in her approach and somewhat chaotic in her thinking. Nevertheless, she had a clear line of command and was in that key sense apparently effective.

When the Prime Minister has political advisers close at hand, the Cabinet Secretary can be compromised, so that confusion sets in about relative responsibilities. There have also been times when there have been ministers in the Cabinet Office. Peter Riddell of the Times, would question whether they can have any valid role. Again under Mrs. Thatcher, the Deputy Prime Minister, Michael Heseltine was in the Cabinet Office. He was both a big fish, and frequently at odds with the Prime Minister. Such arrangements are not helpful to professionals trying to move action along hierarchical lines of communication.

CHAPTER 7

CENTRAL GOVERNMENT AND DEMOCRATIC DEFICITS

Incidentally, Michael Heseltine, (the 'Tarzan' of politics in his day), experienced the role of Deputy Prime Minister under two very different Tory Leaders, Margaret Thatcher and John Major. After his uncomfortable relationship with the former, he felt rapport with the latter. His conclusion was that the power of the deputy derived from that of the leader. Where they agreed, and the leader backed him, the office could be very powerful. Otherwise, it was one in name only.

Now in Cabinet meetings the Prime Minister controls the agenda. As chairman he controls discussions and makes the decisions; the modern Cabinet is in no sense a body which makes its decisions collectively. That is the fiction. The cabinet members are in thrall to the prime minister. If, as individuals running their departmental briefs, they fail to perform to his satisfaction, he sacks them. And if he fails in their areas of responsibility, he sacks them.

A sad development under Blair was the 'sofa cabinet', with members sitting around in easy chairs. The emphasis was on apparent informality with an absence of minutes. Such arrangements could easily degenerate into weekly chats about how government should present itself on issues of the moment.

A Cabinet may have many committees, each with a chairman whom the prime minister appoints and who will naturally answer to him. They will, in any case, have to report back in an advisory capacity.

Even important matters are sometimes decided without all the Cabinet being there, or, as in the notorious case of the Iraq War, without the full legal evidence being either presented or debated. And we only have the Chilcot inquiry to thank for that revelation. Otherwise, it might well have remained secret. Not for the first time cabinet minutes had been suppressed from the electorate.

The former International Development Secretary, Clare Short, gave evidence in the Chilcot inquiry (and received a standing ovation from the public gallery) in which she claimed that discussion of the legal advice by the Cabinet was effectively stopped at a pre-meeting. She asked why the advice was so late, but was not supported by other Cabinet colleagues.

CHAPTER 7

CENTRAL GOVERNMENT AND DEMOCRATIC DEFICITS

She further claimed she had been 'conned' into supporting the war in Iraq. Blair created the impression that Saddam Hussein, the Iraqi leader, was a "monster" who "threatened not just the region but the world". That with hindsight proved to be a hysterical overstatement and the war was a tragic overreaction to it.

Since Lord Goldsmith, the Attorney General at the time and, as such, the government's chief legal adviser, had seemingly changed his mind, there were de facto grounds for conjecture as to what influenced him. The media argued for disclosure in the legitimate public interest, but the government claimed its usual exemptions, not evidenced, that publication would be contrary to "national security", that endlessly elastic concept.

Minister and Departments

It is at the level of government ministers of state that a key interface occurs between the elected politician and the professional administrator. Politicians have often been very voluble about it in their memoirs, whereas in the nature of their relationships, senior civil servants are gagged in office from commenting. Their life-long reticence usually spills over into retirement, sometimes aided by the honours list, that traditional encourager of, and reward for, loyalty.

A major problem with ministers is that they are usually made responsible for some area of government for which they are not prepared, either by background, by knowledge, qualification, or experience. Sometimes they are not very able either, nor remotely interested in the subject-matter as such. This should be worrying, because these are the very opposite of the criteria by which most demanding jobs in society are appointed to.

The demerits would be handicap enough, but they are often compounded, in modern times especially, by remarkably short tenures in post, two years or less. Insecure and unpopular prime ministers frequently shuffle their ministerial pack, in order to attain a multitude of aims, be it appeasing a faction of the party, refreshing the line-up, scapegoating a failure, addressing a scandal. Whereas Tony Benn used to reckon that it would take a competent minister at least six months to find his feet. Not only do

CENTRAL GOVERNMENT AND DEMOCRATIC DEFICITS

you have to get to know your department, and its key staff, there is the ministerial brief to master, as well as accounting both to Cabinet and Parliament.

So what we have par excellence with ministers is the old-fashioned cult of the amateur. Expertise in the affairs of a practical organ of state is a long way down the list of requirements that a prime minister will seek in an appointee. It is argued by way of justification that the minister has experts to advise him. However, some of these politicians may be so ignorant and prejudiced that they lack the intellectual apparatus to properly assess the quality of that advice, particularly in scientific and technical areas. The cultural skew of the nation ensures that many politicians have a higher education background at best in arts-based disciplines. They were poor at sciences and mathematical subjects at school; some are even proud of the fact!

Regarding government departments, Jenkins concedes that its role is so fundamental that we do need a Treasury. But he is not so sure about other departments of state. If they are not working, such as the Home Office notoriously under Blair and Brown, are we really inclined to look inside them properly and go for fundamental reform? They each have a top civil servant, a Permanent Secretary, who is both the voice of continuity and perhaps an obstacle to change. The past may be very little guide to the novel mix of problems now current. But the politician who is Secretary of State is frequently neither very good nor especially experienced. Jacqui Smith, after her spectacular failures as Home Secretary, famously admitted she was out of her depth and could have done with some training!

Time was that the Civil Service guarded state power against its abuse, whether by incompetence or for party advantage. Policy proposals from government ministers were carefully examined to ensure they were both sound and legal. They helped to ensure that Bills were accurately drafted to reflect policy and its objectives.

Now the Civil Service has become seriously politicized, with orders being taken from party officials as well as elected ministers. When David Miliband, who became Foreign Secretary, was in charge of the Policy

CENTRAL GOVERNMENT AND DEMOCRATIC DEFICITS

Unit at 10 Downing Street it assumed an interventionist mode of executive operation, not content merely to provide ideas as a kind of personal think-tank for the Prime Minister.

Civil Servants, short of whistle blowing and almost inevitable dismissal as a consequence, generally have little choice but to go along with the dictates of their political masters. Typically they will spend all their career in one department of state, thus never developing a sense of the wider picture. They may see the minister encouraging budget rivalry and separatism from other departments as he seeks first to follow his own political ambitions.

Ministers, under a parliamentary convention, are accountable for what goes on in their department of state. Conveniently, no clear constitutional rules (as usual) exist as to what circumstances should require a minister to resign. Clearly, a relevant distinction of culpability could be made between the situation when somebody in his department seriously fails, without his knowledge or command, and that when the minister misbehaves. But it isn't.

In the old days codes of honour were more pervasive so lax conventions did not matter so much. An extreme case of gentlemanly conduct oft quoted is the Crichel Down Affair when in 1953 the Minister for Agriculture resigned taking personal responsibility for the actions of his civil servants, who mishandled land transfers.

The trouble is that the modern tendency is to hang on and brazen it out if at all possible. Sometimes an apology is made and the scandal blows over. It can be argued that there are balances, but they hardly have the certainty of constitution. If, for instance, the minister does not enjoy the support of the Prime Minister, he is finished. To some extent the Prime Minister's stance will have to take into account factors other than his own personal assessment, such as the views of his Cabinet and party, perceived pressures from the media. But it is all very hit and miss. Michael Howard, as Home Secretary, successfully used the tactic of scapegoating the Head of the Prison Service when there was a spate of breakouts. The grounds used were that the officer was responsible for operational matters. Similar devices are commonplace to distance the minister along a chain of command.

CHAPTER 7

CENTRAL GOVERNMENT AND DEMOCRATIC DEFICITS

A subtle, but very powerful way of evading democratic accountability when passing laws, is a general one which could have been designed to deceive the public at large. What happens is that a statute receives parliamentary approval as new law, but is in fact just a skeleton, or broad outline. The actual details of legislation are delegated to be filled in later, and at his discretion, by the relevant minister. This is very typical of local government and quango legislation, and another common and often misleading feature is that of phasing. Different sections of the statute come into force at different times, sometimes years apart. It is frequently the case that administrators who will have to implement the measures are in the dark at the outset about these timescales, and hence cannot plan ahead, and have no idea of their practical feasibility. They are just charged with making it work within arbitrarily set timescales and budgets, usually crass assumptions both. All because ministers are in a hurry, anxious to make their mark quickly, then move on (in some cases before they are found out).

The doctrine of separation of powers fails in the case of Ministers. Theirs is a conflict of roles arising from the fact that, as well as being in the legislature, they also have an additional key role as part of the executive, the operational arm of government, which they are responsible for controlling and directing as regards their own particular Department of State.

Finally, one nasty tradition that needs to be stopped in its tracks is the comfortable convention whereby all ex-cabinet ministers are given peerages in the House of Lords. The tradition encompasses many an MP in addition. The practice is completely irrespective of merit, not subject to competition, and is another example of gravy-train politics for the cosy club members.

The Speaker

The Speaker chairs the House of Commons debates and used to be appointed in alternation by the two main parties from among serving MPs, although like many such conventions it has little standing. The practice is to do with the fact that the Speaker is supposed to be politically neutral, an official office.

CHAPTER 7

CENTRAL GOVERNMENT AND DEMOCRATIC DEFICITS

The post was relatively uncontroversial until the time of Michael Martin under the Blair/Brown Labour Administration. Some previous holders, like the former show-girl Betty Boothroyd, had their performances much admired! But then a whole series of incidents and affairs threatened to bring it into disrepute. One such was the arrest within the House of Commons buildings of the Conservative MP, Damian Green, allegedly for leaking privileged information. (This was mentioned earlier in connection with police behaviour.) Speaker Martin, who seemed quite unaware of his powers, meekly failed to intervene, or even ask to see a warrant, which the police did not have (10). A great deal of anger and constitutional soul-searching resulted, with one faction claiming Commons' immunity ,which appeared to be the position for civil, but not criminal offences, another seeking Martin's removal. It then emerged that there was no constitutional machinery to unseat him. He dug his heels in, and in spite of lack of support after his lame explanations, refused to resign.

More serious was his role in addressing public outrage at MPs' expenses. After the Conway affair, in which a Conservative MP paid some substantial sums from his parliamentary allowances to his university student son for research that he could not demonstrate he had carried out, Martin established a review to be undertaken by a special committee that he would chair. The tactic delayed matters for several months. The committee then made two very modest proposals, such as the use of external audit, which the Commons rejected in favour of retaining the existing corrupt system. Corrupt at least by the regulation standards government sternly imposes on local government and, indeed, by comparison with most ordinary walks of life.

The Speaker's role emerged from the shadows of political neutrality in a spectacular way during the Spring of 2009. Michael Martin, as incumbent and a Scottish Labour MP of doubted talent, then became such an embarrassment to all sides of the House that he very reluctantly agreed to step down (10). He had presided over the administration of the fees office dealing with MPs expenses, sought to resist every attempt to secure either disclosure or reform, profited personally from the system. When found out he rounded on his critics in the House. Like a rabbit caught in the headlights, he froze, then bumbled and mumbled his way through procedures he transparently neither knew, nor understood, whispering urgently with the bewigged lawyers in front of him. An already disgraced Parliament he perfectly personified, displaying neither grace nor gravitas in televised performances of high drama and tragic-comedy until, with painful reluctance, he was uniquely made to go.

That this necessary excision should preface a wholesale reform many did not doubt. The media clamour was enormous, the interviewed man-in-the-street invariably outraged. What actually happened was very far removed from the expectations of even a jaundiced electorate.

An election was hurriedly arranged to obtain a new Speaker before the Commons went into July recess (for the whole summer and half the autumn). Ten hopefuls stood from a range of parties and set out their platforms under cross-examination from their fellow MPs, who would then vote in secret ballot. All virtually had to deplore the expenses scandal as a matter of course, but what they proposed to do about it varied. There were pledges of impartiality (which should be able to be taken for granted, yet evidently cannot be relied upon), suggestions that more backbenchers might be asked to speak in debates, calls for a strong personality to keep MPs in order, and somebody well-known to the public, presumably to give the role more prominence (or maybe just because it was Ann Widdecombe who said it). One candidate wanted Parliament to hold meetings all over the country to engage people more.

What did emerge was that much confusion exists, as well as a lot of disagreement, over the role a Speaker should actually have. The constitution, needless to say, is unhelpful. If it had been effective, matters could have been dealt with before they had deteriorated to the point of breakdown. Events did focus attention also on the fact that the weight of hope probably cannot be born by the post, which perhaps should be little more than a chairman of meetings in the House of Commons debates.

Strong arguments exist for stopping the behind the scenes operations that someone like Speaker Martin indulged in, as a faithful lackey of the government. One of his darker roles, for instance, involved the so-called investigation into the 'cash-for-honours' scandal, when the Blair

CENTRAL GOVERNMENT AND DEMOCRATIC DEFICITS

administration was accused of shady deals favouring rich benefactors to party funds. All suspects "escaped".

MPs, having invented a thoroughly corrupt expenses system in their own interests, are not best placed to chose a Speaker themselves, of course. The process looked to have the usual ingredients of political consideration overlaying or, if you will, undercutting, professional criteria.

The new Speaker, elected by his equals by a substantial majority, was John Bercow, a Conservative. It was clear immediately that Bercow was a very unpopular figure, with his own party, at least, which is maybe why the Labour majority took a delight in electing him. He was marked out previously as a possible defector to Labour and a maverick regarding the whip. Tory backbenchers threatened to unseat him after the General Election even before he took office. Tory MP Nadine Dorries called his election "almost a two-fingered salute to the British people from Labour MPs, and to the Conservative party". Once again voting was shamefully on partisan lines rather than having regard to the respective merits of candidates, even after all that had gone before.

Bercow's own previous record gave the public no reason to be confident of his reforming zeal. He himself had been caught out in the expenses scandal, and campaigned earlier for MPs' pay to be dramatically increased. Not long afterwards his wife compounded the controversy by her adoption as a prospective Labour candidate for the general election.

There never has been a time with a better excuse to introduce a radical proposal. The Speaker needs to be chosen by a process independent of Parliament and should be an outsider without political affiliation. He/she should be given strong controlling and disciplinary powers to curb the disgraceful behaviour which is so habitual. He/she has to be above the scheming, a public window on what has long been a cosy and secret society. Please, no more lawyers. They get enough influence in society as it is. Why not try a university politics academic, or someone from the armed forces, but let's not be doctrinaire about it.

There is one final and fitting postscript to show once again that the

CENTRAL GOVERNMENT AND DEMOCRATIC DEFICITS

leopard does not readily change its spots: Michael Martin was subsequently created a life peer in the House of Lords.

Members of Parliament

Certain individual members of Parliament have personal standing arising from their work in constituency, but in public esteem MPs generally are at a very low ebb. This is a joint consequence of both their limited political importance and their behaviour. Roles will be examined first.

A clever way, some would say, that the State provides a less than democratic constitution is that our MPs are 'representatives', not 'delegates'. So, although we elect our MP as our constituency representative, he can speak and vote in the House of Commons as his conscience dictates, quite at liberty to ignore what on some issues he knows is the majority will of his constituency. This blatantly happens on a large mass scale when the House has one of its occasional debates on the possible restoration of the death penalty for crimes like murder. Parliament has not the slightest intention of bringing it back, rope or otherwise, yet is well aware that members flout the wishes of the electorate at large. So it is a common piece of hypocrisy that an MP will campaign on an issue in his constituency, say to save local post offices from closure, but will vote the other way in Parliament at the dictate of party whips.

And regrettably, MPs show much less interest in the gamut of national affairs than we are entitled to expect. They tend to have their specialist interests.

On the other hand, as our "delegate", an MP would have to follow some kind of mandate comprising the elements in, or at least, in line with the ideals and objectives of, some pre-election programme to which the people were deemed to have given their consent through the act of electing him. This would be consistent with democratic principles, but has not been tried in the United Kingdom, needless to say, and could not be refreshed and updated regularly, as it would have to be, without some as yet non-existent consultation machinery.

CHAPTER 7

CENTRAL GOVERNMENT AND DEMOCRATIC DEFICITS

Their role in drawing local issues to the attention of government is, of course, potentially the big one where we want to see them being effective. It is difficult to envisage how they can be other than seldom. First there is the imperative of national business and government policy. Secondly, they are but one of many clamouring voices across a very divided land. They can ,it is true, table questions in parliament for ministers to answer. Presumably, if they are ambitious for office, they will not make a nuisance of themselves this way, or at least mostly confine their enquiry along lines of agreed party policy. Some of the information they obtain by virtue of such processes, or merely by office, will be of use when fed back to local interest groups. MPs very much act as conduits for information flow, perhaps managing to engineer a ministerial visit to their area on occasion.

Concerning the MPs' local roles these have been somewhat disparagingly described as 'social workers', or even 'socialites'. Regarding the former, they have to hold regular 'surgeries' in their constituencies where they will be called upon to give advice. This is usually about putting members in touch with other agencies or people, though it can be more useful to them than that. Sad to say, many an organisation will these days short-change an individual, where they might do their job properly if prompted to by an MP.

The 'Socialite' role is more familiar to most. There may be events like 'Tea with your MP', and he/she will often be an honoured guest and speaker at local meetings and conferences. Every week the local newspaper is likely to carry articles with photographs of the MP associating his/her name with good works or successes. The impression is not always the reality.

Turning to MPs' national roles. They are used by government and shadow cabinet alike more or less as voting fodder. Any ideas of their own which might not accord with the official party line are expected to be suppressed in the public arena. If this does not sound very democratic, it isn't. Add in the various sanctions which the party whips have at their disposal and it is not very nice either.

Backbenchers get very little parliamentary debate time allocated to their

CHAPTER 7

CENTRAL GOVERNMENT AND DEMOCRATIC DEFICITS

pet concerns - in other words, to the affairs their local constituents might hold dear, as well as any special interests. They are small fry in the lake.

MPs in Parliament are considered by some to have another vital role to play - in the formulation and passing of new legislation, with the House of Lords acting to scrutinize and query along the way. There are many problems with the process in practice. Proposed legislation does not usually receive the time and scrutiny needed to ensure its merits. MPs cannot keep up with reading it all, never mind debating it. Bills are subject to a timetable, and when that is up, debate is stopped by 'guillotine'. Both devices ought to be abolished, except in extreme national emergency, as agreed by all the main party leaders. Because, currently, some new legislation gets little discussion, and many a clause none at all. That can only be in the self-interest of rulers in the long run and will inevitably produce some badly constructed law, sometimes serving inappropriate purposes, hard to interpret perhaps, and maybe difficult to enforce, possibly at odds with other areas of existing law.

MPs do have another theoretical power when it comes to legislating. In principle, they can individually put up a private member's bill for consideration, for it to face a ballot among other hopefuls. The lucky winner will probably have little prospect of the bill's eventually passing into law. Even if sympathetically received by the majority, time is likely to defeat it.

A way in which they may somewhat remotely influence policy is that some MPs will get to serve on one or two all-party groups, or even parliamentary committees. The potential of select committees, and thus MPs, to make any kind of democratic inroad is noteworthy. All-party committees are established to receive 'evidence' from leading practitioners on key questions of the day and make recommendations to government. In practice, the 'evidence' consists of verbal opinion from attendees, time available is seriously constrained, and the knowledge and standard of questioning by members of somewhat variable quality. There are those who might say the system serves as a showpiece rather than making a significant contribution, especially when chaired by benign and cloth-eared government plants, and now increasingly televised.

CHAPTER 7

CENTRAL GOVERNMENT AND DEMOCRATIC DEFICITS

Select committees in general need to be made stronger, so they can probe due process. Their scope would be wider than legislation, also encompassing policy review. The chairmen would have to be elected, unlike now, and would not be able to dominate from the ruling party. Their powers of investigation must be increased and the government would have to set out a public and reasoned response to their openly published findings. They could concentrate on the big issues and not be fettered as to terms of reference, or who they could call before them. Hearings would not be behind closed doors and would not just grant audience to the vested interests.

So, in conclusion, MPs have a somewhat complex mix of not wholly compatible roles, in their performance of which they are hindered by considerations of party politics, vast scope, geographical distance, and a lack of power.

We turn next to a consideration of their actual behaviour - another major reason why, despite the valiant efforts of notable exceptions, they are failing spectacularly as a body.

In fairness, it should be said that the actual rights of parliamentary conduct are very complicated, and their application has varied both over time and in different contexts. Consequently, most MPs will not know all the rules, and there is much scope for uncertainty and argument about them anyway.

It is disturbing, nevertheless, that the House of Commons is unable to frame for itself, whilst legislating for the rest of us, an easy to follow and sensible set of operating procedures that would bring government into the contemporary world. If and when it ceases to appear so arcane, maybe the general public might develop more interest, perhaps even respect.

When the Daily Telegraph obtained the details of MPs expenses, which were officially due to be published later in the year (in censored form), they brought them to public attention early, in May 2009, causing public furore over the disclosures (11). People were incensed to learn that, within a very generous and lax system of rules (which Parliament had itself invented), many were systematically exploiting the situation to their own considerable financial advantage. Most of the scams fell into clear-cut patterns, suggesting that information on just how to go about it was internally shared. One trick was to make sure they used their full allowance, by going on a spending frenzy in March just before the financial year-end. Another was to renovate their house just before the term of office was over, so as to maximise profits on its sale. Several scams were variations on a ruling which allowed them to designate which was their second home, as between constituency and London. Furniture and refurbishment could be claimed in expenses on the second home, so as soon as that had been done up, they could nominate their constituency home as their second home instead and do that up as well. When a member of the public sells his second home he pays capital gains tax. But an MP could designate the house their main one and so avoid tax. The change of home designation could be effected as expediency demanded for different purposes, to obtain a discounted rate on council tax, for instance.

Whilst the 'rules' and the willingness of MPs to hide behind them, putting the onus on officials to challenge their claims if they dared, were arguably a protection, in the real world fraud would have applied to at least all those cases of claiming for phantom mortgages, deliberate avoidance of capital gains tax, and the 'flipping' of homes between main and second residence in order to maximize the expenses take.

In interviews people frequently indicated that the principles mattered more to them than the actual amounts, or the details of them. Although the press had many rich and varied accounts of the vast range of items, from large to small, some risible like the infamous house for ducks, which various among their number had claimed for.

Even as the expenses details were remorselessly being exposed, MPs as a group still sought to pass legislation giving them exemption from the Freedom of Information Act in respect of disclosure. They tried to conceal the truth about the trough from the taxpayer, even though all other public sector employees are subjected to such regulation, and rightly so. Over a protracted period of time they defied opposition, not least a ruling by the High Court itself. So we know where their collective hearts lay.

CHAPTER 7

CENTRAL GOVERNMENT AND DEMOCRATIC DEFICITS

Not content with self-protectionism ,MPs again showed their rottenness, and how unresponsive is the system to public feeling, by blatantly introducing new rules allowing them to claim a £25 per night allowance whilst staying away from their designated first home. In spite of public furore over repeated attempts to conceal their claims from open scrutiny, the MPs approved a receipts waiver, so doubling the previous maximum to over £9,000 a year which could be claimed in this way. The action was delegated to a small committee chaired by that paragon of promised reform, John Bercow, the newly elected Speaker of the Commons. It provided yet another method by which the MPs could accrue monies in a way that could not be audited, and in addition effectively bypassed requirements of Freedom of Information law.

Most ordinary citizens probably thought that in the wake of the MPs expenses scandal the fees office management should be sacked at the very least, and the whole edifice dismantled, or at least drastically reformed. Not so, in practice, to start with, anyway. What actually happened was that the senior manager who oversaw the expenses system received an 8% pay rise in 2008/9 at a time when the public sector going rate was around 2% ,and his salary band rose to £125,000-£130,000. He it was who defended the resistance to publication of the expenses details in 2008/9, a good and faithful servant.

Traditional forces are very powerful among the establishment. They were inclined to make the amazing claim, even after all that happened, that the basic structure was sound and only needed minor modifications. They were worried that it would be drastically 'modernized'. And horror of horrors, that there may even be the threat of a written constitution. How shocking that a sadly misguided electorate appears to have lost its trust, for no good reason, in the people they have elected to represent them. And how dreadful if independent outsiders are brought in to regulate this noble body of politicians.

So the public hurt and indignation was further insulted by the so-called pledges of a self-serving polity. These mixed with the cries of media pundits to produce a bewildering rag-bag of suggested changes, set against a back drop where not much of significance actually did change. True, many an MP decided to stand down at the next election (though

CHAPTER 7

CENTRAL GOVERNMENT AND DEMOCRATIC DEFICITS

very few were willing to go immediately, foregoing salary, lump sum pay-off, and pension). But how many of these were genuinely bent, how many merely fallen foul of their party hierarchy, who had seen a golden excuse to deselect them? Worse still, how many were good people truly sick of the corruption all around them and defeatist about their influence to clean things up?

The consequences for MP turnover of the expenses scandal may not be altogether good ones. Much experience was lost when MPs stepped down, as well as not a few who actually did put public before personal interest and had sound reputations in their constitution and across the country. Notable were free thinkers who were difficult to whip. All were tarred with a very black brush, none the less. Yet, also apart from the corrupt, many MPs stay on too long, run out of ideas, lose their zest and reforming zeal. It can happen far too easily in safe seats with complacent local party organisations.

Perhaps predictably after the expenses exposé, but before they stepped down from office at the 2010 general election, some MPs appeared tempted to milk the system still further to maximize their gain while they could. In late March three former cabinet ministers - Stephen Byer, Patricia Hewitt and Geoff Hoon - were suspended from the Parliamentary Labour Party for allegedly "bringing it into disrepute". What they had apparently done was to offer their services to a lobbying firm for cash, lots of it, and had been exposed by a Channel 4 television documentary acting under cover. They denied wrongdoing, and Labour's response was ambiguous in that they dismissed calls for an inquiry. Once again, unfettered previous practice and vaguely drafted rules would bear some of the blame. Nevertheless, for no less than Lord Mandelson himself to describe the affair as "rather grubby" might speak volumes.

The final insult of the now-styled "rotten parliament" was probably when 148 MPs 'retired' at the general election in 2010, with an average £1 million each in final salary, pensions, and resettlement grants. This constituted almost a quarter of MPs, with more to come, and included many who were disgraced by the expenses scandal or other dealings.

After the general election ,of course, there was a massive change in the

CHAPTER 7

CENTRAL GOVERNMENT AND DEMOCRATIC DEFICITS

occupancy of seats, with much new blood entering the fray. But the partly new composition of the Commons did not do enough to change prevailing attitudes towards expenses entitlements. Within weeks some of them were squealing about the new system in a movement commanding support from all sides of the House. There were loud calls for the new rules to be relaxed in the detail in favour of a broader system of 'principles'. IPSA was new, and thereby inexperienced in its role of claims management. It did not help its cause by staffing expensively, and early conceding frequent changes of administrative procedure, as well as by proposing to consult MP s in annual reviews of its operations.

The Media

Another development that ironically erodes our democratic freedoms in practice, when claimed to enhance them, is the way the independence of our views is manipulated. The regular publication of opinion polls tells us the 'national mood' and media comment is increasingly unbalanced, sometimes party-politically biased. It may be very difficult not to go along with the herd.

The British national press is in both structure and practice no servant of democratic ideals. In terms of editorial policy there are more daily newspapers broadly right of centre than on the political left wing, which essentially only has the Mirror, the Guardian, and the Observer.

Another cause for concern is the monopolistic ownership of the press, effectively split between two main camps, whereas democracy would be served better in principle by diversity.

We know that newspapers are divided into the supposedly intellectual broadsheets, such as the Times and Telegraph, and the tabloids, like the Sun, Mail and Express for the masses. The trouble is that standards of veracity are sadly lacking in both, but the tabloids do not even bear the stamp of respectable journalism. In the interests of naked commercialism they seek to distort, exaggerate, sensationalise, trivialise, and selectively report. It should be plain that they are dangerous comics with the capacity to brainwash an electorate over time. In no sense could they

CHAPTER 7

CENTRAL GOVERNMENT AND DEMOCRATIC DEFICITS

possibly be trusted as a reliable source of information about the world. Sadly, they serve to feed our prejudices and pander to base instincts.

However, what may come as a shock to many are Davies' claims, backed up by careful research from the journalism department of Cardiff University, that even in the broadsheets little direct journalistic investigation, or checking of potential stories, goes on(12) any more. The vast bulk of news' material comes from public relations outlets acting on behalf of particular interest groups in society, notably political and commercial ones, or else from organisations like the Press Association, wired from sources and authors that, like those of the public relations firms, prefer, for reasons of self-interest, to remain anonymous, shadowy, hidden, and unaccountable.

And according to Davies, local government, as well as national affairs, is no longer effectively covered by the press in terms of external scrutiny of its activities. Local newspapers used to report in some detail on all their local authorities, including the small parish councils, but not now. In 2006, the Press Association, a very major supplier of news items to journalists, did not employ a local government correspondent. Instead local authorities tend to have their own press officers who selectively fabricate news in their institutional interest on websites or via press releases. Depressingly, this may even suit a largely uninterested and unknowledgeable public, who, even if they realised they were being manipulated, would probably not care much about the issues unless they were personally affected.

Now, if the public were subject to an overt censorship of what they could read, in some climate that reminded them of George Orwell's "1984", they just might revolt. This is the impressive success of current arrangements in the media, because folk are largely unaware of what is going on. Life is miserably hard in Britain today for very many people, so they are not about to lift their blinkers except in extremis. Media pay a valuable role in dumbing down, and providing the soothing balm of entertainment at the end of busy, frustrating, and worrying days. A successful democracy would have the prerequisite of an informed and engaged electorate. Unfortunately, our society has none of these attributes.

CHAPTER 7

CENTRAL GOVERNMENT AND DEMOCRATIC DEFICITS

Clive James noted on BBC's 'Question Time' in July 2009 a dangerous illusion among part of the press that they are somehow an organ of government. He called this "a form of popularism close to fascism".

What we have sometimes are potentially compromising relationships between politicians and media people. As illustration, there were the allegations about David Cameron's communications chief, Andy Coulson, who once presided at the News of the World over a newspaper accused of hacking into the telephones of prominent politicians and others in the public eye to obtain confidential personal data. Millions of pounds have been paid in out-of-court settlements to aggrieved victims as a consequence. It seems at least likely that the Metropolitan Police were aware of illegal activity, but failed to do their duty and prosecute, presumably for reasons of political pressure. They also resisted a considerable groundswell for an independent inquiry. Eventually, and to the belated credit of the 'system', Coulson had to go, whilst still defended by his boss, mostly because the press were divided in ownership and some actively campaigning to stop the monopolistic purchase of BSkyB by the Murdoch chain of newspapers. The ramifications would have to run their complex course, but at once put other papers in the frame as accused of illegal phone tapping, and cast further doubt on the competence and independence of the Directorate of Public Prosecutions, which had failed to investigate. Do we really want a press so free that it breaks the law whilst moralising about the behaviour of others in wider society ? And how could we come to trust its intentions again when we suspect that the authorities have acquiesced?

The major determining characteristic of New Labour with the ascent of Blair was arguably its presentation. Under Alistair Campbell, a former journalist, there was a ruthless, highly professional information machine, which acted as the government's media interface and controlled what went out to the public and how it was formulated. Campbell, remarkably, even attended Cabinet meetings and had authority over civil servants as a highly-politicized supporter of policy.

This generated a serious conflict of interest for journalists. Trusted by the public to obtain the political facts and present them fairly, some nevertheless gave in to the spin, taking the line of least resistance, in

CHAPTER 7

CENTRAL GOVERNMENT AND DEMOCRATIC DEFICITS

case of conflict with the Downing Street Press Office. The public would do well to be uneasy at what is sometimes a cosy relationship between the media and government. Too many people are now making a comfortable career out of moving across the divide in one direction or the other.

The extent of what could be termed truly investigative journalism that takes the lid off what is happening is actually very little. Much political behaviour gets an easy ride because the journalists are in awe of their subjects, or at least apprehensive owing to the positions they occupy.

And then we have the cosy 'embedding ' arrangements, where, say, a war correspondent joins the troops, and gets to report just what the politically correct military commander asks him to.

Parts of the media can be readily manipulated by being fed exclusive stories, by ministers or civil servants. Of course, it is utterly against the rules for civil servants to do the same if they are in any way critical of the regime. And their heads can roll.

Another technique is the use of briefings for the press which are 'un-attributable'. Sources are commonly anonymous and the effect is to enable ministers to conceal their actions and evade accountability.

Government will also float ideas in the media whose effect they are not sure about, and they sometimes prime the public against bad news in the same way.

The upshot of all this, after years of the public being misinformed, manipulated, and just plain duped, is that very few politicians are now trusted at all.

In 1963 television was just beginning to be a factor in general elections, and party leaders were having to come to terms with becoming performers. Tory Alec Douglas-Hume, a reluctant participator, (and possibly reluctantly-chosen leader) saw through it early. He complained about the medium's simplistic 'Top of the Pops' approach, where the best actor, prompted by the best scriptwriter, would be the one to impress. In

CHAPTER 7

CENTRAL GOVERNMENT AND DEMOCRATIC DEFICITS

effect, someone like him, with the smile of a grinning skull, was never going to make it. Image grounds would in future militate against the election of some very good people (as they later did in the classic case of Labour's Michael Foot).

The 2010 general election was the first to screen television "debates" between the leaders of the three main parties (the other parties were undemocratically left out in spite of protest and legal challenge). Most of their other canvassing throughout the campaign was stage-managed among "friends", then beamed out to a national audience at home.

A strange and hitherto unprecedented phenomenon occurred in the aftermath of the first of these United Kingdom television events. What had been billed as the usual two-party race, suddenly apparently became three when the leader of the Liberal Democrats, Nick Clegg, was considered by most commentators to have won the debate hands-down. During the next week, leading up to and after the second television debate, the effect translated dramatically into national voting intentions, as projected by the opinion polls. Their figures differed considerably, but some had the Liberal Democrats in second place behind the Conservatives, with a few even putting them first. All the three main parties, though, were closely positioned, taking around 30% of the votes. Such results would lead to a hung (or balanced) Parliament, with a need for some inter-party cooperative agreement to share power (a staggeringly undemocratic, yet perfectly legal ploy) , or a second general election if that were to fail.

The distortions in the first-past-the-post voting system would ensure that the Liberal Democrats still remained a poor third in terms of the numbers of seats won - a very good argument in itself for a move to a fairer system - but it provided hope for those who were weary of the endless oscillation between red and blue and were yearning to break the mould.

Yet what did the turn of events actually mean? Most certainly it was hard to make attribution to Clegg entirely - only about nine million people out of over sixty million in the country even watched the programme. And that number sank to around four million for the second debate. The populace on the evidence of the content would have remained largely

CENTRAL GOVERNMENT AND DEMOCRATIC DEFICITS

ignorant about Liberal Democrat policies too, or the other leading personalities in their party, for that matter.

Then there was the somewhat disturbing thought as to how fragile, fickle, and superficial many people's voting intentions must be, and how much in thrall to the magic of the 'idiots' lantern?

Perhaps there was a broad sense of exasperation within the nation at the long-term, pretty dismal efforts of most post-war governments? Possibly there was an idea there here was a radical, yet respectable and mainstream alternative voting opportunity, one not offered by the very small parties, or those campaigning on single-issues, or the dangerously extremist.

We are used to seeing the cult of personality fostered by television (or is it merely the slick of presentation); how individuals may be built up, only to be shot down later when it suits the media game. So early questions remained about how artificial the Clegg phenomenon was, how long it might endure, and what the consequences for the Liberal Democrat party.

Coming back to television itself, there is already the problem of virtual monopoly, with little say for the general public. Most output is dominated by SKY, which sells channel coverage to so-called Freeview ,and which dictates to individuals which channels it can have by a rigid system of packages, instead of a la carte options. Nothing appears to be done about the ridiculous spawning of pseudo-channels operating for part of the time, or repeating programmes staggered by an hour, and so forth. A major problem remaining to be addressed is the resulting practice of the endless recycling of certain old programmes, whilst many others seem to disappear without trace at the whim of programme planners.

All have to pay a standard annual licence fee to the state-controlled BBC, whether they watch a lot or a little of their output , and a silly fiction is put about that it is 'our BBC', because there is a supervisory Trust, to which we may complain. The Trust is, of course, mostly made up of government appointees and what really matters is the unaccountable conduct of the ministerial Culture Secretary. For years the BBC has been behaving like a sort of elitist club dabbling in all sort of fields at will and

CHAPTER 7

CENTRAL GOVERNMENT AND DEMOCRATIC DEFICITS

assured of ready central support for its financial requests. At least there were signs under the Coalition of a slight hardening of approach, whereby its exposed cult of massive salaries was moderated, further disclosure of its dirty commercial secrets to some extent required, and a sort of recognition arrived at that its activities needed reigning back in areas where private enterprise could not compete on a level playing field.

Reform

According to historian David Starkey, Parliament is a shadow of its former self.(13) The government now decides not only its own affairs, but the business of Parliament as well. MPs have little in the way of a national role. Those in the ruling party are simply there to ensure the government gets its way by winning the votes on each legal measure that it puts before the House. The debates are skewed, presided over by the Speaker, who, because he is also a sitting MP, has an inevitable conflict of interests. By careful choice of who he calls to speak, he can have a powerful influence over the course of the debate.

The convention of party alternation has broken down, so the government of the day is quite able to appoint one of their own kind, another area in need of constitutional safeguard for the avoidance of abuse. The American system of government is better than ours, Starkey claims. It has a proper separation of powers. Specifically, there is an elected second chamber, which legislates, unlike ours, which delays.

Mary Riddell believes that we have a tacit 'social contract' in which we, the governed, consent to being so.(14) She says the contract is 'fragile' and that society is now 'broken' by the behaviour, not of people at the bottom, but by those at the top. The public have lost faith and trust in politicians as a class because of too many examples of appalling behaviour, much of it financial greed, by some among them. The long-term unwillingness and incapability of MPs to reform their expenses payments has provided an ongoing and rich source of media criticism. Their standards of conduct, self-chosen, are so far removed from what the rest of the community are required (by them) to live by that the transparent hypocrisy of it all is quite corrosive.

Philip Johnston's view was that Parliament had ceased to have dignity

CENTRAL GOVERNMENT AND DEMOCRATIC DEFICITS

and integrity as an institution.(15)   Credibility in the eyes of the British public was at a very low ebb owing to MPs having changed as a breed. He put the blame squarely on the rise of career MPs, a new 'political class', who had studied politics at university, gone into it as researchers or special advisers, and worked their way up the party machine.   This contrasted with traditional recruitment, by which politicians came into it later in life having first established themselves in a career outside.   The case may or may not have been made.   There is no doubt that the nature of politicians has changed in the way he suggests (see 12), but it is perhaps not clear that this of necessity produces a cadre of the self-seeking, devoid of morality and out to exploit to the maximum the public purse.   What is true is that MPs have become even less representative of the myriad walks of life than they used to be, though traditionally certain professions, notably the legal, have benefited.

With feelings running so high among political commentators and the public at large, what were the official responses of the body politic? Aside, of course, from the various draconian pronouncements of the Leaders, and their occasional sporadic action in suspending a colleague from the party, or some such gesture, formal action was announced with great histrionics.

In November 2009 Sir Christopher Kelly, as chairman of the Committee on Standards in Public Life, reviewed, then published details of his proposals to deal with the expenses scandal, proposing radical reforms. On housing, mortgage interest payments could no longer be claimed on second homes, 'flipping' between main and second homes would be banned, and an agency would oversee MPs' accommodation needs in London.   Regarding staff, MPs would have to recruit on the open market according to the established principles of personnel practice, resettlement grants on retirement would cease, many of the allowances would be abolished, all claims would need to be backed up by appropriate receipts and/or other documentary evidence.   There would also be an enforcement regulator with powers of investigation, repayment demand, and fines.

But the enormous reluctance of the body politic to wash clean and become transparent was highlighted in January 2010 by the Daily Telegraph's exposure of secret dealing.   It emerged that seventeen MPs

CHAPTER 7

CENTRAL GOVERNMENT AND DEMOCRATIC DEFICITS

who accepted they had infringed expenses rules during the 2008/9 financial year, in what was said to be unintentional or minor ways, were allowed to repay monies "under a cloak of anonymity", without automatic public disclosure or their constituents being told. Screening from scrutiny was permitted by John Lyon, Parliamentary Commissioner for Standards, under a loophole called the 'rectification procedure', first introduced by the former speaker, Michael Martin.

It involves a private apology to their colleagues on the Committee of Standards and Privileges. In fairness, there appears to be no legal bar on complainants making matters public. However, neither is there a requirement for the Parliamentary Commissioner to do so, and he did not.

Sir Thomas Legg conducted at government request a comprehensive, individual audit of each MP's expenses claims and payments for the period 2004 to 2008, looking for mistakes, and then ordered repayment in cases where he considered it was merited. Unfortunately, his methods played into the hands of those MPs reluctant to pay up, or merely incensed by the principle of the thing. Because he retrospectively imposed limits of what he thought was reasonable to claim where the Commons rules had not, some MPs refused to cough up as a consequence, and their cases had to be reviewed by Sir Paul Kennedy, a retired judge appointed to hear their appeals.

The credibility of the Legg audit was damaged by arithmetical errors and then when Kennedy not only criticized the retrospection, but also upheld no fewer than 44 out of 75 appeals. This meant that Legg cost more than he saved. But the judge's own credibility came into public question, however, owing to his remark that he had discovered "little, if any" examples of intentional wrongdoing. What, in that case, had so exercised the Daily Telegraph and its readers throughout the revelations?

After the main disclosures of the MPs' expenses scandal emerged and the above preliminary work had proceeded, the Government set up the 'Independent Parliamentary Standard Authority', IPSA, and charged it with reforming and operating the system in an attempt to restore public trust in Parliament. It was to be responsible for pay and pensions, as well as expenses.

CHAPTER 7

CENTRAL GOVERNMENT AND DEMOCRATIC DEFICITS

Should that give us grounds for hope? The evidence following the May 2010 general election was mixed.

The first piece to consider is whether the government is ever capable of generating a truly independent organisation when it still decides their terms of membership and key appointments. The chief of the new body was announced to be Sir Ian Kennedy who, it soon transpired, was a personal friend of former Blair spin-doctor, Alistair Campbell. So close, in fact, that they went on family holidays together. He was also on social terms with prominent and influential senior Labour politicians and officials.

Secondly, Kennedy very quickly distanced himself from the Kelly report, making it clear that he felt no obligation to implement its findings. He regarded it as "only one of the bases" for his future consideration of the issues and said that Sir Christopher Kelly was wrong in assuming there was a legal requirement to do so!

When he went further, and openly criticized some of Kelly's key findings, such as that MPs should not profit by selling second homes or employ their relatives, it began to become quite doubtful how much of it would actually come to pass.

The next consideration is one of value for money. The IPSA was established at a cost of over £6 million. It later emerged that it planned to recruit a public relations team at a cost of over £180,000 per annum to deal with external enquiries, whereas none would be needed if the intention was to tell a straight story with an absence of spin. IPSA also turned down use of existing government buildings in favour of expensive leasing from the private sector at over £1 million a year in costs to the taxpayer. It may be worth reminding ourselves that, whilst some of the rationale for the organisation was the policing of MPs' behaviour, the rest of it related to preventing the enormous and inappropriate loss of public funding to myriad unwarranted causes! It seemed possible that IPSA would cost more than it saved!

So could we sleep soundly, safe in the knowledge that Sir Ian Kennedy will do the job the public hopes he will? Well, he started by making

CHAPTER 7

CENTRAL GOVERNMENT AND DEMOCRATIC DEFICITS

tough noises. There would be a new expenses system designed to identify "rotten apples" and "come down on people like a ton of bricks". On the other hand, he was obviously going to take his time, hinting rather depressingly that there could even be a pay rise for MPs in 2011/12. And Sir Christopher Kelly, clearly no admirer, has warned that Kennedy's changes could make some parts of the expenses system "more generous" still.

Just before Parliament was dissolved in 2010, Sir Ian Kennedy came up with the new expenses rules which were to govern conduct in future, with a plan for a sanctions officer to deal with breaches. The package proved to be the predictable sell-out. MPs were cut down to employing one relative, but that was only for any new staff appointed. The existing nepotistic arrangements for continuing MPs were unaffected. Maximum annual accommodation and office claims would be reduced in value and no claims for buying a second home would be allowed, only rent to the value of a one-bedroom flat, if over an hour's travel time from Westminster. Cleaning, gardening and daily commuting would go, as would future resettlement allowances, but there would be extra help for MPs with young children, single parents, and carers for relatives. Travel claims would exclude daily commuting. Despite the reductions, total claims entitlement per MP were likely to exceed £170,000 annually.

This could be disquieting. We shall not give respect to our MPs unless they are subject to serious disciplinary proceedings, including warnings about future conduct, and sackings for breaches of new codes of practice, the kind of public sector codes that apply in local government. Those dismissed should be banned from holding future relevant office, with details published of the sanctions against them. We cannot unfortunately rely on a fickle press to keep the pressure up once they have made money from the exposure and the scandal.

In June 2009 the Metropolitan Police, which all police forces across the country had been told would conduct investigations where appropriate into their local MPs expenses, announced it was "highly unlikely" that any MPs would be successfully prosecuted. Their inquiries had involved the Crown Prosecution Service, as well as lawyers, and were allegedly politically nobbled.

CHAPTER 7

CENTRAL GOVERNMENT AND DEMOCRATIC DEFICITS

They took the extraordinary view that a prosecution would require evidence that MPs misled the fees office, or acted outside the rules of the expenses system. Their probity was apparently otherwise assured, despite the grossly unsatisfactory nature of the expenses system, for whose setting up the Commons was, of course, collectively responsible. This view was not shared by notable senior politicians themselves. For example, William Hague, former Tory Leader, said that "some cases look like fraud". Vincent Cable, the Liberal Democrat economics spokesman, thought some of his colleagues had been "greedy and foolish", whereas others displayed "outright criminality".

Eventually, the Director of Public Prosecutions brought successful charges against only three MPs and one member of the House of Lords. All maintained they had done absolutely nothing wrong. There was talk of using the concept of 'parliamentary privilege' as a complete defence. When they were called to court they hired top barristers and it was announced that they would receive legal aid from the public purse... .

There is no shortage of creative thinking on the subject of Parliamentary reform. Anthony Seldon, a public school headmaster (Wellington College) and historian, called for steps towards a restoration of public trust.(17) He wanted more 'substance' from politicians, the big issues like climate change and capitalist financial instability addressing. Reforms should be radical, and not just of expenses either. Whilst it was maybe too much to expect a willing coalition of major parties to form a national government, as with McDonald and Baldwin in 1931, he did seek their "cooperation" for the nation's interests to be put first.

Politicians need an ethical code of conduct, a contractual relationship with the public, involving the reality of fines and dismissal for wrongdoing. A local trust in each constituency would monitor and evaluate their performance.

Boldness was needed now. Although governments are the weaker now under global conditions, they have real clout still to provide a people's written constitution. And the imperative is to "get real about decentralization", with an elected governor for each county, sucking some power away from the capital, and devolving much in the way of decision-

CENTRAL GOVERNMENT AND DEMOCRATIC DEFICITS

making to local institutions, including the engaged volunteers acting from enthusiasm and a love of their community.

Seldon talks about establishing "a new contract between the electorate and politicians". But there is no contract, either in the sense of an agreement, still less in the meaning of 'legally binding'. We can agree with him, however, that "all political parties have wantonly eroded trust". He is also right to indicate that the loss is by no means confined to the political classes. Rather, it is now pervasive in many walks of life where we feel that we have been let down.

Government ought to display more of Seldon's virtues, such as clarity and determination of purpose, being positive and optimistic, bringing back conviction that there is a practical and desirable alternative to Thatcherism. The quality of political life must become more democratic to be enhanced.

Looking at matters from the inside, the House of Commons Reform Committee (called the Wright Committee after its chairman) in its November 2009 report "Rebuilding the House" set out recommended reforms. These have been usefully evaluated and commented on by the Hansard Society, a non-partisan charity which undertakes political research and aims to strengthen parliamentary democracy. Essentially, the Society welcomes the plan to wrest back from government Parliament's control over its own agenda, timetable, and procedures; in particular the suggestion of 'Business Committees' for the House and for backbench issues. Parliament must become independent of the Executive under the principle of separation of powers. It also notes with approval a democratic plan for elections to membership of select committees via the parties, and to chairs throughout the Commons.

What it finds weak and disappointing, after campaigning for many years, is the failure once again to espouse greater public involvement. It has long advocated a Petitions Committee so that ordinary people can bring their own causes forward for parliamentary consideration.

Partly because they largely operate unobserved, political systems such as that of the United Kingdom are rotten with corruption. They make it easy

CENTRAL GOVERNMENT AND DEMOCRATIC DEFICITS

to exchange individual favours, whether jobs, pay offs, or contracts. Preferment on the basis of who you know has long been the British way of doing things (and not only in Parliament).

For lasting reform to be possible, there are two main approaches. One is to proceed slowly, by small systematic steps, at each stage gathering support for the measure. But it requires enormous perseverance and a tradition of reformers to maintain. The other way is to make wholesale changes all in one go. That can only be done in a democracy when a crisis has undermined public belief in the present state of affairs. But isn't that rather where we are at?

Competition in a capitalist economy always provides the temptation of corruption, imbuing the culture and affecting ordinary people at many levels and in different walks of life with the ideas of getting rich quick or making a fast buck. As an antidote to corruption, democracy would appear in principle to be weak. Somehow, people would have to be given significant incentives to be honest, sad though that conclusion may be. But what would these consist of in a nation where greed is rife and no criteria for the relative evaluation of worth of the jobs structure exists, or is seriously wanted?

The United Kingdom system of government, as it stands, has been caught in the glare of the head lamps over the influence purchased by special interest groups, like particular firms or even industries.

It is not clear that many in the ruling elite are inclined to regard such activities as criminal, still less to try and stop them.

Opposition parties can, of course, expose corruption, unless they themselves are also guilty, but the rot sets in again every time they need to raise funds for an election campaign.

It is quite possible to pass anti-corruption laws, monitor and enforce them. Individuals can be prosecuted and punished, shamed and marginalized. But the major requirement is part of the agenda for democratizing the nation: structural changes in the fabric of government at all its levels, and the massive simplification and transparency of its myriad operations,

CHAPTER 7

CENTRAL GOVERNMENT AND DEMOCRATIC DEFICITS

especially procurement procedures. And this could only possibly work with a sustained commitment from the very top of government itself. Do not on any account hold your breath... .

It is not any purpose of the present work to come up with a systematic and comprehensive programme of Parliamentary reform, although many ideas are put forward throughout. There is just way too much wrong, and it would in an ideal world be preferable to start from scratch. Our governments have done this with other institutions. They should not themselves be structurally immune. Doubtless, the idea will seem abhorrent to the many who have been brainwashed over the years to believe that Britain is best, instead of the increasingly pathetic and grubby little backwater it actually is.

So, if the arguments for reform are accepted, how may the United Kingdom move forward towards fulfilling at least the main democratic ideals in practice?

Democracy is better respected if it promotes - but there is strictly nothing in the concept or constitution that requires this - a climate of mutual discussion and debate in relation to characterizing the problems of society, then formulating the policies and implementation strategies to solve them.

If you agree with the thesis, there are perhaps two main courses for remedial action. Firstly, you can disenfranchise many more who are just not up to it. That would be paradoxical; in order to improve the quality of judgements in democracy you take the anti-democratic course of restriction to a voting elite. Secondly, you can provide better education.

That the second course should be tried seems difficult to argue against, although it would be a slow process, possibly over complete generations, and the outcomes very uncertain. At the moment, governments (and presumably peoples) run scared of incorporating political education in the core curriculum as such in primary and secondary schools. There are stated fears of indoctrinating tender young minds with propaganda, but there are other dangers too, such as that children may begin to see through and challenge the whole rotten edifice of our clapped-out, elitist-serving constitution.

CHAPTER 7

CENTRAL GOVERNMENT AND DEMOCRATIC DEFICITS

Regarding the threat of political brainwashing, this is rich when you consider that the State has seen no such reluctance in the matter of religious education. Logically, the risks are no different in kind. Both subjects spawn dogmas, ideologies, calls to belief and faith, and both are deeply dangerous .With some religions, like Catholicism, there may be the added risk of institutionalised child abuse. And yet, not only is religious education encouraged, and from a very early young age, but it is actually compulsory under English law in schools, with conscience opt-outs for parents brave enough. Moreover, we allow denominational schools to be established, which exercise admission discrimination, and even endow them with powers and state funding to protect their insular practices and building programmes. Undoubtedly, we are in thrall here to tradition and the historical power that the churches have wielded within the law. But these are an irrelevance now except to sectional, vested interest, including those of alien immigrants. Let the churches get on with worshipping God, if they must, instead of tampering selectively with ethical elements in the development of society, where more rational forces need to prevail.

In the run-up to the 2010 general election there was a lot of hysterical media over-reaction in anticipation of the prospect of a 'hung parliament'. It was said that it would be a recipe for disaster, given that Whitehall politics is essentially and historically an adversarial system, with official opposition to government action seen as a duty. The familiar Punch-and-Judy show in the Commons, with the baying of the backbenchers, and a spluttering Speaker calling for order, is undoubtedly in part theatrical, but there are bitter animosities there as well, and, of course deeply entrenched differences of policy. It was further claimed by the opponents of voting reform that this kind of unedifying and ineffectual behaviour would become the norm should any kind of proportional representation be brought in, and that 'weak government' would result.

It is quite understandable that, having been stuck with our unjust system for so long, we might struggle to imagine how any other way could work. Our experience is too insular to take in what happens elsewhere in Europe and the wider world. Or even, sadly, to draw lessons from our own local government, where politicians very often have to make quite implausible alliances on paper hold together in practice. Lib/Lab and Lib/Con pacts are not uncommon, for example, as is the fact that a ruling party may be of different political hue to that of the government of the day. As with most things in life, there are some personalities almost totally unsuited to the sophistication and accommodation needed to make a go of it, and they thrive better in bully-boy, dictatorial environments.

Various commentators are starting to open up interesting lines of thought about the desirability of new political mechanisms within a democratic model. Sutherland wants an end to ideology and so sees the role of political parties as outmoded, except as small sectional interest groups.(18) The idea is for professional recruitment experts to appoint government ministers by competitive process. The ministers would be held to account by a Parliament to which ordinary people were appointed by lot.

Random selection is viewed by its advocates as the best way to avoid corruption and tyranny, as well as factions, but it is entirely possible that the process would generate an extremely unrepresentative parliament. To adopt this kind of measure always seems like a cop-out when it is difficult to find a fair way. So look and try harder. Few things should be more important to us as a community.

Similar negative remarks are made about the independent MP. Vince Cable, for one, strikes a note of caution. He admits that "independents and celebrities have been breaths of fresh air", but suggests they need a "platform" for policy decisions. He implies that only a party can deliver an appropriate platform, presumably viewed as an interlocking set of policies across the spectrum of society's problems.

A telling illustration of the impact of independents is Martin Bell, the man in the white jacket and former journalist. Another character of unshakeable integrity, he was so incensed at the disreputable behaviour of the then Tory MP for Tatton in Cheshire, Neil Hamilton, that when Hamilton was discredited he stood against him as an independent candidate on an anti-sleaze ticket at the general election and won. But after a noble term in office, tilting at windmills like Don Quixote, Bell went on to other things, as a man of many talents. At the next general election the seat was won back again by the Conservatives, another Tory grandee, George Osborne,

CENTRAL GOVERNMENT AND DEMOCRATIC DEFICITS

later Chancellor of the Exchequer, being installed. As a Shadow cabinet minister he, too, subsequently had allegations of corruption levelled at him, claiming regular mortgage and interest on his second home and, notoriously, for a chauffeur to take him to London. It seemed that the constituents of Tatton had short memories and had learned nothing, despite the fact that Hamilton and his wife, once unseated, became media personalities, shamelessly cashing in on their disgrace.

So such forays are seemingly destined to failure under a strong party system, unless there are large numbers of independents all at once.

There has to be fundamental boundary reform to give the current system any semblance of democracy. At the moment some 60 to 70% of MPs are in safe seats, so that no matter how high the swing nationally, it is most unlikely that they will not be elected. There are far too many places in the country that are 'true blue', or 'red through and through', effectively disenfranchising those voters who would prefer an alternative candidate. With the 'first past the post system', their votes count for nought. The situation is entrenched, so lasts for generations, and provides the incumbents with a guaranteed life, as long as they do not do something very foolish to incense the electorate.

A similar fault is paralleled across local government also, of course, and would need a radical overhaul of traditional geographical boundaries to try and balance up the council vote. It is probably well-nigh impossible, whereas proportional representation and abolition of political parties could both be effective solutions.

Sinecures have got to be broken. Long tenure leads to loss of ideas and energy, complacency, sometimes corruption. So another way to do it is to have strict time limits on the period MPs and Lords members can serve. Just as with American Presidents, two terms (or up to ten years) would appear realistic to give attractive opportunities for the talented and the development of valuable experience in post.

Likewise the relative rights of MP and constituency voters need balancing up. If an MP crosses the floor of the house to join another political party because of changing beliefs, he can no longer be said to represent the

CENTRAL GOVERNMENT AND DEMOCRATIC DEFICITS

majority of local electors who voted him into office. But he is within his legal rights to stay on, and often does so. In a proper democracy a by-election would have to be called. Theoretically, and absurdly, you could have a scenario where the MP's change of affiliation eliminated the majority of the ruling party, giving a quite disproportionate influence to, say, a humble backbencher. Conceivably, he could even precipitate a general election, unless the ruling party agreed supporting arrangements with one of the minority parties to keep them in office against votes of no confidence and potential defeats on major planks of policy. An MP potentially in such a position would have huge influence and could virtually name his price.

Another useful way of improving balance would be the proposal whereby a petition signed by a minimum of, say, 5% of the constituents would automatically trigger a bye-election.

We have seen earlier how small the position of MPs has become in practice. In neither national nor local roles do they count for very much in terms of either influence or power. In truth, they exist primarily as voting fodder, to feed the party machines.

And there is another big argument in favour of reducing the number of MPs in the fact that much sovereignty has been surrendered to Brussels. Some three-quarters of our regulations now come from the European Community, thus considerably marginalising their traditional work as legislators.

The constituencies are also surely entitled to proper representation, which may be ought to mean full-time application to the job.

Not content with voting themselves large salaries and very generous expenses by ordinary standards, lots of MPs have second and even third jobs. Debate in society is unresolved as to whether being an MP should be regarded a full-time job; some argue that if they do other things at the same time they bring more current and valuable experience to bear on their political life. But if they are allowed to 'moonlight' it is surely not right that they pass regulations fettering much of the public sector from doing likewise. On balance it gives people quite the wrong impression if

CHAPTER 7

CENTRAL GOVERNMENT AND DEMOCRATIC DEFICITS

their MP's attention is seen to be considerably divided. What sort of attitude is it for those who govern, or aspire to, which says that passing the country's laws or running departments of state is only important enough for doing on a party-time basis?

Decent remuneration for MPs should first require it to have an important role. Pay needs to be high enough not to be a barrier to entry, yet not so large that it attracts candidates mainly for the money. Simplifying the system to cut out the problems caused by expenses would suggest an independently set and reviewed salary as sole remuneration - perhaps some fixed multiple of national average wage, say 2½ to 3 times.

The working day in the Commons is eccentric. Effectively, debates are in afternoons and evenings, sometimes going on very late. It must generate an unhealthy lifestyle not conducive to normal life. Attendance at debates is spasmodic, with the emphasis on MPs only being there for the all-important votes.

Where issues are not considered 'important' to the major players, the enthusiasts will be there talking to a virtually empty chamber. So they need to move to a 9-5 system, an ordinary working day.

Compared to the entitlement of most ordinary mortals, MPs holidays are indecently long, especially the summer recess, which runs from mid-July to early October. Speaker Bercow says shorten it from the twelve weeks, so they would go back at the start of September instead. The proposal would be in keeping with Bercow's post-election promise to "demystify Parliament's rituals and make it more accessible to ordinary voters". Some at least of the extra working time could be devoted to committee attendance, examining putative legislation, and dealing with matters in constituency. Votes for the week could be taken on a particular afternoon when the House was sitting, the above presuming that something like present roles would continue.

If the MP lives in or near to London the accommodation problem does not arise, but for those from other areas with far to travel there could be free use of public accommodation to be set up around Whitehall. There can be no question at all in future of second homes allowances, which have

CENTRAL GOVERNMENT AND DEMOCRATIC DEFICITS

been totally discredited by the MPs' behaviour. Likewise, office facilities, including staff, would be provided centrally and communally.

There could be safeguards concerning quality too, with MPs without sufficient experience outside politics within the wider working world not being eligible to stand.

Lastly, but by no means unimportantly, the nature of the Houses of Parliament and their methods of conduct of business are hopelessly dated and quite inappropriate to serve the rigorous requirements of modern government in the 21st century.

Parliament is laughably archaic. The design of the Commons and Lords debating chambers, for instance, encourages confrontation, with parties baying at each other from seats on either side. Whereas, tellingly, the new Parliaments for Wales and Scotland are circular, like King Arthur's round table.

Dress is ridiculous for Lords and officials, all gas and gaiters. The language is over-formal and constricting, such as having to put points in the interrogative, like 'would he not agree that…', and references to 'the honourable member'.

And some of the rituals, like the Queen opening Parliament preceded by a weirdo called 'Black rod' are frankly risible.

Unfortunately, and to our shame, there are real barriers to securing major change in something as archaic and complex as the Parliamentary system. First, are the vested interests in positions of power. Second is the public apathy, and a lack of consensus even among would-be reformers. Thirdly, there is the transient concern of media, rightly seeing that most of the population live for the moment and have short memories. So the conserving forces play for time. If a band wagon does not roll quickly, the window of opportunity disappears, especially when new issues press.

It has to be stressed, for the avoidance of doubt, that, whilst in a book all this talk about the State must perforce be in the abstract, the real State is

CHAPTER 7

CENTRAL GOVERNMENT AND DEMOCRATIC DEFICITS

not a theoretical, obscure and neutral-sounding concept at all, but a manifestation of terrible power and awful judgement over our lives.

If the public have to meet the State half-way in forging an actual future democracy, they will need a great deal of organisation and an abundance of determination. They need to harness, for instance, a so far critical, yet transiently-interested media, committed only until the next good story breaks, feckless and uncaring beyond measure. The people have to be able to dig in, for a long-sustained and cooperative effort, well beyond their personal concerns and normal horizons.

Let them be in no doubt whatsoever that the whole might of the ruling classes will be ranked against them to stop the State becoming democratic.

Unprincipled politicians can have a field day when theorists like Saward play into their hands by saying things like: *"The most difficult questions in democratic theory concern efforts to square idealism with realism. Strictly denying any democratic credence to systems that in some specific respects fall short of the ideal would be going too far"*. And again: *"democracy is about where a system ought to be going as much as where a system is"*. To the political rogue, and there are many of them, this vote of confidence must seem like manna from heaven.

Their self-interests will be protected with all the unscrupulous measures and coercive force at their considerable command. Lies will be told, laws will be broken or changed, information suppressed, threats made, punishment meted out, if it will but help the cause of those in power.

There should be no naïve illusions, however reasonable-sounding their weasel words, that the elite are uniting in common cause with the masses in some glorious enterprise to make all our lives the better. At the heart of darkness the nation has to decide what kind of government it will consent to. If it does not, it may get even worse then we have... .

CHAPTER 7

CENTRAL GOVERNMENT AND DEMOCRATIC DEFICITS

NOTES

*   1.   How the European Union Works, European Commission Publications, Brussels, 2007.

*   2.   Turner, Chris, EU Law, Hodder Arnold, Second Edition, 2006.

3.   Bailin, Alex, and MacDonald, Alison, 'Speedier, wider justice', The Guardian Weekly, 2nd April, 2010.

4.   Coleman, Vernon, England our England: A Nation in Jeopardy, Blue Books, Barnstaple, 2002.

5.   Clements, Richard and Jones, Philip, Public Law, Oxford University Press, Oxford, 2009.

6.   Rees-Mogg, William, 'Reform the Monarchy? Let's wait for a century', The Times, 2009.

*   7.   Bogdanor, Vernon, The New British Constitution, Hart Publishing Ltd., Oxford, 2009.

8.   King, Anthony, 'The British Constitution', Oxford University Press, 2007.

9.   Morris, Nigel, 'Speaker admits police did not have search warrant'.The Independent, 4/12/08.

10.   Grice, Andrew and Russell, Ben, 'Labour rebels push Speaker to the brink of humiliation', The Independent 9/12/08.

*   11.   The Complete Expenses Files, Daily Telegraph, June, 2009.

12.   Davies, Nick, Flat Earth News. Chatto & Windus, London, 2008.

CHAPTER 7

CENTRAL GOVERNMENT AND DEMOCRATIC DEFICITS

13.   Starkey, David, 'This Week', BBC 1, 4/12/08.

14.   Riddell, Mary, "General Election 2010:   Trust is in tatters", Daily Telegraph, March 2010.

15.   Johnston, Philip, Daily Telegraph, 2009 and 2010.

16.   Oborne, Peter, The Triumph of The Political Class, Pocket Books, Simon and Schuster UK Ltd., 2007.

17.   Seldon, Anthony, Documentary, Channel 4 Television, March, 2010.

18.   Sutherland, Keith, A People's Parliament, Imprint Academic, Exeter 2008.

CHAPTER 8

PUBLIC POLICY

The Nature of Policy Studies

Social Science Methods

An Approach to Public Policy:

  1. Planning

  2. Decision-Making

  3. Implementation

  4. Evaluation

Policy Strategy

Limitations of Public Policy

Major Challenges for Society

CHAPTER 8

PUBLIC POLICY

The Nature of Policy Studies

The aim of the chapter is to characterize policy studies and assess what light it throws on public policy, both the processes and the outcomes. An approach to policy studies is outlined involving four stages, before looking at each stage in more detail. The chapter concludes by considering some of the main limitations of public policy itself, then underlines some of the major challenges we are facing in society.

Policy studies is the academic study of policy. It is multidisciplinary, within the social sciences, drawing on the relevant subjects as may prove useful. Clearly, it needs a working concept of 'policy'. It can then in principle investigate, using its methodologies, policy in any institution and field. However, the scope of the present work is limited to the public sector alone, and with especial reference to central and local government.

So starting with policy, Hogwood and Gunn(1) try usefully to disentangle various popular and loose meanings of the word. It can be as broad in the public sector as anything that government decides. Often the term is used as a label for a department or jobs which are related to policy in some way. And when politicians speak, they may pray in aid 'policy' as what they would themselves set in motion to achieve a general goal or a specific aim. This will not do, however, from the perspective of a formal student of the genre. It lacks the necessary precision. All the same, public policy deals with those problems which governments, central and local, seek to solve.

'Policy' in general usage is rather a woolly term, which does not help matters. It can be a plan, programme, scheme, or a stance or position which is subscribed to. The plan may or may not indicate the actions required to put it into effect. And there is often the accompanying idea of the policy being underpinned by some principles, or at least beliefs. There is usually also an implication of purpose. This could be strategic or tactical. And an unstated implication is that policy is rational.

CHAPTER 8

PUBLIC POLICY

We are not going to do any better in the literature in pinning down 'policy' as a term. Whenever we see that a concept which is in popular parlance, has changed over time, and is subject to many connotations, there is likely to be an unavoidable propensity for misunderstanding. So the academic study has an inherent weakness, which might prove serious in actual usage.

To make things worse, 'policy' is something which has to be decided, but many decisions are too small or too trivial to be called policies. You could also argue that political movements are too large to be considered as policy. The manifesto of a political party, for instance, is really a collection of intentions, each of which might perhaps be specifically formulated as a single policy, though very often isn't.

Nagel[2] characterizes policy studies as the study of "the nature, causes, and effects of public policies", but he might well have added the environmental context, and how problems come to be 'defined and constructed' also. Because different subjects contribute, and each has its own methodology, public policy is blessed with many methods. But by the same token, no one theory about public policy is likely to have applicability across both the public and private sectors. However, the present remit is with the public sector alone, so most of the reference will deal with public policy studies and theory only.

Parsons[3] sees policy as the arena in which there is the potential for a great coming together of various disciplines, all of which have relevance to it. Notable in a long list are political science, philosophy, economics, sociology, management, and administration. 'Policy studies' has the capacity, he believes, for integrating the insights of the different disciplines in ways that are beneficial. We may be able to judge that claim later.

Social Science Methods

Before we look at public policy in more depth, it is necessary to consider methodology further in principle at this point because the standing of the contributory social sciences in relation to physical and natural sciences is controversial, as has already been seen in an earlier chapter. Significant thinkers argue that social sciences can never attain the objective truth

CHAPTER 8

PUBLIC POLICY

characteristic of the 'proper' sciences. It is just a collection of personal viewpoints, a subjective swamp in which one opinion is as good as the next.

Because the human world is a good deal more complex than the natural one, the tasks of the social sciences in seeking truth are that much harder. It is obvious that humans cannot be experimented on in the same way and that their behaviour may be subject to considerable irrationality and erraticism. Yet these caveats need not be taken to entail that truth in the social sciences it thereby unattainable in principle.

A word is in order about the paradigm, or framework consensus, within which science is regarded from the stand point of the present book for purposes of enquiry. The author takes the mainstream and 'positivist' view that current physical and natural science is tentatively true as far as it goes, the most complete account and understanding we have ever had, and with methods more likely than any others to find truth. Some 'post modern' views are defeatist, suggesting that truth is relative (to places, people, states of affairs), or unattainable. 'Critical theory' stresses the inevitability that the researcher views social phenomena through a lens of his own values, so we could not find objective truth, whereas 'constructivism' states that we actually invent our realities as mental constructs in which the social phenomenon and the knower's contribution are inextricably linked. The positivist views post modernism as a false trail to nowhere, but can see both critical theory and constructivism as providing important tests for scientific enquiry to guard against the twin dangers of bias and subjectivity.

Public policy operates within the context of social institutions, so it is appropriate to start with sociological theories about them. These aim to explain their origin and existence, and are typical of social science.

The first, Talcott Parsons' functionalism, claimed they helped society to remain stable and organised(4). Society was regarded as having different compartments, like education, politics, the economy, religion, law, and so forth. Each compartment developed institutions which contributed to the general well-being. Societies were regarded as moving towards equilibrium, but with social problems as possible dysfunctions within the system.

CHAPTER 8

PUBLIC POLICY

However, not even all functionalists were optimistic about finding social solutions, a serious drawback, of course. In the 1960s functional theory fell into disfavour because it did not account for conflict in society, the reality of coercion being exercised by institutions, and it failed additionally to deal with problems of class. The theory seemed to imply that people worked towards the community's ends and that these were fully and appropriately represented by the state. None of which then, or now, seems to be particularly plausible.

Needs theory suggests that social institutions arise out of serving human needs. But one trouble is that they do not have an inevitable existence. Additionally, there are many ways of organisation, so all their tasks, even essential ones, could be dealt with in a different manner. Cultural diversity is not thereby adequately addressed.

Rational choice is a third theory of social institutions which might seem more promising. They are the result of choice among people coping with their situations. Both the solutions and the situations could be changed over time, as may the institutions. In many respects the theory is fine, but it cannot account for the needs, unfortunately.

Clearly, then, the three models do not lead to unambiguous conclusions, hardly surprising when they see things differently. One fundamental rift by way of example is in regard to causative factors, whether people are fashioned by their society and its culture, or by their biology and psychology. If more than one factor obtains which are they and what is the relative magnitude and nature of their interactions?

Another source of disagreement relates to deviance from social norms and its toleration. Some see it as a natural and healthy individual reaction to society, and one of little importance if on a small scale. On the other hand, quite how the various theorists would deal with contemporary drug culture, as an instance, is both intriguing and moot.

The above should be sufficient to show that application of theory in the social science can be a very cloudy matter. It is now fitting to explore, at least in broad outline, some main methods of research within the social sciences. These are quite heterogeneous, and so it cannot be assumed that

CHAPTER 8

PUBLIC POLICY

all the subsequently discussed findings of policy studies were obtained in the same way. It will always be necessary before using any findings to come to a conclusion about how these methods measure up as accurate and reliable pointers towards some kind of truth.

Now a commonplace positivist method in social sciences[5] is the survey, very commonly used, and capable of wide-ranging application, from small to large scale, simple to complex in subject matter, varied in purpose from those which count frequencies of some phenomenon to explorations of how factors relate to each other. Data-collection is regularly by interview, which can be structured in advance, or questionnaires for subjects to complete. The tools need to be designed for purpose and field-tested before use.

Typically, the target population is sampled, in a variety of statistical ways, so that scientific conclusions are dependent on proper application of the technique and mathematically rigorous analysis of results. Of crucial significance are the size and nature of the sample and the estimation of error.

Developmental research introduces a valuable time dimension, looking at change over a period. Trend analysis is one example, here a parameter is measured at intervals, so that its quantitative changes can be calculated, and visually graphed. If forward projections are then made into the future, we can derive estimates of what will happen. Of course, to turn a projection into a prediction is a pure act of faith if based simply on the numbers alone. What we need is a good underlying understanding of the cause or causes of the trend, since projections need to be tempered by any likelihood of how the causes may change over the period in question. The research method is descriptive, as opposed to experimental, but can still in principle attain a degree of scientific sophistication if properly applied to suitable phenomena (that is, where we reasonably understand the causal factors involved).

Those social scientists who reject positivism tend to have a few beliefs in common. They want to investigate the social world from the perspective of the individuals involved. The researcher cannot stand outside the framework and derive objectively true results, but must essentially immerse himself in the subjective world of his studies, as the only way he can capture the direct experience of human beings in particular situations.

Once this is conceded, we are no longer able to aim at exposing the ultimate underlying reality, but we may be able to make some sense of our world. The social reality is largely constructed by man, so can appear puzzling to outsiders of the culture concerned.

There are three large schools of thought in non-positivist social science, each with its own different theory of knowledge. They all reject the idea that human behaviour is controlled by general laws.

Phenomenology looks to our own consciousness as the key to reality. We perceive the world and bestow it with meaning, but we remove ourselves from all preconceptions of it by a kind of introspection which subjectively examines the culture and symbols of the social reality.

Schutz[6] says that we interpret the behaviour of others by experience in our own situation, coming to organise and classify accordingly. Much is socially learned and differs from one context to another, so that we appear to live in 'a world of multiple realities'. These will sometimes have different rules and so require changing behavioural responses.

Ethnomethodology is the second manor approach, also dealing with every day life. It stresses field work and wants to look even at very ordinary events, the practical activities and circumstances. It is sceptical about the semblance of social order. The discipline aims to know how social interaction works, what practices and views people use. It explores both the construction of meanings and the mutual interdependencies, sometimes emphasizing the role of language, sometimes the wider situation. Researchers in ethno- methodology are liable to challenge their subjects' ordinary assumptions in their workaday situations, which can be disconcerting. They believe the technique is helpful in getting underneath to causes. However, since they regard each situation as unique, conclusions are singular, not of widespread generality.

The third methodological force is called symbolic interactionism, although as a school it is rather loose in its collection of common assumptions. But practitioners dwell on people's creation of meanings and their symbols, see it as an ongoing process, liable to change, and one which operates in a social context. So the focus is on the actual interactions, rather than individual actors, with its consequences in producing greater personal dynamism, people changing as a result of their interactions.

The three approaches are themselves subject to serious criticisms. For one thing, they are restricted to qualitative rather than quantitative research. Secondly, they tend to be relativist rather than objective. So we cannot apply the findings in other circumstances. Thirdly, their revelations about people's intentions are too restrictive of purpose for a social science. Actors can be poor witnesses, or hopelessly confused, or simply falsify their account for numerous reasons. Their understandings, even in their own milieu, will probably be incomplete. What comes across may well be emphatically understandable by lay men, but in the way literature rather than science is.

Such methods can ignore important factors, like unequal power among participants. If they are about negotiating meanings there has to be a wider (and unexplored) structure of meanings which people draw on. So there is a social objectivity out there which is being denied, let alone merely ignored, by the methodology.

Among particular research techniques used by non-positivist social scientists are personal constructs, case studies, and action research.

Personal constructs are built up by the research from the subject's account of the important elements in his life, such as people, places, objects, ideas, events, and institutions, as well as his adjectival descriptions, set along polarities, such as warm-cold, quiet-talkative. The data is collected on grids and can be subject to various analyses.

Case studies look at units, whether an individual, group, or community. They are observed, sometimes with the researcher acting as a member of the unit, sometimes not. Researchers optionally can remain under cover. Data is collected, in all sorts of ways, and can be qualitative or quantitative. The subject-matter is ordinary experience but inherently messy to organise. Whilst there are risks, the method can be adapted for positivist social science. It could hold out the prospect of findings for the smaller unit of research, say a hospital, being given a wider currency (across the health service, for example).

Action research, by contrast, aims to acquire accurate knowledge of a narrow problem for a given purpose. It intervenes in a modest way and examines what effects this has. What is radical is that the subjects and the researchers work together, the subjects evaluate the findings, and changes can be made even as the research continues. It is used par excellence in working environments in which the goal is to improve the subjects' performance. Once again, in principle there is nothing to stop the conclusions being transported into other situations elsewhere, provided they are inherently generalisable, accurate, and obtained by a rigorous methodology that non-positivist social science so often lacks.

What should emerge from this brief overview, which is far from comprehensive, is the undoubted strength in coming from a non-doctrinaire stand point. An effective social scientist should take a flexible and eclectic approach to the choice of research methodology, now using this method, now that according to the way his work develops in practice. A judicious selection of methodological mix could have a very beneficial effect on research outcomes, since nothing appears to stand reliable enough on its own.

On the other hand, from the point of view of the recipient and potential user of the research findings, it behoves him to ask searching questions both of the methods and of their practical application.

Social science positivists assume that objective evaluation of the whole policy process and its component parts is attainable. Critics are sceptical, tending to view the policy analysis as value-laden, essentially a political process, not a scientific one.

Non-positivists nevertheless have a varied armoury of evaluative techniques. One simply involves testing the claims and arguments involved. Another weighs up after unpacking the inherent values. A third is radical: it casts the evaluator as facilitator and mediator of

CHAPTER 8

PUBLIC POLICY

discussions among all concerned with the policy, as makers, practitioners, or end-users, as well as representatives of wider society. Policy as learning experience can make some people edgy. Yet this would be a rare manifestation of liberal democracy in action, wouldn't it?

An Approach to Public Policy

Now in addition to utilizing social science methods in researching policy insights, we can also use philosophical analysis, which will later be outlined in the policy context. This is not surprising in view of discussions in a previous chapter as to how science and philosophy may improve management practice.

A fundamental truth of analysis is that we do not come to policy studies; indeed, cannot come to them, as they really are. Irreducibly, we can only describe, and to do so we should build some kind of model to approximate in (hopefully) all the relevant ways, without damaging distortion. In the ideal case we operate inside a framework of thought which comprehensively covers the phenomenon under investigation and its properties. Of course, our frameworks in socio-political life are always less than ideal. We are forced to resort to pictorial maps, analogies, and metaphors in language to convey our (partial) meanings. Attempts to comprehend all the many factors and forces which shape social problems inevitably fail to some extent or other. At the very least we will need models of the institutional bureaucracy and of the community at large.

Policy analysis is concerned with the whole policy process from start to finish. Crucial is the way problems are identified and defined, since that will significantly influence how they are tackled. But new policies do not emerge from a vacuum. Unless the problem is new, and perhaps few really are, totally, the new policy has to be set in an environment where there is already an existing policy. There may also have been previous ones. The situation can be quite messy and illogical. We bumble along. And new policies may already be being suggested and perhaps formulated even as the new ones are tried out. Agendas are set and controlled and the new policy allocated, in ways the analysts look at, to a place with a given priority in a list of policy initiatives in other fields. Those in power, and how they are influenced, will be relevant subject-matter, as will their ideological bases.

So, with this preamble in mind, how are we to proceed with policy studies? A rather well developed approach to the policy process is that which recognises certain stages, which are undergone in a sequence from start to finish. When these stages are linked up by returning to the beginning again, with refinements, the process is called a 'cycle'.

The idea is somewhat of a simplification of reality, but it is a popular framework which can be subject to experience and refined in the light of it. It is therefore the approach that will be adopted here.

Before we do, it is only fair to explain the opposition among some theorists to 'stagist' (policy cycle) approaches to policy theory. Sabatier[7] does not regard it as possible to separate such stages as agenda-setting and policy-making. Rather, you have to look at the networks of players and identify policy 'sub-systems' which are made up of 'advocacy coalitions' with beliefs and resources, markedly varying in their relative resistance to change. There is scope to consider fundamental and less important (sometimes hidden) values and their limited capacity for negotiability, as well as the change agents themselves.

With regard to 'analysis', there are two layers of usage in public policy. The policy process itself can be analysed. Likewise, individual policies may be split up into their component parts. A policy is examined in the light of earlier ones in the same field, and critical scrutiny provided. It can be instructive to follow how the policy was made, in what political circumstances, and for which people. Both problem and policy have to be constructed, so analysis is not some neutral stance, but an active participation.

Sociologists have sometimes been keen on social surveys to establish 'the facts'. Positivists could then deal with these problem facts by analysing and addressing their causes. In order to aid the planning and formulation of policy, or look at possibilities, option analysis and research can be undertaken, and decision theory applied to the policy choices made. It is then important to track implementation, since policies are variously

PUBLIC POLICY

effective and can have unintended consequences. Finally, analysis can throw light on any need for corrective feed back to adjust the timescales and impacts of policy implementation in a subsequent evaluation phase. It all seems quite logical and is the basis for a stagist approach. This will now be discussed in more detail.

Schematically, quite a few stages can be sent out as follows:

     (1)   problem awareness;
     (2)   problem definition;
     (3)   identification of options;
     (4)   evaluation of options;
     (5)   selection of policy option;
     (6)   implementation of policy;
     (7)   evaluation of results;
     (8)   feed back of intended improvements.

Although the approach is deeply flawed, it is widely and still considerably useful. Some of its shortcomings are that in real life the stages do not exist in quite such a clear-cut manner, but are intertwined. Secondly, stages give the actually muddled processes a spurious air of logic they do not manifest in practice. Nor will they always proceed in a linear direction. Crucially, the model fails to account for the external factors that are also relevant, or say how they are to be included and involved.

Now it is important to emphasize that what we have here is an academic overview, designed to bring order and understanding to what is usually a very messy and unsystematic set of processes in reality. There are no doubt myriad ways of looking at the subject, but the methodology to be adopted is a simplification of the stagist approach show in outline above.

The first three elements - problem awareness, problem definition, identification of options - are all to be subsumed under 'planning', called the first stage.

The next two elements - evaluation of options and selection of policy option - will be the subject of 'decision making', the second stage.

CHAPTER 8

PUBLIC POLICY

'Implementation' then stands on its own as stage three, and is called by some 'delivery analysis'.

Finally, analysis of results and feed back of intended improvements are to be dealt with under the heading of 'Evaluation', the fourth stage of the policy processes.

There is another refinement which the chapter's stagist model of policy process could benefit from, to add machinery for looking beyond evaluation, asking 'what next?'. Here the analogy of a cycle rather than a linear sequence of stages fits better, because once the wheel has gone full circle, it is natural to ask if it should stop, or start all over again. The post-evaluation phase needs to be an active one with discussions between evaluators and implementers, followed by the latter's practical take-up of a remediation or improvement programme. It should again be stressed that what has been said has got to be seen very much as an idealized notion of reality, one which falls a long way short of characterizing practice for the most part.

For a start, many managers and administrators are untrained and unqualified; most politicians are de facto amateurs. The problems of society press, the constraints of time and resources limit, so the wrong questions are frequently addressed in the wrong way, and lessons not learned because of dogma, and failure to evaluate. So many factors are usually involved that very careful and objective studies by social science experts would be needed to make sense of successes and failures. They rarely happen. The media often do not help, by their cynicism and never-ending bias. But the rulers frequently cover up, or establish long-term enquiries with restrictive terms of reference and loading membership to deliver favourable messages. Another thing they do is think very short-term and tactical. Many initiatives and promises give the impression of having been hurriedly dreamed up by a small group of trusted advisers and scribbled down on the back of a fag packet. 'Policy' would be too grand a word.

We now proceed to examine what insights some of the key researchers in policy studies have discovered, stage by stage.

CHAPTER 8

PUBLIC POLICY

1. Planning

The 'planning' stage is possibly too grandiose a title, given that it can cover a very heterogeneous collection of activities, or states of affairs. It is reasonable to talk of a pre-planning phase, in which the public might be apathetic. There could be little realisation in most quarters of need for a policy. A problem area may not even have been identified. There might be minimal demand, or support. The level of organisation of related effort in institutions, the community, or the polity could be very low, or non-existent.

A useful framework is Easton's model of the political system[8]. This essentially looks at a range of 'inputs', which lead to policy-making, and then 'outputs'. Putting some flesh on the bone, for the policy process, 'inputs' are a variety of flows from the environment which become mediated through channels like parties, interest groups, the media. Among the many conceivable 'outputs' are the actual application of the policy, its enforcement if necessary, debates about interpretation and merit, attempts to legitimate it, or reinforce its support, modifications to the policy in the light of experience, with possible later retreat from it, or even repudiation.

Jones shows forcibly how the planning stage can be much more complicated than the layman might well perceive[9]. He cites the following distinction:

Issue $\rightarrow$	problem $\rightarrow$	policy
(people sleeping on the streets)	(homelessness)	(more housing)

As soon as the sequence is set out it immediately becomes obvious that not all would agree on anything beyond the issue, if that. For example, there will be differences about whether the matter is a public or private one. And whether more housing should be provided. And if so, by whom, at what cost? And so on.

How a problem comes to be defined and structured can differ greatly, another difficulty for theorists. People need to be able to recognise the problem, so it has to be given a name and an easy-to-remember explanation. It then requires placing in some category of responsibility. Issues stand a better chance if they won't go away, or are not very technical, or are fresh. Events may act as indicators that something ought to be done.

Boundary analysis is important, to show the constraints and limitations within which real policy has to be framed. These are legion, but key ones will typically include the historical tradition and culture, economics, and geographical factors.

In this first stage of the policy cycle, it may take some considerable time before there is an agreed awareness among rulers, or the people, that there is a policy issue.

Cohen places emphasis on the media for creating social problems in their interaction with the public[10]. A story breaks, which the media disseminate widely. The coverage, especially if the story is deemed newsworthy, can be disproportionate, simplified, and exaggerated. Public reaction might then lead to a clamour, reinforced or initiated by the media, for political action. So, to a great extent, news is manufactured and so are the social problems.

It may be tempting for politicians to respond positively and without much reflection, but both media and the public can be very fickle and short-term in their interest. Increasingly, options for dealing with issues will be thought up by experts behind the scenes, working to pre-determined parameters of what is politically acceptable to their masters.

Lowi provides a division of policy issues into broad categories[11]. These are for distributing resources, regulation and control, setting-up or reorganisation of institutions. The types do not, however, drill down to give any flavour of the myriad, underlying social problems, nor are they contextual, so they have limited use. And there are other possible categorizations, needless to say.

Hogwood adds to the mix 'lumpy' policies, which are to do with goods that cannot be divided up, and issues of principle, which are agreed or disavowed[12].

CHAPTER 8

PUBLIC POLICY

What should also be included are dimensions of complexity and the relative requirements for technical expertise. Then there is the no-change policy.

Next is the topic of agenda-control. A fully-worked theory would show the dynamics of what is frequently covert in the political process. The emphasis is usually on that which makes it to policy formulation, whereas it is just as instructive to see how issues are screened out, or downgraded, deferred, repackaged, and so on.

As could be expected, there are some quite cynical approaches to the topic of agenda control. Pluralists might like to have a process of competition between groups open to free speech and public debate, within a neutral outlook born out of initial impartiality (Dahl)[13]. But Schattschneider[14] claims it is rigged in favour of the most powerful players-parties, institutions, and pressure groups. They tend to pack the agenda with their own priorities and squeeze out the rest.

Cob and Elder[15] show how an issue can force through onto the agenda if it has the right kind of trigger. An international dispute or a technological breakthrough could be exemplars, providing an immediacy or a momentum to carry it along.

But if the putative agenda item is resisted, the controllers may seek to provide tactics like public reassurance, token gestures, longer-term monitoring, or simply discrediting its proponents. As we have seen, the role of mass media is increasingly important for such tasks. Sadly, the public cannot rely on professional impartiality from them.

Crenson[16] does not see agenda-setting in terms of public involvement, anyway. Instead, he emphasizes the personal importance to the agenda setters of the policies as costs or benefits to themselves. The agenda may still have a sense of order about it, but it is likely to be linked to the politicians' ideological vision. Marx would agree with the last point. So-called 'deep theorists' study the agenda construction from these kinds of perspective, regarding the main influences as essentially hidden ideas, such as beliefs and values among the rulers. Marxists remind us that the rulers are good at influencing the way people perceive social reality

CHAPTER 8

PUBLIC POLICY

(Gramsci). So the idea of the policy process as involving a free and democratic definition of agenda problems is quite false (Marcuse).

Institutional approaches seek a corrective to models which stress political roles. Selznick(17) takes a sociological view that institutions as well as individuals seek self-fulfilment and self-protection, which can go beyond the purposes for which they were set up. Laid-down policy from above may therefore undergo changes, intentional and otherwise, at the organisational level. Institutions can be like a layer-cake, with heterogeneity even between levels (quite apart from the agendas of individuals).

The theory of "group-think" was discussed in an earlier chapter on leadership and also seems suited to exploring the dynamics of small groups like the Government's Cabinet, which will suffer the limitations of insularity and a common ideology. They may over-estimate their ability, close ranks, and close minds. In the government of Gordon Brown, to give an modern example, Janis' (18) counter-proposal that the leader should encourage members to express their doubts and arguments seemed very unlikely to be adopted. Neither is the seeking out of challenges from independent, external experts. It is well-known that the weak tend to surround themselves with sycophants.

Given these varying analyses of agenda-setting, it is maybe now clearer that current modes in national government are woefully inadequate, and perhaps considerably harmful to, the citizen's well-being. A general election once every five years or so, and lip-service to a party manifesto the public have allegedly voted for, are virtually the only fig leaves for the ruling party's modesty.

2. Decision Making

The second major strand of policy studies is decision analysis, or the theory of decision- making, although it can be particularly difficult in practice to separate from the planning phase.

Some theorists take a stance on the rule of rationality in decision-making.

CHAPTER 8

PUBLIC POLICY

They talk of assembling all the relevant information, comparing the options objectively, then deciding in a rational way. This is only an instrumental approach, because the actual goals could well be normative, consistent with the beliefs of the decision-maker. Theory focuses on the limitations of a rational outlook, seeing incomplete knowledge, a changing environment, and unknown consequences as potential weaknesses, along with the decision-maker's own human failings.

There are many theoretical stances which focus on singular elements in decision-making, often making assertions that these are the crucial or main ones in the process. A few of them will briefly be outlined below, but they are all obviously simplistic.

A common approach is to see decision-making, on a first-order approximation, as governed by power. Elitists will view the power as concentrated. Pluralists see it dispersed among many hands. Marxists stress economic aspects and the class struggle. But these are only examples. There are, of course, other nuances. And possibly a surprising number of thinkers who down-play the importance of power as a predominant factor.

For instance, Deutsch[19] is a thinker who believes in the value of systems analysis for understanding decision-making. He disclaims power as the primary driver, arguing that information flow through a network of communication channels is the major factor. It enables self-regulation and control, so that much happens anyway without direct decision-making.

It is but a small step then to the idea that the capability of government to make rational decisions is somehow improvable by computers. Reduce the (flawed) human element and all will be well. Machines will out. The only remark that will be made about the suggestion here is that we have in it a perennial theme of science fiction.

Then again, there are managerialists, who consider decision-making in the public sector to be rather like that in the private, business sector. Some envisage that industrial management sciences will one day coalesce with the public policy sciences. To some extent this has been willed to happen, or at least, business theory has been much applied from Thatcher to Blair within government and other public bodies. It is only fair to say that the results are contentious, some would say catastrophic.

A good deal of the foregoing is rather unsatisfactory, so are there any fresh ideas? Vickers[20] attempted to reach the essence by analysing the nature of judgement in decision-making. The attempt grapples with the reality out there and the nature of the problem, the values behind the decision, and what needs to be done and how. Vickers made an important distinction between 'reality judgements' and 'value judgements'. The former relate to the objective nature of the policy problem. But the latter look at the significance of such facts in the world. They give meaning to mere information and say what 'ought' to happen. The next step involves action judgements, about what to do and how to do it.

Vickers is quite radically different from those who would set goals and then evaluate decision-making in terms of whether/how they were met. His model takes on board some of the greater complexity we normally experience, the ongoing adjustments, and the fact that problems are seldom solved with the neatness of cross word puzzles, if at all.

Kaufman's[21] Integrative Model has been much used to understand decision-making in local government, which can get very conflictual, although it has a much wider application than that. The model has the great strength of being compatible with a wide range of theories, and, interestingly, introduces cognitive psychology alongside more traditional organisation theory, so it is applicable at both individual and institutional levels. The core ingredients to go into the decision mix Kaufman sets out as preferences, perceived options, external events, and states of affairs in the wider world, as well as the foreseen consequences for all the players. Preferences can be a complex amalgam of values, knowledge and opinion. Options will have to take into account resources and timescales. And the wider environmental context can introduce many extra relevant factors.

Some recognise that problems are mostly complicated, not well-structured, full of dispute and uncertainty. This can lead to the view that there is a limit to how successful decisions could ever be in addressing such problems, and how rational they need to be. If they are to reflect the

PUBLIC POLICY

mess, decisions will also require irrational inputs, easily obtained by rendering the decision-making process more open and participative. Experts are still seen as valuable, but on tap not on top. In a way the conclusion is quite the contrary of what complexity needs to unravel it, the added confusions of amateurs.

Lindblom(22) somewhat in this vein regards decision-making rather less grandiosely, as just 'muddling through'. It is likely to be by negotiation, trial-and-error, untouched by theory. It may not be big and it may not be final either.

The co-called 'public choice theorists' had a big impact on politicians and the people, mostly during the 1980's. They looked critically at public sector bureaucracies - government departments, agencies, local government - and drew attention to self-interest and expansionism among bureaucrats as a danger to be combated. Tullock(23) recommended market forces techniques like privatisation, or at least contracting work out. It was sensibly recognised that not all bureaucrats had the same intentions. Motivations, too, differed widely among individual officers. There was quite enough here, though, to feed the prejudices of those who could see no good coming out of any bureaucracy. Rather more moderation might prevail following spectacular falls from grace of many a private-sector firm or manager, and an acceptance that there are certain residual and important (one might say 'human') needs in society that cannot be met by the market. Officers are not necessarily to be accused of acting out of self-interest either. It might just be one reason why they did not opt to work in the private sector. So it is becoming clear that managerialism can be too crude. In so far as business theory and ideology is useful in the public sector, and can be, the not-so-easy trick is to ensure that it marries with what is important to retain in the public sector, not to ride roughshod over it and miss all the subtleties of merit.

And one way of showing some of these is to have recourse once again to philosophy. Various, broadly philosophical and psychological, outlooks lie behind policy decisions. It may be worth briefly mentioning a few of them, since they rarely obtrude in the obvious way that the wearisome and largely sterile left-right political debate so typically does.

CHAPTER 8

PUBLIC POLICY

There is for one Etzioni's[24] communitarianism, which points to a very large gulf between the individual citizen and the State and asks how the fragmentation of community in the modern world can be reversed? His solution in principle is to renew and revive the important institutions which stand between these extremes, like the family, community schools, and voluntary bodies. Protection from the worst excesses of both market forces and state regulation would be joint objectives.

Habermas'[25] critical theory approach to policy analysis focuses on the overuse of rationality in its models. Social understanding is the key, promoted by improved discourse, language, and participative argument.

Additionally, psychological angles have attempted to throw light on public decision-making. Lasswell[26] somewhat alarmingly (but with growing supportive evidence), is convinced that many politicians are mentally unbalanced. Failures in their lives have driven them to seek compensation via power. It is well-known that political advancement can be accelerated out of all proportion to ability. The barriers of selection that would defeat them in ordinary walks of life do not apply in the same way. So many exploit the fact to our detriment.

There have besides been some very disquieting studies of group psychology in a decision-making context. Janis, as we have seen earlier, is notable. The main idea is that people in herds can be dangerous and irrational. The mob, the crowd, distorts the judgement of individuals. There is a tendency to 'mass think', or should that be 'unthink'?

Finally, as has been noted, decision analysis studies the nature of choices, when and how they are made. Values and beliefs are implicit or explicit in decisions, so these have got to be explored to make sense of the choices. Decisions occur at many different stages in the policy process and at different levels in the organisation with different actors. What is starkly seen by many philosophers as a dichotomy between facts and values, which are fundamentally different immiscible entities, might strike decision analysts as a fuzzy meld. Among the diverse practical and operational decisions to be taken, there are also obvious key ones like what information to take into account, what problems to define, which policy options to consider and choose, how to implement, monitor and evaluate the policy over what timescale and with what resources.

The sheer variety of problems and organisations charged with solving them must cast very serious doubt on the feasibility of decision analysis as an approach likely to produce general guiding conclusions about decision-making which are usefully transferable to all other decision contexts; or even predictive of likely future decision-making behaviour. Whilst it should in theory be possible to give an insightful analysis into the dynamics of singular decisions, we are probably up against that seemingly perennial limitation of the social sciences, namely, that the only true generalisations tend to be the trite ones.

3. Implementation

The third strand of policy theory is delivery analysis - the study of the implementation of policy. There is an immediate danger here. Lay people, and too many politicians, rather take this stage for granted. We have decided the policy, so get on with it. What's the problem? But the simplicity is deceptive (Van Horn(27)). Nor does the policy-making end here. All throughout the implementation phase the policy itself is being put to the acid test of whether it actually works. The demarcation between decision and delivery is too sharp. It can give the stagist theories a bad name.

Gunn(12) wanted to know why implementing a policy is so difficult. His analysis concluded that many conditions are required for success, apart from appropriate time and money. There should be just one agency charged with the responsibility for implementation, good communications, and adequate briefing, so that all concerned know what is to be done and how. The agency should not be externally fettered or interfered with during its work, and the staff have to be given a suitable environment and release from other duties to be effective. Many analysts correctly point to the potential tensions and inhibitors up and down essentially hierarchical delivery systems.

The practitioners themselves are likely to follow policies or methods imposed on them to the literal letter. They too have views; they may be highly educated professionals in their own right. One way, it is said, that the implementers can be taken on board is by providing them with some influence over the actual decision-making as well as some discretion on how they proceed. That does not really happen systematically in local government, so the waste of talent is striking. One reason is that when senior managers interact with strong politicians they tend to be cautious. Delegation becomes a perceived risk for them, if they will be the ones held to account.

The implementing administrators must all be in the position of knowing exactly what to do, understanding the policy, and being willing to carry it into effect. This last point cannot be relied on, and is likely to become more difficult as society becomes better educated and politicians more dishonest. Much will depend too on how whistle blowing rights and their enforcement develop. Successful implementation relies on the assumption that the policy is at least a half-way decent and sensible one, which may perhaps be asking a lot.

Another stumbling block is that policy has an ethos as well as a content. That is to say, implementation can look to an agreed goal, yet aim for it by other methods than the one prescribed. Implementation tends to take place nowadays in a managerialist framework. There are various operational management methods in common usage, for example, PERT, which stands for the Project, Evaluation, and Review Technique. Sometimes critical path analysis can be helpful, especially where there would otherwise be artificial hold-ups owing to vital resources not being in place at the time they were needed. In the planning phases SWOT analyses are undertaken - Strengths, Weaknesses, Opportunities, and Threats. The first two parts of this forecasting technique focus on internal matters, whereas the second two are external factors.

Ever since Thatcher, delivery of public policy has been from a variety of institutions, in combinations called 'mixes', which vary enormously between policies. The major components of the mixes are governmental agencies, like quangos, and the public sector combined with private and/or voluntary sector. In local government, councils have been encouraged, or forced, by central government to contract out increasing

PUBLIC POLICY

numbers of their services to private or voluntary providers. Refuse bin collection is one instance. Other services have been routed through quangos instead, by grant aid direct from government. The Youth Service, formerly run by local education authorities directly, is an illustration of the principle, then taken over by a national body operating locally called Connexions. Sometimes new legal frameworks have been devised to encourage public/private partnerships, as in some new building of schools, colleges, and hospitals.

Implementation in the public sector involves a large number of people in a mix with some vested interest in the outcome and whose interest in public services is at best a subordinate one. As a result there can be a lot of scope for disagreement and dysfunction. Providers of public goods and services are no longer exclusively the direct providers employed by the public body concerned, although it will have a monitoring as well as a procurement role.

Enforcement is unfortunately an essential element in delivery today. Without it outcomes are much less certain among heterogeneous institutions. Boulding[28] rightly emphasises authority. He has three variably utilized dynamics: the coercive, the remunerative, and the normative. Governments tend to operate by a combination of fear and threat, by payment to induce cooperation, and by appealing to people's sense of values. It is obvious that an enforcement balance will vary considerably in states with different political systems. But it also does so between policies within a state, and then again between the delivery institutions.

Another way of getting a leverage for successful implementation can be to emphasize delivery to the public as consumers. Advertising and access for citizens would be improved and quasi-markets set up to provide choice of supplier and product. Some of the obvious drawbacks include the fact that not all public goods are marketable in a commercial sense, that standards can even be driven down (by price, usually), and that Joe Citizen is sadly not always the best judge of where his own interests lie.

CHAPTER 8

PUBLIC POLICY

4. Evaluation

Evaluation looks at how policy is acted upon. It is the fourth and final stage in our policy process model. In each case there will be a combination of tools and techniques to study, both for the actual implementation and for the subsequent evaluation of its effectiveness, as delivery model and, hopefully successful, policy. The outcomes of the policy, both intended and not so, need to be explored.

Evaluation is shown as the last part of delivery analysis, although really it can be, and should be applied to all stages of the policy cycle. It has to concern both appraisal of the policy and of the people involved with it, if it is going to be thorough-going and professional.

Dealing with the former, a light-touch evaluation may be little more than observing the consequences of the policy in operation. But these days we really need to know scientifically whether there has been an effective causal link between the goals, the inputs, and the outcomes in the community. Certainly for major policies, when large resources have been committed and much is at stake.

One of the main techniques for that is cost/benefit analysis, where a balanced view is taken of whether the results in their impact justified the outlay of finance and other resources. Performance may have to be measured in a variety of ways for the purpose.

In simple models of evaluation there is suggestive feedback which can lead to more policy changes. Sadly, the process is rarely that systematic . As de Bono[29] pointed out, policy is sometimes concerned with just moving away from the past. It seems more important to escape from a zone of discomfort than find the ideal solution to a problem.

'Formative evaluation' functions during the policy implementation phase. Rossi and Freeman[30] explain its intention to answer, with details, three main questions, as follows: Is the programme reaching the target populace or something else? Is service delivery going as planned? Are the resources being used consistent with those allocated?

CHAPTER 8

PUBLIC POLICY

Typically, management information systems (MIS) have been developed to provide those responsible with ongoing process feedback. Computer systems have to an extent allowed the collection of relevant data to become more routine. The process is quite empirical and can be very effective in generating performance indicators, P.Is, one danger being that they can become accountancy-dominated and start to overshadow the relevant policy values themselves.

'Summative evaluation' also features in Palumbo's(31) schematic policy cycle, but not for the implementation phase, rather in assessing its impact. The method looks to comparative measurement, whether of 'before' and 'after' elements, of a group that was subject to the policy as compared with one which was not, and by collating results from different parts of the country. Unfortunately, the scope for interleaving such findings with political ideology and values is legion, leaving them highly dubious in the hands of the political apologists. That is quite apart from the already discussed difficulties of running social research experiments. So summative evaluation is as good or bad as its interpretation.

Evaluation in local government can involve monitoring of the performances of staff, typically on an ongoing basis, at least annually. A key instrument is the appraisal interview with the line manager, so that targets are set and performance in attaining them is assessed. Human Resources strategy, often put in place by the relevant professional department (what used to be called Personnel), plans to change people's behaviour where they are individualistic so that they are more committed to the aims and values of the organisation. Much skill training could be provided for particular tasks, like interviewing job candidates, giving presentations, and inevitably handling computers. Of course, an officer may well have divided his time and effort among a variety of projects. If the evaluations are run by different departments they might not be matched up.

The processes of staff appraisal can be invasive. Feelings and desires, as well as working relationships, come under scrutiny. The climate quickly becomes one of staff unease and a lack of trust in the management, as professional autonomy is undermined. Managers can also become dissatisfied with the process, as they find it interferes with their relationship with staff. It is also disappointing that, although these techniques themselves need evaluation in the context of the organisation, they rarely get it. Stick more than carrot, or at least the threat of it, can be quite demoralising with conscientious and committed staff. As such, performance is likely to decline rather than improve, an irony indeed.

What is especially relevant is to guard against, in any evaluation, political attempts to massage and distort ahead of the facts becoming known. Terms of reference of any review committees or audit firms, as well as their chosen personnel and modes of appointment, could be of moment here.

Bardach(32) mentions that an existing policy is rarely formally terminated when matters move on. This is because there is no political incentive; it smacks of an admission of failure. Policies can be expected to last a long time, and many will have a great deal of money invested in them. Termination, or its threat, can cause a lot of conflict, with some defending present practice up to the hilt. There may be no continuity when the policy changes, so we can be left with loose ends, services ended, loss of finance. Much can depend on skill in how it is done. Timing is important. A valued policy can best be terminated when a crisis (or invented one) focuses attention elsewhere. Any wording, devised for best possible image and construction, may well be the vital overriding concern. A kind of legitimation can frequently be indulged in; media campaigns to embed the alleged advantages of the policy in public consciousness. Open retreat from a policy is rare for the reasons stated. Covertly, the party may start to position itself slightly differently, possibly by a subtle change of emphasis, or begin to steer its priorities in another direction.

Classically, if you want to terminate a policy Machiavelli(33) supplies a range of political tricks, such as distract the community, discredit the achievements, redefine the problem, slow the process down, call for a long-term review, make positive noises to belie your negative actions, and so forth. Perhaps needless to say by now, they are all alive and well in the United Kingdom today.

CHAPTER 8

PUBLIC POLICY

Policy Strategy

Mulgan has done some interesting work on how governmental strategy takes shape in its attempts to attain important objectives(34). Various elements need to be harnessed in the cause, notably finance, people, and technology. The public sometimes has to be worked on to secure their 'commitment', or at least tacit acceptance.

It is important to talk about strategy, which is about longer-term goals, because government is mostly concerned rather with the immediate situation. It wants quick gains, instant and easy successes. It sees a week as a long time in politics. It knows that, even if strategies pay off, present incumbents are unlikely to be around to receive the plaudits.

Unfortunately for them, strategy is neither easy nor certain. There is no magic formula, but we do know it needs leadership from the top and sustained efforts by large numbers of people lower down. They need time, resources, authority, and detachment from the more immediate tactical considerations.

Knowledge is key: so strategy makers, who can be politicians and/or managers, need to be able to find and collate relevant sources, internally and externally, not easy in itself. Expertise these days will have to be brought in on many a specialist topic. The knowledge of generalist civil servants must inevitably fall behind. Some policy fields will be relatively stable, with a strong knowledge base already, but others will be changing and will need careful monitoring.

'Joined-up' government is a popular slogan and common criticism of the way it actually operates, where the left hand and right hand etc. The reality is that government has a vertical departmental structure based on important functions of state. The necessary horizontal correctives to such organisation which would ensure a measure of 'joined-up' government remain a formidable challenge, though many initiatives have been tried at one time or another. These include having a super-minister to oversee departments, joint ventures, joint departmental budgets, shared staffing and training, joint appointments of ministers, interdepartmental

PUBLIC POLICY

committees and task forces, information exchange, use of social networking insights, peer reviews, and so forth.

So really there needs to be synergy between top-down and horizontal pressures and supports, as well as bottom-up pressure and support from the public. Power is an essential ingredient and the mix will vary. The public need rights - to service, standards, choice, information, funding, and redress, but don't always get much of any.

So what is public strategy about? Well anything and everything of future major importance; like energy and transport. So it will be necessary to study and research the complete environment, to look at trends and causes, models and forecasts, resources and timescales. Government also has a responsibility in this unstable world of managing risk, which of necessity means planning ahead, assessing dangers on impact and likelihood, developing contingency structures for coordinating 'disaster' responses and the like, and acting as steward to pool risks via social insurance schemes and funding preventative measures. Frequently, government acts only after a tragedy, not only too late but too little. It has not exercised foresight, nor now does it harness the available expertise with a coordinated and comprehensive response.

Many governments just muddle through on almost everything, never mind risk, and strategy is barely applicable as description of anything they do. But if they are wise, they will at least have a plan for developing public trust in them. This can take a long time.

It requires honesty, integrity, as well as competence, qualities in short supply in contemporary governments. It requires politicians to admit and apologize for their mistakes, and to show how they will not be repeated. It needs mutual communication and cooperation, with no attempts to conceal or twist the truth.

What it means is that the public relations gurus will have to go. What is at stake is the ability of government to be able to change public perceptions and behaviour when these are wrong. Such cultural change can take a generation or more.

CHAPTER 8

PUBLIC POLICY

Limitations of Public Policy

Now that policy studies has been characterized, and some of its insights examined from the point of view of a stagist approach to policy processes, it is an appropriate time to reconsider what the discipline has to offer as a whole. The question is what benefits, and perhaps burdens, does policy theory, and then practical public policy, produce for a wider society that will be hoping to improve its lot?

Just after World War Two Lasswell(35) had a (utopian?) dream that there will ultimately be a mutually beneficial working dialogue between policy makers, policy analysts, and society at large. Policy-making should be aiming to generate values which are positive for the development of individuals and society. He sees participative democratization as the key. Services will be decentralised and delivered more locally, by bodies more politically accountable to the local electorate, and not autonomous external consultants and non-elected quangos. The public will no longer be passive recipients of policies remotely decided on high, but their interactions will make a positive difference. Legitimacy of decision making, and trust between the people and public bodies, sorely need to be restored. Citizen's social awareness and responsibility have to improve, and their freedom to exercise real choices ought to be greatly extended. This is Lasswell's vision.

Yet contrast it with current reality so many years later. One reason why public policy can fail is that the populace are not knowledgeable or responsive enough. Many attempts these days are being made to help citizens get the best out of the public sector, but this is relatively new. Part of the approach is inevitably long-term. It seeks through education to inform the next generation better about the rights and opportunities of citizenship and how public institutions work. Another strand is to increase the spirit of consumerism within the public services. What is made available is attractively packaged, more intensively advertised, and marketed to the public, who are regarded as consumers. This is no mean task. Aside from the fact that much public sector delivery is not commercially viable, the notion of choice can be a bogus one. People can, and do, drop out, or at least fail to engage, out of apathy and disillusionment. Where purely local needs are being met within a community, and delivery is born of consultation with the very consumers who will be affected by it, there can be a much better chance of success.

Going back to policy studies, Lindblom[22] rejected policy cycles altogether and questioned the rationality of the process. He called it, in contradictory style, *"the science of muddling through"*. He thought policy processes too interactive and complex, with the competition of many inputs and interests, to conform to some grand model. Taking Popper's line of cautious 'social engineering', he advocated incrementalism. Matters should proceed piecemeal and by small steps, since we cannot really predict outcomes. Other commentators have thought this a very appropriate characterization of actual policy development in local government during the heyday of the Local Education Authorities, LEAs. Only they called it 'disjointed incrementalism', partly in jest.

Government eventually grew tired of it, owing to uneven results across the country, local eccentricities and party opposition, and because they came to want to drive through new policies to do with curriculum and academic standards via a centralised machinery, heavy on legislation and target-setting.

Apart from impatience, Heineman[36] has usefully shown the limits to analysis in political contexts. Politicians might easily suffer from a surfeit of information and advice, they may interfere with and damage the analytical process, they can derail it to annouce, instead of the merits of prospective new decisions, the achievements of previous ones. Analysis itself has been known to fail to give sufficiently practical guidance. The biggest weakness, nevertheless, is likely to be the relative lack of status and power that the analysts suffer from, being either public servants or hired consultants. They are hopelessly outgunned when offering an opinion, whatever their grasp and knowledge. Part of the national culture is to distrust experts, so the politicians happily feed on it. A classic illustration was at the height of the 'credit crunch'. With the nation's economy in crisis, the prime minister, Gordon Brown, failed to call together a standing panel of the best economic brains to advise him. He knew best, and he also knew that to consult brooked delay and possible contradictions. Some would have sneered it off as a sign of weakness.

CHAPTER 8

PUBLIC POLICY

So it is understandable, then, that Edelman(37) takes a sceptical view on the theme of presentation. 'Political fictions' are displayed before the public. The rulers wish to do certain things, and so they may not be above inventing problems, or posing them in misleading ways, for which their proposed actions are likely solutions. His analogy is with a theatre, where political performers play before the people as audience in the hope of attaining, maintaining, and then enhancing their support. This, of course, is deception on a grand scale. Edelman wants to put the public wise to it, and thinks that policy analysis is the vehicle for the task!

However, Taylor(38) is more cynical than that. He believes that public policies almost invariably go wrong, anyway. He tells us why. When a policy is implemented it generates uncertainties, and these can lead to further problems. Various illustrative examples are cited. One is of a policy to provide financial help for single mothers, so they do not have to go out to work and neglect their children. A difficulty is that the measure could also give single women the incentive not to marry, whereas societal attitudes incline to the view that marriage is desirable for family well-being. A lover would have to live elsewhere to protect her benefit. The problem gets worse in one sense as the children, though still dependent, get older. Then there may be social pressure for single mothers to go back to work. So immediately the policy is tested by the situational changes in the woman's life. A simple framed policy will be certain to fail, or produce unintended consequences, which may be regarded as undesirable. On the other hand, a complex policy will be very difficult to frame (in a way that is socially acceptable) and may be even harder to sell.

The public presentation of policy option by politicians is seldom sophisticated, as election campaigns will readily testify. Nick Clegg, as leader of the Liberal Democrats , remarked in January 2010 that policies were a matter of (his) "convictions". So we are presumably supposed to trust his possibly deeply held beliefs. Well it won't wash any more.

Of course, policies (and publics) need to be treated with a deal more respect. If you were being scientific about it, you would want to know a whole raft of things about any one specific policy proposal - for example, what inputs of resources would be needed, in terms of costs, manpower, skills, distribution, timescale, and how it could be afforded. Would the

CHAPTER 8

PUBLIC POLICY

monies, for instance, have to be diverted from other policy streams and, if so, how and with what effects? What outputs could we expect from the policy, both qualitatively and quantitatively? What would be the direct and indirect effects of the policy, and how would success be measured, by whom, and how communicated to the people?

The public would be right to be deeply sceptical, if not downright cynical, about the efficacy of any and every public policy. After all, politicians have been introducing it, and endlessly changing it, for as long as we can remember, yet just look at the truly pathetic state of the country that has resulted.

Coming back to the research methods themselves, and noting their huge variety, not forgetting the ideological rifts among their respective adherents, are we in a position to trust that any of them can attain truth? Unfortunately, the jury still has to be out at this stage, however keen we may be to resolve the matter, which is quite vexatious, given there is so much at stake. If there could be profound insights, the view here is that only a positivistic social science, with sophisticated and rigorous application, can one day have even a remote chance of succeeding. Assuredly, we are just in the infancy of development of newish social sciences, considering their very problematic subject-matter, and a golden age might possibly dawn for them, as it did for physics, and is now occurring in molecular biology.

What we should get used to asking, routinely, when any research findings are announced, and not just in the social sciences, are questions to do with pedigree. Who conducted the research, on whose behalf, on what terms of reference is one such set, enabling us to get a feel for whether it has been independent, following where results lead, or motivated to serve somebody's pre-ordained interests, be they commercial or governmental. Another set of questions would aim to establish the methodology, the statistical basis, and elements like sample size and choice (for surveys), as well as limits of accuracy. Only by looking first at the whole basis of the project in depth can it be established whether the findings are even worth looking at. It has to be said, because institutions and media have shamelessly misled a public largely vulnerable owing to its scientific ignorance.

CHAPTER 8

PUBLIC POLICY

Finally, faced, as we are, with the bewildering array of theories and approaches to policy studies, of which only a very small, but hopefully representative, sample has been given here, what are we to make of them? Do they represent value for the considerable amount of effort that has undoubtedly gone into them? Can they provide useable insights, albeit from less than finalised research techniques?

Well, it seems hopeful that some appear to chime with experience in part, or have relevance in specific settings. To that, very limited, extent they are useful. Yet as candidates for a policy 'theory of everything' not one of them remotely begins to measure up. Maybe none ever can, in the nature of things.

Major Challenges for Society

Public policy studies have been discussed with their systematic approaches to public policy. The severe limitations of what can be achieved by public policy have also been indicated.

So we have to turn to the kind of agenda which any public policy must face. It does not need to be comprehensive here. Nor does it dwell on the terrible global problems that stem from politico-religious or environmental concerns. These are dealt with in the chapter on social progress. Nonetheless, it is a formidable list, and in the wrong hands will be crippling.(39)

The defects of capitalism - such as vastly disproportionate rewards of wealth and the ruining of people's lives when private enterprises fail - will need to be addressed by public policy, if they are to be addressed at all. The private sector will not do it. Social welfare and health policies will be sorely tested by the relatively large numbers of the elderly. Capitalist failings, including fraud, in the administration of private sector pensions funds, together with government irresponsibility over many years in not investing to meet public sector pension liabilities, have left public policy with an almost insurmountable burden, which can only get worse for many years to come.

CHAPTER 8

PUBLIC POLICY

Britain will struggle to supply food and water, affordable and enough housing, a stable economy, a culture of quality, institutions fit for purpose, decent environments, a functional infrastructure, and a minimum of internal conflict, some of it racial, along with significant rights to privacy and security of personal information(39), and a non-politicized police force.

Look at our disjointed transport system - the over crowded and cracking-up roads, the prohibitive expense and shocking standards on rail travel. Observe the breakdown of law and order. Rue the remorseless deterioration in postal services. Struggle to pay the exorbitant domestic fuel costs, whilst reflecting on the lack of a coherent plan to develop a sustainable energy supply. Watch, helpless, as our manufacturing industries fall into foreign ownership and are then disbanded.

There is nothing remotely in the history of Britain to inspire confidence that all these challenges, and many more besides, will properly be met. Quite the contrary is the likely case. The public policy theory discussed above is surely enough to show how and convince that politicians will conspire and fail in what they do and what they don't.

CHAPTER 8

PUBLIC POLICY

Notes

1. Hogwood, B.W. and L.A, Gunn, Policy Analysis for the Real World; Oxford University Press, London, 1984.

2. Nagel, S.S., 'Conflicting evaluations of policy studies'; in Lynn and Wildavsky (eds),1990.

*   3. Parsons, Wayne, Public Policy; Edward Elgar Publishing Ltd., 1995.

*   4. Albrow, Martin, Sociology: The Basics, Routledge, London, 1999.

*   5. Cohen, Louis, and Manion, Lawrence, Research Methods in Education, Routledge, London, Third edition, 1989.

6. Burrell, G., and Morgan, G., Sociological Paradigms and Organizational Analaysis, Heinemann Educational Books, London, 1979.

7. Sabatier, P.A., 'Toward better theories of the policy process', PS: Political Science and Politics, 24: 147-56.

8. Easton, D., A Framework for Political Analysis, Prentice-Hall, Englewood Cliffs, N.J., 1965.

9. Jones, J.A., 'Federal efforts to solve contemporary social problems', in Smigel (ed.), 1971.

10. Cohen, S., Folk Devils and Moral Panics, Paladin, London, 1972.

11. Lowi, T.J., 'Four systems of policy politics and choice'; Public Administration Review, 32: 298-310, 1972.

12. Hogwood, B.W. and Gunn, L.A., Policy Analysis for the Real World, Oxford University Press, London, 1984.

CHAPTER 8

PUBLIC POLICY

13. Dahl, R., 'Who Governs?: Democracy and Power in an American City'; Yale University Press, New Haven, Conn., 1961.

14. Schattschneider, E.E., The Semi-sovereign People; Holt, Rinehart & Winston, New York, 1960.

15. Cobb, R.W., and C.D. Elder, 'Participation in American Politics: The Dynamics of Agenda-building', John Hopkins University Press, Baltimore, Md., 1972.

16. Crenson, M.A., The Unpolitics of Air Pollution: A Study of Non-decision Making in the Cities; John Hopkins University Press, Baltimore, Md., 1971.

17. Selznick, P., TVA and the Grass Roots; University of California Press, Berkeley, Cal., 1949.

18. Janis, I.L., Groupthink; Psychological Studies of Policy Decisions and Fiascos; Houghton Mifflin, Boston, Mass., 1972.

19. Deutsch., K.W., The Nerves of Government: Models of Political Communication and Control; Free Press of Glencoe, New York, 1963.

20. Vickers, G., The Art of Judgement: A Study of Policymaking: Chapman & Hall, London, 1965.

21. Kaufman, S., 'Decision making and conflict management processes in local government', in Bingham et al., 1991.

22. Lindblom, C.E., 'The science of muddling through'; Public Administration Review, 19: 8-88, 1959.

23. Tullock, G., The Politics of Bureaucracy; Public Affairs Press, Washington, D.C., 1965.

CHAPTER 8

PUBLIC POLICY

24. Etzioni, A., The Active Society: A Theory of Societal and Political Processes; Free Press, New York, 1968.

25. Habermass, J., Legitimation Crises; Heinemann, London, 1976.

26. Lasswell, H.D., Psychopathology and Politics; University of Chicago Press, Chicago, Illinois, 1930.

27. Van Meter, D and C Van Horn, 'The policy implementation process: a conceptual framework'; Administration and Society, 6: 445-88, 1975.

28. Boulding, K., Three Faces of Power, Sage, Newbury Park, California, 1990.

29. de Bono, E., Atlas of Management Thinking; Temple Smith, London, 1981.

30. Rossi, P.H., and Freeman, H, Evaluation: A Systematic Approach, Sage, Newbury Park, Cal.; 2nd edn., 1993.

31. Palumbo, D.J., 'Politics and evaluation', in Palumbo (ed.), 1987.

32. Bardach, E., Policy termination as a political process'; Policy Sciences, 7: 123-31, 1976.

33. Machiavelli, Niccolo, The Prince, Everyman's Library, 1908.

*   34. Mulgan, G., The Art of Public Strategy, Oxford University Press, 2008.

35. Lasswell, H.D. and A. Kaplan, Power and Society, Yale University Press, New Haven, Connecticut, 1950.

36. Heineman, R.A., W.T. Bluhm, S.A. Peterson and E.N.

CHAPTER 8

PUBLIC POLICY

Kearney, The World of the Policy Analyst: Rationality, Values and Politics; Chatham House, Chatham, New Jersey, 1990.

37. Edleman, M., Constructing the Political Spectacle; Chicago University Press, Chicago, Illinois, 1988.

38. Taylor, I. and L. Taylor (eds), Political and Deviance; Penguin Harmondsworth, Middlesex, 1973.

* 39. Coleman, Vernon, What Happens Next?, Publishing House, Trinity Place, Barnstaple, 2009.

CHAPTER 9

LOCAL GOVERNMENT

Background
- The Public Sector
- Local Government

Structure
- Organisation
- Re-organisation

Public Service
- Remuneration
- Working Life
- Whistle blowing

Finance
- The System
- Council Tax

Public and Private Sectors
- Privatisation
- Public Finance Initiative
- Council Business Roles
- Concluding Remarks

Futures

CHAPTER 9

LOCAL GOVERNMENT

BACKGROUND

The Public Sector

The public sector, in its provision of basic goods and services, is complementing the private sector, which does not, or cannot do so. It is vast, one of the largest sectors in most economies, although not in the United Kingdom ever allowed to become as big as the private sector. It is also very heterogeneous in type of institution and purpose, consisting of public corporations (firms owned by government), the national government itself, the Crown, the armed forces, the judiciary and court system, and quasi-autonomous non-government organisations (quangos). Then there is local government. So different are the natures, structures, objectives, sizes, conditions of employment, funding, and accountability of public sector bodies that they may have little in common, other than that they are not wealth-creating.

A further word should be said about 'Quangos', because there are very many of them, they are little understood by the public, and they are the opposite of democratic institutions[1]. Essentially, a quango is not elected, works for central government one way or another, and spends very large sums of public money. Quangos are the deliberate creation over some years without public consent of organisations that carry out some role or other that mostly used to be the province of local government. Nobody knows for sure how many there are, since definitions differ, but estimates can easily identify 5,000 or so of them.

So when government ministers drone on about bureaucratic waste, and turn their predictable fire on hapless local authorities, they conveniently forget to mention their own created quangocracy, which they have done very little to prevent the expansion of, never mind curb. A lot of quangos operate behind a veil of secrecy. Their meetings are in many cases not open to the public, minutes and reports are not published, they are not subject to external audit, they do not comply with public codes of conduct concerning freedom of information, or keep registers of members'

CHAPTER 9

LOCAL GOVERNMENT

interests. Some quangos nevertheless have good people, albeit appointed in partisan ways, and do useful work, like housing action trusts, or learning and skills councils.

Quangos would be virtually non-existent in a truly democratic society, but the processes by which they could be reduced would not be easy, or without risks and problems. Since most people are ignorant of them in any depth, and that goes for politicians as well, there are likely to be glib suggestions such as just get rid. This would be a tragedy for some talented staff and their dependants, and would in some cases lead to genuine losses for society. In other situations the work would be transferred to existing institutions, which might be deflected from core purpose, or otherwise weakened. Again, it could be very easy for government to obfuscate, and to make exaggerated claims as to the money that was being saved.

The organisation 'Justice', which comments on the paucity of it in the United Kingdom today, issued a timely warning when the new Coalition government produced its Public Bodies Bill. This was intended to enable and facilitate the agenda to abolish or reform many of the quangos. The long list of hundreds was set out with many a fanfare.

What caused the most outrage should have been the sweeping and dictatorial nature of powers proposed to be delegated to ministers behind the backs of the Commons and Lords. Hitherto, constitutional arrangements would have required separate legislation on each quango to change its statutory regulations, at least accompanied by the usual modicum of parliamentary scrutiny and debate that primary legislation has to undergo.

Also important for government watchers to track (if they only could) was the claim about financial savings resulting from the apparently draconian (and certainly doctrinaire) proposals, predictably brought out without consultation. Because the feeling soon emerged that the Coalition's typically breathless rush to judgement had produced very flawed plans based on superficial views of bodies whose work they had not had time to properly understand. Their stated intention to save money, oodles of it, by the measures, was also put in doubt by window-dressing. For instance, an organisation might nominally be closed down, like the Financial Services

CHAPTER 9

LOCAL GOVERNMENT

Authority, only for the staff to be absorbed into another arm of government instead (here the Bank of England).

The second named goal, to increase accountability, you may be assured would aim at clarifying top-down communications between a quango and its political masters, not a greater transparency to the people.

The unstated and overriding reason for the enterprise, of course, was neither cost-saving nor accountability, but part of being seen apparently to be cutting away the unhealthy fat from an obscenely bloated public sector; one which it claimed New Labour had fed and fed.

It is not the plan of the present chapter to treat these (very disparate) public sector organisations at length, so only one will be singled out here for comment - the National Health Service, NHS.

The government runs the NHS by central direction (2). In spite of claims that there is devolution to local levels, the health trusts mostly work on delivering national targets and in ways prescribed by Whitehall. The top-down approach is one with complex management structures at different levels, prompting those who are right-leaning politically to talk about bureaucratic waste and to threaten yet more reform. The larger part of the vast cost, of course, comes from overpaid professional doctors, whose trade union, the British Medical Authority, is a very effective negotiator.

Despite assertions that patients are to be freed to choose their provider, there is no real competition in the NHS. If there were, specialists would be matched to area demand. 'Joined-up' provision generally is a big and long term weakness of government bureaucracies. So, for example, the case management of a patient might need effective links with local authority social services departments, and hospital nurses would be deployed around patients rather than tasks, as is the modern fashion.

Opinions differ about the popularity of the NHS, as much depends on individual experiences against a back -drop of political spin from both sides. One suspects, though, that, whilst the British may be inclined to regard it as their favourite public institution (not a difficult choice, perhaps), it is perceptions of performance they are mainly judging it by.

CHAPTER 9

LOCAL GOVERNMENT

As the nation, aping America, becomes more litigious, vast numbers of claims for criminal negligence are made against the NHS every year. People will not be endeared either by the fact that thousands of operations are cancelled annually for 'non-medical' reasons.

The public finds it hard to understand why, as one of the richest countries in the world, we come a long way down the league of tables for advanced societies of deaths which could have been prevented. And they are coming to realise that the standard of care they receive is very variable between hospitals, and from one part of the country to another. If they do not experience it themselves, they may know others who have contracted dangerous bacterial infections whilst in hospital - some ten per cent of patients got something horrible in 2009.

The Coalition government sprung a nasty surprise on the electorate very early. Beforehand it gave plenty assurances that the NHS would be safe in its hands and no upheavals contemplated. It then undemocratically prepared the groundwork for future privatisations with its unilateral proposals to undertake immediate and wholesale delegation of service commissioning to the already overworked GP s, abolishing the layer of Primary Care Trusts at a stroke and simply dismissing the fate and value of their managements as though they were a needless on-cost. Outcry came from Opposition parties, the general public, all the medical bodies representing professionals in the field, but where are the constitutional safeguards to prevent this kind of extremist and destructive action?

Local Government

Turning to local government itself, which used to own and manage hospitals, it must be difficult for young people to contemplate the extent to which council authorities have declined in importance and scope since the First World War. Before the Labour Attlee Government in 1945 at the end of the Second World War local government was a leading supplier of energy, both electricity and gas. Even banks were owned by some cities and towns, as well as bus companies and street markets. Post-war until 1970 local authorities were a major builder of new homes, as

CHAPTER 9

LOCAL GOVERNMENT

well as acting as landlords for the council house rental sector. Until the end of the 20th Century local government ran the Police.

But while these shrunken authorities still expend billions of pounds annually, they are only the local guardians and agents for most of it. The key decisions on how much they are allowed to spend, and what it can be spent on, are decided by central government, who put up about three-quarters of the money from general taxation. Much of the residue comes from the locally levied council tax. In the words of Professor King: "it is scarcely too strong to say that modern local government is neither local nor government". What it is, on the other hand, is the "local administration of national policies", with some residual discretion for local priorities on a small-scale(3).

One reason this could have happened is that the constitutional position of local government is weak. There is nothing in place to safeguard the public's right to elect local councils, or for these to have particular, specified purposes. That fact should sit uneasily alongside the history of devolution which has occurred in parallel to Scotland, Wales, and Northern Ireland, enfranchising their people. It seems ironical so soon after successful devolution to Wales and Scotland that not only was there little interest in regional government in England, a few homogeneous areas like Tyneside perhaps excepted, but that the populace were apathetic about having a local democracy running their cities, towns and villages through accountable local representatives. Even though many of them would have been brought up in the area and passionately concerned about its well being.

Cynics and optimists might say that there will always be local government: if nothing else about it is considered worthwhile, central government often finds it a convenient scapegoat. Others will point to the resilience displayed by local government during many years of attack. Mrs. Thatcher, who hated it for personal reasons, supposedly to do with how her father had been treated, saw off the mining unions, but could not crack local government, although its powers underwent deliberate and major retrenchment on her watch.

Two important illustrations of the sounding of retreat will be briefly

LOCAL GOVERNMENT

mentioned. The Police and Magistrates Courts Act 1994 hived off the police services from their local authorities and set them up as independent, precepting on the Council tax for part of their funding. Council representation is now outgunned by central government nominees and the Chief Constable himself.

In housing, during the 1970s, Mrs. Thatcher allowed tenants to buy their council houses off the local authority at massive discounts. The Housing Act 1988 gave a right to various bodies, like housing associations, to take over council housing as landlords. The rules were heavily stacked against councils, which were not allowed to raise private finance. Transfers were accelerated under New Labour, the (predictable) result being that the country became chronically short of available housing stock. Local authorities no longer built them and so-called 'affordable' housing became rather a rarity.

The remaining services provided by local government can be categorised three ways as needs, like education, housing, highways or refuse, protections, such as fire and police, general amenities, like libraries, museums, and leisure centres. Whereas formerly all the services were directly supplied by the local authorities, nowadays they are increasingly provided by other local agencies exercising powers from government. Local authorities are required to collaborate with an expending range of new partners, who also contribute to local governance in both policy-making and delivery terms. Some commentators envisage local government retreating to a more limited role as main commissioner of services supplied by other institutions. This happens already, in part, through the purchase of places in social care homes, for example, but its scale and durability remain conjectural.

Regarding councillors, for local government is an elected democracy, there are a few key points to be made. Firstly, as to representation in the sense of how the cadre compares with the community at large: essentially, women, ethnic minorities, and all ages apart from the elderly, are under-represented among councils. Whilst some practice positive discrimination, over which arguments may be finely balanced, and which can make a statistical difference, it is hard to see how much greater proportions of the working population can be recruited, short of making councillors jobs' full-time, well-remunerated employment.   Various allowances, notably for attendance, are paid these days, but for some reason people at large regard the idea with enormous resentment and hostility. While councillors' roles in the community have become much more demanding and time-consuming, often involving personal and family sacrifices.

A second key issue relates to the way councils operate, and to the potentially serious structural flaw introduced by the Local Government Act 2000. That was an objectionable piece of legislation in that it forced local authorities to abolish their tried and very well-tested committee structures for services and finance and introduce instead a system that central government had not the slightest intention of abiding by itself. A case of do as we say, not as we do. Specifically, councillors were divided in role into 'executive members' and 'non-executive members' (there were one or two variant models on offer, but this was the main one adopted). The 'split' was between a small executive of the ruling party that made policy decisions and took public responsibility for them, and a non-executive reduced to general overview and specific scrutiny of them. Within the executive, commonly an individual would take at least urgent decisions, whereas others would be made by the executive members in the cabinet as a whole. The vast majority of councillors, whether in the ruling party or not, would act in the non-executive roles where they could intervene during any or all of the stages of policy planning, implementation, and performance, potentially calling in evidence as part of formal consultations with a whole range of local individuals and organisations.

In order to ease government's untrusting suspicions about council operations and their possible democratic deficit (or more likely deviance from the national agenda), a monster has been created. Delay and inefficiency is certainly built-in, unless individual executives leading departments go unchallenged. But without high levels of cooperation with political friends and foes alike there is a recipe here for paralysis.

One very commonplace observation among local government officers is that nobody else appears to understand them or what they do. And they are frequently confused with civil servants, which they are not, the latter being employed by central government. It is generally conceded that historically local government has been very poor at explaining itself to a wider world, which always seems at best indifferent, sometimes downright hostile and prejudiced. This sets authors a serious and important challenge, especially at a time of media indifference, with very few journalists left specialising in the field nowadays.

Voting turnout in local elections is not high and never has been. There are those that say it is only national politics that counts and that the low interest suggests we do not want or need a locally-based democracy. In the run-up to the 2010 general election, with local elections due to be held simultaneously in many areas, the media made scant reference. One method to increase it, apart from making it a legal requirement as many democracies do, would be to have a local income tax, so we had more at stake. Another would be to break up the party stranglehold, whereby people could actually feel they could get rid of a council they did not like, instead of knowing that it would endure because of its permanent majority of whichever political colour. On the local scale, of course, many of the electorate have a much bigger chance of actually knowing some of the candidates and there is no doubt that their personal visibility ,and the esteem with which they are held in the local community, can count at least as much as the issues. And that standing is liable to be based on assessment of actual performance and personal qualities.

Whilst national issues and events are naturally more prominent and dominant, they are less likely to touch our lives on a day-to-day basis than local affairs. And when the effects of politicians on the national stage are so widely criticised, even disparaged, why do people seem content to let local democracy die by default, leaving matters largely at their mercy? If some councillors are rogues, at least they are local rogues, easier to rumble, get at, and evict from office. The sinister alternative, coming in all over like creeping sickness, is the already-mentioned quango, where central government sets up an institution to deal with a narrow area of policy implementation across the country and run it with their non-elected appointees. Appeal machineries, if they exist at all, are likely to be nominal. So, if something like the age of Orwell's Big Brother is at hand, it is partly because the public collectively have been too politically naïve, uninterested, and complacent to see him coming.

CHAPTER 9

LOCAL GOVERNMENT

Although we may have dealings with the local authority, these are likely to be over mundanities like bus travel passes, rubbish collection, library books. We can form the impression that it is dull, whereas it is in fact subject to a constant ferment of change, both externally and internally driven. And the character of the local authority is going to reflect traditions in the area, and so differ in noticeable respects from others elsewhere, despite the commonality of service delivery.

One very unfortunate feature is that something may be going awry in one department and can give the rest a bad name by association. A notorious, and tragically recurring scenario, is that of the neglected or abused child who dies, whereupon it then emerges that the local social services department might have done a great deal more to prevent the tragedy. These cases are not numerous, though one is too many, but they are very high-profile and extremely emotive. Whilst people think they can relate to the situations, they mostly cannot begin to understand the complex mix of professional interactions and responsibilities, although they rather think they can. Sometimes more venom is heaped on the hapless public servant than on the guilty parties within the malfunctioning family. So enquiries are held, practice guidelines changed. Heads have to roll.

Understandable, then, that local government is neither really comprehended ,nor trusted by the populace. In part because it has been rubbished by governments and the private sector, and because we have to pay for it and are not sure just what we get for our money, or whether it is worth it, anyway.

One major problem in England is that local councils are still, in spite of it all, the natural focus for people with all manner or community issues, but quangos, as well as other 'governance' manoeuvres have rendered their coordinating role in the local environment that much more complex, if not well-nigh impossible. After all, quangos are not always obliged to cooperate with them, anyway.

Local government working with the community sector is probably a great deal more formalised than it used to be, and for essentially one principal reason, the demands of central government. Essentially, government has its own agenda, which it seeks to impose through use of local bodies as

LOCAL GOVERNMENT

agencies for delivery in what is known as the 'voluntary sector compact'. Local authorities, voluntary bodies, charities, community groups generally, are thrown into collaboration as their only real way of obtaining significant public funding. Additionally, central government lacks trust in the agencies, especially if they are campaigning or sectional in interest, so over-regulates their activities, and is forever searching for some organisation which is truly representative of the people. It certainly does not regard elected local government itself as such. Indeed, it sometimes bypasses institutions in favour of a direct dialogue with creations like citizens' forums and focus groups, or to individual members of the public via local referenda and opinion polls.

The approach has undoubtedly produced gains. For one thing, local consultation is much more likely to be genuine in the lead-up to local authority policy formulation, with correspondingly more community-sector influence, whether representative, or more probably otherwise. But the wider goals of organisations can be squeezed out; whether they like it or not, they are in effect signed up to a national cause, delivered through specific projects. The working practices are full of injustices and tensions, with voluntary staff operating on the cheap alongside paid professionals.

Now some go willingly to water, and others are forced to drink. Likewise, councils vary greatly in their relative keenness to involve the public in participative ventures. The methods attempted, driven by central dictat, have expanded in type, from the rather traditional public meetings and consultation documents, to more zany approaches like interactive websites, community-run activity schemes, citizen's policy 'juries', and consumer satisfaction polls, as well as 'visioning' exercises to look at future possibilities. Is it all in the lap of the gods?

STRUCTURE

Organisation

Until 1965 about a quarter of the population of England and Wales lived under a single-tier, all-purpose authority, called a 'county borough'(4).

CHAPTER 9

LOCAL GOVERNMENT

Unitary reform, when it came, was therefore a relatively straight forward matter in those areas.

What was altogether more difficult, and confusing, was the three-tier system then operating in the rest of the country outside London; that is, in the county areas. They had county councils, districts, which could be called urban, rural, or non-county boroughs, and with a patchwork of parish councils in some rural areas.

London, with its proximity to Parliament, was always a special case. It has undergone various changes of structure over the years and is not typical of the national model, being close to Whitehall, so it will not be discussed here further.

In county areas, the County Council, as major authority, provided a raft of often more strategic services across the whole county. These would include education, social services, transport coordination, area planning, and main highways. The minor authorities, the district councils, dealt with housing and the more mundane functions, like refuse collection and street maintenance.

It is difficult to characterize in general terms the levels of cooperation between major and minor authorities over the years. Certainly, there were obvious areas of overlap, such as the (town) planning function. In other functions there was a built-in right of representation. For example, school governing bodies always contained members appointed by the minor authority. For many years it was also allowed for politicians to double-track, so that they could be members of both the major and minor authority simultaneously. Officers never cease to marvel at how smoothly the average politician removes one hat, then dons another.

Nevertheless, the degree of rivalry could be a significant factor, as were differences of outlook and priority. As major authority, too, the county council had to balance competing interests from localities across the whole piece. Yet a common stumbling block, as always in British politics, was the party allegiance. Disagreements could range from the tiny- minded to the fundamental, with major and minor authorities sometimes within the control of opposing parties.

CHAPTER 9

LOCAL GOVERNMENT

As briefly alluded to above, there is also in England a third-tier of local government, called parishes, with over 7,000 parish councils. These were created by the Local Government Act 1972. It is not usually given prominence because it is small beer, but plays an important role with the little things. If it were not for parish councils, many a village might wait in vain for the main council to renovate its dilapidated street furniture, for instance. Possibly surprising, Parish Councils have so far survived the unitary authority movement.

The Local Government Act, 1972, also invented six metropolitan counties, such as Greater Manchester, Merseyside, Tyne and Wear, covering conurbations with large populations of between one and three million. Their responsibilities covered a range of services of an environmental nature - highways and transport, planning. Within these areas a lower tier of metropolitan district or metropolitan borough councils was set up to cover the majority of local functions, with some overlap on planning matters with the metropolitan counties. One such metropolitan borough was Birmingham, with over a million inhabitants.

The Local Government Act, 1985 abolished the metropolitan counties, partly also to prevent conflict between the tiers. Another reason, though, was that they tended to promote regional policies which could be in opposition to national ones. Essentially, the metropolitan counties were of a different party political colour to the Conservative government of the day, so it was seen in some quarters as blatant gerrymandering.

When the dust settled on this reorganisation, which had swept away a good many district councils, the main remaining criticism was that there were still far too many authorities, with some not large enough to be financially viable. Also, it had done little to remove people's confusion about local government. So review started again before very long had elapsed, leading to the reorganisations of 2006-08, which are discussed in the next section to illustrate important points about democracy.

One cautionary note needs to be sounded first. Whilst it is easy to look at structure simplistically, and to want, say, to espouse a straight forward arrangement of authorities, there are inherent dangers, of which fortunately most politicians involved are well aware, at least in relation to

LOCAL GOVERNMENT

their own geographical centres of operation. What looks good and rational on paper may not work too well in practice. Structure is not the key to effective performance in local government, although poor elements can certainly be a hindrance. Relevant factors make the equation multivariate. Nor is it rooted in time, despite tradition playing an important part, still less is it the same everywhere, neither does one size necessarily fit all. What would serve us badly here, when contemplating another local government review, are remote politicians with dogmatic beliefs and only a modicum of local knowledge, where the dynamics, of whatever character, are invariably complex and subtle. And it requires a stamina and resolve which political communities only seem able to muster very rarely. So the results may have to last a long time even where they have not been properly designed to do so.

The Bains Report of 1972 had a profound effect on the subsequent development of local authority structures at the level of departmental management and their relative pay. Its emphasis was on integrated, or 'corporate' management to bring unity to the council, in contrast with the fragmenting effect of traditional departmental approaches, which allegedly were not so well coordinated. Parallel departments had also developed independent structures, so the hope was that duplication and financial excess could be reduced, as well as council problems being addressed in a more cooperative way internally.

Bains was enthusiastically taken up across the country. At members' level the model of an all-powerful Policy and Resources Committee was recommended, answering to Council in the last analysis, but with policy-making and executive roles. Other committees too were to be given delegated authority, not merely being advisory, but this nevertheless meant that the Education Committee, representing often far and away the largest function, number of staff and external institutions, such as schools, was rather cut down to size. It was easy to see how its areas of interest could overlap and conflict with those of the Policy and Resources Committee also, and they did.

Officers did receive more delegation of powers, but the recommendation was for a Chief Executive, who would lead and chair a management team of around six Directors. They would each be in charge of a

LOCAL GOVERNMENT

directorate formed by amalgamating small departments. For an illustration, there could be a Director of Technical Services, who would manage former departments like architecture, planning, environment, and engineering.

It is difficult to generalize about the success or failure of these models. People are always more important than structures. Nevertheless, some of the inherent weaknesses did emerge in places and should be pointed out.

One was the transcendent role of a dominant and influential chief executive, sometimes from a business background, where previously you just had a town clerk, who ran the legal department and was 'first among equals' among his colleagues at the management table. A few of these new characters threw their weight around, upsetting member and officer alike, completely failing to grasp the complexity and subtlety of local government culture, and they had to go. Some tried to build up departmental hierarchies of their own. Others meddled. Authorities like St Helens Metropolitan Borough ostentatiously did without a chief executive after a bad experience.

Nevertheless, there was a tendency to bear down on the freedoms of directorates. If you were in Education, for instance, an increasing amount of your time would be taken up with meeting the corporate demands of the wider authority instead of the school clientele and national government. Some longed for the days when specialising politicians on the Education Committee were dedicated to 'the Education Party' and the Chief Education Officer had the influence which came of being a nationally respected expert in the field.

Critics of Bains feared it would become a bureaucratic monster and they were not wrong. Directorates were often put together with strange bedfellows - professionals with little in common, although certainly budget and policy rivals. They were accordingly difficult to control. Education might be thrown in with museums, or libraries. Sometimes a 'centralizing' directorate, like finance or administration or personnel ,would spring up and grow powerful. As their structures developed, initially quite layered, the already large directorates, like Education or Social Services, would be asked to thin out their managerial staff. The

CHAPTER 9

LOCAL GOVERNMENT

corporate pressures led to comparability of pay and structure across functions, irrespective of the disparities in importance of posts and their responsibilities. Recruitment norms widened and qualification requirements with relevant experience tended to dumb down. Education had recognised postgraduate standards, but some of the newer departments lacked tradition.

There is little doubt that local authorities through the Bains proposals were responding to another fashionable idea from industry. They did as they always did, by looking over their shoulders and following suit. Not all had the same level of understanding of the practical purposes of Bains, and old traditions of operation died hard. If councillors were disorientated and some heads of service felt their areas to be under siege, they were, of course, right. Education was a particular loser. It had been common to run district-based administrative units in counties, and these were the mainstay of day-to-day and personal working relations with the schools. Under corporatism they were frequently reigned back, reduced in number or even abolished altogether, leading to a sense of remoteness.

Whatever the prevailing views on the ground, it was not long before the government decided that Bains reforms had failed. They were off again on yet another costly Local Government Review.

The government gave local government and their electorates various reform models to choose from ,since they were adamant that the traditional mode of organisation and conduct of business was not streamlined enough for the modern world. They pointed in their critique to 'inefficient and opaque decision-making' behind closed doors by caucus groups in the majority party, too many committees and meetings, too much time spent by councillors away from their communities. In other words, it is tempting to remark, all the sorts of vices that government knows only too well afflict Parliament too.

The source for these proposals was 'Freedom Within Boundaries', a Local Government Management Board publication in 1997. They were pure 'New Labour' with Blair claiming they would improve efficiency, accountability, and openness. The models they offered were broadly of three main kinds. The first was a directly elected mayor, who selected a

LOCAL GOVERNMENT

cabinet from the councillors. They became local 'ministers' with executive powers in given areas of work.

The second model allowed for a directly elected mayor and a council manager, the latter having delegated powers for even strategic policy as well as day-to-day operational decisions.

The concept of a mayor directly elected by the public is American. As a high-profile figure he/she could become more effective in communicating with the electorate and government. He/she would also cut down on red tape and would speed up decision-making.

Not surprisingly, though the system is alive and well in London, which has elected very charismatic mayors, in Ken Livingstone and Boris Johnson, it has been rejected almost everywhere else. Councillors were frightened at their potential loss of influence, the dangers of corruption and dictatorship, possible erosion of powers, the lack of representation. And the public have been less than enthusiastic, even though it does not take much of an up-swell of feeling within the rules to force an election.

The third optional model was a cabinet with a leader elected by the Council. The key proposal was to separate the role of councillors into two. One group would form 'the executive'; the other group becoming 'representatives'. The executive would naturally formulate policy and be responsible for its implementation. The representatives, on the other hand, would be in tune with their constituents, as well as acting as scrutineers of the executive.

The operation of executive leaders for local government service areas has given more power to the former chairman of service committees, so that it puts a high reliance, not always justified, on both their ability and their willingness to take proper advice from key others among council and party members, and from the professional head of service.

Arrangements can exist to 'call in' their decisions for scrutiny before implementation, which leads to the creation of elaborate edifices and in-house rules in itself.

CHAPTER 9

LOCAL GOVERNMENT

Decisions may come more quickly, but are not necessarily the better for a lack of shared deliberation. Not everything in local government needs to be done in a rush, anyway. Many an issue will certainly wait. It can take quite a time for good policy to formulate.

So the structural changes which occurred in local government under the Blair government were complex. They were in addition characteristically profoundly undemocratic in their modes of operation, quite deliberately so.

Reorganisation

As we have seen, reorganising local authority structures and boundaries is something that United Kingdoms did from time to time during the 20th century. It was never easy and not cheap, so as well as ideology it required political determination and the timing to be right, at least from a central perspective. It usually created havoc on the ground.

Mixed models were the common outcome, and no attempt ever attained the sense of completion, finality, and irreversibility that the Blairite one has, although there remain parts of the country that it never reached.

The Labour Government under Blair believed in, and sought to bring about, a one-type-fits-all sort of local government to every part of the country - the Unitary authority model under which one council caters within each locality for all the services provided. It looks at this remove in time to be here to stay, whether or not it has all-party support and, sadly, whether or not it succeeds.

One of the great problematic facts of life is that all governments seem to view the structure in public bodies as crucial to their operational capability. But it ain't necessarily so. Manpower capacity and quality are much more important factors, as are appropriate levels of resourcing. Governments fiddle with local authorities because they do not trust them, and because they can.

In the 1990s the two-tier system in Wales and in Scotland was abolished

LOCAL GOVERNMENT

by the Government in favour of unitary authorities. They clearly wished to do the same for England, but the way they went about it was dishonest, extremely long-drawn out, deceitful, and very costly, both financially and in terms of local authority staff and their morale.

A Local Government Commission (known as Banham after its chairman, a former head of the CBI) was then (for England) set up to explore and review structure and boundaries for all the local authorities. It operated from 1992 to 1995 and had to advise the government on such matters as community and democracy, efficiency and effectiveness.

The Commission was required to produce a plan for each area, consult locally, then report back to government with final recommendations. In the case of Cheshire, which will serve as an illustration, Banham proposed retention of the existing two-tier system of county and district councils. The idea was entirely consistent with the government's guidance to the Commission: whilst it expressed a preference for unitary solutions, it also made it clear that the two-tier system could continue in areas where it was thought best. But the Banham Report for Cheshire was rejected. He was humiliated in the Commons and told to think again. (This was the internationally respected Banham, the man brought in to advise on the fairness of democratic elections in Rhodesia.) The Commission did so and Cheshire's fate was the retention of a reduced size of county council. Their areas of Halton and Warrington were hived off as separate new Unitaries.

Banham became generally critical of the exercise nationwide because there was a lot of interference by successive ministers during the process. Not only were recommendations of the Commission referred back, but they kept changing the guidelines. The government's actions were actually declared unlawful by judicial review in the High Court in 1994, but Banham was replaced nevertheless.

There are, of course, theoretical arguments available for and against unitary authorities, but available evidence is sparse and difficult to weigh. The kinds of reasons government used in favour of the unitaries were reducing costs, improving services, better leadership, and greater community involvement in the running of their services. Yet ultimately

LOCAL GOVERNMENT

the government's preference for unitaries was based on unsubstantiated ideological conviction.

The present purpose is not to argue especially for one model or another, and the account here does not attempt to do justice to those Cheshire districts that pressed for the unitary model. Rather, it is what the behaviour of central government tells us about our 'democracy' that is the focus.

The case study should matter a great deal to people, for no matter what view they take of the relative importance of local government, if government is prepared to behave in such a manner with the populace over a 'small matter', just what would it get up to when the stakes are high?

In 2006, when the next tranche of Local Government Reorganisation started, there was existing legal machinery in place about how the structure of local government could be altered. Matters would be referred to the Boundary Committee, which made recommendations to the Secretary of State. The next stage was legislation in Parliament to enact changes or, if relatively minor proposals, Orders could be placed in the Commons by the Secretary of State to give them effect.

Illegally, however, the government ignored established procedure and instead gave the Secretary of State complete control over the whole process and the decisions. They were enabled to do so by a variety of states of affairs: firstly, they had a large majority; secondly, there was public lethargy and general lack of interest. Thirdly, and very significantly, local authorities are creatures of statute in the United Kingdom. Consequently, unlike in some countries, their existence has no constitutional protection here.

The government was deceptive. It forced through some massive changes, yet in March 2006 the Local Government Minister, Philip Woolas (he who later lost his constituency seat in court for illegal canvassing at the general election in 2010) said:

> "Restructuring without local agreement is 99.99% ruled out. I'm not aware of anywhere that's likely".

CHAPTER 9

LOCAL GOVERNMENT

The scope of the LGR was large across the country. Two-tier local government was replaced in seven county areas by nine new unitary councils. Seven county councils were abolished, along with the many district councils in their areas. Unitary authorities were created to cover all the functions of the councils in five county areas. In the cases of the other two county areas, including Cheshire, each was divided into two, with a total of four unitaries created to cover them. Parts of England affected included Cornwall, County Durham, North Yorkshire, Devon, Cheshire, Shropshire, Somerset, and Wiltshire, so it was relevant to a lot of people.

Cheshire County Council was not broken, but they fixed it anyway. The same probably goes for many of the other authorities disbanded too.

Chisholm and Leach have written at length and critically on the subject of the way government conducted the 2006/8 LGR. Cambridge Professor Chisholm was a member of the Local Government Commission for England during the 1990s; Leach a Professor of Local Government at De Montfort University Leicester(5).

Existing authorities were required to put bids in to government setting out their proposals. The government's own criteria by which local authorities should be judged were fivefold, as follows:

     (1)   strong, effective, and accountable strategic leadership;
     (2)   neighbourhood flexibility and empowerment;
     (3)   value for money on public services;
     (4)   affordability;
     (5)   supported by a cross-section of partners and stakeholders.

Unfortunately, for the existing local authorities, it was difficult to be exact about the precise criteria the government was using, because the literature shows the wording changed somewhat as the process went along. Time and again Chisholm and Leach analyse inconstancies and inconsistencies of wording in government statements on the various reorganisations. The most charitable view is that it wavers as a result of less than precise drafting. At worst, there is evidence provided of true intention hidden behind bogus argument.

CHAPTER 9

LOCAL GOVERNMENT

Consider criterion 5. This seemed to imply a prior need to convince a whole range of local people and institutions before change was adopted. However, Baroness Andrews, for the government, said:

> *"We deliberately did not look for public support, we did not require local referendums, and we did not make this a test of public opinion."* She also said:
> *"Let me be clear about what the definition of 'broad cross-section of support' actually means..... It is, essentially, about whether the new unitary authority genuinely meets its objectives and will work for local people".*

Clearly, the government was distrustful of public opinion and produced a false criterion so as to look reasonably democratic when it was in fact being dictatorial and paternalistic.

The government's own statements about the various reorganisations showed confusion of thought over the strategic leadership criterion. It found it difficult to think of reasons why strategic leadership would be improved in unitary cities. And it said that a desirable component was "shortening the distance between governors and governed". But that is to confuse it with local empowerment.

The affordability and value for money criteria were quite simply not met. A figure of £75 million was reported by the government as the saving from reorganisation by the creation of five unitary councils. But the transition costs were drastically underestimated, with independent sources claiming an overall cost of £116 million. Some places included the shadow new authority in the lead up to reorganisation costs, others did not. Ongoing and IT costs were not properly accounted for in the government's calculations, Chisholm and Leach concluded. There was also an understandable tendency of bidding authorities to underplay the area governance, or bureaucratic costs, and harmonisation and re-branding, especially given government's plans for engaging and empowering communities at a very local level, another potentially unfulfilled success criterion owing to the limitations on financial underwriting.

CHAPTER 9

LOCAL GOVERNMENT

In practice, affordability and support were not taken as seriously by government as the other three criteria. And even with these, the desired outcomes did not necessarily have to come with the reorganisation, but it was said could be attained later by the new authorities some way further down the line.... . So, against a rather mobile backdrop, it was very difficult for any of the councils to formulate fully evidenced and reasoned bids, though naturally some of their efforts were objectively much more impressive than others.

The authors concluded that the government was "guilty of malpractice in the way it proceeded, especially in not following the law and rules" (established for reorganisations in local government).

To quote from their findings:

> *"Unreliable data were accepted (by government), inconsistent decisions were taken, and misleading information given as the basis for those decisions. Parliament was misled, and there was a large element of political deception".*

It is instructive to consider the change from the standpoints of the arguments adduced in advance of it, and also of the behaviour of central government, to see what light they throw on democratic process. In reality the decision- making had the mere semblance of democracy about it. There was tokenism.

For one thing it was contrary to the expressed wishes of the Cheshire people in the local consultation process. The Labour government's decision was prominently opposed by the redoubtable Gwyneth Dunwoody, Labour MP for Crewe, one of the district council areas, who said:

> *"I have rarely seen a decision taken with such cynicism and with so little respect for the interests of the average voter".*

Cheshire County Council was abolished despite providing over 80% of the local services as a government 'excellent-rated' authority. The government itself admitted that the County Council's bid to survive met all its criteria for bids.

CHAPTER 9

LOCAL GOVERNMENT

Cheshire Schools Forum, representing over 330 secondary, primary and special school heads and 4,000 governors, firmly opposed the break-up of Cheshire County Council in a letter to the Secretary of State in October 2007. The worries were about funding adequacy and the loss of specialist expertise and services, threatening the existing high level of standards, as well as change overload in schools.

Martin Bell, former independent MP for Tatton in that area of the county, stated his views that:

> *"there is no sense, financially or administratively, in splitting Cheshire. The division is profoundly undemocratic".*

The Centre for Sustainable Urban and Regional Futures at Salford University produced a report which questioned the split-county model for Cheshire on economic grounds, no distinctive economic units having been identified to coincide with the areas of the proposed two unitaries(7). Neither did the pattern of travel to work provide evidence for a split either.

Even Cheshire's Labour leader criticized the process (8). C.C. Bateman highlighted the fact that it was so long drawn-out that staff had been unsettled by its uncertainty for ten years. He was also unconvinced that the quality of service to the public would not be adversely affected.

One aspect of the national reorganisation review was that local authorities affected by proposals were legally fettered in relation to public advertising of their cases. How is that for freedom of speech ? (9).

Chester City Council was the key local authority which in its submission advocated the unitary split, subsequently adopted by government. But, following an adverse report it commissioned from the financial consultants, Deloitte's, Chester withdrew support for its own bid! The financial figures were exposed as seriously in error, using simplistic estimates that, for example, unreasonably assumed the disaggregation of services would be cost-neutral, as also the integration of IT systems.

The Secretary of State in written record to Cheshire's Chief Executive admitted there were 'risks' in the financial case for creating two unitaries.

CHAPTER 9

LOCAL GOVERNMENT

For the Cheshire review the government commissioned its own independent financial report on the proposals. The County Council (10) asked the Government to release all the information which they had used to come to their decision. Especially relevant here were the dealings Government had with the Institute of Public Finance, because the body was understood to be commenting on financial material supplied by the County and the boroughs in their submissions arguing their cases. The Government's response was to decline, and to claim a legal exemption under the Freedom of Information Act. People will draw their own conclusions as to whether concealment was within the spirit of democracy and if government and local government were playing the game according to the same set of rules.

The Secretary of State, Hazel Blears (she who later lost her ministerial job for fiddling expenses), had announced the decision when Parliament was about to recess for Christmas. The verdict came after a mysterious delay, ostensibly for further consideration, while the other structural changes nationally were announced on 5th December, 2007.

Mrs Dunwoody, herself a former Labour cabinet minister, accused the government of using a written statement as a device for limiting questions in the House of Commons.

Because several of the authorities being abolished then pleaded that they could not meet the set time scale for reorganisation, a House of Lords committee examined the position, concluding that the government should reconsider it (11). But the request was denied. It is a long standing experience in local government that timetables imposed on them tend to be very tight. Central government, on the other hand, can, and does, take just as long as it likes. Only one side probably had the good of the people at heart. Even though they faced the abolition of their positions, local officers and members were expected as a matter of course to maintain their traditional selflessness in the face of a perceived community need for continuity of services and to cooperate with all to enable a smooth and seamless transfer of power.

The Labour Government had announced the decision late 2007 to abolish Cheshire County Council and all the Cheshire district councils from April 2009. It had lasted 117 years and was to be replaced by two new

CHAPTER 9

LOCAL GOVERNMENT

councils, covering East Cheshire and West Cheshire respectively (6). These divisions never existed hitherto in any geographical or socio-economic sense and were quite alien to the communities involved.

Regarding local government reorganisation, the Labour Government since the 1990's had an ideological commitment to bring the reality of unitary authorities to the whole country. Bear in mind that it had taken central government at least seventeen years to achieve the goal, given that it set up the Banham Commission in 1992. Strong decision-making could have achieved it in about two years with a simple change of law providing for the practical lead-in time for a smooth transition. Sham democracy can be worse than non at all, since it destroys trust and wastes everyone's time and money, whilst maintaining false hopes.

The fact that local government has always been the cat's mouse was again scandalously demonstrated under the Con-Dem government ,which soon announced and set about with relish and barely concealed glee wholesale butchery across the public sector and in local government in particular. Tories have always had an ideological distaste for public sector 'bureaucrats', whom they deride and disparage at every opportunity with unthinking mantras that roll off their silken tongues. It is very hard to see in such a climate why public servants would want to stay in post and take a pride in their work when the sleaziest salesman in the private sector appears to be more highly regarded. So much for the vacuous Con-Dem slogan that "we are all in it together."

So it is worth now looking at Local Government employment in a little more detail to understand , and perhaps even empathise , with their situation rather better than the Tories do.

PUBLIC SERVICE

Remuneration

The pay you receive in working life may not be the sole consideration, but it is a very large factor in determining the kind of job you do and the satisfaction you derive from it.

CHAPTER 9

LOCAL GOVERNMENT

The young therefore need to be told before they enter working life that in theory pay in the private sector is unfettered, whereas the Government of the day, any Government, will seek to control pay quite strictly across the whole public sector, and all of the time. Again in theory this means that your pay in the private sector is likely to have much to do with market conditions, while in the public sector in practice it will be decided to a large extent by Government policy.

The result is that year after year the public sector is held back by Governments seeking to appear prudent and responsible in their handling of the economy. Of course, in reality the situation is much more complicated. For one thing, token attempts might be made for some public sector workers to 'catch up' after years of relatively unfavourable treatment, maybe in response to union pressure and direct action.

But it is easy enough for the Government to put a lid on it most of the time, because media distortion encourages public attitudes that claim productivity in the public sector is artificial and that what these workers do is actually no better than a drain on the nation's resources.

Typical of the sentiments arraigned against staff pay rises was a Times leader in June 2008 (12). The consumer prices index, an official measure of inflation, was 3.3%, and the local government union, Unison, had rejected an offer from the employers of a pay rise of 2.45% in favour of industrial action. The tenor of the article was that the Government was likely to be engaged in a conflict essential for it to win. It suggested no money was left in the national kitty at a time of rising unemployment in the private sector. It did acknowledge the 14% pay rise won by the militancy and picketing of the tanker drivers, but made no link in justice or equity. This is the old, old story, of course. There never is a good time for local government to be seeking a pay rise. There was a hint that they were being irresponsible. The stance became laughable within a few months with the arrival of the credit crunch, precipitating bank collapses. Billions of pounds were then found by the Government for the bail-outs of failed institutions, greedy and incompetent bank managers. The culture and state of law was such that there was much uncertainty over whether any of these miscreants had even acted in criminal ways.

CHAPTER 9

LOCAL GOVERNMENT

At one time it was conveniently said that, although public sector pay was generally lower than that for 'equivalent' jobs in the private sector, the compensation was in relative security of tenure, and perhaps better pensions. But now it is very clear that, whilst the private sector is no more stable, public sector jobs, in addition to being for the most part dead-end, are coming more and more under threat themselves. A whole range of destabilizing influences can be at work, such as short-term contracts, internal and external reorganisations, the introduction of private sector measures like reducing the levels of hierarchy, (and thereby promotion opportunities) ,accountability via Government target-setting and media scrutiny, and many more besides.

In talking of the 'public sector' it is important to make certain qualifications clear. The sector is fundamentally heterogeneous; in short, it contains a wide range of disparate groupings, as we have seen, with few interests in common and doing a vast range of considerably different jobs. This is significant if you are looking to energize public workers as a sector (which rarely happens), and may well help to explain why, with few exceptions, groups have been as putty in the hands of central government. In local government the preponderance of women, many earning a second family income, damps down militancy. A majority do not even join the union that might help to protect their livelihoods.

Then again, the public sector contains groupings with a wide range of popularity ratings. For instance, nurses always get the sympathy vote, the Fire Brigade are viewed as essential, but local government officers are regarded by many as a waste of space.

The groups differ enormously in their influence over Government. This is partly a matter of public opinion and prestige, but more to do with strong and effective union-like organisation with some, such as the doctors, and political affiliations with the legislature and executive, as with the judges.

So even within the limitations of relatively low pay settlements across the public sector, there are some groups that will do very nicely thank-you and others that will mostly feel shafted.

CHAPTER 9

LOCAL GOVERNMENT

It is, of course, true that not all the main parameters remain fixed. Some groups have varying popularity over time, teachers being one of them. And the relative position of a group within the pecking order can change markedly too.

Witness when Mrs. Thatcher as prime minister decided that the police needed a leg-up the ladder. You then had callow youths with minimal training being paid more than qualified teachers and the young married constables being provided with subsidised housing.

For all that, it is depressing for a typical public sector worker to observe that, over the many years since the militant 1960s, other groups have still found it necessary from time to time to flex their muscles over strike action. They tend themselves to have a sense of vocation all too easy to exploit.

To return to the rank and file teachers in elaborating the point, in spite of their strategic role of aiding to invest in human capital, in preparing us all for our adult lives, and despite the relatively new lip-service paid by Government to the importance of education, teachers have been unable to improve their relative lot in society at large. And goodness knows, they have seldom been out of the media pleading their cause. Perhaps it is time for them to undertake some social engineering with the tools of their trade, by trying to inculcate communitarian values in the next generation of hapless workers.

Local Government has become subject to the business trend for a sharply tapering, pyramidal hierarchy, with a few well-paid managers at the top and quite flat plateaus underneath. So career aspirations are realistically modest and have been so long-term, at least since 1945. Given this, public attitudes of low esteem or downright hostility, and the reducing job security, it has to be seen as some kind of wonder that people continue to volunteer at all. Perhaps they have absorbed the ethic from their parents, been attracted by carefully pitched higher starting rates, been plainly misinformed or naïve, or have simply nowhere else to find a refuge.

Ironically, the international banking crisis and credit crunch, which will have long-term effects not all easy to predict, could make public sector

CHAPTER 9

LOCAL GOVERNMENT

employment, even local government, more attractive to job seekers. Much will depend on political responses to the private sector's opinion on the private/public divide. They have already caused a major review of, and reduction of benefits in, public sector pension schemes, which are based on final salaries, once they become unable to sustain their own (frequently much more generous) schemes. Traditionally, local government pensions can only reach a ceiling of half-salary ,and that after a full forty years of service. Gross financial and political mismanagement may have been largely to blame, but the public sector were nevertheless seen as unfairly advantaged. One terrible mistake made by Government was not to invest contributions, but to meet annual pension calls out of general taxation.! It could all go sour again, if a battered economy fails to regenerate sufficient well-paid private sector jobs in the post-credit-crunch era. It will inevitably happen, anyway, as the proportion of pensioners in society demographically increases as a growing burden on the employed.

One feature, however, is laudable. In the interests of open government the grading of each local authority post has to be published and available to scrutiny. The public are entitled to know what their servants 'earn', if this term has any semblance of meaning left in a country of such gross inequities. There are those who think that the secrecy enjoyed by the private sector in these matters is a strong encouragement to exploitation, and their concealment of profit margins a recipe for dishonesty.

It should not go unsaid, finally, that there have been some attempts in public sector in recent years to ape the private sector when it comes to paying large salaries to those at the very top. The same kind of huge salary disparities as have characterized the private sector have developed in the public sector too, though rarely at such high levels. For example, principals of colleges of further education boosted their salaries by over fifty percent in eight years to 2009. Meanwhile hundreds of staff in over fifty colleges had been made redundant. It is not uncommon for chief executives of larger councils to receive more than the prime minister in salary, but not in associated allowances. They have no second homes or personal staff paid for by the taxpayer.

Similarly, scams have developed at the top in local government regarding

CHAPTER 9

LOCAL GOVERNMENT

the employment conditions of council chiefs. Some do not last long before falling foul of the local politicians and have received large severance deals not related to length of service or their achievements in post. In March 2010 an Audit Commission report highlighted 37 cases over two and a half years at an average pay off at over £250,000. Whilst they undoubtedly need some protection against dismissal at political whim, because of 'personal differences', some have quickly gone on to another lucrative job, the so-called "boomerang bosses".

It is clear that these developments are resented, both by politicians and the public. They want to rein them in. But not especially because of the little folk. The general attitude appears to be that local government is never entitled to better than the private sector. If the latter suffers, so should local government take a proportionate share of the pain. The stance might be reasonable, except that it is always one-sided. Private profits are unfettered. Local government is never allowed to benefit from bonuses, share options, perks of any kind, and staff rarely even have the option of a salary review based on private sector comparators. The arrangements for chief executives in local government are legal and contractual: such events are commonplace in the world of industry and commerce, where they largely pass without comment, but must result in higher prices.

The pre-election talk in 2010 from all the main parties about the need to curb public sector pay was superficial.

It overlooked or discounted the massive injustice stemming from the banking bail-out and the continuing, mostly unfettered practices, of paying vast bonuses in that industry to its top people.

It announced no intention to address the problems of unfairness stemming from uncontrolled high-end pay in the private sector.

It said nothing about the fact that top pay in the public sector is usually considerably smaller than that in corresponding private sector positions.

We need to expose and discredit the shallow private sector claim that to attract the best staff top 'going' rates have to be paid. Just how rare are

CHAPTER 9

LOCAL GOVERNMENT

these talents? How come they are worth scores or even hundreds of times more than ordinary mortals?

And it was silent about the argument that many staff in the public sector with relatively high earnings actually deserve their pay.

Dishonestly, it tended to gloss over the quite small savings to be found from clobbering what is really a very small group of workers.

To suggest, as Gordon Brown did, that those on "over-generous" salaries would be "named and shamed" did nothing for the morale of the public sector, or his reputation either.

And it was barefaced hypocrisy too. Governments generate public sector waste on a truly spectacular scale all by themselves - by myriad behaviours such as hiring armies of private sector consultants, generating numerous unnecessary ministerial and political advisory posts, spawning large numbers of quangos, setting up legion enquiries, contracting to develop a whole series of sensationally costly and failing IT projects. The now abandoned NHS computerisation project, for instance, wasted £30 billion, despite expert warnings at every stage, which went unheeded.

The clamour for transparency over top remuneration packages in both public and private sectors seems hard to take exception to, unless you have dark secrets to keep. Private firms get away with it very often, because they are to an unhealthy extent allowed to do what they like.

Even in the public sector we still did not know what all the high earners received. Shamefully, the so-called 'stars' at the BBC refused to tell us their 'commercial secrets' and we did not require them to, although we knew they got millions. So the official 'Public Sector Rich List' was incomplete in 2009. Nevertheless, it did reveal no fewer than 806 public sector workers with annual salaries over £150,000.The BBC alone paid 85 executives more than the Prime Minister.

In December 2009 the Reform think tank, a Conservative-leaning organisation, exposed something of the reality that pre-election politicians just dared not do. In order to reduce employment costs by 15%, and save

CHAPTER 9

LOCAL GOVERNMENT

£27 billion per year, one million public sector jobs would have to be lost, not footling little measures like restricting pay rises, leaving some unfilled posts vacant, or cutting back-room boys out of the administration. For the credit crunch deficit to be addressed, in other words, there would have to be very substantial reductions in 'essential' services, as well as in front-line staff.

In full recognition of the imminent storm ahead, as the general election drew nearer there were demonstrations in London in April 2010 against the looming prospect of public sector cuts. …..

Working Life

It would be nice to report otherwise, but the present section regrettably must serve as a serious word of caution to all those young or not so young people who might contemplate a future career in local government. The sound advice at the outset is don't. But if you are tempted ,at least read on first and mull things over. Better still, talk to those who have suffered first hand.

Staff at more junior levels are not necessarily going to be aware of the influence of central government on their local authority employer, but they would be wise to try to track what is going on, at least in broad terms.

Local Government, as has oft been said, is a creature of statute. Its powers and duties derive from the legislation of governments to which it is beholden in ways which can be quite unsatisfactory for local people, as well as for those unfortunate enough to toil within its walls.

It cannot control its own destiny. Those in national politics will not come clean on their game plans, will lie and dissemble, will probably change their minds, or be rapidly replaced by colleagues with other ideas.

Some might say that endless cycles of new policy initiatives, and even wholesale reorganisations of staff structures, were a result of political dogmas unsullied by contact with reality, desperate attempts to shore up a

CHAPTER 9

LOCAL GOVERNMENT

government's fading reputation for competence and achievement, the cult of 'newness' from inexperienced ministers anxious to make their mark and knowing that only instant 'results' might do the trick before they were found out.

The almost wholly unconstructive opposition between left and right nationally can have very serious effects. Much hot air is expended for cheap advantage by our leaders seeking either to expand public sector employment or to reduce it. A buffer of the expendables has grown up; these unfortunates gain employment with Labour and disappear again under the Conservatives. The mechanism is, of course, of enormous political usage, the more so if it remains unrumbled by the electorate at large. Both parties make capital; one by 'creating jobs', the other by 'reducing bureaucracy' in an ongoing tide of ebb and flow.

A major difficulty for staff is that councils have increasingly lost their powers of independence as well as some functions. More and more, local government has become an instrument by which central government carries out its policies on the ground. So it has come to expect, and resigned to live with, the frequent edicts, about-turns, and breathless schemes foisted on it from above. Laws are passed, helpfully interpreted for practitioners by quasi-legal administrative circulars (without central liability), timescales drawn up, deadlines set, and monitoring regimes put in place, usually requiring regular feedback on exacting lists of questions. So if you are the kind of person that finds satisfaction in setting his own agenda for social change, rather than carry out someone else's, forget it as a career path altogether.

Government attitudes and behaviour at a time of major economic setback, such as the credit crunch in 2009, are instructive for all those in local government. When the credit crunch started to hit employment, its first major impacts were in the private sector, leading to the usual press howls of protest that the public sector was unfairly cushioned. Some economic theorists suggested that it would behove government in the short-term to bolster state employment to help ride out the recession, but the 'Labour' government officially could not see it. Their stance was that inflation was low, and people could no longer afford significant council tax rises during the downturn, so council tax rises had to be kept to a minimum. The

CHAPTER 9

LOCAL GOVERNMENT

predictable outcome was that by February 2009 the Local Government Association was claiming at least 65 local authorities had already made staff cuts, with 70% expecting to have to resort to additional job losses. Typically, government tried to face both ways at once. Communities minister John Healey said that *'councils should not cut jobs, as an easy option, but residents must come first'*. Government had also set draconian 'efficiency savings' of £1.5 billion, and placed a financial penalty cap on council tax rises above 5%. Typically, councils respond by removing backroom staff rather than front-line professionals, leaving them denuded of support.

The tendency of central government to reorganize the structure of local government quite frequently has already been examined. It is worth while pointing out the likely effects on staff when it happens. If a large local authority is forced repeatedly to reorganise, hive-off, merge, or contract with private sector institutions, it loses ethos, identity, and strength. Good people go, clowns are appointed to strange new jobs by ill political judgement or bias, staff live with gnawing uncertainly for months, if not years, their job descriptions unilaterally torn up. In the turmoil public service deteriorates because of the internal focus of institutional attention. People are deskilled as they clamour to fill the available posts, competing with their friends and colleagues, to become, often as not, more square pegs in round holes. Sometimes they are moved to different sections, buildings, even towns. They lose touch with the bulk of their former workmates.

Management cannot cope. Shadowed by tough-minded 'advisers' from their Finance and Human Resources departments, and given well-nigh impossible briefs and timescales by central government, it becomes enmeshed with intractable problems of staff careers and morale. Relationships break down. A growing number of employees start to suffer from work-related stress. Sickness absence rises.

The old political guard collapses, to be replaced by fresh-faced innocents of whatever motivation in a pluralist society which contains growing numbers of extremists and others to whom United Kingdom culture is alien.

LOCAL GOVERNMENT

We will see later how Government's contemporary love affair with the private sector led to regulation requiring more services to be contracted out, or with competitive tendering between in-house and private sector outfits, and could easily do so again for services as yet untouched. The role of the local authority in such situations becomes merely that of the 'client', 'buying' external goods or services.

It used to be thought that anything of an uncommercial nature would have to stay in the public sector. Until, that is, governments hit on the idea of creating artificial markets where there are no real ones. It is so easy for them to siphon off actual or potential liabilities and launder them within national accounting figures, thus creating environments more attractive to the business community. This happened with the railways, so why not in local government?

When that was done with the Prison Service, the private firms employed staff who were cheaper and less experienced to cut costs and maximize their profits. Unfortunately, a company called Group Four let a succession of prisoners escape.

Since more local government staff and members are now involved in novel financial arrangements, the scope of greed and corruption has probably increased. Its future consequential rise is a reasonable prediction to parallel the corruption of capitalism in the private sector. Employees could be tempted, or unwittingly sucked in, as it becomes a common mode of behaviour in the outside world.

The Local Government Act 1999 brought in the duty on local authorities to deliver services of 'Best Value' across all functions ,so as to produce 'continuous improvements'. They must meet set standards by means that are the most 'effective, economic and efficient' feasible. They must consult their 'stakeholders', notably tax payers and service users, and undertake regular reviews. Managers find themselves every year formulating Best Value plans, which include performance indicators (PIs), performance standards (PS), and performance targets (PTs). They have to prepare comparisons with past years and against other local authorities deemed relevant, publishing their reports for senior management, the Council, and the external auditor. He may inform the national Audit Commission, which has inspection powers, and reports to the government minister responsible on performance 'progress'.

The constant threat hanging over staff like the sword of Damocles is that of performance. They know that at any time government, or even their own council, may seek to put out their service to an external agency. The trouble is that the PIs are almost always based only on what is measurable. Government by targets put a premium on numbers, but these do not tell anything like the complete story with regard to quality or humanity.

Something else for a would-be officer to bear in mind is that their roles in local government have been changing virtually ever since the Thatcher years. Much would be called experimental if it had ever been scientifically tested and assessed, but is, sadly, rather more a reflection of central government's vacillating trendiness. To some extent the mode has brought in new kinds of worker: in other parts it has 'required' existing staff to acquire new skills and undertake new roles.

The kind of general management training received in-house has changed out of all recognition. In contemporary times there has been one-way traffic, with private sector consultants being imported, at great expense, to teach the ignorant public sector how things are done in the real world and how, henceforth, they will be done in local government.

Managers from the private sector would be surprised to see how little personal assistance, or even secretarial help is now available, except at the highest echelons and for the council members. Nor is eye candy employed for purposes of image or marketing. They would be frustrated by the artificial deadlines, the numerous internal reporting mechanisms, the focus on relative trivia, the elaborate networks of communication, the slowness of decision-making, and much else besides standing between them and client or organisation-centred goals. Some sections could grow so wrapped up in applied navel-gazing that the outside world comes almost to seem like an irrelevance.

Turning to staff structures, the prospect of employees becoming embroiled in a high-profile case in the media is not so remote as once it was. In 2009 the nation was shocked by news of several sadly fatal child

CHAPTER 9

LOCAL GOVERNMENT

abuse cases (13). Attention focused on the alleged shortcomings of local social services departments which had apparently not exercised appropriate supervision and intervention with 'toxic' families. The Director of Social Services in Haringey was subsequently sacked. The Government made it clear that they supported this decision, and there was much popular agreement. (In a sequel the Director took her case to law, suing for wrongful dismissal and produced documentary evidence of pre-judged political bias) (14).

It later emerged that in 2004 the Council had appointed a new managing director, or chief executive, who restructured its departments. Whereas before there had been specialists in charge of these departments with the relevant professional expertise and qualifications, and hierarchies with clear lines of reporting, now came departmental leadership from managers who in some cases came from different disciplines, including the Social Services Chief. Accountability between layers had become weaker. The notion behind these changes was that if a manager were competent, he could run any department without knowing what a practitioner did. This is a desperate mistake in a politically-run institution like a local council. Tradition has it that elected members do not need, and do not usually have, qualifications in the fields of the institution's responsibilities. In this local government mirrors practice in central government and it could be a matter for considerable debate. So it is all the more important that at least the officers know what they are doing in such a structure.

A strong argument could be made out evidenced with myriad examples of where the tradition of lay control has also sadly let down the nation at both levels of government. It is perhaps a price people are willing to pay for a modicum of democracy (for it is little more).

But given that ,and the strong pressure local government departmental heads can be under from their politicians, they need to be able at times to represent and defend their department's direction, development, and operations with an expert's authority and insight. Neither is it good for a department's morale when career professionals are overlooked in favour of unqualified managers from outside the discipline. What has made it more difficult in the case of social services and education is central government's legislation to abolish the former Education and Social

CHAPTER 9

LOCAL GOVERNMENT

Services separate departments in favour of amalgamated departments representing children on the one hand and adults on the other. At best this was the coming together of two disparate professions.

Recruitment practices are also well worth prior consideration by prospective local government employees, because, once in, there may be no way of getting away out again.

In local government there has been a massive hypocrisy for years about jobs. All have to be advertised by law, although some can be restricted internally to the organisation. But in reality many of the advertised jobs are not available in practice. The advertising and interviewing process is costly and laborious. Applicants have their hopes raised, only to find there is no competition. This can mean the job has not been released for filling after all. More likely, it has already been allocated to a specific candidate and everyone just goes through the motions. Those who have ever tried to obtain posts in other local authorities than their own can usually attest to experiences of losing out to the mysterious local candidate, frequently never met and interviewed on another day. Parochialism can be a stultifying force.

Be prepared for some fairly amateur interviews. Recruitment has been delegated quite a long way down some hierarchies, owing to pressures of work, and not all officers will be trained at interviewing. And remember too that indifferent performers could tend to appoint in their own image at all levels.

Promotion is said to be a function of ability, interpersonal skills, and performance in bureaucracies, which supposedly use objective measures. But it isn't. That is not the British way. Who you know and whether your face fits will count for much more.

Remember too, that local government has councillors as well as more senior officers. All are above you and could have a significant effect on your future progress. A key change is the payment of council members, who were traditionally unpaid volunteers. Leading members have sometimes become full-time, lines of demarcation from senior officers blurring owing to their new quasi-business responsibilities.

CHAPTER 9

LOCAL GOVERNMENT

It is fair to say, however, that most local government staff will not usually have much of a working interface with councillors, unless they are dealing with a matter of one of a councillor's constituents, when he might intervene if the constituent is aggrieved and complains to him.

The Council needs to be confident of its working relations with chief officers and other very senior staff who interface with them regularly. This means it is commonplace for appointments at third-tier and upwards to be made by the members themselves, variously advised by relevant officers on professional and legal points. Unfortunately, just about anything can happen. Subjective factors may be very prominent, such as, notoriously, small-minded tendencies. Some capable officers have had their careers effectively blighted because they could only 'cut it' with officers and were unable to break through the 'crass ceiling'. The academically minded are especially likely to fare badly.

There is a long-standing and socially dangerous malaise which detracts from the importance of local government. Yet it was not always so. Back in the 1960's local government was seen as a decent and honourable career with a steady job, a sound path, and a role of some worth to the community. It was considered a suitable vocation for graduates, and one offering intellectual complexity and variety, albeit in a rather dull and unexciting environment. It had undeniable power and influence. Notable authorities had deeply-rooted local traditions and styles, and were strongly independent of central government, although some could be depressingly insular too.

But by the time Blair came to rule in the 1990's, local government was mainly regarded as a repository for uninspired 'pen-pushers' of limited vision, who wasted the valuable resources of the community in worthless employment. They were described as 'jobsworths', especially by the political right wing, the prejudice being that they were untalented and doing fake jobs, artificially invented by those with a vested interest. Such views have been fostered by branches of the press, represented notoriously by the Daily Mail and Express.

From the perspective of a local government employee talk of local democracy can seem very heady.

CHAPTER 9

LOCAL GOVERNMENT

Their hope may more modestly be that public service is perceived by the general populace at least in a neutral way, as 'work carried out for or on behalf of others', preferably in a positive sense, as in the dictionary 'usefulness' or 'beneficial act', 'assistance', or 'facility'. Very sadly, public employees these days are going to encounter more feral elements in society and a growing proportion of negative and hostile reactions, underpinned by resentment of having to pay for them via the council tax, and more akin to the dictionary description of 'servitude', as 'subjection to irksome or taxing conditions', or even 'slavery'. The implication is that they deserve little consideration themselves, one sometimes carried into practice by their own hierarchies.

The rot set in with Thatcherism. The changes imposed on local government from Thatcher on were not, and are not ,confined to reorganisation and abolition of authorities, skewing finance towards central objectives, and imposing new structures for councillor decision-making, as well as enforcing new partnerships with the public and private sector. There were other drastic changes for the workforce too in ways to do with officer relations and management. Numerous initiatives have come, and to some degree, gone, but turmoil and uncertainty are now a way of life for staff. Some of the government initiatives may seem rational and reasonable in principle, but soon take off in practice into mind-boggling complexities in the detail.

It is hard to be sanguine about the prospect of any Council being a particularly happy place to work for long. Consider the toxic mix of ingredients. We have central government looming over all like the sword of Damocles, suspicious, interventionist, critical, controlling and constraining. We have disparate politicians within a very complex system of major and minor parties and independents, yet forced to collaborate in some ill-conceived structure which dominates the formality of their conduct of business, whatever informal modes they (will undoubtedly) devise behind the scenes. We have varying influences and relations between politicians and the professional officers, between departments, within departments between sections, in a milieu of constantly changing, often externally imposed, organisational structures. And then there are the critical media and a disenchanted and disconnected public. ....

352

CHAPTER 9

LOCAL GOVERNMENT

A UNISON (union) survey in 2005 entitled 'Sustaining Communities-Taking the Strain' showed "a workforce under pressure, undervalued, understaffed, and under resourced". Verbal abuse by service users was experienced by nearly half and 16% reported bullying by their own managers.   .

Wilson and Game have an apt summary of the workforce: *"councils remain, by any standards, ... large-scale employers of extremely heterogeneous workforces. ...(with) more than tenfold pay differentials between jobs ... . They have at the top a range of well-paid senior managers and professionals, and beneath them a vast army of lower-status administrative, clerical, manual and non-manual employees. These people are essential to the process of service provision, yet the financial rewards they obtain are often relatively unattractive ... .   With many having to rely on state benefits to the low paid in order to survive, the surprise must be not that 2002 saw the first national strike of local government workers for 23 years, but that it has not become an annual event".*

Wilson and Game's conclusion is that: *"It would be miraculous if local government staff were not on occasion to feel dumped upon and demoralised".* Sad words, but probably rather understated. In the experience of the author many would say the "occasion" lasted most of their working lifetimes.

Whistle blowing

A final section is appropriate here to explore the rapidly changing climate with regard to whistle blowing in the workplace, with some, but not exclusive ,emphasis on the position of local government. The reason is that standards of conduct in society generally are slipping, with local government far from immune. The propensity for malpractice is probably greater than at any time past. Certainly we can have a heady mix of amateur politicians, senior managers under a great deal of pressure, unforgiving governments, prurient media, and a baying public, not to mention considerable financial temptation in the myriad zany schemes that politicians cook up. A local authority has many legal powers, yet all have limits, and somebody will be tempted to go beyond them or instruct someone else to do so.

The legal position is briefly as follows. Both fraud and corruption are concerned with financial practices contrary to law.

'Corruption' is to do with bribery, acceptance of illegal gifts, not declaring a financial interest in a piece of Council business, bending the rules to give individual favours like a reduced rent to a tenant, or selling authority assets for personal gain.

Much 'fraud' is by the public making claims for benefits when they lack entitlement _a common occurrence. Fraud from inside the organisation, by staff or council members, can involve accounting irregularities like creating imaginary creditors or claiming false expenses.

The Public Interest Disclosure Act 1998 theoretically protects employees who disclose corruption in the workplace.

In local government, however, many authorities still have no effective procedures. Where there is one, the employee would normally go through a senior officer, but this can lead to difficulties. Years ago the Nolan Committee, investigating standards, had recommended to Government that there should be a procedure for 'whistle blowing', to allow disclosure in confidence, and that this should be within the management structure. They called for there to be a 'monitoring officer'. In its advice to the Nolan Committee, ICSA, the Institute of Chartered Secretaries and Administrators recommended that the monitoring officer should be a specific senior officer with the assigned role of looking after the administration of the code of conduct, rather like the Company Secretary might do in industry. Nolan suggested that the Chief Executive could be the appropriate officer. But was this a good idea in that he would be potentially compromised in relation to subsequent appeals? A common model is for whistle blowers to refer up the executive chain, perhaps with the departmental director as appeals arbiter. If you are the whistle blower your line manager may be the person complained about, or for various reasons possibly not a wise choice to make. Mechanisms need to be sufficiently flexible to adjust to these kinds of sensitive problem, but are they?

CHAPTER 9

LOCAL GOVERNMENT

The protection afforded by the Act to the whistle blowers is against detrimental treatment or unfair dismissal. However, it depends crucially on what the whistle blowers are exposing. They are covered if they disclose information and reasonably believe it concerns criminal action, a miscarriage of justice, or environmental damage.

Unfortunately, officers of integrity can be in the wrong place at the wrong time. They may ,through no fault of their own, become witnesses to dodgy dealings. They take a risk if they bring matters into the open. Victimization is an all too human response by the aggrieved, who may be in a considerably stronger position of managerial authority or political power. Rather than address the deficiency, pressure to remove the whistle blower from his job can sadly prove overwhelming.

Many civil servants have to sign the Official Secrets Act, whilst in local government staff on the interface with elected councillors are placed in 'politically restricted' posts. It may be a feature of some British employment more generally, but it is certainly true of the public sector, that in post staff lose some of their democratic rights of free expression. On pain of dismissal ,for instance, they are unable to express publicly any criticism of the organisation for which they work. And their views on key areas of policy are rarely welcome further up the hierarchy either.

This can hardly inspire confidence in institutions among thinking people. A scientist would say that it is only through analysing its weaknesses and then taking remedial action that an institution can ever hope to improve itself. Such examination is unlikely to occur, or may lack the necessary insights, if the experiences of its own practitioners remain unwanted and unvoiced.

One of the key weaknesses is that the law is framed far too narrowly. There are multiple other, arguably legitimate, reasons why whistle blowing may be desirable in both principle and practice. Not all unethical behaviour is a matter of finance and money. Officers and members can be encouraged to break the law, give unfair preferment to certain clients or job applicants, to lie, make false promises, and so forth. Then there are serious line management issues such as contraction of the chain of executive command. This is when A manages B, who manages C on

CHAPTER 9

LOCAL GOVERNMENT

paper, but B is unable to manage C in reality, because C and A are in alliance against him/her unofficially. Such deliberate undermining of authority can, of course, render B impotent. If A is well established further up the line, B may well have no effective recourse, either in law or procedure.

Whistle blowing regulations have too many grey areas and leave too much discretion to individual local authorities. An example occurred in Wirral Borough Council in 2009 when it generated a public furore over its extensive plans to close a raft of libraries and community facilities. Some of its staff were incensed by the proposals and claimed that the Council had unreasonably fettered their rights of protest, despite the fact that the cuts would put jobs at risk.

The Council's official line was that staff had ample rights of expression. They could, for instance, take matters up through their trade union (if any), or at staff consultations and briefings, or with their line manager. Outside of working hours they were also free to protest as ordinary citizens, it was said.

Not exactly, according to staff who complained to the media. They had been advised, they claimed, under threat of sanctions, not to communicate with the press, or participate in any petitions, or speak at public meetings.

Now, this is a case where there will be disagreement about the truth of the matter. Feelings ran high. Yet it should not be so. Institutions in this country just do not seem to be big enough to accept criticism from within their own ranks. Those in authority tend to take it as a disrespect, undermining their security.

The problem was in part that the case had a high-profile. The public were incensed and the media paid a lot of attention. Government reacted, very unusually, by calling in the authority's decision, to be reviewed at a public enquiry. The inspector subsequently produced a damning report on the Authority's consultation conduct and decisions, which the Council tried to suppress, before it eventually caved in and changed the policy.

Nationally, however, the government behaves no differently. In February

CHAPTER 9

LOCAL GOVERNMENT

2009 it was claimed that Prime Minister Brown's key adviser, Sir James Crosby, had allegedly sacked an HBOS executive, Paul Moore, in 2005 when he warned that the bank's sales culture was irresponsible and would get the bank into trouble. His internal 'whistle blowing' up the line, he alleged, had previously led to bullying tactics against him. Once the credit crunch occurred and HBOS crashed, Moore felt able to go public with his allegations. By this time, Crosby had been advising government and the banking world as deputy head of the Financial Services Agency, FSA. He denied Moore's allegations, but resigned nevertheless. The affairs showed that whistle blowing can be effective, especially if backed by a persistent media campaign of investigation.

More dramatic still, and possibly one of the most significant cases of whistle blowing in British history, was the 2009 exposure, by a former SAS Officer, John Wick, to the Daily Telegraph, of the whole of MPs' claims for the four-year duration of the Parliament to that date. The resultant campaign of daily newspaper exposures of MPs' exploitation, of what was in itself a very generous, lax, and corrupt expenses system, led to a massive outbreak of public anger, with pressure on individuals to resign and pay the money back, and for the parties to deselect and sack them.

There were very immediate political responses across Whitehall, leading to promises of a complete reform of the system, with independent, external management and scrutiny of it in the future, as we have seen earlier. What Parliament (on a free vote) had consistently voted to keep secret in the past they then tripped over each other to condemn. The party leaders competed to look tough, only succeeding at the time in offering up a few scapegoats.

There were in addition many, but mixed, calls across society for wide-ranging changes to other aspects of Parliamentary conduct, notably pleas to rectify the constitutional short comings, and to balance up the eroded power of Parliament as against the government of the day.

While when all is said and done, more will be said than done, what Wick had achieved was truly unprecedented. The whistle blower had acted ahead of the scheduled release of details set for July, (reluctantly agreed by the Commons when the courts upheld a Freedom of Information judgement against it), when he saw that the Speaker's claims office was conniving with MPs in helping them to sanitize their expenses forms before publication. Amazingly that still subsequently happened, with key details being blanked out. Matters had moved very fast. When the first wave of exposés began, the Speaker talked tellingly of legal action against the whistle blower. In his moral code it was Wick who was the wrongdoer! A few weeks later, the Speaker had been forced to resign in shame, or at least to create an impression of Parliamentary outrage at its own conduct. Wick was justifiably able to assert that *"I have played my part in history"*. He went on to say *"It is now for others to decide on the best way to move forward and punish those who have been exposed"*.

It is a nasty feature of British culture that whistle blowers are usually persecuted. In both public and private sector institutions a great many employers fail to grasp the important public morality involved. They have yet to accept emotionally, even in principle, that it is right to protect the whistle blower. If and when we get to that stage, society will have advanced in maturity. As the Wick's case, and many others show, whether we are talking of victims or the ordinary spiteful, some of the whistle blowers can ex officio have much to say that it is in the public interest to be revealed.

All the cases that had gone before were potentially dwarfed in 2011 by Wikileaks, an internationally-based internet organisation which obtained and then published many communications from bodies, notably the governmental , which they had sought to keep secret from the general public.

The attempts by political players in Sweden, the United States, and Britain to use legal processes to harass and discredit Julian Assange, Wikileaks' founder, are well known. They confirm what very many citizens long suspected, that the authorities have been hiding much that it is in the public interest to know. Their natural inclination is to withhold information unless their own interests can be served by disclosure.

So the so-called democratic deficit, in so far as it relates to incomplete information in the public domain ,such as aspects of foreign policy ,has been demonstrated as never before. Governments have been outflanked by the relatively new medium of the internet which they had struggled in vain to control.

What should come of this at the very least is rather more professional behaviour from politicians, diplomats and their staffs in their working lives where they purport to be acting in our name ,since they will never in fact know for sure whether or when their sayings might be exposed. They may have to raise their game a little in some cases.

But views among the political class can be very entrenched. Many are unlikely to concede that a knowledgeable electorate is a prerequisite for the empowerment of competent politicians and a key safeguard as to their continuing integrity. Hilary Clinton's attitude, as US Secretary of State for foreign affairs, may be typical among the political establishment. Leaks constituted a 'breach of trust' ,she said , whereas we might be more inclined to claim that was the non-disclosure.

Some right-wing Americans claimed that perpetrators of such leaks should actually be executed for placing 'national security' in jeopardy. So we should all worry ,and if we are brave enough, we should start to whistle….

FINANCE

The System

Although structure and restructuring are very prevalent features of many a local government officer's working life, as we have seen, what dominates at all times is money. It usually acts as a sort of straightjacket.

The present section therefore covers aspects of local government finance, a vexed subject which ultimately suits nobody in its present state, despite being based on a laudably transparent and well-developed set of accountancy rules, elaborately audited, locally and nationally, and administered via a cadre of professionalized and technical staff.

CHAPTER 9

LOCAL GOVERNMENT

The field is a complicated one, so a start will be made by the exposition of a few key financial terms and background information (1).

An important technical distinction is between 'capital' and 'revenue' finance. The former is for expensive, long-lasting investments, like school buildings and roads. The latter is for cheaper and short-lived items. Capital is borrowed money which is paid back over a generation or more as local taxpayers receive the benefit. It results in local authorities having a high proportion of loan debt, which is an unavoidable annual charge paid to their creditors.

About 85% of local government net finance comes from central government, notably through the rate support grant, RSG, so only 15% stems from local sources. The result is a serious democratic deficient owing to central government's controlling interest over the bulk of local finance.

Although calculated on the basis of very complex formulae which claim to take account of local need, allocations to local authorities of rate support grant are clearly at government discretion. This means that party political considerations can play a major and unsatisfactory part. A Labour government will not wish to appear generous to a Conservative-controlled council, and vice-versa.

The so-called Barnett formula involved is widely criticised. Objections are that it is completely obsolete and in need of a fundamental replacement. Historically, it was rushed in as a stop-gap many years ago. Now governments lack the energy and reforming zeal over problematic issues that do not catch the public eye.

Specific grants are given by central government to local government for special purposes. They are welcome, but obviously serve to deliver national rather than genuine local aspirations.

Central government encourages certain project involvement in local authorities by providing incentives to bid for development funding. Schemes can be 'novel' (or untried) and pump-priming is used to suck in the Council before in later years the government pulls out and expects the project to continue, free-floating on local finances. Needless to say, such schemes are prone to collapse, and do so after the raising of hopes and expectations.

Government financial management of the public sector, being remote, can be quite crude. A clear illustration occurred in the wake of the credit crunch. Colleges of Further Education are nowadays no longer funded through local education authorities but nationally, via a government quango, the Learning and Skills Council, LSC, which had embarked on a major programme entitled 'Building Colleges for the Future'. Alleged mismanagement at the national level had resulted in colleges having a cash-flow problem to the tune of £170 million because of delays in receiving funding. The chief executive of the LSC resigned, because colleges had been placed in this position as a result of making progress on their projects with LSC encouragement.

One of the features of local government budgets is that, since they are cash-strapped, and a high percentage of the base budget is already committed, councillors have relatively little scope for their pet schemes. The lack of financial scope which local government is constrained by is hard to over-emphasize.

Much staffing expenditure is outside its control, notably for teachers, where salary levels and pay increases are dictated by national salary agreements to which individual local authorities are not parties, and which may well form their biggest items of revenue cost. Local government is legally required to implement many such a statute with serious financial implications. The charitable view is that when government legislates, the cost implications on the ground are difficult to calculate, so it is hardly surprising that local councils perennially claim to have been under provided for in this regard. So why not remove the very large teachers' salary bill to Whitehall?

Local government does raise 'council tax', to be discussed later. But it is not a buoyant tax from the point of view of revenue raising. Strongly condemned across local authorities, the government's capping legislation allows, they think, too much central control over their expenditure. What happens is that a spending norm is fixed each year. If a local authority

LOCAL GOVERNMENT

then plans expenditure above the norm, its rate support grant is reduced. Beyond a set ceiling the grant may be cut by a high, punitive amount. It is a blunt instrument, one that takes little account of the situation on the ground and generates bad relations as well.

Local government does have some other sources of income. They can charge rents and fees for services, but are never allowed to 'profiteer' like the private sector. They have received business rates on industrial and other non-domestic properties, except these again are set nationally. And they can sell land and property, but, of course, when its gone its gone.

There are unresolved moral debates about charging, whether local authorities should charge, and if so, whom, when, and how? These can naturally dampen down the activity somewhat. Practice differs among authorities regarding usage of other income sources, so the proportion of revenue raised is variable too.

Concerning the working of national funding, the rate-support grant is decided annually, about five months ahead of the new financial year, and thus allows local authorities little time to plan their future expenditure, especially given that party political agreement is needed locally and there may well be requirements for elements of public consultation. Worse still, the Councils are not given budget indications ahead, unlike universities, which are subject to quinquennial agreements that offer scope for much-needed medium-term planning.

Because of the one-year settlements, there is another distorting effect on expenditure. Budget managers always suspect they are going to be asked to make cuts next year, so the last thing they want to do is under spend in the current financial year. If there is nothing essential they will find something less important to fund. This is commonly why there is a spate of small road maintenance schemes taking place round about February and March, for instance. In other words, the system itself encourages a certain amount of inefficient and wasteful expenditure. This is deeply ironical, given government's endless economy drives for the public sector to mend its ways.

What, finally, are we to make of the system, a culmination of years of development across many national administrations? The key word is 'function'. In a country which cannot make up its collective mind about what functions it wants its local government to carry out, or even if it wants a local government at all, it is probable that we shall continue to bumble along, permanently miserly and resentful in our attitudes to what is spent, and highly suspicious and intolerant of those who do so on our behalf.

Reform of local government finance in this country is sorely needed and long overdue. It has repeatedly been ducked by governments, partly owing to the inherent complexities, no doubt, but not least either as a consequence of the centralist tendency. There are plenty of clues out there as to what to do. Other western countries usually give their local government powers to impose a range of taxes on different groups, so that the local take can be three times as much as here. And their taxes are not crude and regressive like the Council tax, but geared rather more to individual ability to pay and to their extent of service usage. And allied to granting greater financial powers, continental countries would tend to provide a less fettering regime of central regulation and control.

The system of local government finance in the United Kingdom is regarded by the Congress of Local and Regional Authorities of Europe (CLRAE) as both unduly centralist and quite undemocratic. Since authorities have only one (Council) tax by which to raise revenue, and this not only generates only about a quarter of the total needed, but is also capped, local leadership is too constrained to be especially effective. Under what is a politically-motivated dictatorship, favouring or punishing authorities over expenditure can depend a lot on their party affiliation.

Much local authority expenditure is effectively fixed - buried in the base budget and so not amenable to quick release for other purposes. So decision-making about the budget tends to be at the margins, where small percentage changes might be made. Nevertheless, the sums involved can be big, if the council is a large one. And even if it is not, the scope for decision-making will not easily be disregarded by the populace whom it affects.

Tony Travers, of the London School of Economics, called the local government finance arrangements by central government :

LOCAL GOVERNMENT

"a spectacular example of a command economy control system in operation. The former Soviet Bloc never managed this kind of all-embracing and intricate control. A computer in London dictates the fate of a primary school roof repair in Wirral or a secondary school's music teacher in Cornwall."(15)

Council Tax

Council tax is very unpopular. And it is one major reason why local government can easily get a bad name. So it is to council tax we now turn to consider just what it is about it that generates such profound feelings of disapproval within much of the community at large.

A good deal of that residual element of funding which is raised locally comes from the Council tax, levied on the capital value of people's houses. The valuations are split into a series of price bands which are very crudely drawn, so that quite modestly priced houses will attract the same tax as mansions! Most of the bands are at the lower end, needlessly introducing grading distinctions among the less expensive houses.

Numerous commentators have campaigned over many years for the reform of the Council tax system. As will be argued, nothing short of its complete abolition will do, whether you replace it with the local government system of income tax, that proponents argue will rekindle a basis for local democracy, or use the local corporation tax take to aid Council not national funding, or otherwise.

It is unjust in principle to have a tax system based on the value of houses, however organised and for whatever purposes. The reason is that there are many people in this country who are 'capital rich', but 'income poor', and for all sorts of reasons. A progressive tax, such as income tax, takes more from those who earn more; there is at least some correlation between demands to pay and ability to pay. Yet this is sadly not the case with the Council tax.

As the above considerations render it unpopular, successive Governments have talked from time to time about reform. But it has never happened in

CHAPTER 9

LOCAL GOVERNMENT

all the years from 1990, when the present housing valuation and banding was carried out, until 2009, when there was still no sign, apart from a cosmetic consultation paper about procedures, published in 2006. Governments know it would be a lot of effort and could be very unpopular.

So the position is quite ludicrous. Houses are placed in valuation bands according to their market sale value on 1st April 1991. The vast majority of houses were obviously not actually sold that year, never mind on that day, and so their valuations are merely hypothetical, based on estate agents' guesstimates of what they would have cost at the time. Crude comparisons with allegedly similar houses that ostensibly did sell at genuine market value in 1991 are utilized.

In spite of its very dubious basis, the citizen is usually in an extremely weak position if he seeks to challenge his house valuation. The State has devised an ingenious set of administrative and legal procedures which seemingly give the citizen rights, but in reality are cleverly biased against his successful exercise of them - a recurring hallmark of the United Kingdom's sham democracy.

This is the story. Mrs. Thatcher as prime minister had tried to reform the old system of local authority rates by bringing in the poll-tax (or community charge) in 1990. As a flat-rate cost, although with exemptions and rebates, it was so unpopular that defaulters among ordinary citizens were prosecuted and there were riots in the streets. The scheme was hurriedly dropped, but not before Mrs. Thatcher had lost her job. The poll-tax is generally regarded as an important plank in her political demise, and a potent reason for government reticence over future reform of the Council tax. However, the current system is so unjust that it is amazing it has not engendered similar strife, although a few brave pensioners have gone to prison over it.

Council tax was first introduced in April 1993. Payers were then given just eight months to appeal against the banding of their home before losing the entitlement. The trick removed at a stroke most people's democratic rights in the matter. In the words of the Department for Communities and Local Government in 2007: *"Since that initial period for appeals ended, usually only people becoming taxpayers in respect of a particular dwelling for the first time may appeal, and in these circumstances appeals must be made within six months."*

However, if you do move house and appeal, which will include a relatively small proportion of home owners, the barriers in your way are very onerous. It is a useful model for judging how a system measures up to the principles of democracy and justice.

Your local Council will refer you to the Listing Officer, who works at the Valuation Office, a separate government quango. When you give him notice of intention to appeal he will send you the relevant papers, but he may also try to discourage you from proceeding. It can take the form of placing an onus of response on you by a particular date, in the absence of which he would deem you to have decided not to go ahead and would ask the Tribunal to dismiss the case without a hearing.

You might think that such coercive and unilateral representations from the Listing Officer would prejudice his case with the Tribunal, but not a bit of it. It is thus of relevance to examine the nature of the Tribunal itself. Members are appointed, not elected, and some are partly chosen by the very local authorities which stand to gain financially from high banding decisions. The Tribunal presidents are appointed by Government, so ensuring that their interests are paramount. They even share in the decisions to choose each tribunal member.

So what we have is a large quangocracy - a bureaucratic edifice set up by the State to evade accountability to the citizen. We have Valuation Offices all over the country with their professional Listing Officers and administrative support staff, no fewer than fifty-six Valuation Tribunals at the time of writing, and a Valuation Tribunal Service, VTS, to supply the tribunals with an administrative support framework of their own. It would be interesting to see just what costs could be saved by the country if it were to abolish house valuation as the taxable principle.

The dice are loaded against appellants in other ways too, apart from the make-up of the Tribunal. For one thing, the Valuation (Listing) Officer can in effect withhold evidence from the appellant, by making it available

LOCAL GOVERNMENT

only at his office by appointment after written application. And since these offices are situated regionally, not necessarily locally, many appellants would have quite a journey. And any evidence the appellant might have can only be considered at the Tribunal hearing if the appellant has sent it to the Valuation Officer at least one week beforehand.

The appellant may attend the hearing in person, but if he is unable, or unwilling to do so, if he submits a written appeal it will be considered in his absence. The Valuation Officer, however, is always entitled to be present, or to be represented, and so will have his say.

The Tribunal restricts appellants to using material from the valuation date (1991), whilst itself allowing the Valuation Office submissions to relate to subsequent years right up to the present day.

The tests required to 'prove' the correct banding are very crude and narrow. Only one 'equivalent' house sale in the area is needed, the Valuation Officer can go by the sale prices at other times if there were none in the area in April 1991, the houses do not have to be the same, no criteria of similarity are laid down, he is not required to evidence that fair market price was obtained, or to mention any special factors surrounding the sale.

In any case, no valuation of a house can be accurate to more than about 10%; it is a very inexact science with many disparate factors to take into account. Where the valuation is close to a banding limit, this can make all the difference as to which tax band the house is placed in, and accordingly, how much tax is due.

An argument the Valuation Officer will use is that the house is in the same band as others in the area. But, as we have seen, the claim is meaningless when in reality most citizens, whether aggrieved or not, have been disenfranchised from formal objection!

Turning now to complaints procedures when the case and then the appeal have been lost, there are features here that are similar to others in different arenas of public administration, namely a restriction of grounds for appeal. How you were treated personally, when officers handled your

LOCAL GOVERNMENT

case is about it. Whilst the really worthwhile rights - to challenge policy, the distribution of power, its exercise and abuse - do not exist.

So what of a final recourse to law, then, when all else fails and maladministration is so artificially constrained? Once again, they have seen you coming. Appeal against the Tribunal decision can only be made on a point of law, so for most of the few who reach that stage there is no possible redress. And another convenient time restriction weeds out the stragglers. Appeal must be within one month of the Tribunal's notification of decision, no later.

Legal appeal has to be made only to the High Court, and this sits in London. Your document is required in triplicate, accompanied by a substantial fee. A lack of lay knowledge and experience virtually necessitates your being legally represented, by a solicitor and barrister, at great expense. You had better win, for there is the threat of large legal costs being awarded by the Court against unsuccessful appellants!

This particular public administrative system has been gone through in unusual detail to illustrate that the devil is often right in there. Unless citizens are personally faced with situations in which they follow their vaunted rights to the bitter end, they are more than likely to remain blissfully unaware of their limitations. Justice may sometimes be attainable in this country, but there are many, deliberately designed, financial and legal barriers to put off all but the most bloody-minded and persistent. It exposes the true nature of the relations between citizen and State. They can always use their coercive powers to keep you in line if you have the temerity to question and oppose.

And, of course, it's about your house and your Council tax, so like as not it will be the local authority, not the government ,that you will blame.

PUBLIC AND PRIVATE SECTORS

The present section makes some observations about the growing interaction in local government between itself, with its public sector ways and values, and the private sector. As we have noted before, ever since

CHAPTER 9

LOCAL GOVERNMENT

the days of the Thatcher government in the 1980's, central politicians came to believe in, and tried to develop, schemes in which the public sector could benefit from the private, and vice versa. The intention has taken many different forms, some of which will be briefly discussed in what follows.

Privatisation

The concept of privatizing local government services raises strong public feelings, not to say prejudices. Local Government Acts in 1980 and 1988 introduced, and then widened, the number of services that had to be subject to tender, so that sections and departments directly employed by Councils were placed in rivalry (Compulsory Competitive Tendering, CCT) with private firms. The contracts - such as for refuse collection, building maintenance, catering - were time-limited, and after three years the service would be reviewed and re-tendered. Of course, once an in-house section had failed to secure a tender ,the staff left local government employ and the internal capability was lost to the private sector for the future thereafter, though some were re-engaged by the successful bidders, at least to start with. Over time the process would result in much smaller local authority staffs and some transferring to the private sector would later lose their jobs.

With rules encouraging acceptance of the lowest tender, and the constant problems of under funding, some unacceptable failures in provision have resulted from private sector delivery. A combination of low budget, firms seeking to maximize profit, and relative inexperience among local government officers in monitoring private sector performance standards, placed elderly patients at risk of neglect or poor treatment from badly trained and inadequately vetted carers. These scandals broke in 2009, having been exposed by television reporters for 'Panorama' working under cover.

They are potentially widespread, the private firms in question working across many different local authorities.

There is little doubt that the process could, and probably will, go much

CHAPTER 9

LOCAL GOVERNMENT

further one day. Whereas it is now mainly manual, the Local Government Act 1992 identified white collar professional and technical areas for tendering. The list included, lawyers, accountants, human resources, and information technology staff, all with an across-the-authority role. It was a close run thing, but a stay of execution lasting years resulted from subsequent Local Government (structural) Reviews and Reorganisations, and the New Labour Government, which had, or claimed, a 'third way' in many things, including here. It introduced instead a 'Best Value' regime, to be discussed latter.

So what are the lessons to be learned from privatisation? The first is that ideology rules. People are likely to be prejudiced for or against it rather than prepared to look at matters objectively. The second is that there is no private sector magic formula to make things work, nor are all public sector ventures inadequate. There are stories of success and failure covering both public and private sector attempts to run services efficiently and effectively. The third is that because privatisation still has an association with the political right, and nationalisation is regarded as a tool of the left wing, there are liable to be swings of emphasis, one way or another, depending on who is in power. The process is complicated by the fact that many a local authority will have a ruling party opposite in colour to the prevailing government. And so it is almost certainly going to be a political football for a long time to come. Which will be in few people's interests ultimately. It would be an insult to science to call the situation 'experimental'.

What is rather curious is the tentative way in which government proceed, prompting the question as to whether this privatisation by stealth arises from their fear that it might be contrary to majority public wishes.

Just possibly the lessons, and others too, will be learned. Meanwhile it will be the electorate as usual that suffers.

Public Finance Initiative, PFI

Although invented under the Conservative government of John Major, PFI was enthusiastically taken up and expanded under Blair and New Labour from the mid 1990s when they came to power.

CHAPTER 9

LOCAL GOVERNMENT

In these deals the private sector would pay for and own new schools, hospitals, and some other local government services. The companies would then run the institutions for up to fifty years, recovering their money by annual charges to the taxpayer from leasing schemes. There would be no government borrowing to count as public debt, but the firms had to borrow their own, probably at higher rates, ultimately adding to the public burden considerably. This was compounded by the complex bidding process and the consequent need, as government (wrongly) saw it, to draft in highly-paid private consultants. As one union critic put it, it was "like paying for your house with a Barclay card" (at prohibitively high interest rates).

Whenever you have public sector and government officials negotiating contracts with big business, the public sector is liable to get a raw deal. It is men against boys, expertise against lack of experience or ability. Increasingly, the rules were skewed so that the public sector assumed the risks and the private increased its profits. Public bodies were forced to cooperate, or they did not get their building schemes approved.

If ever there was a prime example of central government acting both deceptively and wastefully it was PFIs. Deceptive because its main reason for use is so that the private sector borrows the money, so keeping the item technically off the Treasury's public sector borrowing requirement. Wasteful in that the private sector always requires a profit element which would not stop at ordinary building costs, but would include public payment for use over the lifetime of the asset and compensation for the capital risks involved. The latter can be a sick joke when firms get into financial trouble and have to be publicly bailed out anyway. Of course, to a local authority anxious to replace, say, clapped out school buildings, PFI, if not attractive exactly, may be the only way it can proceed, even though the asset might remain in private ownership (a raft of headaches stored up for a future generation to deal with).

Vince Cable, as Liberal Democrat Treasury spokesman, had been sceptical about PFI for a long time. After the credit crunch firms involved in financing PFI schemes came to government for state help with their funding gap. The obvious principle appears to have been missed, that the private sector surely cannot be entitled to PFI perks if the scheme is

LOCAL GOVERNMENT

essentially public-funded. In that scenario, government might as well go back to its traditional public sector funding models instead. They could still be able to use public investment as a way to stimulate a flagging private sector economy, if desired, maybe with school and hospital replacement programmes, but there would be rather more flexibility over restriction of overheads and long-term costs, he pointed out.

Council Business Roles

The Rates Act of 1984 made it a legal requirement for local authorities to consult local business. In the 2000s the 'Best Value' movement ensured greater and ongoing consultation with local authorities' "stakeholders", including also taxpayers and service users. But that is about accountability of a local authority to the community it serves. It helps to ensure that at least the better organised and more vociferous among them get a hearing, which council members can then take into account in decision-making. It has some of the dangers of specialised lobbying, although it is difficult to argue against the general reasonableness of purpose. It looks as if it could be a useful element in democratic participation.

Yet that is not the business role of local government to which this section refers, which is the way the local authority provides advice, support, and even resourcing to local business enterprises. The role seems odd given the above relationship of accountability of local government to business, if not actually incompatible with the democratic relationship. Perhaps they can come to the same thing. That business expresses what it wants of local government and the latter attempts to comply.

Is this how things should be? Traditionalists will probably say 'no' on the grounds that there is/should be a fundamental public/private divide, with no blurring around the edges, that the public sector is inadequately funded even to serve its own priorities let alone tinker (for that is all it could do) with private sector aims.

It may seem surprising, and it is certainly illogical, that whilst the general trend is to reduce local authority powers, they have also received an important new one in recent times. The Local Government Act ,2000 introduced a power to promote the economic, social and environmental well-being of the area, with their trading and commercial potential thereby being enhanced. But it is difficult to see how this can lead to anything other than wasteful use of scarce resources to play at, and/or prop up, private sector activities.

A good illustration of what can result was the decision of Wirral Borough Council in March 2010 to invest some £12 million in a super-fast broad band infrastructure for the benefit, not of the Council tax payers, but private sector companies in the area. They clearly saw a role for themselves in stimulating the local economy, but that was not what they were elected to do. Particularly when the previous year they said they could not afford to keep some of their libraries open.

A more moderate kind of quasi-business role undertaken by local authorities was to broker job-orientation courses for the academically weaker or disaffected post-16 youth to link them into the world of work. Nationally this was taken over by Connexions, a government quango with a shop in local high streets. Clearly the local education authority was well-placed to arrange to address defects in basic education, parental guidance. It formerly ran youth services, which then also became bound up under Connexions, operating in a variety of structural modes, more or less distant from local authorities.

One trouble is that economic development is just too tasty to be left alone, it seems. Often the bids to the European Union for regeneration funding are left in local government hands for the area. When firms come in, of course, lured maybe by the low rentals and available buildings, they may or may not bring their own workers and continue to use their external suppliers. Anyway, this is just competition among areas, so somewhere else loses out.

Possibly it is one way local government can appear important, to be doing a proper job in the real world. Councillors like the fringes, because bid money is usually about innovation and is high-profile. It has not already been committed and accounted for in detail, or locked into the base budget year on year and so, in effect, untouchable.

CHAPTER 9

LOCAL GOVERNMENT

There is certainly a chance to play at politics. Small traders can be subsidized, or even formed, in order to promote such concepts as gender or ethnic equality on the ground.

In the past local authorities have faced legal restrictions on their rights to trade (confined to trading with other public bodies), or to make commercial charges for their services. Public sector in (unfair?) competition with private sector tends to be frowned on, as with the BBC's commercial arm, and in all these quasi-business ventures there is a question of the risks to the safeguarding of public money and its possible misappropriation.

It is nevertheless predicted that the steady confusion of roles will continue, that what looks like a loosely principled mess to separatists will get worse, fuelled by an ebb and flow of government initiatives in the main, quickly arrived at and just as quickly forgotten.

The initiatives can take many forms in different places. One rather small local authority with very poor relations with its electorate nonetheless boasted a "dedicated business support team". The idea was that a package would be provided for a small local firm comprising the networking services of a local authority-employed 'account manager' working with partners of the Council like the Federation of Small Businesses and the Chamber of Commerce. A Council-run "Business Forum" provided companies with information, exhibitions, events, conferences, workshops, training support, apprenticeship opportunities, and accounting advice.

Most of it would be very small-scale and involve tiny businesses. The controversial issue would be whether direct funding should be provided from public taxation without some reciprocal arrangement to share in any profits?

And must local authorities proliferate their activities into lots of little pies, and thereby weaken their impact, instead of concentrating on key core purposes and being decently funded to carry them out?

An illustration of the murky waters into which local authorities are getting themselves these days was the connection in Chester between the City Football Club and the unitary West Cheshire Council. The latter actually owned the ground and the Club went into administration unable to pay its debts. Previous attempts had been made to broker a deal whereby the Club could pay a rental to the Council, but the risks of default seemed to be high. Some might ask just what a local authority was doing with public money to own such a property, and to be involved in propping up a private company in the first place. Par excellence a football club, which had no doubt been run with that walk of life's usual amazing and irresponsible sense of values and tendency to profligate waste. The former owner and chairman was later charged with attacking a policeman in a public bar and was considered by some in the game an unfit person to run a football club. Meanwhile, just up the road the cash-strapped Wirral local authority was sponsoring Tranmere Rovers .

Another development has been the offers of financial help to first-time homebuyers who cannot obtain a mortgage loan by conventional means. This begs lots of questions about why ratepayers should be expected to subsidise people towards property ownership when they clearly cannot afford it and should be in the rental sector. Surely the credit crunch has been a more than adequate demonstration of the folly of such a plan, still trying to throw public money at the chronic credit seekers, those whose defaulting on loan repayments partly led to the international mountain of toxic debt in the first place.

The public/private divide is in such ways a destructive one, since it tends to polarise prejudices running deep in society. The noble thing to say would be that the dichotomy in United Kingdom society is to be deplored. They have an intrinsic interlinking, although mechanisms can vary a great deal, with each capable of having profound effects on the other. Somehow, ways have to be found to transcend the predictable and polarised hostilities and to produce a mutual outlook which is mature, objective, and integrated. But it is, or should be, predicated on priority and key public purposes. When you have little money you have to cut your cloth accordingly.

And the national debate on what are the true, appropriate financial ends of a local authority is long overdue.

CHAPTER 9

LOCAL GOVERNMENT

Concluding Remarks

The issue of interaction between public and private sectors is always a sensitive one, and comes to a head on funding matters.

Bad feeling between the sectors is endemic, and easily stimulated by the political parties and the media.

Predictably enough, temperatures rose in the wake of the credit crunch. In the aftermath, when the government had borrowed billions of pounds to bail out the banking sector, and some prominent private companies, came the cries for the public sector to share the pain. A prominent pundit was the Head of the Audit Commission, Steve Bundred, who asserted in July 2009 that public sector pay should either be frozen, or subject to "severe" restraint to help rebalance the public finances. He even claimed it would be "a pain free way of cutting public spending". As though to echo the sentiment, Alistair Darling, the Chancellor said: "we have got to be fair with regard to people who work in the private sector".

Adding their voice, the Institute of Fiscal Studies warned that the United Kingdom faced a post-election 'decade of pain' in its public services owing to the scale of financial cuts that would be necessary. If government sought to protect particular areas of expenditure, the extent of retrenchment for the rest would be that much greater. A figure of over 16% cuts was postulated for the three-year period 2011-2014.

The Conservatives in opposition were itching as usual to take up their traditional sport of public sector bashing. Cameron, the party leader, made a pledge in 2009 to end "the age of excess" in public sector pay. The attitudes behind this, of course, were shared by many of the public, as well as some Labour politicians. Terry Rooney, the MP, and Chairman of the Commons' Work and Pensions Committee, in September 2009 called for high-earning public sector workers to have their pensions capped at a modest £50,000.

The debate, as ever, had the propensity to polarise fundamental issues about division and fairness across society.

CHAPTER 9

LOCAL GOVERNMENT

In the wake of wanton government failure to regulate the vast excesses of bankers and others in the private sector, Vince Cable had called in vain for an end to the bonus culture. Even after the credit crunch countless top managers in both public and private sectors, not just in banking, but in organisations such as the police and the BBC, had been exposed as receiving enormous bonuses not linked to performance in the sense that failure did not disqualify. Despite the recession, large bonuses continued to be paid - even in banks where the government was now the majority shareholder, raising the fear in public sector quarters that the private sector was not only out of, but also too powerful, to control.

Unison general secretary, Dave Prentis, representing local government workers, protested that low-paid public sector workers should not be expected to pay for a recession caused by bankers, speculators, and government. That was probably going to be part of the reality, nevertheless. There is a kind of inevitability about their place in the pecking order, which is humble even by the standards of the public sector. Finally, if there are any positive gains to be made from the rifts they are surely to do with cooperation and the development of mutual understanding. Sectors are well enough connected at the level of the economy as a whole, the one creating the resources, the other humanizing the effects of the first.

However, whilst they are interlinked, that does not mean they, always or maybe even often, have to work together, straying over into each other's familiar territory and areas of expertise. We should take a step back and critically examine the current mish-mash of the activities to determine just what it is that we are trying to do, then resource them properly, or leave well alone.

FUTURES

In conclusion, it must be apparent from the foregoing that not all is well in the garden of local government. Its many years have been a turbulent history of massive changes. Functions have been stripped or added. It has been structurally reorganised many times. Powers have sometimes been strengthened, but mostly reduced. Government has piled on duty

CHAPTER 9

LOCAL GOVERNMENT

after duty, kicked it around like an old toy, at times used it as a fall-guy, or worse, campaigned publicly to question its honesty, competence, even raison d'etre.

In their collectivity the public are far from blameless, either. Their esteem, rarely strong, has sometimes collapsed into apathy or cynicism. They show little interest on the whole and are too ignorant of how local authorities work to intervene effectively. Much of their prejudice, pro or anti, is fuelled by a strident popular press, playing on the public/private dichotomy, a sort of politics of envy, splitting roughly along main party lines.

The government has several methods open to it in order to stimulate change in the public sector generally. One is via legislation, another is to collaborate with industry and commerce. A third option is to use the academic world to promote and spread new ideas, and we have already seen the use of quangos. The fifth way is, of course, to decentralise, to act locally via public sector organizations. And when you do that, you have to take account of local government, even if you decide to go round it.

In trying to assess what the future has to hold for local government, or even if there is to continue to be one, it might be instructive to look at some of the ways central government has intervened already to change the modus operandi.

John Major as prime minister in the 1980s introduced 'The Citizen's Charter', in which the main idea was to try to get local government closer to its people. Whereas the tradition had been that the authority provided a service to its own standards and by its own ways, the public were to be encouraged to become active customers, with some say at least in how things happened. Although the movement came and went, it did produce a lasting change in the way people perceive councils and how they treat the public. There is more informing now, through customer service centres, complaints procedures, user surveys. A limitation was, however, that this was only about consumerism, not democracy as such.

Then, as we have seen, there was Compulsory Competitive Tendering,

CHAPTER 9

LOCAL GOVERNMENT

CCT, designed to make local authority services compete with the private providers for the privilege of continuing to deliver them in-house. The Tory hope was clearly to reduce the size of local government, simultaneously generating greater efficiencies through their unshakeable belief that private is best. Cameron echoed the refrain during the 2010 general election campaign.

CCT declined, partly because local authorities became adept at playing the game, winning in house contracts themselves, so privatisation did not go as far as intended. There were some notable failures, too, of private sector providers. A change of government abolished it, and Blair introduced Best Value instead, with statutory force.

It required councils to produce annually a Best Value Performance Plan, BVPP, showing how they could achieve 'continuous improvement' across all their responsibilities. The document was intended to become the main method of accountability. To produce their element of the plan, managers would first have to conduct BV Reviews, using 'the 4Cs': challenge, compare, consult, compete. Each service would be challenged to justify itself and show why other approaches were not adopted. It would have to compare its performance with similar providers, consult all local stakeholders to set better performance targets and an action plan to attain them, then demonstrate it was competitive against other possible providers.

Many local authority staff regarded the tasks as just plain silly, or yet another attempt by government/senior management to make life impossible for them on top of their normal day's work. Research by Cardiff University soon established that councils were not very impressive on the challenging and competing roles. After all, much of their work involves responsibilities that have never been commercially viable or of the slightest interest to the private sector. It would be surprising if they could manage the comparison role effectively either. Local authorities differ from each other so much in how they are organised and operate that comparing like with like would usually require visitations to each other's patches to conduct in-depth studies in other parts of the country! Inspections by the Audit Commission added yet another time-consuming headache.

CHAPTER 9

LOCAL GOVERNMENT

After the 2001 election a new ministerial team seemed to recognize the stultifying effects best value was having. Local government had become overwhelmed with centrally imposed requirements. The answer was to be Comprehensive Performance Assessment (CPA) ,which incorporated best value, but unfortunately for those on the receiving end, did not replace it.

In essence, whilst the laborious reporting machinery remained, incentives were offered to local authorities in the form of lighter inspection, and some freedoms with regard to budgets and grant expenditure, the removal of capping for the high-scoring councils. Low ones were subject to intervention, however, with Audit Commission staff being 'engaged' to work on 'improvements'.

Local Public Service Agreements (LPSAs) were also invented, the idea being to form a partnership between a government department and an individual local authority. The council would commit to attain specific, measurable service targets, beyond the BV plan, the government would help, and would provide cash rewards for success.

Government then produced the mutated concept of a Local Area Agreement, LAA, perhaps seen as an idea too far in that it is very difficult even for practitioners to understand. The LAA worked through the Local Strategic Partnership, LSPs, in cooperation with numerically strengthened Government offices for the Regions, and brought all the local players together.

It seemed very positive, but behind it was the congenital lack of ability on the part of central government both to trust local authorities and to concede that local people generally know what is best for their area. The deep irony is that the local elements of an LAA are required to be 'joined-up', whereas the government departments involved so palpably are not.

In a related initiative, as though unaware of the disorganised mix of players stimulated by quangocracy, New Labour had earlier tried to push a possible new role for Local government in its leadership via partnerships of many stakeholders' through a plethora of funding schemes for service delivery. 'Wicked issues' was the term coined to describe the unyielding and perennial problems of the community, such as urban

LOCAL GOVERNMENT

neighbourhood decay and families lost outside the economy. There developed partnerships with other local authorities, with other public bodies, such as NHS primary care trusts, and with private firms. Sizes, areas of operation, and purposes differed widely. Issues might come from areas like education, health, employment, sport, regeneration, legal services, even the arts.

As so many partnerships emerged, the concept of the Local Strategic Partnership, LSP, had been born. These were set up throughout the country, not just in deprived areas either, to coordinate the efforts of the partnerships. Membership would include local authorities in the area, other public, private, and voluntary sectors, and local residents. The LSP would be required by government to write, carry out, and review a Community Plan which aimed to improve the community via its social, environmental, and economic aspects.

Was this feasible? The Audit Commission had expressed concern. The model had been centrally imposed, on variously willing parties, seemingly without discrimination as to its optimum conditions for applicability. A lot of time and cost could be wasted discussing how to work together. After all, what had been done to fetter powers of bodies which were not traditionally subject to detailed operational control by government? Some of the members of an LSP could be more easily coerced then others, but inevitably the accountability of all was weakened since very difficult to apportion. And where was the glue that was supposed to keep an LSP together?

Nobody knew what direction local government would next take off in. Some made a distinction between the 'Old Localism', which a small minority seemed to want, strong local democracy via local authorities controlled by elected politicians, with a much higher proportion of locally-raised finance, and greatly enhanced devolved powers, if not functions, to pursue a distinctly local rather than national agenda. Then there were the 'New Localists', spawned under Blair and advocated by David Miliband, who were careful to put the national agenda centre stage, but to be locally delivered. They need careful watching by local government supporters, for they did not see devolution inevitably being focused on local authorities. They seemed to want broader and more

CHAPTER 9

LOCAL GOVERNMENT

variable 'governance', and it is clear that there would be rewards for good and faithful servants, penalties for the rest.

'Local governance' is a term they used to deal with the fact that councils were no longer the only local institutions involved in government. LSPs were one example. What we have is an emerging and variable dog's breakfast of different governmental and non-governmental agencies working together fluidly by partnership and contract using a variety of strategies.

Local governance can become quite woolly, as accountability gets blurred in combinations of all sectors - public, private, and voluntary. Tasks, too, can be vaguer than 'provision' or 'control' or 'direction', becoming more to do with 'enabling' and 'networking' for instance.

We may reasonably predict that regionalism will not be much of a player in this. An early casualty of recessions, it seems to suffer from a lack of natural support in many parts of the country, and is seen by many politicians and theorists as a tier too far in government.

If the new localists devolved power, it would be with many strings and for highly specific purposes. 'Experiments' might ensue with all manner of recipients down to neighbourhood levels in towns and below. Some kind of financial voucher schemes could be used, in theory, to put choice and power into the hands of individual consumers; that is, voters.

Then again, total destruction is a real possibility which cannot be ruled out. Local government could be abolished altogether. Many, many people might like that.

And the organs of the State which would have to sprout up locally in its stead would be essentially just delivery vehicles run, like as not, by separate government departments. On past performance these would be quite unlikely to operate in a 'joined up' way, as is now required by government from the existing public institutions. Nor might they be at all friendly to deal with...... .

Yet in spite of what has happened to it, local government has shown a

LOCAL GOVERNMENT

remarkable resilience. It does try to adapt to all these crazy things the State asks of it. It attempts to serve its local community and to do what it thinks is right.

What we need to ask, as a nation, is whether it is good enough in a supposedly civilized country, to continue to blunder on at the whim of Johnny-come-lately political chancers? Should we not instead seek a public consensus on future development, a blueprint to guide us forward, with a national agreement on appropriate roles to transcend the party political proclivities that have been so damaging and deflecting of purpose?

It may become a vote for abolition, of course. In which case the public needs a prior understanding of what would almost certainly replace it - quangocracy on a very large scale. Ad hoc national bodies would spring up with local outlets to undertake state agendas. They would not be democratically accountable and their intentions would not necessarily be explicit. They would be difficult to appeal against also.

Alternatively, if we wished to proceed more positively, it would first be necessary to inform people properly about the nature and worth of the institution, and to convince them of the importance of personal participation in pursuance of the values of community. Once such a cultural change had been visibly demonstrated by real achievements on the ground, it just might then be possible to convince the State to devolve more of its power and responsibility, including financial capability. To be genuinely effective such a revolution would need the association of concomitant financial reforms, ones that would ensure continuity of funding over the medium-term, a rather higher proportion of gross domestic product committed to the sector than hitherto, and a simplified and uniform basis for local resourcing. To give just one example, we would not have had such a serious shortage of 'affordable houses' if local authorities had been allowed to build them over the last twenty years.

Councils do experiment to try and involve the local electorate more, but it is far from easy. One idea is the 'area forum'. When Wirral Borough Council tried it, they set up twice-yearly meetings in each locality with a small budget and the aim of bringing together politicians and residents, as

CHAPTER 9

LOCAL GOVERNMENT

well as representatives of the Police and the National Health Service. The forums were mostly poorly attended, however, unless there was a burning issue, and in spite of local coordinators surveying people's wishes. All that resulted was an opportunity for a small number of committed activists to talk. The apathy may, of course, have something to do with the lack of ability of the forums to influence policy or expenditure except at the margin. Things take time to nurture and catch on, particularly when it comes down to a matter of changing people's behaviour.

Since they must assume there is still much to play for, it is very important that local authorities retain a strong sense of their own identities, especially while they are being buffeted around by central government. That is, not to take an independent and disapproving stance, but look to their survival chances, at least in a rational evaluation, improving them by living according to certain principles. (16). Try, within available resources and influence, to address the real local problems, focus on a few key objectives and action them well, create a climate of openness to new ideas, get a reputation as a thoughtful innovator only of sound ideas. Deploy staff to look after the short, medium and long term timescales, introduce simple and easy to understand strategies, and finally, use constructively critical ways to evaluate and improve performance behaving as an organic institution, where people matter on the inside as well as the out.

The right kind of innovation might just help. Where a local council is really into sustained innovation, it needs to experiment a lot in a formal and transparent sense, setting up pilot projects to see whether they work, and assess their feasibility for scaling up across the area. Suitable noises and support have to come from the leadership, both council members and senior officers. It is difficult within a demanding and somewhat unforgiving society, yet somehow we have to get used to regarding most public project failures as a normal price of experimental innovation and not to mind too much admitting them. Whilst the blame culture can easily have deleterious effects, it might be defused in part by more systematic integration of risk management and a better-informed understanding of the concept.

What is it to be? So far, with the Coalition government it is really none

CHAPTER 9

LOCAL GOVERNMENT

of the above. The plans are to roll back public sector employment, and especially local government ,perhaps, to produce a State in which the private sector is by far and a way the bigger sector, and thereby the country should become in theory much better able to pay its way in the world. So local government is squeezed by huge budget cuts, whilst skewing central allocations towards the Tory strongholds. Since Labour Councils are usually to be found in urban areas of the north and midlands, a disproportionate burden of cuts is aimed at the communities who are already relatively deprived. Simultaneously ,there is increased delegation of decision-making ,so that the local councils have to make the very unpopular choices as to what key facilities they will curtail or disband . The government cynically claims that it is not responsible, of course ,implying that it might have made more acceptable decisions if it had been in charge, but we are, after all, living in a democracy…

Cameron himself had a very controversial vision of "the Big Society" in which voluntary groups ,charities, and community-minded individuals would somehow come forward to keep the really worthwhile activities going in spite of a lack of financial resources……

CHAPTER 9

LOCAL GOVERNMENT

NOTES

1. Wilson, David and Game, Chris, Local Government in the United Kingdom, Palgrave Macmillan, Basingstoke, Fourth Edition, 2006.

2. Butler, Eamonn, The Rotten State of Britain, Gibson Square, London, 2009.

3. King, Anthony, The British Constitution, Oxford University Press, 2007.

4. Byrne, Tony, Local Government in Britain : Everyone's Guide to How It All Works, Penguin Books Ltd., London, Seventh Edition, 2000.

5. Chisholm, Michael, and Leach, Steve, Botched Business, Douglas McLean Publishing, Coleford, Gloucestershire, 2008.

6. Murphy, Liam, 'Twin authorities to replace county', Daily Post, Liverpool, December 19, 2007.

7. The Centre for Sustainable Urban and Regional Futures, Salford University, 'City Regions, County Regions and Sub-National Governance', 2007.

8. News Release, Cheshire County Council, 18th December, 2007.

9. News Release, Cheshire County Council, 30th January, 2008.

10. News Release, Cheshire County Council, 15th October, 2007.

11. Press Release, House of Lords, 21st February, 2008.

CHAPTER 9

LOCAL GOVERNMENT

12.   Times, 'Pay Load', 25th June, 2008.

13.   Rotten Boroughs, 'Winter Chill', Private Eye, No. 1228, January/February, 2009.

14.   'No Sorry from Baby P Chief', The Mail on Sunday, February 8, 2009.

15.   Travers, Tony and Esposito, L, Nothing to Lose but Your Chains: Reforming the English Local Government Finance System, Policy Exchange, London, 2004.

16.   Mulgan, Geoff,The Art of Public Strategy, Oxford University Press,2009.

CHAPTER 10

EDUCATION

Philosophy and Education

Curriculum

Staffing

Organisation

Final Thoughts

CHAPTER 10

EDUCATION

Philosophy and Education

In a sense 'education' is the odd subject out in this book. That is because, although, like any other subject, it has a philosophy of its own, potentially or actually, it is not itself a fundamental subject in the sense of being an end, but is, rather, an instrumental one. It is about how to teach and learn all the other subjects.

It does, in point of fact, have a not undeveloped 'philosophy of education', with a plethora of quite contradictory theory accumulated over the ages and loosely underpinned by such more scientific disciplines as psychology and sociology. From philosophy it tends to take potted ethical and aesthetic ideas.

The philosophy of education, notwithstanding, does contain some rather grandiose elements(1). It has a component called 'curriculum theory', which purports to examine, and of course tell us, what is worthwhile, or even essential for humans to study.

Unfortunately, in modern times philosophy of education, with a few notable exceptions, like Russell and Dewey, has failed to attract the serious attention of the foremost thinkers of the age thus far. To compound its problems, the disparate rag-bag of ideas that comprise it is prone to a seemingly insurmountable drawback, namely, that we have all been to school and therefore we all reckon to know what it is about.

Still worse, the subject is bedevilled by politics. Left and right wings, with their largely incompatible ideologies, wrestle it back and forth in practice. The effect is that change in Education is endless; despite there being no agreed indicators to decide whether it is being successful or not, or even what direction to go in.

The fact that education of some kind or other is an obvious necessity for us all in a complex, advanced contemporary state makes the need for consensus and regular review essential. If we actually lived in a democracy we would

CHAPTER 10

EDUCATION

conduct a major national debate involving the populace, including older children and teenagers, who are its main recipients, to decide such basic questions as what to teach, to whom, how, and why, with what purposes and yardsticks of success, and in which organisational and institutional modes. We would then keep it under regular review. Since in effect we lock up our offspring throughout their childhood and adolescence in the company of teachers (one suspects partly for pragmatic reasons of child minding quite unconnected with the nature or value of education), it seems reasonable to provide at the very least a cogent justification. Once examined, it surprisingly turns out to be anything but self-evident.

A classic contribution to the philosophy of education is the eponymous work edited by the guru, R.S. Peters(2). It essentially considered clarifying the concept of education and its aims, looked at aspects of curriculum like integration and planning, analysed the nature of teaching and learning, and ended with social and ethical arguments in its favour. There was an interest at the time, elitist in leaning, to make a clear-cut distinction between 'education' and 'training', emphasizing the perceived inherent superiority of the former. It was also desired to stress the value of education 'as an end in itself', and a general preference for a 'liberal' education, unhelpfully seen as the development of 'mind' (and perhaps academic attitudes also). It was suspicious of vocational emphases and the values of a consumer society. Instrumental concerns, and their potential for distortion of educational purism, these authors had an inclination to resist, but they did valuable work in, say, starting to unpack the clues that methodology gives to what is 'indoctrination' rather than education(3).

'Indoctrination' is a term pregnant with emotional overlays of a derogatory kind. One strand is that the teaching strays from giving a balanced treatment of the various opinions on a topic to claiming the rectitude of one distinct approach. The teacher is steering and willing the student to come to his own preferred beliefs. There is an intentional element with indoctrination, as with teaching, but one which suppresses a broad-minded rationality, one that would weigh up the relative strengths and weaknesses of each position. The above might be sufficient guidance by which to distinguish 'teaching' from 'indoctrination', except that some commentators can muddy the waters. On the one hand they can leave quite vague the tenets and tests of 'rationality'. On the other they may claim, as Barrow does, that *"to influence...children*

CHAPTER 10

EDUCATION

towards the acceptance of certain patterns of behaviour…is not in itself to indoctrinate." (3)

Can we be at ease that our teaching always respects the distinctions and keeps well away from indoctrination? Do we really mind over much, notably when the views being conveyed coincide with our own? Should we not look more closely at syllabus and methodology? And another reason why we probably don't is that we are used to dealing with young children, where we encourage them to behave in ways that do not come naturally to them, where they are at an age which renders them unable to understand our reasons, and which we seek to impose by varying methods and degrees of coercion. When they are older, of course, they have become conditioned to behave in certain ways automatically as a result. Do we then go back and try to analyse and explain the underlying rationale? One false track was the idea of 'child-centred' education. In the hands of some extreme educational advisers and primary teachers it became a movement that threatened to undermine adult purposes in favour of letting the little darlings do exactly what they wanted. They would have been much better off developing psychological insights into child development instead.

Another important concept to be analysed in the 1950's and 60's was 'culture'. 'Culture' started to be considered along with social attacks on classical elitism and began with the rise of popular art forms.

That Education should seek to convey our 'culture' is not superficially to be doubted by many. Once again, the multifold problems emerge with a closer examination of what exactly 'culture' means.

Traditionally, Education in the United Kingdom has been associated with cultural elitism, which it has tried to convey. Barrow provides a useful characterisation of it as follows. There are works of art (used in the sense of all the arts, whether music, sculpture, painting, literature, film and so forth) which are better than others. These are known as 'high culture' and are more worthwhile than popular or folk culture, such as television and popular music, and other non-cultural leisure activities. This 'fact' stems from their inherent qualities, which those educated in culture have a heightened ability to understand and appreciate. It seems to follow that

CHAPTER 10

EDUCATION

perhaps only a minority will ever be able to develop the requisite insights, or even be interested in so doing.

There is an offensiveness about cultural elitism in contemporary pluralist society which stems from its polarisation along both political and intellectual lines. It can quickly become snobbish and class-ridden. Wrongly tended it can stiffen resistance to Education altogether.

But which is right tending? Any attempt to decide what is definable as culture has to overcome one of the oldest and most intractable of all philosophical problems, namely how to be able to ground universally acceptable criteria for aesthetic excellence.

The most likely answer is that there are none. But that is a bleak prospect affording no way forward for educationalists, so it is not socially acceptable. However, if there are artistic standards, what are they and who is entitled to determine them? Lastly, what benefits should derive to students as a result of a cultural education?

The truth is we really have little idea. What we do have is largely unexamined practice. A loose political overlay from government gives a framework within which there is still ample scope for educationalists in positions of influence to call the shots. The result is a very complicated hotchpotch of behaviour which feeds on both tradition and current fads and fancies.

One of the key areas of philosophy of education in the 1970's was the theory of knowledge, sometimes called epistemology. Hirst, a main proponent, concluded his analysis by claiming that there are seven 'forms of knowledge', named as mathematics, physical sciences, human sciences, history, religion, literature and fine arts, and philosophy(4). He argued that they are distinguished by their "conceptual structures and the truth criteria involved". It is important to grasp that these forms of knowledge are meant to refer to knowledge of the world, and not, tritely, of their own subject matter. The thesis was subject to much criticism. Hirst himself later came to concede his doubts. They included the concession that history and the social sciences are "logically complex", and that the arts and religion may not contain knowledge at all.

CHAPTER 10

EDUCATION

At any rate, the work opened up serious epistemological uncertainties which are still being grappled with. Far from informing the absolute nature of knowledge, it muddied the waters somewhat. But for those hoping to hang curriculum planning on it, Hirst was clear from the outset: his forms of knowledge were not "to be regarded as providing a pattern for curriculum units. A total curriculum pattern could be composed in an infinite variety of ways, and needed defending not only in relation to the fundamental categories of objectives, but on psychological, administrative and other grounds as well". So an end then, if he was right, to what was just a pipe dream for the tidy-minded. If we cannot logically derive curriculum from something bedrock like truth, then it remains perennially prey to the political struggle, both from educationalists and from outside the service. And where is the satisfaction in that, except for those who get their way and remain in a fool's paradise?

Unfortunately, enlightenment has not really emerged so much as confusion in the contemporary world of philosophy of education either. The subject has branched out, (for instance into 16-19 education) and been subject to new influences such as continental perspectives and post-modernism, which can have a negative effect and lose any certainty. Although it is now less conceptually introspective, and more open to outside ideas and practices like feminism, where is its influence on the mainstream of educational practice? As with the insights of educational research, there seems to be an unhealthy dislocation from political policy and management in Education. As additional indictment, education as a service is not good at communicating with, and learning from, its own parts, be they theoretical or structural. The primary, secondary, further, and higher education sectors each have their own, mainly separate (dare we say blinkered?) traditions.

Curriculum

As readers should be aware from a previous chapter's discussions on the concept of value, it is not a bit of use trying to justify curriculum content by appeal to its intrinsic worth. There will be manifold opinions and intuitions, but no consensus. So all the arguments to be assembled here will perforce be instrumental ones. Yet in a changing world curricula are, or need to be, evolving entities.

CHAPTER 10

EDUCATION

Unprincipled pragmatism may not be a bad guide when we come to curriculum reform either. We can start from where we are, with the subjects and topics we teach, and proceed to seek practical justifications first to retain each given aspect, second to reject them. Legitimate decision criteria may well include such non-emotive factors as difficulty, relevance, usage, obsolescence, size, and so forth. Next we can proceed to consider new candidates for inclusion. Environmental content, for example, would first be examined to see if it could easily be integrated into existing subjects like the sciences and geography. Or whether this would lead to unwieldy fragmentation or duplication.

Does this happen in practice? Well, after many years of bumbling along, the watershed for curriculum reform was the speech in 1976 by the Labour Prime Minister, James Callaghan, at Ruskin College, Oxford, which started the so-called 'Great Debate'(5) . He criticized the effectiveness of informal methods of teaching of the 'three Rs', the relevance of the curriculum to economic needs, and the examination system.

When Mrs. Thatcher then came to power she expressed interest in the primary sector reforms to raise standards in English and mathematics, nothing more. Yet the National Curriculum came to pass. How?

The jury is still out. But the civil service wanted it and the Department of Education and Science, DES, was very influential. Its interest was central control, previously ceded to local education authorities and schools. Education reformers in the university academic world also wanted it. And governments came to see it as linked to Britain's international competitiveness.

Now the National Curriculum is a wondrous thing(6). It is monitored for government by the Qualifications and Curriculum Authority, QCA, an appointed quango. And it has been compulsory in state schools since September 1989, having been introduced by the Conservative government under the 1988 Education Reform Act.(7)

The National Curriculum is divided into four 'key stages'. Stages 1 and 2 respectively cover the infant and junior years of primary education.

CHAPTER 10

EDUCATION

Stages 3 and 4 are concerned with secondary education, stage 3 covering the first three years, stage 4 taking the last two years to the (minimum) school-leaving age of 16.

It is easy to get bogged down in the myriad technical and bureaucratically-exacting detail of this elaborate construction, the administrative bane of many a teacher's life. For instance, there are for each subject at each key stage 'programmes of study' which prescribe the content, 'attainment targets' which prescribe pupil performance requirements, assessment arrangements at each of eight 'level descriptions' within every attainment target, 'planning guides', 'schemes of work', 'cross-curriculum dimensions' and annual reporting regimes. This is an Alice in Wonderland world of spurious objectivity and complete over-elaboration.

The National Curriculum is ennobled by much high-sounding yet hollow rhetoric about its 'values'. These are 'enduring' and underpin the Curriculum. They relate to 'the self', 'relationships', 'the diversity in our society', 'the environment'. The 'common good' is mentioned, along with truth, freedom, justice, human rights, and the rule of law. 'Families', including those of 'different kinds', are valued, as are 'a healthy and just democracy', 'a productive economy', and 'sustainable development'.

By having a 'statutory core' the National Curriculum is able to 'establish an entitlement and standards', as well as 'promote continuity, coherence, and public understanding'.

Pupils are to be prepared for 'the world of employment' and to 'contribute to community cohesion', and other responsibilities of adult life.

Running along with this, as is typical of the shallowness of political thought, there is no underlying theory by which to ground and justify the National Curriculum. The best they come up with is how a subject contributes to an 'area of experience', with the whole constituting an 'entitlement' for every child. The list is one of nine adjectives, similar to, but not entirely coincident with, the subjects themselves. The ones that are the same are: human and social, mathematical, physical, scientific, technological.

CHAPTER 10

EDUCATION

The ones that are different are: aesthetic and creative, linguistic and literary, moral, spiritual. The first two of these are obviously covered by Art and Design, the second two by English. Moral and spiritual will usually be assumed to belong to religious education.

Shockingly, however, no content for moral education is prescribed. It is church denominations that have the most say in devising local syllabuses for religious education. These presumably also encompass the 'spiritual' dimension, whatever that is supposed to be beyond ordinary mental well-being.

Not surprisingly, the driver for the National Curriculum was not educational principles at all but an approach aimed at gingering up teachers by imposing pseudo-market conditions. Competition was introduced via such devices as published school league tables and public consumerism.

According to Phillips, a major inherent flaw of the National Curriculum was that the ill-informed politicians used as reformers those 'experts' from within the education world who were out to radicalize it. So that, for instance, there was an emphasis on child-centred learning (for greater fun), as opposed to didactic methods, and relativism rather than objectivity of knowledge, which infected the construction of subject content.

Regarding the nature of the National Curriculum content we need to consider key stage 4, because there the subject matter is at its most mature, for the older pupils.

Statutory programmes of study for all are to be found in the following subjects: citizenship, English, ICT, mathematics, physical education, and science.

Religious education is also a compulsory subject. There is something called 'personal, social, health and economic education', which is encouraged, but not legally required.

It is instructive to see what has been dropped as a requirement from key

EDUCATION

stage 3 just prior to the two-year run in to GCSE examinations. The list of subjects is: art and design, design and technology, geography, history, music, and modern foreign languages.

Comparisons of key stages 3 and 4 subject listings show the massive diminution in the compulsory element between them. When the National Curriculum originally came in there were the three 'basic' or 'core' subjects, which still remain - namely, English, mathematics, and science. But they, together with seven others, formed the so-called 'foundation subjects'.

It is still possible to take examinations in all of them, in principle. But unfortunately for student choice, it can be quite misleading to argue that key stage 3 compulsory subjects can all be taken at GCSE level, in practice. It depends. Choice is guided on ability, but timetabling decisions also have to be made by schools, as few will have the resources to provide a complete range.

A notorious case is the long-term decline of the study of sciences in secondary education. A survey in 2009 revealed that over half the schools in England and Wales did not allow any pupils to offer at GCSE the three standard sciences - physics, chemistry, and biology - quite unlike the position a generation earlier. Academic experts are convinced the situation makes it an uphill task even for brighter students looking to succeed in these sciences at 'A' level and on university degree courses.

Reasons are not solely to do with school resources either. The sciences are not culturally valued in our society very highly, and good teachers of them are in short supply. Then there are the competing interests of other subjects and the personal predilections of school management. A main factor, all these others notwithstanding, is that the subjects are difficult.

Other matters have not, of course, stood still since 1989 either. The QCA ran a consultation on primary curriculum review during 2009, for example, and a new secondary curriculum had come into force in September 2008. But this was all within the constraints of the main established framework.

CHAPTER 10

EDUCATION

The Rose Report on primary sector curriculum reform thought there was too much in it. They recommended an antidote to "over-prescription and over-crowded content". The solution, it contended, was a move to more thematic, less subject-based, approaches. The themes are listed as 'understanding' in: English, communication, and languages; mathematics; science and technology; physical health and well-being; arts and design.

Using themes is similar to a well-established method in primary schools, one sometimes referred to as 'teaching by topics', where a topic will draw on a range of relevant subject areas.

The report did stress, however, that it would not want to see the demise of subject teaching, or "cross-curriculum studies". History and geography would come in under the human/social/environmental theme. Key priority was to be given to literacy, numeracy, and technology.

Cross-Curriculum 'dimensions' have become a quick political fix at secondary levels too. Supposedly reflecting major concerns in the wider world as they develop, such as 'global and sustainable development', they typically mirror political concerns like 'cultural diversity' in a country swamped by unchecked immigration.

So with the preface of our dubious enlightenment from the theory, let us now examine curriculum content further. It is important because we all have in principle a democratic stake in it. Neither the teaching profession nor politicians have any monopoly of either knowledge or wisdom.

There are some practical problems with a national curriculum, if you decide to have one, of course. Not all are impressed with the resulting uniformity, it can stifle the creativity of good teachers, and a serious drawback is that if you do not get the content right, and have (like us) inadequate machinery for updating it, what is left out can come to loom disproportionately in its significance.

Something that is socially divisive, and thereby difficult to defend, by the way, is the fact that the National Curriculum is mandatory in the public sector, but not in private schools. Since we are repeatedly told that education in the private schools tends to be better on the whole (certain

CHAPTER 10

EDUCATION

individual state and private schools excepted), we might wonder from that alone at the merits of the National Curriculum, but it is true that we are dealing here with a very complex, multivariate social phenomenon. Factors like relative financial resources, class size, teaching quality, and attitudes of learners, as well as parental backing, would seem to be very significant, for example.

Leaving aside the abstruse issues about subject content, teaching methods, and the age/ability of the child, in coming to decisions about just what subjects to include in the curriculum, national or otherwise, there are many prior considerations, few of which are ever publicly unpacked. The sort of relevant matters include the outcomes of learning we expect from these subjects, both in terms of the knowledge they impart and the methods they employ, how subjects relate to our culture, the modern world, the economy and working life, leisure and pleasure, and values.

Now a fundamental, and unsolved, practical problem immediately emerges, namely that of curriculum overload. Difficulties are compounded because of fringe pressures, often politically driven, for new material to be added to the curriculum: typically in response to some prominent media issue of the moment, such as an aspect of health and safety, or drugs, or the knife culture, or nutritional standards in relation to junk food and obesity. There is an inertia effect that has a tendency to act one-way; it appears easier to add to the curriculum than to justify taking away from it.

Another key issue, and one which does argue for a degree of impartiality and detachment in the decision makers, is that subject specialists can be blinkered and biased - they are liable to extol the virtues of their own subject and play down the relative importance of its rivals. Nor do they take responsibility for how they might all fit together. In general there was a lack of a coordinating vision.

The education philosopher, White, had a novel justification for including almost anything of cultural relevance in its broadest sense - students should be exposed to as wide a range of subjects as possible, so that they could ultimately reject most of them on the basis of at least some partial knowledge, instead of the usual blind prejudice and ignorance. A rather cynical-seeming view, it nevertheless encapsulates some unpalatable

EDUCATION

truths, not least the fact that most efforts of most teachers with a not negligible proportion of pupils are probably fore-doomed to failure.

In any case, and fundamentally, the National Curriculum had no philosophical basis.

The preamble could continue, for this is a profoundly complex field - no less than the current sum of human knowledge and it methodological endeavours - but the argument will now be rested in favour of looking at some of the subjects of the potential curriculum themselves.

It is not the intention here to reflect on every subject and evaluate its case for curriculum inclusion, still less to detail an appropriate syllabus content within the subjects. Rather, a few broad cases for inclusion or exclusion will be outlined. These alone will not comprise a complete corrective to the ongoing malaise, but they do serve as exemplars of the kinds of debate that urgently needs to be enjoined.

In making positive steps to curriculum reform it is important to take a perspective view of society as a whole, perhaps comparing it with others. When you do that with the United Kingdom, you find that statistically-speaking most of us are rather poor at science and mathematics. This is both long-term and culturally embedded. It is so pronounced that prominent members of the establishment, politicians and the rest, openly boast that they struggled with these subjects at school. Hardly surprising then for career structures to be so arranged that those with liberal arts degrees tend to have more openings available to them, leading to higher salaries and positions of greater influence and social prestige. Media, thinly populated themselves by the scientifically educated, are inclined to caricature scientists as eccentric and rather unworldly. Somehow, in spite of the inherently greater difficulty of the sciences, the problem, which is profoundly serious, must be solved for the benefit of a populace otherwise hopelessly ill-equipped to understand or properly function in the modern world. If politicians for instance remain unconvinced, let them consider this: without the existence and proper deployment of high-calibre scientific expertise, the country will undoubtedly sink towards third-world status. It may do so anyway. We only have here a necessary condition for prevention, not a sufficient one.

CHAPTER 10

EDUCATION

Next comes a plea for inclusion. Analytic philosophy is missing. In France, for instance, it would be highly valued and very prominent, but not in the United Kingdom. Why not? Essentially, the reasons are historical and cultural. But it is unpopular here today because it requires hard thinking, so is difficult, exposes weaknesses in thought, so can be humiliating, and has a tendency to be critical and attack sacred cows, such as religion, and politics, so is viewed as threatening, even offensive. Also, and this is a very large factor, it does not obviously lead to specific jobs in the world of work, where employers are unlikely to understand it. It seems remote by caricatured image in its ivory tower, whereas it can, and usefully should, inform almost every aspect of our lives. It rarely appears in schools, except perhaps in a bit of 'thinking' for juniors, and sixth-form minority time. A glance at public debate should be enough to convince. The general standard is very low, whereas philosophy could help a great deal in sharpening up our reasoning powers, and our abilities to frame arguments and assess their strengths and weaknesses without lapsing into excessive emotion or personal attacks.

Philosophy is valuable for all sorts of reasons, of which an illustrative sample is given here. Janet Radcliffe Richards highlights the fact that most questions of public interest have philosophical aspects and so need philosophical methods to address them properly. It helps to avoid "contradictions and confusions"[8]. It is just an extension of ordinary reasoning, but sharper and more systematic and critical.

The lack of philosophical rigour in public debate is tragically dangerous. People have begun to see through the more obvious party stances and tactics of politicians on television programmes like BBC's 'Question Time', for instance, but are largely unaware of their own prejudices. When writ large across virtually the whole of society, it leads to poor decision-making and a decline in valuing the intellectual life. We have to be able to recognise and appraise evidence, to distinguish it from mere rhetoric.

It helps us to see that disagreement is so frequently a clash of unpacked, and rarely examined, values, or about a rigidly-held ideology whose rectitude has been taken for granted.

401

CHAPTER 10

EDUCATION

Philosophers themselves seldom help, of course. Too many are remote figures, researching obscure topics in over-technical language, not attempting to communicate with the layman, regarding themselves as above the fray, detracting from the positive image that might see their aid enlisted, as was Mary Warnock's over the successful legal reform concerning the enablement of 'test tube babies'.

By contrast now follows a plea for exclusion from the curriculum. It involves the vexed subject of religion. In the United Kingdom there are church schools and state schools within the public sector. Some of the church schools are 'controlled', which means that the local education authority has a majority voting interest on the school governing body. Obviously, those (usually called 'aided') schools controlled by various denominations of church, notably the Anglican and the Roman Catholic, can and do make their own arrangements within laws they have themselves, through their ecclesiastical hierarchies effectively negotiated with the State. Whatever you think about how appropriate it may be for churches to have such schools and powers, and the author is convinced it should be illegal because of indoctrination and irrationalism, there is surely no argument, except perhaps an archaic one from tradition, for the state schools within the education system to be anything other than secular. What is here meant is that state schools should not, as now they are legally required to do, start every day with an act of collective worship involving the whole school (parents only having a right to withdraw their child on grounds of conscience). The service implies that the state legally sanctions the position, brooking no argument, that there is a God and that he should be worshipped. It cannot be an educational stance, but indoctrination of tender minds pure and simple. Neither is it appropriate to opt everyone in, with the onus on them to opt out, if their children can withstand any resulting social pressures.

Secondly, 'religious education' so-called is enshrined in the curriculum by law. Atheists and agnostics have no choice here but to attend lessons. The churches even get the dominant view in deciding the syllabus content. In fairness, though, whilst secularism plays little or no part, there is at least an attempt to teach about the major faiths from a comparative point of view.

CHAPTER 10

EDUCATION

One subject of potential concern in curriculum design is history. The argument that all children should learn to develop some kind of reliable perspective on what came before them (in uncivilization) seems unexceptionable. However, given the great propensity for political interference, actual practice needs to be carefully watched.

It is a commonplace that history tends to be written from the viewpoint of the victorious in conflicts. Indeed, the difficulty of evaluating the accuracy and objectivity of historical accounts for all sorts of reasons is one of the important messages to be imparted in the classroom discussions about historical research methods that it is hoped would be deemed essential. Minorities also need to be heard and their positions and behaviour made clear.

Politicians are tempted to want to infect children with their own political values, whilst proscribing such an approach from the subject teachers. Watch out for topics like "citizenship", in which so-called 'British values' may figure prominently, whatever they might be. There is also likely to be a bias in favour of British history in an attempt to inculcate nationalism.

As presumably curriculum designers are aware, content must ensure an effective balance between the abstract and the concrete. Students need real examples to illustrate principles, so deepening understanding and aiding the memory. One appreciates that history is too vast for all of it to be encompassed in the school syllabus. A similar problem of scope and selection applies to geography, and to many other subject too.

Finally, in such a brief perusal of the state of curriculum, many adults are struck by the thought of how ill-prepared for life the education system leaves them, even if by conventional standards they have been 'highly educated'. That has to be a serious indictment of the curriculum. It is said such are the preoccupations of adulthood that children would not be interested in them. Well if so, why does the system insist on teaching them about ancient history, or algebra? The argument simply does not wash. A stronger one is the pragmatic fact that teachers are generally not trained to deal with such subjects and there is no teaching tradition for them. Essentially, we are still

EDUCATION

emerging from the domination by classical interests and the liberal arts from the grammar school days.

So what is meant by 'life' subjects, if not the drawing of nudes? The list here is not comprehensive, but suggestive. It would include developing personal qualities, parenting skills, domestic financial management, the problems and solutions of relationships including marital, job skills, insurance, wills, pensions, household cookery and cleaning, DIY skills, the main aspects of house maintenance, how to deal with contractors and traders, consumerism, health and safety, common legal problems, key aspects of the law and the legal system, what used to be called 'British Constitution', political knowledge and awareness, saving and investment, the banking system, dealing with public authorities, and, not least, how to complain.

It seems utterly wasteful and extremely aggravating that most of us emerge into adult life very deficient in many of these areas, whilst it cannot be denied that some rather piecemeal aspects are likely to be covered haphazardly to some extent. Happiness and effectiveness are going to depend significantly on our ability to understand and rationally cope with the increasingly complex and fast-moving world and society around us. By this, possibly harsh yet necessary test, the present curriculum woefully fails almost everybody. Politicians like to claim that public sector schools are underachieving. Curriculum irrelevance may be a far greater threat.

To show the unsatisfactory kind of method by which we proceed, the 14-19 curriculum was not in safe hands with the Blair government because of the disputatious ideas of the legion players, all with vested interests(9). A common strand had been the political wish to reduce compulsory elements of the National Curriculum. For example, the 2002 Green Paper, and a 2003 discussion document "14-19: Opportunity and Excellence", stated an intention to virtually end the National Curriculum at 14, dispensing even in the short-term with all subjects except English, mathematics, and science, with religious education. A rag-bag of broadly life skills and physical education would also remain a requirement. Out to join arts and the humanities as optional were now modern foreign languages, and design and technology.

CHAPTER 10

EDUCATION

What government wanted to do was improve the status and standing of vocational studies, providing flexibility for students to learn at their own pace, and a continuity with the post-16 curriculum increasingly to be related to their future world of work. The movement was not aimed exclusively at those of lower academic ability. On the contrary, it was hoped that brighter students would turn to vocational studies in preference to the time-honoured and prestigious GCSE Advanced levels.

A major problem with all this, apart from a woeful lack of consensus, and an initiative-weary teaching force reeling from years of imposed change, was the messing about that ensued with regard to the actual system of examinations to be designed at both 16 and 18 years of age. Some imagined new vocational GCSE 'O' levels at 16, and hybrid subjects incorporating both academic and vocational elements.

A 14-19 Reform Working Group was set up under a former Chief Inspector of Schools, Mike Tomlinson, to design an English-style Baccalaureate on the successful continental model. Tomlinson's approach found favour with the Education profession partly because he intended to retain and "build on all that is good in the current system, including the real and great strengths of A levels and GCSEs". The bedrock of proposals was a new Diploma with four levels: two below GCSE, an intermediate level at GCSE, and an advanced one for A level.

But, in the event, the government rejected the plan in 2005. It had been opposed by some of the business sector and a general election was coming up. Instead it opted for a three-tier diploma system in fourteen different occupational areas to run alongside GCSE and A levels. Tomlinson protested in vain (and sensibly) that the scheme would inevitably perpetuate (and probably exacerbate) the unresolved status tension between academic and vocational qualifications. The Education profession was united behind his disappointment.

The Brown government then announced in 2007 the launch over several years of yet more diplomas. But these would now begin to cover academic subjects too!

All the diplomas would compete against the existing qualifications until a

EDUCATION

complete system review, no doubt with its usual lack of prejudice, to be undertaken in 2013. Their actual fate could instead depend on the outcome of the general elections in 2010.

In conclusion what must come across from an examination of the history of the National Curriculum is that there is more to success than mere rationality. It has to be competently channelled. The experts proved to be self-centred about their subjects and an inadequate overview was taken of how it would all fit together. Politicians did not have the wit to arbitrate; therefore the whole project became distorted by obsession with outcomes, as 'measured' by performance testing.

Staffing

The next area for scrutiny will be staffing of education, although the specific focus is on teachers, rather than those who also serve, be they 'managers' including heads, administrators, or other support staff. There is no interest here in assessing the contribution of these groups, which is not to suggest they are not important in themselves.

Rather, the point is that media and public concern tends to be with teachers, who form the vast majority of staff within the Education Service, and who consume the lion's share of all the resources. So what, then, needs to be said about them and their lot? Do we get value for public money in what is the key determinant of quality in education as process?

Let it be made clear at the outset that, in the opinion of the author, the vast majority of teachers in this country do a very fine job for modest reward. The nation is in many important respects well served by a dedicated group of workers. But, nevertheless, there are some notable reservations to be discussed, mostly systems failings.

In one way of looking at it, teachers are victims of their predecessors' success. In Victorian times the village school master was part of the hierarchy to be looked up to, along with the vicar and the local squire. He would have been one of the few with 'an education'. Since then, of

CHAPTER 10

EDUCATION

course, we have developed schooling for the masses. A lot of parents are rather better educated than most of their children's teachers now. Thus it is understandable that teachers' status has slipped on that account alone and so has become a matter of obsession for some of them.

Teachers consider themselves to be part of a 'profession'. The term is used repeatedly, and without any apparent sense of contradiction, in their unions' negotiations over pay and conditions. Primary teachers especially assert their professionalism, and it seems to be a mark of insecurity in part and also reflects a lack of confidence. Strict semantics may see the term 'profession' as applicable only to walks of life which are fee-earning. They do nowadays have a Teaching Council, which supposedly regulates standards, including qualifications, although this can also apply to manual trades.

Turning to the matter of insecurity, it may seem a strange idea at first, since pay and pensions are state-guaranteed, but it is a sign of the times. Fundamentally, modern governments do not trust public servants, and teachers are just that. In recent years particularly they have seen the rise of accountability mechanisms based on stick rather than carrot. The major one is OFSTED, with the dreaded school inspections. Time was a teacher could close the door of her classroom and be largely left in peace with her charges to teach what she wanted and in her own way. Then governing bodies assumed formal powers to mediate community wishes and provide scrutiny. A national curriculum was imposed, specific methods of notably literacy teaching encouraged, formalised and individualised, pupil progress records introduced for the teachers to keep up, a regime of regular testing developed for each stage and age of learning, and statistical measures invented to monitor 'added value'. When you compound this with the internal demands of the school hierarchy, the hostility and litigious nature of some parents, the reduced sanctions available to deal with (rising) pupil indiscipline (a reflection of society), and intrusive media, it is perhaps remarkable that they stay. Yet the vast majority do. The teaching force as a whole is rather resilient. However, it is worth reflecting what good the experience does them and whether blatant exploitation of their vocational values by society is the best civilized way to improve our (and their) qualities of life and the standards of education in their charges. As has had to be said so many

CHAPTER 10

EDUCATION

times to modern governments, trust is easy to break down, very difficult and slow to repair. Target chasing, beloved of New Labour, is by its nature only about the measurable. The trouble is, so many of the valuable things in education, like encouraging a child's interest in a subject, or his self-confidence and esteem, are not amenable to measurement in any way.

Money, of course, is. A word about remuneration may therefore not be out of place here. An element of the declining respect for teachers could have something to do with the fact that their salaries are comparatively unremarkable. Numerous are the teachers who cannot afford to live in the catchment area of their school. What makes it worse is that examples abound of trivial activities in wider society, like football, attracting a fortune. Many trainers, who have taken shorter courses at lower levels, such as driving instructors, and alternative therapists can easily command better pay. On the other hand, public sympathy could lack because teachers' pay disputes are high-profile. Their annual national conferences receive media coverage. The more militant threaten strike action from time to time. They could certainly be the envy of local government officers in at least having a platform and seeming to boast effective negotiators. Yet governments have the power to change a public sector group's position in society, as Mrs. Thatcher upgraded the police force in the 1980's. There is little sign of this happening to teachers; their sheer numbers would always militate against it anyhow.

The 2010 pre-election Tory promise to make teaching "brazenly elitist" by such measures as not providing financial help for those trainees without at least second-class university degrees, and paying of the student loans for those with top grades in science and mathematics, was seen as liable to be a false dawn. The Labour government's scheme 'Teach First' similarly provided incentives to get "the best graduates into the most challenging urban schools".

Experts were sceptical. Was this just window-dressing, measures affecting the few? Whilst high ability and graduate knowledge were important, were not many of the most successful teachers also those with personalities suitable for their pupils, a love of teaching, and inherent ability to do it well. And the question of what training they should receive is begged.

CHAPTER 10

EDUCATION

On the subject of teachers' pay there is one important exception to what has been said; head teachers have had a handsome leg up. Once again, the movement started with Thatcherism. When the government decreed that local education authorities should delegate financial, and much other institutional management, to schools, the measure opened the flood gates. Head teachers suddenly started to argue that their responsibilities were now on a par with captains of industry. Secondary heads, for instance, had annual budgets in some cases of around £2million or more. Much of the claim was bogus, of course. Nearly all the budget was already committed (to inflexible staffing costs), and LEAs continued to provide a deal of specialist support and management advice (much free of charge), with regard to estate management, for example, and budgetary expertise.

The Local Management of Schools, LMS, as it was known, demonstrated another unpleasant characteristic to the unsung town and county hall staff, namely that head teachers, in their single institutions, were worth paying royally for the work local government administrators used to do for a pittance for all their numerous schools. Nor did their levels of pay rise to meet the challenge of their new roles in training and advising these fledgling managers. It was all in a day's work. They would see some of the heads, unqualified in their new fields, falling at the first hurdle. Convinced their skills would be found out, or unable in principle to sanction the radical departure, lots of heads took early retirement rather than face the upheaval. Later on, most on both sides came to regard LMS as on the whole a success, or at least a change very unlikely ever to be reversed once schools had tasted greater 'freedom'. The officers in education and treasury departments could also ruefully watch as the new system tempted the bad apples in the barrel to excess. There were, and are, quite frequent cases nationally where head teachers abuse their managerial powers. Details vary, but typically involve inappropriate use of funds for personal gain, or the appointment of relatives to posts within the school. One recent example was of a principal who notoriously ran her own management consultancy agency during school time. Harder to gauge are the cases where heads fall foul of their increasingly empowered governing bodies. Fault could lie anywhere, perhaps a function of interpersonal skill failings.

Management courses have now been introduced specifically designed for head teachers. For how many of them, though, is it a thin veneer on top of their ingrained pedagogic professionalism? In America you would have a management expert running a school. That could not happen here without a massive cultural shift first.

There is a difficulty altogether over the training of teachers, both primary and secondary. In the case of the primary sector, teachers spend three or four years after the sixth-form in colleges of education on a qualifying course. The emphasis is vocational, heavily on the theory and practice of education, with strong elements of classroom experience. An academic subject is also studied, but the depth and breadth may not be much above school advanced level, if even that.

Time was in the late 1960's, when colleges of education had three-year training courses leading to teacher certification. To provide an academic gloss, new Bachelor of Education, B.Ed. degrees started to be encouraged, wherein the three-year course was essentially extended by another year.

A problem with primary teachers as a group is their relative lack of a good tertiary education. Mathematics, recognised to be a national weakness, is a crucial, bedrock subject which a lot find too difficult for them. Some cannot even pass GCSE mathematics, although attempts have been made to make it a prerequisite for teaching qualifications in state schools. So long as the situation continues, and it has been culturally and generationally embedded, primary schools will struggle to provide a competent mathematical foundation for their pupils. Primary children do, of course, learn rather elementary mathematics, but it is a fallacy to assume it does not require a very good grasp among teachers to stimulate effective learning. Understanding is what is needed by the pupils, not just accuracy in being able to follow mechanical procedures, and this comes from teachers who have studied mathematics to advanced or even degree levels.

Phillips argues that the chief focus should be the primary school, because, she says, that is where most damage is done. You can see what she means if she is looking for academic rigour and depth of understanding, because the primary teaching force as a cadre, though very well meaning and dedicated to the children, just isn't generally in that sort of league. The dilemma is cross-cultural: some subjects really need to be introduced quite early in a child's life, where we are looking to have the foundations soundly laid. That is especially true in the sciences and mathematics, for you cannot build a complex edifice on unstable ground. A poor start tends to handicap pupils for life in these disciplines.

Concerning recruitment, a serious, culturally endemic feature of our primary education is that it is gender-biased. Men are greatly outnumbered by women in primary teaching, and the balance gets considerably more pronounced for younger children in the infant department. That may say something about role preferences between the genders, also the notion that rather more men still have an expectation of better advancement and/or remuneration in other careers. It could be true that some local authorities have practiced positive discrimination in favour of promoting more women to even up perceived imbalances. Nevertheless, it is probably not healthy for boys and girls to be taught by just female adults, especially where they come from homes without fathers. Appropriate role models can be difficult to come by in the social jungle. They are needed by both sexes from both sexes.

For would-be secondary teachers to qualify, the university degree is the requirement, together with a year of postgraduate studies in education, PGCE, including a component of teaching practice. Now it seems as if one stream is light on subject expertise, the other on pedagogic knowledge and practice.

Some features of teacher training have undoubtedly improved, such as the larger proportionate emphasis on classroom practice rather than theory, and the system of mentoring, so each new entrant has an experienced teacher to act as his professional guide. Nevertheless, it should worry the government and the general public that around half of trainees do not make it into teaching at all. Teaching is notoriously difficult, even for some a debilitating way of earning a living. If the training achieves one thing, it usually removes the rose-tinted glasses, but not the thousands of poor teachers, almost all remaining in post, professionally protected.

Now the shortcomings of teacher training are not, unhappily, confined to the school sector. They are structurally present in further and higher education also. Colleges of further education, for 16-19 year olds in the main, have always had a tradition of recruitment from more experienced people, who have first pursued jobs, or even careers, in either the private or the public sector. They were not until the 21st century expected to have undergone any course at all on teaching theory or practice before they joined, although short in-service courses came to be encouraged. What allegedly helped them is another further education college tradition, that of lecturing rather than teaching. The model does provide what appears to youth to be a more adult (and therefore maybe more attractive) environment than school, yet it in principle sets students at a disadvantage compared with those who obtain individual and small-group tuition in school sixth-forms from qualified teachers.

More attempts are being made to professionalize the lecturing cadre in further education. A national body, the suitably named 'Lifelong Learning UK', LLUK, introduced new teaching qualifications in September 2007, replacing the previous qualifications. All prospective further education teachers now have to complete those qualifications at some time, but interestingly, for many this process will be in-service. Tellingly, two levels have been introduced. The Level 5 Diploma gives qualified teacher status akin to primary and secondary sectors. The Level 3 / 4 certificate qualifies staff as 'associate teachers'. Their responsibilities are restricted to using pre-prepared curriculum materials rather than designing their own, and will be more confined to specific subjects, levels, and types of student. It will be an area of professional conflict, if teaching assistants in primary class rooms are any precedent to go by. Whilst all teachers in further education under new government regulations need to register with the Institute for Learning, one suspects that the older guard may not in the main qualify, and it will probably take a generation before students have the benefit of a fully-trained teaching force.

The universities also place a low valuation on teacher training in terms of their criteria for academic appointments. Almost all the emphasis is on the academic qualifications, and the research experience and capabilities, of the applicants. Once again, a teaching qualification is not a requirement, and lectures for the many are the predominant teaching tool. The better universities are starting to address this problem, however.

CHAPTER 10

EDUCATION

In America the polarity is recognised organisationally by a structural split between institutions that specialise in degree-level and postgraduate research, and those which teach to such levels. In Britain all goes on under the same roof. The universities are seeking to renew themselves and compete internationally, so they are always on the look-out for the brightest prospects to continue and start the new research traditions. It almost goes without saying that they are having to do so, as usual, with indifferent remuneration and a reducing financial resource per student from public funds, at least in the times of recession.

Of course, the fact that a teacher is 'qualified', according to some recognised and accredited course of study, is no panacea for ills. Nevertheless, if university expansion policy remains determined to see up to half of the age cohorts, and perhaps more, requiring educating to 'degree level', then the need for good and student-centred tuition is essential. Staff/student ratios will have to increase, at considerable cost, in order to spoon feed the weaker brethren. The almost inevitable alternative, it is feared, has to be a dumbing down of the advanced nature of courses.

Organisation

Organisation is the next important illustrative topic. Often it has served as a very wasteful diversion, given that it is something governments think they can use to improve things. But the sad reality is that politicians can do little right here. There is ample evidence demonstrated historically by their constant meddling and inept fiddling about. Valuable resources are consumed which do not address fundamental problems.

The organisational framework of Education in this country has always left something to be desired, and the history of its development has been an uneven one, racked with dissension and social divisiveness. Even in modern times there has been much uneasy compromise and poor decision-making, because the nation, or at least its politicians, educationalists, and religious leaders, just cannot agree on the nature of the organisation best suited.

CHAPTER 10

EDUCATION

To start with the youngest children, the debate about their pre-school experience is endless. Some think they are best at home with mother, others would have them at the earliest possible age out there in social groupings. Some believe in the play-way; others want to introduce a formal educational experience, at least in part. The balance of pre-school provision, and ancillary support, such as child-minding, is very piecemeal across the country. Both the public and voluntary, as well as private sectors are involved. There are some stand-alone nursery schools, as well as nursery classes attached to infant schools. Staff quality and training qualifications are very variable and costs differ significantly. It is incomplete and a mish-mash. It is what you get when the country puts its priorities into other things. It is a disgrace and a shameful response to the promise of a new generation. What it needs as an absolute minimum and new starting point is a statutory and universal framework for pre-school educational entitlement and provision.

Part of the problem derives from the fact that successive governments have failed to make education legally mandatory before a child is rising five. As children enter formal schooling in the infant reception class, or perhaps earlier, sometimes in some places they will have the benefit of state schemes designed to compensate for socially deprived backgrounds. Attempts may be made to develop parenting skills and belief in the values and importance of education for those families judged to be in need. But these initiatives are expensive, and they are not backed by a national political consensus about means. Systematic and comprehensive development is a long way off and yet the first few years of a child's life are crucially defining. Findings of psychology seem to suggest that early intervention of the 'right kind' is vital for children to get a head start in education. The trouble is to find agreement on what is the right kind.

A key pointer was the Early Years Foundation Stage (EYFS). The 2002 Education Act introduced this statutory framework for the pre-school curriculum. Formal emphasis on letters and numbers especially was not welcomed by all, although both structured and unstructured 'play-way' approaches of the child-centred theorists were largely disparaged. Prescription was opposed by many influential educationalists, who thought it would make young children too anxious and rather put them off learning.

CHAPTER 10

EDUCATION

Structurally, it has yet to be decided over many years whether children are better off in dedicated infant schools, or in larger primaries. Both models are commonplace. But expediency comes into play. When the population declines there is pressure from the government for Local Education Authorities to reduce the number of places available. A very common way to do this is to combine an infant school and a junior school into one primary school covering the whole five to eleven age range, so saving at least one headship in the long-run, and possibly immediately if the incumbent is able and willing to move on, or retire. So much for idealism over primary structures then.

An important matter that is reasonably well-handled is the very local provision near to where families live, although many still have long distances to walk to school, measured in miles, and not always exclusively in isolated rural areas. There are petty bureaucratic arguments over transport cost provision, and parents who deceive with their cars.

But all local authorities are legally required to have transparent school entrance policies at primary and secondary levels, with independent appeals panels to arbitrate on parental disputes. Obviously, not all can access a place at the school of their choice in situations where supply is over subscribed by demand. However, the policies have to be based on objective and reasonable criteria, such as having siblings or living in close proximity, and placed in a priority order of application. Every now and again a cause celebre emerges, yet the rules are well tried. They are a necessary protection to ensure a balance of decision-making between competing interests. Some parents will cheat to get the school of their choice. Such devices as addresses of convenience within the catchment area are common enough and can now attract legal sanction. Some head teachers will plot to keep what they consider the undesirable children out. Miscreants need dealing with seriously. These civil wrongs could be regarded as criminal, the guilty fined, named and shamed in the media, and ill-gotten place offers withdrawn.

What repeatedly goes wrong is when a church school decides to deny access to pupils on denominational grounds. Unfortunately, there may be a nearby primary school, but of a religious nature possibly refusing access, or the wrong denomination by choice. Even in a mostly secular society in the 21st century, large numbers of parents have to accept as a matter of sheer practicality a school influenced or run by a religious body they do not believe in. This is offensive to more than atheists and agnostics; it adversely affects minority denominations and religions too.

Some 'experiments' occurred from the late 1960's with the age of transition from primary to secondary schooling. Middle schools were tried in places like the West Riding, pupils leaving infant schools, not for junior schools, but to these institutions covering an age range from 8 to 12 or 13. The plan did not catch on, perhaps partly because the middle schools could not attract enough graduate secondary-trained teachers. The fashion left a fairly standard model of junior transition at the age of 11 to "big school".

And so it became, with the all-ability entry comprehensive school movement of the 1960's on, and rising birth rates just after the war, as the baby boomers themselves started to reproduce. There again, the nation was divided about the framework and model of secondary education it wanted, and governments fudged the issue in favour of local democracy at the time. Some espoused comprehensives as egalitarian, and many grew to factory size of around 2000 pupils. They were mostly mixed, as with the primary sector. Other areas retained the conventional post-war model of academic grammar schools for those passing the 11+ examination, and secondary modern schools (of lower status and a more practically-oriented syllabus) for the rest. So the inherent social divisiveness of the post-war era was deliberately perpetuated, even in the supposedly egalitarian public sector.

The comprehensives were founded on a near-impossible ideal on the other hand: that of total social inclusion. In fact, the vast majority deviated greatly from it. One way was single-sex, another restricted to a particular denomination, some served specific ghetto areas, others ruthlessly setted by academic subject, or streamed their intake into classes by previous attainment. The word 'comprehensive' was a convenient and clever misnomer. Such schools are rarely a microcosm of society. No great American experiments were tried, of bussing pupils across town to create a better socio-economic, gender and racial balance.

CHAPTER 10

EDUCATION

Just as serious, there was no organisational agreement universally on the age of transition to further education establishments. There still isn't. Many comprehensives only cover 11-16, thereby putting off a lot of bright academic teachers, while others are 11-18 with large sixth forms. In particular areas you have the 'mushroom' concept - a structure in which all the comprehensive schools bar one are 11-16. The odd one out is the 'mushroom'. It is 11-18, and its sixth form has to be large enough to cater for the whole town. Except that there may also be a college of further education locally, to which some 16 year olds will preferentially transfer.

Because there were, and are, so many 11-16 comprehensive schools, sixth-form colleges grew up to look after the 16-18 age range. In effect the academic elitism divide was recreated at 16-19, because those who did not stay on beyond the minimum school leaving age of 16 either dropped out or went to the area college of further education. Broadly speaking, the sixth-form colleges tended to concentrate on academic teaching to 'A' levels, with the aim of getting students into university, whereas colleges of further education offered mostly vocational courses variously linked to the world of work.

There were some attempts at rendering the 16-19 age range 'comprehensive', but these were short-lived. Here and there was floated an integrative idea, that of building a so-called 'tertiary college', which would all be on one campus, and combine every function of both sixth-form colleges and colleges of further education. It did not happen. The national pattern remains a wide dichotomy, with all the traditional social divides and the career consequences that entails.

A curious historical development was the education advisory service. Local education authorities long ago recruited experienced teachers from schools to a central force deployed by the management to ensure teaching quality. Traditionally, and remarkably, the service started with physical education, that most crucial of academic studies! In time councils came to employ notably primary advisers, frequently former head teachers of infant and junior schools, and secondary advisers, commonly from specialist subject posts as heads of departments in secondary schools. Advisers also arrived for further education from senior posts in the colleges, then under LEA control.

CHAPTER 10

EDUCATION

Now, the range of secondary subjects is broad. LEAs varied in their resources and policies to provide posts to cover it with specialist teachers. Smaller ones had no chance, but all remained with serious omissions.

Whatever effect they had on teaching quality, you could say that the system had other inherent weaknesses also. For one thing, the relative autonomy of schools meant that their welcome from head teachers varied. For another, they cultivated a professional independence which saw them as a cadre reluctant to be managed by each other, let alone by LEA management itself. One very important deficit over the years was a resultant failure of LEAs to prescribe curriculum, locally, except perhaps around the fringes, the major determinants of which, prior to the National Curriculum, continued to be an unpacked combination of historical practice, the wishes of head teachers, and the demands of universities mediated through the examination boards.

One of the deeper ironies was that teaching, a self-styled profession if ever there was one, felt it had to be supported by this army of advisers, and at considerable financial cost. Somehow, whenever politicians talked of bureaucratic waste, it was the administration and management they referred to, not the education advisory service.

Over time this service established very cosy relationships with some schools and teachers. When, by another ironical twist of fate, the Government set up OFSTED as a national body to inspect schools more regularly than Her Majesty's Inspectorate had been able to manage, it needed a lot of staff in a hurry, and recruited many LEA advisers, along with some emergency-trained lay people, to do the job. For more than a few advisers the change in relationship with schools that entailed was quite enough to put them off altogether. A practice emerged of LEA advisers working as inspectors for some of the year. The compromise was that they temporarily joined a team in another LEA, and inspected schools there where they were not known and had no relationships to spoil.

The breakdown of trust between central government and local councils was behind this populist inspection movement, which continues. A somewhat peevish illustration of the relative privilege of LEA advisers was the prohibition on LEA officers with teaching qualifications from serving under OFSTED.

The debate, of course, quickly moved on to inquests over allegedly "failing schools", the lack of suitability of performance targets to evaluate worthwhile but nebulous aspects of school life, such as 'ethos', and the statistical dubiousness of calculating what 'added value' teaching produced in schools of different socio-economic mix.

There were some good things. Subject choice became less rigid and more diversified. There was heightened awareness of the need to prepare for the jobs market. Partial democratisation of decision-making on the staff and with the community improved with the advent of the national reform of school governance, bringing in a wider range of lay people, including parents, (but also formalizing the risk of conflict).

Other matters deteriorated along with the enforced delegation of budgets to schools from Local Education Authorities in the late 1980s. Greater financial constraint and awareness and school discretion sometimes led to a selling-off of school playing field land for housing, the decline of school dinners and nutritional standards in favour of fast foods from commercial outlets. There were also heads, mercifully few, who suddenly fancied themselves as entrepreneurial managers. Others were sadly tempted to put their hands in the till.

Then in 2009 the Nuffield Review published the results of a major study into secondary education. Among the depressing findings came the indictment that the Education system was failing less academic teenagers, whose aptitudes and aspirations were not being catered for. The bottom half were leaving school unprepared for further study or work training. The authors, led by the educationalist, Professor Pring, and consisting of researchers from the London School of Economics, and Cardiff University as well as Oxford University, blamed the origins on the National Curriculum, because prior to that technical school traditions were alive and well, absorbed into the comprehensive movement.

Since its introduction in 1988 the effect had been to introduce a test-driven culture in which it had been easier to focus on written examinations to the detriment of practical skills. As consequence success was perceived far too narrowly, and traditions of practical subjects like woodwork, metalwork, home economics, science, and geographical field-work had all declined. The failure of the system with regard to less academic pupils was seen to be both endemic and persisting.

Reforming schools is very hard work. There is far more to it than typical political responses like helicoptering in whizz-kid head teachers on ridiculously high pay and rather short-term contracts. Though this looks good. And it may fool some of the people some of the time. Re-organising schools is much easier. Bureaucrats are good at such things. So it is that a bewildering array of new 'kinds' of school have been invented over the years, and the practice continued under the Con-Dem government's reactionary reformer, Education Minister, Michael Gove.

After the Second World War the Attlee Labour government approved of the continuance of a variety of so-called 'direct grant' secondary schools, which governed themselves, but were given some state financial support in return for providing a proportion of free places to non-fee-paying pupils who had academically won local authority scholarships.(10) But if this was the cream of the state sector, the Wilson Labour government gave them away under its 1965 comprehensive school reform plans. Many opted out of the state system to become private schools instead.

The 1988 Education Reform Act did a great deal to proliferate the types of school. Secondary schools were allowed to opt out of the local education authority control (seen by Mrs Thatcher as some great evil), but remained 'grant-maintained' state schools. They had a lot of direct state funding, more than LEA schools received, but governed themselves without local interference. An obvious attraction for them was the power to doctor the intake in favour of the more middle class.

During the 1990s 'specialist schools' were invented. These were state schools, but controversially allowed to select up to one tenth of their intake on academic grounds.

Some schools were permitted to become City Technology Colleges

(CTCs), if they could raise a certain some of money from local, usually commercial, sources.

Under Blair specialist schools were diversified to include emphasis on broader ranges of subjects, such as languages, arts, sports, business and combinations thereof. Self-funding targets were reduced and schools encouraged to apply.

New Labour renamed CTCs 'City Academies', partly a response to failing schools and perceived poor standards, but partly to demonstrate that they were very much in favour of the private sector. The City Academies (later just 'academies') would be sponsored by business and industry, who were to take a leading role in their management. The plan was to greatly expand the numbers of these institutions which had rather stalled.

It was another aspect of cutting LEAs down to size. They were advised by government instead to experiment with new forms of public-private partnerships, opening up more and more services for schools to competitive markets (if they existed, or could be coaxed into being).

Under the 1997 Education Act all state schools were required to make a determination as to which of four types they wanted to be or become. The categories were the long-established ones from the 1944 Education Act used by church schools of 'voluntary-aided' (governing body-controlled), 'voluntary-controlled' (local-authority-controlled), and the secular equivalents 'foundation', run by their governing body, or 'community', run by the LEA. Some foundation schools formed charitable trusts with an outside partner, such as a business firm.

Within these categories are state schools with particular characteristics which differ from the mainstream. As well as 'academies' and the original 'city technology colleges', there are still grammar schools in some areas, selecting their pupils by examination at 11+. There are also 'faith schools', a sop to such religions as Islam, where they have more freedom in relation to religious curricula, admissions, and staffing.

The plans are clearly designed to encourage schools to leave the LEA

CHAPTER 10

EDUCATION

family and widen the kind of sponsorship to be attracted, to increase the number of academies, as they function independently of the local education authorities in their area and receive their funding directly from central government. With every major creation and abolition of school types the government has hoped to reduce number in the LEA sector. The ethos of each academy is shaped by the sponsor, so far including religious groups and charities, as well as businesses and universities.

Teachers' unions have been sceptical about the movement, claiming that they are more generously funded than local authorities are allowed to do, so having an adverse effect on other public sector schools in the vicinity. Typically, the schools chosen to be academies have better academic and social credentials, so success can be claimed more easily.

There have been other problems. Alarm bells rang over the behaviour of some private sector sponsors, notoriously so in the case of Sir Peter Vardy, who, as a successful car dealer (!) set up the Emmanuel Schools Foundation, which demanded to teach as fact his religious view of literal creation of the world as in Genesis and additionally seemed to be discriminating against the entry of children from poorer families. Criticism has thus been prompted that putting academies in the hands of people whose expertise lies in other walks of life is no recipe for school improvement, and something of an insult to teachers and professional LEA administrators.

In what has been called privatisation of state schools by stealth, the government in September 2009 announced the removal of the requirement for up-front payments of £2million by private sponsors of proposed school 'academies'. The suspicion exists that a framework is being steadily created for future governments to allow state schools to be run for profit, with the tax payer-owned property assets stripped by the private sector. This is the trend. Both Conservative and Labour seem to agree with the principle of having, and indeed significantly expanding academy numbers. In the Tories' case academies would take the place of the long-promised roll-out of new grammar schools across the country.

Yet, the reverse, only complete abolition of private schools and equitable redistribution of their assets among comprehensive state schools, could

CHAPTER 10

EDUCATION

provide even a starting point for the makings of a just and fair society. It isn't going to happen.

The fundamental bifurcation between public and private sectors still enshrines part of the serious class divides that separate the nation. It embeds the basic elitism whereby the affluent buy places at independent, private schools and the less well-off and poor attend state schools provided 'free' by the local education authority from taxation, and considerably dictated to by central Government. Undoubtedly such a state of affairs leads to separate social networks and opportunities for the privileged few.

Private schools are relatively much less regulated, being allowed, for example, to select their own pupil intake, to disapply the national curriculum, and to recruit teachers who may lack the approved paper qualifications. The last point may help to account for the fact that with some of the slighter private schools, parents may well be buying an inferior education, snob-value apart. The more successful and famous have always had close ties with the establishment, leading to career conveyor belts into areas such as merchant banking, law, the civil service and the armed forces.

A report published in 2009 by Kent University in association with the London School of Economics showed that pupils who attend private schools earn a third more than their counterparts from state schools on average. The study covered 10,000 United Kingdom individuals who were at school during the decades 1960 to 1980 inclusive and was adjusted for differences of family background. It did not unfortunately shed any light on the workings of so-called old boy networks as such, which have understandably always preferred to operate discretely.

In July 2009 the Milburn Report was published. A former Labour cabinet minister, Milburn chaired a study for government on access to high-status jobs. The report, from an 'independent' panel of experts, claimed that prestige professions - law and medicine were cited - were being closed to all but the wealthy families, and retained an attitude of exclusivity.

If 'socialists' in power had wanted to conquer elitism through the

CHAPTER 10

EDUCATION

Education system, they could be seen to have failed at both primary and secondary levels and from 5 to 19 years of age. Many Labour cabinet ministers in any case sent their children to private school, their protestations and justifications being an elaborate study in hypocrisy.

The playwright Alan Bennett, as a working class northern grammar school product, remains of the view that private schools should all have been abolished.[11]. In his view too much damage has accrued to social inequality to justify their continuance. But neither can he see that such radicalism could be achieved without terrible social upheaval and unrest. The alternative of state education becoming good enough to match the private sector no longer has any plausibility after government's numerous failed attempts. 'Bleak' is his word to describe the situation and its future prospects.

At university level things were apparently different, but only because there was a government movement towards mass access to high education within a generation. That rather glossed over the entrenched inequities between institutional status and resources. Nobody was blind either to the stubborn resistance of a disaffected element in the working class towards ambition of any kind beyond life on the dole.

Pre-war a university education was the preserve of the rich and the aristocratic. A few bright grammar school boys, and it was mostly a male world then, won state scholarships to attend. Oxford, Cambridge, and London were the main universities of prestige, with a few old-established civic universities in the big cities, like Edinburgh, Manchester, Bristol and Leeds.

After the second world war expansion was at first moderate. New so-called 'red brick' universities were established, often perversely in places of relatively low population density, like Lancaster, Norwich (University of East Anglia, UEA), and Keele. The latter was especially notable for helping to pioneer novel new degrees, in combined liberal arts, for example.

But alongside them grew up the 'polytechnics', so we had a socially and economically divided higher education system. The 'polys' had

CHAPTER 10

EDUCATION

emerged out of a variety of post-school colleges characterized by offering at least a few courses of post-advanced level difficulty. Locally, they might have had a mining, or other technological bias. Narrowly-based 'monotechnics', like vocational fine arts colleges, were also absorbed, so that what developed was the vocational alternative to university academic studies.

Political attempts were made in vain to promote the polytechnics as of equal standing to the universities, but the public did not wear it. So polytechnics were allowed to call themselves universities as a result of the Conservative Further and Higher Education Act, 1992 and that pragmatically expanded the number of universities. Because the Council for the National Academic Awards, CNAA, was abolished as the polytechnics degree-awarding body, the institutions became able to award their own degrees internally. The question needs to be explored whether external moderation has been sufficient to maintain academic standards since. Short-term effects at least resulted in lower state funding for the universities as polytechnic facilities were improved. A new national body became the government's umbrella funding agency.

Several expansions of the higher education sector occurred to the end of the 20th Century, the government's now stated (and popular) intention being to expand university education opportunities towards half of the cohort. Current debate is undecided whether the expansion has itself led to a reduction of educational standards, though most people think they know. Cynics would say that the policy has certainly massaged the unemployment figures for the young at any rate.

The expansion was predicated on largely unanalysed international statistics showing allegedly similar trends in countries that were economic rivals. Government, and population, increasingly saw the value of education instrumentally, as a stimulus to full employment and economic growth. As rising student numbers grew ever more costly, universities were starved of commensurate funds, and parents and students hit with swingeing costs for a higher education hitherto free to the previous generation. This continued under the Coalition, with a vicious plan to cut university funding by 80% and treble the tuition fees. Students still signed up like lemmings in spite of the mounting evidence that graduates

CHAPTER 10

EDUCATION

will struggle to find jobs and careers suitable to their abilities and training, or even find jobs at all from some subjects, in times of recession especially. What the phenomenon might do for social unrest when students discover their life opportunities blighted is a story yet to run. But such large changes in our society are only superficially planned by our leaders and crudely implemented. If they want economic success ,where are the concerted attempts, for example, to marry the subject course outputs even numerically to anticipated demand for specific expertise and skills?

Of course, if the new understanding is that you now have to pay for your degree course, what chance that any post-graduate courses may be state-funded? The short answer is very little. For most people the burden of further advanced study will prove too much, especially given that many will be paying off debts on student loans from their undergraduate days for years and years thereafter.

Now this is likely to be very important, in principle and in practice, the former because access will once again depend on money rather than ability, the latter because a good deal of degree-level qualifications fail to provide the specific professional or technical skills and qualifications required in jobs, and a certain number of the gifted will also be needed to go on to postgraduate higher degrees to sustain the universities' research and teaching capacities. Part of the shortfall will doubtless be met, as ever, by personal and parental sacrifice, or in good economic times by sponsorships from industrial and commercial employers. But only part. More will fall by the wayside. It is in our society now quite an extraordinary slog just to get on a lowly rung of some putative career ladder, unless you have influential connections or an obvious shortage skill. Appeals to the public are unlikely to help. Undergraduate bashing is a popular sport, all the more so because the masses are woefully ill-educated, a fact which they can hardly hope to conceal on any day of their public lives, and are accordingly very resentful. Envy readily turns to persecution.

It shows, too, the superficiality of media campaigns, which are all about opportunities for pupils from financially poor homes to become graduates. What is the earthly point of making that financially possible,

CHAPTER 10

EDUCATION

when they still cannot get good jobs and careers because they can't afford the professional courses that would qualify them to practice?

Needless to say, a good university education is far from everything, anyway. Life skills and an attractive, outward-going personality are arguably rather more important - in the workplace at least.

Hoggart talks of the plight of bright scholarship candidates for Oxbridge entrance.(12) To an extent they leave the rest of the class behind by being unusual and having flair, qualities that do not equip them to succeed in later life outside academia. Not all are brilliant; some have a kind of intelligence that makes them do particularly well in examinations, but not necessarily at other things.

One ever-present opportunity and threat to higher education is the government's efforts to use the universities to stimulate the business economy. An interesting structural departure in this regard was the decision of the Brown government from June 2008 to abolish the separate department for further and higher education and merge the functions instead in a new Department for Business, Innovation and Skills. It may or may not have been hugely significant that the works 'higher education' did not appear in the title, but it doubtless was that a very controversial figure like Lord Mandelson was appointed to run it. The move was immediately condemned in principle by the University lecturers' union, which interpreted it as a downgrading of importance of the sector and a potential threat to academic values. It remains to be seen what this might have done for job creation and the filling of these posts by appropriately qualified graduates, since the Labour government fell at the 2010 election.

It is interesting to speculate what effects will occur from the seeming equivalence of established universities and former polytechnics as bodies offering undergraduate courses, because the public even now do not regard them as such and they have different traditions. By and large former polytechnics still concentrate on vocational subjects, the established universities on research. Entrance qualifications are accordingly higher in the universities, but less academically clever students attending the former polytechnics may be rather better placed

CHAPTER 10

EDUCATION

when it comes to the job market. Should the country be run by less than its brightest, as it increasingly is?

There are notable exceptions, of course. The divide is not strict, so that, for example, medicine, an obviously vocational subject, is catered for by the universities when it comes to producing doctors and vets. Then again, traditional universities have particular affiliations to certain employers. And for many employers it may still be more important what institutions a postgraduate recruit attended, school and university, rather than any subject he may have happened to study.

Because of the very high numbers of university students now, it is very clear that a public debate is needed to decide the way forward for university funding in the years ahead. Almost everywhere in the world universities are funded by the state, to a greater or lesser extent.

One of the risks here from the structural positioning of higher education as a responsibility of the government department for economic development is the possible emphasis on the skill needs of industry and commerce to the detriment of wider culture. No change of priority would be expected under the subsequent Tory-driven Coalition.

In the first decade of the 21st century expectation has grown that students and their parents should meet an increasing proportion of the financial burden. That is unrealistic unless you want to revert towards universities being the province of only the richer families again, or unless you want to eliminate the university students' alleged financial incentive in obtaining a degree.

The prospect would unfortunately be relished by more than a few. There is a nasty vindictiveness in United Kingdom society towards thinkers and a belief that they are being carried by the rest. An exemplar is the Demos think tank report of December 2009, which wants to set up a national civic service scheme so that graduates can put something back into society, and also demands students pay a higher rate of interest on their loans to fund it.

The plain fact remains that without adequate resources being expended on

CHAPTER 10

EDUCATION

our main seats of higher education the country will sink inexorably to third-world status. There are already signs. Perennial prejudices about academic values do not augur well for our likely fate. Our state is a very rich one. The issue is what we choose to value in relative terms.

Whatever the state of the economy, however, at any given time, the country needs to be able to make up its collective mind, bearing consideration of all the relevant arguments and every vested interest, as to just what kind of university system it wants, and what proportion of national wealth it is prepared to allocate to achieve the desired outcomes. Hard decisions might well have to be made over such long neglected fundamentals as which institutions are to survive, what subjects with their respective student capacities, and which proportion of the national age cohort will be allowed to qualify for entry.

One final organisational sector remains in the education world - that of adult learners. To those who are charged with balancing the public books this group is a further headache. Because their ideals are also costly.

There is a concept of lifelong learning as <u>entitlement</u> for adults, with tenets such as the following:

a)   a statutory right to learning in the workplace;
b)   universal access to basic skills courses regardless of age;
c)   learner-involvement in all levels of decision-making about their learning;
d)   widening participation in higher education and the provision of a second chance later in life.(13)

Unsurprisingly, the great dearth of public funding for lifelong learning stands in the way of aspiration here. Government tends to divert resources towards vocational courses for young unemployed people, whilst LEAs are starved of funding for the 'leisure and pleasure' adult education courses they have a legal duty to provide. Older members of the community in particular lose out and another of life's civilizing and culturing aspects is placed at risk. A long tradition of liberal arts stands in danger of neglect in consequence.

CHAPTER 10

EDUCATION

Because of Blair's government lifelong learning was a vehicle for international economic competition. People had a responsibility to update their skills throughout their working lives and needed to invest in Individual Learning Accounts, with government financial support. Stewart Ranson opposed the concept, calling for lifelong learning to develop a new political and moral order to sustain personal development. The idea was capable of many different interpretations. As usual, a national consensus was lacking. So not surprisingly, Individual Learning Accounts had to be suspended in 2001 following widespread cases of fraud. But not before another quango, the Learning and Skills Council (LSC) had taken over the field for all adult education outside the higher education sector, divorcing it from local democracy.

Final Thoughts

In conclusion, it is fitting to consider the future, not perhaps with a crystal ball, looking into the further mists of time, but with a firm eye on current weaknesses, trends, and what one might like to see happening, as well as what most recently went before. Suggested reforms in the foregoing will not be repeated here and there is no attempt to give a complete account.

If Blair was some kind of neo-socialist, one who believed in values like social justice and inclusion, equality of opportunity, and community cohesion, whilst nevertheless being suspicious of the public sector, which he saw as oppressively self-interested, he significantly failed to overcome the problems of squaring these values with his love affair for private enterprise operating in the education sector. He regarded 'comprehensive schools' as a dirty term to the middle classes and spoke up for choice and diversity of provision. So it was hands off the remaining grammar schools for one thing. Education was to stay, as it was under the Tories, a "market-driven commodity driven by consumer demands". Blair put it as his top priority, and considerably increased spending, replacing many a clapped out school building, pressing equipment for computer technology, and attacking high class sizes for the infants.

"Standards not structure" was one mantra, the emphasis on teacher accountability to parents, through published and more frequent school

EDUCATION

inspections and league tables for school performances in external examinations, becoming even higher in profile.

There were, however, serious critics, such as the Campaign for State Education, CASE, which wondered what values underpinned the (simplistic) assertion that diversity in schools was a good thing, and could not understand why three types of state school (community, foundation, and aided) were needed.

The government came to have a curriculum problem of its own making, because it continued to say there was a 'curriculum entitlement' for pupils, whilst at the same time jettisoning parts of the National Curriculum for older secondary pupils and creating specialist schools which placed greater emphasis on given subjects.

A main feature characterizing the era was the chasing of national targets, notably through the examination system, which became an arena of spectacular dispute and failure, one of the most notable among them being the A level papers marking debacle in 2002. It was the final straw that brought down the then Education Secretary of State, Estelle Morris, a nice and earnest ex-teacher who was in any case self-admittedly out of her depth. The issue was complex, but there were accusations that examination boards fiddled the marking. Others pointed the blame at hurried and misguided reforms by government bringing in 'modular' units of study within subjects and the new Advanced Subsidiary (AS) level, taken at the end of the first-year sixth-form. Later attacks whittled away at the attendant over-examination of pupils at different ages, the so-called Standard Assessment Tasks (SATS), whilst further scandals involved late marking resulting in university places for A level students being put in jeopardy. Government reforms to standardize local authority computing and centralize the student loan system also ensured many university students did not receive their finance on time, but months after courses started.

The end for New Labour was not predicated on failures in the class room and it is not very easy to anticipate what will come along next in the field of Education. Even supporters do concede, however, that New Labour is unrealistic in its expectations that standards can rise a long way. It seems to think that the odds of social deprivation will be overcome with the right kind of application, and even inequality reduced. It has rather foolishly alienated potential allies to these causes by bashing teachers and local bureaucrats along the way.

Bullying in schools is officially opposed, but the kind where governments deride teachers and bureaucrats goes on regularly. The Children's Secretary, the aptly named Ed. Balls, publicly stated in January 2009 that he was becoming impatient with head teachers who looked outside the school to find causes for their pupils' poor examination results. Poverty was not to blame, he said. On the contrary, it was down to leadership failings on the staff. Mr Balls pointed to the required performance targets and threatened to change the management, or governance, of schools that did not attain them. The option of private sponsorship was mentioned, a characteristic feature of New Labour approaches, as we have seen.

There is, in fact ,an endemic set of problems regarding school leadership, arising from the mix of responsibilities, perspectives, and powers of those within the legal framework. You have the time-honoured problems with those head teachers who are naturally undemocratic. There is the interface with a lay governing body, which can get rapidly out of its depth. From time to time, but perhaps surprisingly not all that frequently, major problems spring up somewhere, usually down to personality differences and communication breakdowns. A prediction is that this will get rather worse without the dispassionate guiding hand of the LEA, and as new Trust Schools test their new-found autonomy.

Phillips blames both main political parties for the way society has pursued the cult of individual freedom as an end in itself. Teachers' problems with trying to raise performance have been exacerbated by declining standards of pupil behaviour and a corresponding loss of acceptable sanctions.

Secondly, it has done nothing to curb, or even abolish, private schools, so the certainty of indefensible inequalities remains.

Thirdly, the resentment of teachers has been further stoked by the political marginalisation of matters they regard as important - like serious debate over the content and purposes of education. Their morale has

CHAPTER 10

EDUCATION

declined for many reasons, not least the erosion of their disciplinary powers and the development of cheap para-professional assistance, questioning their skill base, especially in primary schools.

When you politically over-prescribe - a constant danger in bureaucracies - there is an obvious sense in which you deny the teachers' professionalism, undermining their confidence and security.

A revealing indicator of government attitudes was their March 2009 announcement of a fast-track school teacher qualification scheme. Currently, a graduate does a year of training leading to the PGCE teaching qualification certificate. Little enough you might say, although it is similar for solicitors. The proposal suggested cutting the qualification period to six months for "good people" with "life experience behind them". The press characterised the move as an attempt to help bankers and other unemployed financial sector workers in the City following the credit crunch crashes. Teachers' satisfaction at the shock to the system waiting in store for such 'high flyers' in the tough, real world of the class room is sadly tempered by the realisation that, as usual, it is the children who will suffer the most. They only get one chance and deserve much better than being on the receiving end of cheap social engineering.

The state has never unfortunately been as thorough-going in its approach to prescribing an education when it isn't being unkind to those who must implement its policies. There is the let-out for the affluent of a private schooling. There is also the shoddy area of 'home education', whereby parents are allowed to withdraw their children from state schools and educate them at home instead. Since legal responsibility for a child's education is vested in its parents, and the powers of the local education authority are very weak in relevant regards, fears exist that some children may be getting very impoverished education and social experiences there. The local authority is not provided with a national template for what would constitute a reasonable education and it has no statutory duty to monitor the quality of home education. Parents are not under a duty to keep the council informed, so tracking children can be somewhat difficult.

CHAPTER 10

EDUCATION

That fact leaves them wide open to all manner of potential abuses, including physical maltreatment, neglect, sexual exploitation, forced marriage, and domestic servitude, such as looking after siblings, or being sent out to work for the family. Reform is badly needed, but why were safeguards for children ever considered less important than parental freedoms here?

Another serious cultural weakness is the link between education and working life. Given that so much money is expended on the education and higher education of students by the time they graduate, it seems an amazing waste that as a nation we neglect careers advice in the way we do. People with academic qualifications have traditionally been left largely to their own devices to find a way, whereas it would be the rational course to try to harness all the vast array of talent to natural interests and abilities and the common wheal. The Institute of Careers Guidance pointed out during early 2010 that the government typically skewed expenditure to aid the no-hopers likely to remain forever outside the formal economy.

As we have seen with the National Curriculum, one of the many reasons why teaching can be such a miserable experience these days is the incessant culture of testing and performance-recording. Complaints have at least led to a reining back of the former intent to programme it in for almost every year-group. Pressure is now a defining characteristic of the school week, for teachers and pupils alike. This does not breed lovers of learning, or better teaching either.

In the latter stages of the Blair government there was a considerable retreat from the National Curriculum. In primary schools, for instance, literacy and numeracy took centre stage. The primary national syllabuses in geography, history, design and technology, music, art, and physical education were disapplied as compulsory elements.

In lower secondary, at Key Stage Three, one quarter of taught time was removed leaving a day a week for schools to do other things at their own choice.

To some extent the measures were a reaction to the disaffection of the profession. The 2006-8 Primary Education Review had confirmed the seriously negative effects of government policy. Teachers were under stress because of government pressure on them and a perceived lack of trust. Pupils were in many cases demotivated by the over-formal and didactic methods imposed on the staff. Quality had declined in the face of narrow curriculum and the focus on preparation for testing.

Whatever politicians might say, the fundamental challenge of educational standards runs deep-seated in wider society. Difficulties for educationalists have been greatly increased by the atomised and fragmented nature of that society. Crime levels, truancy, family breakdown have all risen. Phillips characterizes it as "no blame, no shame, no pain", the latter a reference to social indifference with regard to the unfortunate, a deregulation creed that was an abrogation of political responsibility.

Compounding the problems in some areas the New Labour concern to ensure 'social inclusion' had been hopelessly undermined by the swamping effect on local services of unfettered immigration. Government responses had been laughable. Citizenship curricula and tests for new arrivals, normative curricular exhortations to schools, had fed resentment and barely scratched the surface of resource provision. Local authorities were largely left to cope as best they could, with very mixed results.

Perhaps the emerging devolved governments of Scotland and Wales, with their opportunities for fresh and innovative approaches, may yet show England the way, if it has but the inclination.

Because one of the great weaknesses with Whitehall is the centralising and controlling tendency, which is far too entrenched[14]. Working for an LEA, or now in schools, since the delegation of many responsibilities to them under Local Management of Schools initiatives, staff are peppered with edicts and forms to fill in throughout the working year. Local discretion is seriously constrained, as the government, through the civil service, sets out precisely and in minute detail, how schools should be run. Frequently, the requirements will need additional money to implement, but will not be forthcoming. The attitude is very often one of expecting that priorities can be adjusted on the ground at will and compensating economies made.

An illustration is the government's Standards Fund, which accounted for around 10% of school budget. Expenditure had to be competitively bid for by schools across over fifty changing projects, ministerial pets. There is much skill in effective application, which can distort provision away from the most deserving.

Teachers became adept at playing the games. And as a result of the Labour government producing an examination results-driven culture of accountability and reward, they have inevitably resorted to numerous tactics to improve their school's rating. These include drilling students in the facts, allowing them several drafts of their coursework, with suggestions, before formal submission for marking, choosing easier examination boards, subjects, and syllabi. Some of the ploys are of dubious morality, but then self-preservation is a powerful incentive.

Despite such manoeuvres and the striving, it is difficult enough to be optimistic, for all the pontificating and posturing of politicians in power. The Chief Inspector of Schools, Christine Gilbert, in her 2008/09 OFSTED report on the state of education, talked about "too much that is mediocre and persistently so". A third of state schools, providing for well over two million children, still failed to offer a good education. There was reference to a "stubborn core" of incompetent teachers, blamed here for failing to prevent disruption and truancy among pupils by giving dull lessons. In fact some 60,000 pupils avoid school daily, 8,000 are expelled, and 25,000 leave school at 16 with no GCSE qualifications whatsoever.

It will not be the total answer, but it should help if the teaching force were to be toned up intellectually in terms of having better qualifications of entry. Interestingly, the Commons Education select committee came to the same conclusion in its report of February 2010. It said graduates should come in with a minimum eligibility of a lower second class honours degree, whilst primary school entrants should have 'A' levels. It wanted movement towards Masters level degrees in teaching and learning on top of subject degrees. 'Chartered teacher status' would be conferred

CHAPTER 10

EDUCATION

on those licensed to practice with the appropriate level of qualifications and extent of successful practical experience in schools. A requirement to renew their licence on a regular basis would enable the unsatisfactory teachers to be progressively weeded out. These are worthy, if somewhat elitist aims. What has derailed such sentiments in the past has been government desperation to ensure our teaching force was large enough.

It seems almost inconceivable that as university education costs to students inexorably rise, there will not be at some point a partial collapse of applications. Students and their parents are, of course, caught in an unpleasant dilemma. If they do not take up the place, what is the alternative, in a land of diminishing career, even job opportunities?

Elitism, one way or another, seems impossible to combat in higher education. The pressure for international leaders among our universities to break free of the government stranglehold on their student income will see its reassertion sooner or later in terms of affordability to applicants. And whether students are state-funded or no, the considerably differential qualities of institutional performance will not be concealed for long.

What we are saying here in the last analysis is that there will be some dead trails and many a false dawn. Half-baked experts will continue to emerge and infect the profession with their ideologies from time to time. Politicians will tamper, bringing in their structural and reformist fads. The teachers will soldier on out of their subject value convictions and love of the young. Yet the limitations on the possible achievements of this disjointed collectivity in Education will always be severe and less then our hopes. They are chained by the frailties of human nature, the hopeless flaws in a society that has to be coerced into cooperation, and has not the remotest idea what it wants to achieve, or how to get there. But then again, this applies to many a field of human endeavour, so why would we expect Education to be somehow immune?

CHAPTER 10

EDUCATION

NOTES

* 1 Blake, Nigel, Smeyers, Paul, Smith, Richard, and Standish, Paul, Eds., Philosophy of Education, Blackwell Publishing, Oxford, 2003.

* 2 Peters, R.S., The Philosophy of Education, Oxford University Press, 1973.

* 3 Barrow, Robin, and Woods, Ronald, An Introduction to Philosophy of Education, Methuen & Co. Ltd., London, Second edition, 1982.

* 4 Hirst, Paul H., Knowledge and the Curriculum, Routledge & Kegan Paul Ltd., London, 1974.

* 5 Phillips, Melanie, 'All Must Have Prizes', Little, Brown and Company, London, 1996.

* 6 The National Curriculum, Qualifications and Curriculum Authority, London, 2009.

   7 Fowler, W.S., 'Implementing the National Curriculum', Kogan, Page, London, 1990.

   8 Radcliffe-Richards, Janet, debate "Does Philosophy Matter?", British Academy, 2003.

* 9 Chitty, Clyde, Education Policy in Britain, Palgrave Macmillan, 2nd Edition, 2009.

* 10 Jones, Ken, 'Education in Britain: 1944 to the Present', Polity Press, Cambridge, 2003.

   11 Bennett, Alan 'The History Boys', Faber and Faber Limited, London, 2004.

   12 Hoggart, Richard, 'The Uses of Literacy', 1957.

CHAPTER 10

EDUCATION

13   Campaigning Alliance For Lifelong Learning, manifesto, September, 2008.

14   Butler, Eamonn, 'The Rotten State of Britain', Gibson Square, London, 2009.

CHAPTER 11

FUTURE PROSPECTS

Only a fool would try to foretell the future, but most of the trend indicators and objective appraisals of the present lead to very pessimistic conclusions.

Leaving aside the appalling threats to the whole planet of climate change and other environmental disasters, and dismissing also the intractable problems of international relations, it is pretty clear that the inmates are now running the asylum. We do not have very high ability in positions of power, nor the means to find and put them there, to provide even a glimmer of hope.

As Butler put it:

"Because they identify the state's interests as their own, the ruling clique feels perfectly entitled to change the constitution, override the rule of law, and extinguish liberties to achieve their purposes".

Moreover,
"They have no clear process for taking decisions, leaving nobody accountable for what is decided".

We have seen how politicians are hopelessly lost in damaging and false ideologies. We have rued their multifold human failings at our expense.

An important question we should all ask is just what it is that politicians contribute? They make speeches, yes, but mostly written by others. They pronounce on policy, certainly, yet these are largely worked up by clever graduates behind the scenes. As with the phoney job of the professional football 'manager', they tend to have almost everything done for them, apart from their own spot in the light.

The primitive state of social theory relative to that of the physical and life sciences has been demonstrated. So we must surely now know that in its present form, manifesting as management, political, or economic theory, for instance, it is incapable of solving most of our serious societal problems.

440

CHAPTER 11

FUTURE PROSPECTS

Powerful arguments have been adduced against the contention that society progresses as a whole. Instead we lurch on pragmatically, mostly as families and individuals in isolation.

It has been shown that, even for something as precious and fundamental as education, we can neither agree on what we want, nor how to attain it. And that this has always been true in the United Kingdom in modern times.

Some politicians are fond of glib and superficial statements which take for granted that schools are better off once they have their freedom from the LEA. But consider for a moment the sort of support services which an admittedly large County Council LEA (the kind Labour tried to abolish) could provide for all its schools - primary, special, and secondary. Financial services would include management advice, accounting, payroll, superannuation, payments to creditors, income and debt collection, and insurance. Legal advice would be available. Human resources might well include personnel management, providing a supply teacher agency, management and governor training, health and safety management for food, people, and premises. Services for the buildings would cover caretaking, cleaning, grounds maintenance, maintenance, energy, and general property management. Information Technology solutions could be supplied for both administration and curriculum. Stationery and supplies, printing, and book and educational resource facilities could also feature, together with careers advice for pupils.

The lists are indicative rather than comprehensive. To have these all on tap from one locally-based, friendly source, and economically provided, prevented a great deal of lost effort, anxiety and time for busy school staffs, or the need to expand their internal administration and greatly improve expertise to organise a plethora of external outlets. And remember, to obtain these services from other providers will require additional payments of built-in profit elements which the schools can neither quantify nor control.

Quite significantly, Shireland Collegiate Academy in Sandwell was downgraded during 2010 by the government's OFSTED inspectors and

CHAPTER 11

FUTURE PROSPECTS

described as "inadequate" in standards. Before it became an academy and had its 'freedom' it was rated "outstanding". There will be more of these, because political 'solutions' do not meet the case.

The brief survey of key institutions, like the Law and Parliament, points to their being unfit for purpose, but with deeply-entrenched and powerful resistance to meaningful reforms.

Enough evidence has been adduced to build a strong, cumulative case that democracy may not work in any known manifestation, although the least objectionable system to ordinary folk, and representative democracy certainly does not work. The disjunction between the people's wishes and their representatives' actual behaviour is just too great.

The urgently needed movement towards participative experiments within a democratic model is dependant for success not only on the willingness of the ruling classes to relinquish power, but also on how keen the electorate are to participate and how good they can become at it.

For such a quest to be even plausible, except if token ways ,would require the complete prior rewriting of a modern constitution, along the lines advocated in the book, together with a bill of significant citizens' rights, and the subject to be given an ongoing and positive profile in the education curriculum of the nation, so beware the dubious promises of self-styled reformers.

Even after all that happened in the rotten Parliament of 2005-10, the politicians still attempted to deceive the voters on a massive scale. Very reluctantly conceding in the run-up to the general election that to pay for the crunch deficit there would have to be financial cuts and tax increases, they steadfastly and coyly refused to explain how the debt repayment would be achieved. In the last week of April the prestigious and independent Institute of Fiscal Studies, IFS, the country's key economic think-tank, published a damning report exposing the lot of them. What should have been the key and critical issue for the general election had been kicked on until the day after tomorrow.

There had been downright lies about protecting front-lines service jobs in

FUTURE PROSPECTS

the public sector. The local government union, UNISON, predicted that their job losses could eliminate vital services on the ground. Examples included day centres, care for the elderly, meals on wheels, children's services, and libraries, but schools could go short of teachers, hospitals have to lose nurses. The actual scale of cuts envisaged was likely to be the largest since World War II. Unemployment was set to rise dramatically as Austerity Britain took hold. And prospects of a prolonged recession seemed high.

It has not been part of the book's intentions to provide a full and detailed account of capitalism. Yet enough has been said to strongly evidence its very serious failings and horrific dangers in its present form.

Private firms for private gain are just that, with largesse dispersed or withheld at whim, their purposes narrow and simple, aimed at focusing gain on elite minorities. By now, through all the economic ups and downs, it ought to be clear that nothing in them lasts apart from greed. They will not, sometimes cannot cover all their costs without taxpayers have to prop them up to protect them against their own market. And their 'goods' are just a means, at least for them, to profit to the firm, especially its senior management, and the shareholders.

It is true that gains are far from easy. There can be much competition, and the public, fickle in its wants, whilst even variable over needs. But business is not here to serve society. And, since it is the dominant mode of organised activity in it, this should truly scare us all.

There is something very sick about company structures at the top. Why do they need large numbers of 'non-executive directors', who sometimes collect fat salaries for turning up at a few meetings a year to give the benefit of their valuable advice? And what about the mountainous waste spent on puerile advertisements, business trips abroad, first-class hotels and travel, luxury company cars?

It is always said: these are the wealth creators. But look at the morality of what they often do. Drive competitors to the wall, steal the best ideas, price out the needy, create wants for the greedy. Drug companies hold the sick to ransom. Cars are designed for speed and appearance rather

CHAPTER 11

FUTURE PROSPECTS

than safety. Lots of firms produce dangerous goods, like weapons or alcohol, or sell silly services such as luxury hotels for pets.

Another unacceptable face of capitalism is the cartel. Monopolies are conceded by most of those not working in them to be bad for society. As sole supplier they can hold a market to ransom and charge what they like. But cartels have similar defects. In the energy industry we have just such a model, encouraged by government, which deliberately oversees it in a weak manner inimicable to consumers' interests. At times of economic recession, almost coinciding with high and unwarranted price hikes tied to the oil, not gas industry, great distress was caused to the less-well-off, who struggled to pay their fuel bills.

Private cartels are unfortunately not confined to energy. Banks are the prime example, of course, but leading law and accountancy firms should not be forgotten, especially as they play such an important role in protecting and covering up unsavoury practices in industry and commerce contrary to the public interest.

The multinational firms are so powerful that there does not seem to be any known, effective way in which the national interests may be safeguarded. They ruthlessly move their plants and profits around the world at will, evading taxes along the way. Even in Britain with indigenous companies, it is often difficult to trace ownership and responsibility, still less so when they live in alien cultures on the other side of the world. An Indian firm bought out one of our fundamental industries in the former British Steel on Teesside, then closed the plant, producing a blighted town in Redcar from the massive job losses , the United Kingdom government spluttering with ineptitude (or was it just indifference?) A similar thing happened in Birmingham, only this time the government actually paid an inefficient American firm, Kraft, to take over the iconic chocolate manufacturer, Cadbury, against the wishes of its Board ,as well as the public. Kraft then promptly announced the intended closure of a Bristol factory it had promised to keep open.

If you leave a market alone it does not behave rationally or morally, neither is it stable. The economic (right -wing) orthodoxy that says markets will solve the problems on their own is a mysterious belief. Even

CHAPTER 11

FUTURE PROSPECTS

dafter is the notion that rational intervention by human beings will invariably impair the market's working, although in fairness the right kind of interventions have to be made and this is a difficult skill.

Capitalism is a huge and impressively successful confidence trick, among other things, because it is only really in the interests of the lucky few, who benefit grossly, whilst the rest feed off relative scraps. We all know this by the multifold salaries of those at the top of businesses in comparison with their rank and file. Excuses about possible redistribution of wealth are always made, including the derisory notion that it would be de-motivating for the wealth makers, who would then leave and operate elsewhere. The real reason is that big corporations are now in effect more powerful than the state.

Firms have famously been compared in their behaviour to psychopaths, their sense of social responsibility ,for one thing, being virtually absent, unless there is money in it. There are also many greedy individuals whose self-committed behaviour needs to be regulated in the public interest, but is not and almost certainly will not be. As we now know, they include the dark artists of investment banking_ dodgy financial products, currency speculation, tax avoidance ,the fake auditing of the (cookery) books.

Now the political map of England always shows the different regions have very little in common, and this must affect the way the government behaves at times. A very notable difference is that the north of England broadly votes Labour, while the south is essentially Conservative. Unsurprisingly, the capital is in the south with most of the real wealth, so it is largely illusory to talk of a united England let alone a United Kingdom.

A hopeless and crucial problem with England (which also applies to the Disunited Kingdom), is its irreconcilable major rifts. And in particular the class war, always potentially liable to break out in a rash, if it ever really went away. We are deluding ourselves, too, if we think it is remotely feasible to resolve the North/South divide. Some might equate the two, but that would be simplistic. It is, at any rate, possible for people of all classes in the North to look disparagingly at the South, to regard it

CHAPTER 11

FUTURE PROSPECTS

as a fundamentally alien place. Especially, so the capital. London is a magnet, a great creative engine, yet consumer of disproportionate resources, with grand and multifarious facilities. It has little in common with even the rest of the South. Politicians ensure it is getting more so. So there is quite a strong argument for the North to secede and go it alone.

Home traders provide a microcosm on a domestic scale of much that is wrong with practical capitalism in the United Kingdom. As anyone who has tried it will know, the problems of employing contractors to remedy faults or effect improvements at home are legion. Knowledge of what the job entails is virtually essential, and of the contractors themselves a great advantage, but there is ultimately little defence for the hapless consumer. Sooner or later almost everybody will get their fingers burned. And partly because Parliament seems to prefer rogues' charters to proper laws protecting the householder.

But even if you find an honest firm, and are not unduly messed about regarding when the work is actually done, there will probably be insurmountable difficulties concerning the estimate.

Firstly, it is common practice for customers to be provided with quite inadequate quotations, where very little is specified and most of the costs (and all of the profits) are concealed. It is really too easy for contractors to just think of numbers. Even when they do not, and the job itself is satisfactory, many a customer must still be left wondering whether he has received value for money.

In fairness to contractors, there is a case to change the conventional business practice whereby potential customers are not charged for estimates. What happens in effect is that much abortive, and costly work, goes into this. And sometimes the customer calls the firm in for little good reason. The customer who actually signs up the contractor in effect pays a subsidy on behalf of those that do not, including people dealing with overpriced insurance jobs, the feckless, the indecisive, and the plain bloody-minded.

On the other side of the coin, however, the law could help the customer

CHAPTER 11

FUTURE PROSPECTS

by setting out model estimates - which would itemize such matters as labour, materials, transport, equipment, insurance, administration, and expertise - in a comprehensive manner and be a requirement in the different main fields of work.

Profit need not be a dirty word, but what is wrong with its open declaration, within legal ceilings? Secretive behaviour in the private sector has led to obscene levels of gain at times, and it would be chastening, as well as more economic, for firms to have to show it to more than just their accountant and (maybe) the tax man.

It is also necessary to counsel against the practice of fixed price quotations ahead of work. Typically, what happens is that the price is agreed by both parties with only a vague indication of the time which will be required. When it goes on longer the contractor supposedly carries the extra cost, but he will probably have a generous margin built in.

Yet, when it takes less time than scheduled, the consumer in effect pays for the longer job.

One of the hardest aspects for consumers to cope with is that the estimate and the work are often carried out by an entirely different calibre of tradesman. Typically, the workers are never seen until the boss, armed with his smooth patter, has got them hooked. Then they could get the B-team, unsupervised and just out of school.

Finally, one of the nastiest aspects of capitalism is the way it can erode moral outlook and behaviour amongst the ordinary populace .The criminologists, Karstedt and Farrall ,have surveyed widespread examples of financial cheating across the classes: so much so that they do not believe we now have such a thing as a "law-abiding majority". People see others bending or breaking the rules and getting away with it, so the temptation to follow suit gets the better of them.

Public-private animosities surface whenever there is a national or local emergency or disaster, a useful example being the grounding of commercial air flights as a result of atmospheric ash clouds from a volcanic eruption in Iceland during April 2010. Rather predictable

CHAPTER 11

FUTURE PROSPECTS

reactions occurred. One was the quite questionable assumption that it was the government's responsibility to get all the stranded tourists home. Another was the bleat from the airline operators calling for government financial subsidy. A third came in the form of very narrow and uncaring interpretations by airlines and insurance companies of what little entitlements travellers actually had in the circumstances.

Some salutary lessons could come out of the affair, if people were disposed to learn them. It showed, for one thing, how thin is the veneer of organised society at such times, how poor the contingency planning, and how slow and inadequate institutional responses can be in both public and private sectors.

When the norm turns out to be 29,000 flights in Europe per day, a temporary crisis can serve to highlight the extensive rape of the planet and force us to reconsider the necessity of journeys and the relative merits of different modes of transport. Philosophically, it can provide much-needed time to slow down, to savour the challenges of adventure and greater self-reliance, to value journeys more highly and to emphasize the destinations less.

The spectre of swingeing public sector cuts may eventually focus the minds of the unbiased on the possible demerits of capitalism as it now is in the United Kingdom. What it will not prepare for are the hideous mutations that capitalism may even now be undergoing. For example, the world economy may increasingly come to be dominated by China, with its known propensity for inhuman, authoritarian government and its less well-known flirtations with a capitalism controlled by a communist state, not a free market, and able to pursue politically calculated, and economically delivered, policies in relation to trading 'partners' and competitors. What West and East alike appear to be banking on is that consumer societies seemingly produce non-engaged, complacent citizens who will willingly forego more than a few democratic freedoms for a lifestyle which gives them fun and goodies. Always, that is, so long as any suffering is other people's.

When we scan society for an overview of all its ills, ultimately it is not the public sector and its services that are the major problem here. Whilst

CHAPTER 11

FUTURE PROSPECTS

these bureaucracies undeniably can be inefficient, that is not a supreme vice. They are nevertheless fundamentally and relatively humane in their operations, grappling as they do with complex social issues. Their greatest, and seemingly irredeemable, flaw is the political overlay - what their masters ask them to do and how to do it, as well as what they don't. In spite of even this, they are our only, only chance of a decent, civilizing life. If the private sector is brought in to improve the public sector, as has been the aspiration of governments from Thatcher to Blair to Cameron, whatever they cannot make a profit out of they will tend to devalue, want to hive off, or close down. So there will be activities in local areas of value to the people which cease to be done ,or which community and charity groups will be exhorted to take on for nothing out of the goodness of their Big Society hearts.

Capitalist and Conservative voices are very effective in clamouring to keep the public sector severely pruned and constrained from growth. They are fond of pointing out the financial burden to society that the poor old private sector nobly bears. Yet consider the limiting case where the public sector becomes vanishingly small. Suddenly, we are all at the mercy of powerful economic forces which are in no way driven by the welfare of society at large. Just as we cower helplessly before the power of nature when we cannot control it.

The Con-Dem government seemed to think that as they slashed jobs in the public sector, so they would rise in the private sector instead. But this is irresponsibly simplistic; even allowing that the dispossessed workers were in the same place as the potential new employers, how? Would they have the right skills, would private sector attitudes be welcoming or prejudiced against them ? And where would the new resources come from for the firms to expand their work forces? No, a complex mix of market conditions would have to be in place, no doubt including at least short-term government subsidies, and effective lending by the banks.

There are those that would argue that the rich have the potential to solve our economic woes. Others say that political interference will drive them away. But we are the sixth richest country in the world. Total personal wealth in the UK runs into trillions of pounds and makes the national debt look tiny. The poorest half of the population own under 10% of the

CHAPTER 11

FUTURE PROSPECTS

wealth, on the other hand. So graduate the income tax fairly across many bands and ensure proportionate taxes on assets too.

Finally, of the multifold specifics, what shall we finally predict ? Our leaders have demonstrated complete incompetence in controlling the economy, so many of our people will continue to suffer as yet untold financial difficulties.

The gap between rich and poor, which widened under the Blair/Brown 'socialist' governments, will never be controlled, since no government dare take the measures necessary for a major redistribution of wealth, and they probably even lack the power.

Ordinary folk will continue to have little say and most social policies will fail. Public services will not cease to be merely moderate, by and large, and very many completely blameless public sector workers will lose their jobs as a sacrifice to the credit crunch deficit and other capitalist weaknesses.

Laws will proliferate and mostly be variously irrelevant, unworkable, or objectionable. Attacks on personal freedom will remain prominent and the police politicized.

Society will continue to fragment, caring for disadvantaged groups reduce. Problems stemming from excessive and inappropriate immigration will get worse as they outbreed us.

Media distortion will heighten, suppressing and distorting the truth.

For most, in this jungle, standards of living will be hard enough to maintain let alone increase, as we decline remorselessly towards third-world mediocrity. Except, of course, for the relatively few. And they will rule; as it was in the beginning, is now, and ever shall be......

www.ingramcontent.com/pod-product-compliance
Lightning Source LLC
Chambersburg PA
CBHW050448270326
41927CB00009B/1656